Fractured Focus

Fractured Focus

Sport as a Reflection of Society

Edited by

Richard E. Lapchick
Center for the Study of Sport in Society,
Northeastern University

Lexington Books
D.C. Heath and Company/Lexington, Massachusetts/Toronto

Library of Congress Cataloging-in-Publication Data
Main entry under title:

Fractured focus.

  Bibliography: p.
  1. Sports—Social aspects—United States—
Addresses, essays, lectures. 2. Sports—Social aspects—
Addresses, essays, lectures. I. Lapchick, Richard
Edward.
GV706.5.F7   1986   306'.483   85–45745
ISBN 0–669–12860–0 (alk. paper)
ISBN 0–669–12288–2 (pbk. : alk. paper)

Published simultaneously in Canada
Printed in the United States of America
Casebound International Standard Book Number: 0–669–12860–0
Paperbound International Standard Book Number: 0–669–12288–2
Library of Congress Catalog Card Number: 85–45745

The paper used in this publication meets the minimum requirements of
American National Standard for Information Sciences—Permanence of
Paper for Printed Library Materials, ANSI Z39.48–1984.

The last numbers on the right below indicate the number and date of printing.

10 9 8 7 6 5 4 3 2 1

95 94 93 92 91 90 89 88 87 86

For Robert Lipsyte, who has bridged the gap between the sports journalist and the scholar while maintaining his life-long commitment to honesty, integrity, and dignity in the pursuit of creating an informed public

Contents

Foreword

George H. Sage
President,
North American Society
for the Sociology of Sport

Much is written about sport, but most of it is journalistic pablum, consisting of game scores, attributions by athletes and coaches about why they won or lost, and promotional stories about individual athletic achievements and team quests for championships. Most sport literature does not confront readers with questions about the larger social issues and consequences of modern sports forms—ideological underpinnings, power relations, social costs, and so forth. Instead, readers are fed a diet of traditional slogans, cliches, sacred cows, and ritualized trivia about sport. There tends to be a blissful unsophistication about the social relations that control sport. Sport and society are typically presented as discrete institutional arenas, with sport seen as a realm in which character is built and virtue pursued.

Journalistic writing has little feeling for or sensitivity to the constitute character of sport as an element of culture, nor does it deal with the class character of sports. Indeed, its approach is unreflecting and uncritical; it accepts the dominant sport forms and allocates resources accordingly. It tends to reinforce the established social order and reigning consensus, not out of cynical self-interest or subservience to dominant interests but rather out of a naivete about the ideological meanings inherent in contemporary sport forms.

What is tragically missing in the literature on sport is the quality of mind that is essential for grasping the interplay of humans and society, of biology and history, of self and world—a perspective that the late C. Wright Mills called "the sociological imagination." One consequence of the uncritical literature that pervades sports is that the conventional public wisdom posits sport as an apolitical, democratic activity separated from "real life"—simply an institutionalized form of the human play impulse. The one concession to a possible social contextual role of sport is that it will make participants good citizens—loyal, willing to sacrifice for the good of the group, and courageous; that is, it will develop character.

There is a need for a social-analytical perspective in the literature on sport—one that views formal sport as an integral element in the reproduction of the prevailing structure of society. A crucial step in understanding cultural activities of any kind, sports included, is to situate them within their social and historical contexts. Unfortunately, only a small band of social scientists study sport, and their communication outlets are scarce, limited to journals read mostly by other social science scholars of sport.

One of the greatest potential of social analysis is the development of an understanding of the social and material basis of culture and consciousness and the way in which relations of power and authority structure various cultural products, such as sport and games. One function of a book of this type is that the ideas of scholars who have made contributions to serious and critical social analysis of sport are given a wider reading. At least one important outcome of such a reading is the development of an expanded social awareness and an elevated social consciousness in relation to social order and change and the role of sport in society.

Richard Lapchick is well equipped to undertake the preparation of such a book. In addition to his credentials as a social scientist, he has been a social activist for more than 15 years. Indeed, he has devoted his entire professional life to fighting injustice, discrimination, and exploitation with exceptional conviction and courage. The costs have been enormous—both physically and psychologically—but he has been undeterred. As a civil rights activist, Lapchick had devoted years to racism in America and South Africa. In 1975 he authored *The Politics in Race and International Sport: The Case of South Africa.* And in 1978, while he was national chairman of the American Coordinating Committee for Equality in Sport and Society—an organization that campaigned to end all sports contacts between the United States and sports teams from South Africa so long as sport and society in South Africa were segregated—Lapchick was attacked and brutally beaten for his actions on behalf of human rights. That attack and his work on confronting racism in American sports are described in Lapchick's widely acclaimed *Broken Promises: Racism in American Sports,* published in 1984.

Lapchick's present position is director of the Center for the Study of Sport in Society, headquartered at Northeastern University in Boston. The Center was established in an effort to redress the shameful exploitation of American athletes; its focus is on the needs of athletes at all levels of sport. The Center works closely with professional athletes, teams and leagues, the mass media, and universities to bring degree completion programs to professional, Olympic, and amateur athletes, to provide outreach counseling to younger athletes, and to support minimum academic standards for high school athletes. In carrying out its programs, the Center is becoming a prominent force in the study of sport and education.

What is even more appropriate about Richard Lapchick being the editor of this volume is that most of the readings are drawn from *Arena Review* (originally called *Arena Newsletter*) and the *Journal of Sport and Social Issues*

(*JSSI*)—journals started by Rich Lapchick. In 1976, he founded ARENA, the Institute for Sport and Social Analysis, to provide a forum for serious social analyses of sport, and he started the two publications to provide communication outlets for the work of ARENA. With the first issue of the *JSSI*, Lapchick wrote:

> The *Journal* is to become an alternative source of opinion for academics, journalists, athletes, and sports fans. . . . [It] will attempt to provide a variety of perspectives, clear-eyed views and new and provocative ways of looking at sports problems. . . . The *Journal* will deal with various problem areas of sport, including: the political economy of sport, women and sport, race and sport, children and sport, health aspects of sport, and international politics, the responsibility of the sports media, athlete's rights, and sport as a builder/divider of the concept of community.

True to the original mission, *Arena Review* and the *Journal of Sport and Social Issues* have served as voices for articulating serious analyses of sport issues and suggesting the need for social change to make sports more humane and joyous cultural products.

The readings that Lapchick selected from *Arena Review* and the *Journal of Sport and Social Issues* to be included in this volume are essays and research reports dealing with the social issues that Lapchick identified as needing study in the first issue of the *JSSI*. They represent the work of a group of scholars who have been in the forefront of the social analysis of sport.

Lapchick writes in the conclusion of this volume that the "objective of the book has been to move the reader to think critically about sport." The book succeeds in doing this. Readers cannot help but be moved to concern and compassion for the issues facing contemporary sport. They will surely become aware—if they were not before—that there is much more to sports than game scores and striving for championships. As elements of contemporary popular culture, sport has far greater social significance than is usually acknowledged. It is only by understanding how sport relates to the larger society that change will become possible and alternative sport forms and content can become realities.

Acknowledgments

The overwhelming majority of the articles in this collection come from the two publications of the Center for the Study of Sport in Society— the *Journal of Sport and Social Issues* (*JSSI*) and *Arena Review*. Therefore, the first people I would like to thank are the editors of those publications: Jim Frey served as editor from 1978–83, when ARENA, the Institute for Sport and Social Analysis, was the official publisher. Leon Chorbajian and Jordan Gebre-Mehdin have been co-editors since Northeastern University's Center for the Study of Sport in Society took over the role of publishing. Their careful selection of articles made a wealth of material available to choose from for *Fractured Focus*.

I would also like to thank Dean Richard Astro of Northeastern, who agreed to make a financial commitment to the *JSSI*, the *Arena Review*, and, ultimately, to the Center itself; Robert Bovenschulte of Lexington Books, who contacted me about doing a series of books on sport and society and then provided a major source of encouragement after an agreement was reached; George H. Sage, one of the nation's most prominent sports sociologists, for writing the foreword to this book; Kareem Abdul-Jabbar, for contributing part of his own *Giant Steps* for this work; Mark Asher and the *Washington Post*, for giving me permission to use their excellent three-part series on abuses in college sports; and the *New York Times*, for allowing the use of its extraordinary four-part series on drugs in baseball.

When I think about sport and society, I immediately think of Robert Lipsyte and Harry Edwards, who, with some other journalists, scholars, and activists, have opened the eyes of the American people to the impact of sport on society. Bob and Harry have been active in this area for more than two decades, and I thank them for their contributions to this book.

Finally, I thank the staff—both official and unofficial—of the Center for the Study of Sport in Society for their support in this project. I must especially single out Tom ("Satch") Sanders, who has been my sounding board; Jacques Eusebe, who has helped with technical details; Leon Parker, who helped collect material; and Robert Malekoff, who provided invaluable assistance with the final preparation of the manuscript.

Introduction

Ten years ago, I was among the founders of ARENA, the Institute for Sport and Social Analysis. ARENA was created to be an alternative voice for scholars, journalists, sports fans, and perhaps most important, athletes. Entering a sports world that seemed to speak as a monolith, with heroes and hero-worship, one of the first things we did was to start a vehicle for that voice—the *Journal of Sport and Social Issues* (*JSSI*) and its companion piece, *Arena Review*.

The good news about sport has been trumpeted by the media for decades. Sportswriters and broadcasters have too often become sports promoters. The public has been saturated with all the good things sport does for society—building character, motivating individuals, generating teamwork, and instilling discipline through structured competition. Sport has been a powerful social equalizer in this country: Blacks have been led out of poverty and into the mainstream through sports. Women have broken down "feminine" stereotypes through sport competition and, by asserting themselves on the playing fields, have become ready for executive positions in the corporate world. Sports contact with other nations has built international harmony, understanding, and peace.

The underlying assumption of ARENA and its publications, however, has been that sport is a *reflection* of society, not a panacea for all its ills. Our methodology has always been a diverse one, encompassing sociology, anthropology, political science, history, psychology, physical education, and journalism. Over the past decade, we have examined the problem areas of sport, such as the exploitation of athletes, racism, sexism, youth sport, violence, gambling, drugs, and the whole international dynamic—from the Olympics to ideology to the controversy over South Africa.

The Center for the Study of Sport in Society (CSSS) was initiated at Northeastern University in June 1984, and by agreement between Northeastern and ARENA, the *JSSI* and *Arena Review* became publications of the Center. The mission of the Center was not only to study sport and its impact on society but also to try to bring about changes by developing an educated and self-empowered athletic community. As it begins its third year, the sustained national response to the efforts of the Center has demonstrated an overwhelming need for both an increased understanding of sport through a better body of knowledge and a program to address the problems inherent in sport.

Fractured Focus is, for the most part, a compilation of articles published in the *JSSI* and the *Arena Review*, all of which have been updated either by the author or the editor. New articles have also been added—on abuses in college sports, on drugs in baseball, on the youth of Kareem Abdul-Jabbar, and on the boycott of South Africa.

The purpose of this book, like that of the Center's publications, is to counterbalance all the writings about the joys of sport with a critical look at the less glamorous side. Although all the writers have attempted to be objective, many have a strong and sometimes passionate point of view. The book's importance lies in the fact that its contributors are among our finest scholars, journalists, activists, and athletes. Such writers as Sage, Eitzen, Edwards, Lipsyte, Asher, and Abdul-Jabbar bring a unique voice to this volume in their discussions of the issues confronting the world of sport in the 1980s. People in the field who have fought to bring about change not only assess problems but suggest solutions: Harry Edwards on the abuses of college sport and their effects on all athletes but particularly on black athletes; George H. Sage on the National Collegiate Athletic Association (NCAA); Rick Horrow on violence; Tom Tutko on youth; Donna Lopiano on women's sports; and Bob Lipsyte on the sports media. As editor, I have chosen articles that address both sport in America and sport on the international level. The chosen themes may concentrate on problems that are decades old, yet events of 1985 have seemed to highlight reasons for their inclusion.

No issue so dominated the sports pages in 1985 as the state of disrepute of intercollegiate athletics. Not only were amateur athletes being paid big dollars (witness Tulane and Kentucky, two universities long thought to be paragons of virtue), but few athletes were graduating in revenue sports (a *USA Today* survey showed a graduation rate of 27 percent at Division I basketball schools over the past decade), and cheating was rampant.

Black athletes continued to be the most exploited. Memphis State University—a 1985 Final Four participant—had not graduated a black basketball player in 12 years; and the University of Georgia had graduated only 4 percent of its black athletes. The situation was the same at too many other schools. Pursuit of the dream of a shot at the pros, despite the 12,000 to 1 odds against it, apparently is costing a disproportionate number of young blacks a chance at a meaningful education that could prepare them for life.

There were fewer women in athletic administrative positions in 1985 than 10 years earlier; only 53 percent of women's teams were coached by women in 1985, as opposed to 92 percent in 1973. Moreover, the proportion of athletic budgets spent on women's programs was not growing.

The size and scope of youth sports has continued to expand rapidly, while the effects on the education of our youth seem to get worse. A study by Harry Edwards revealed that up to 30 percent of high school athletes in basketball and football were functionally illiterate. Even at the high school level, many athletes had already become primarily performers, not students, as eligibility was stressed over academics. A new Texas state law, introduced in 1985, mandated minimum academic standards of a C average. It was called the most controversial piece of legislation in Texas since the civil rights laws were passed.

Violence in such sports as hockey and football has been on the rise for many years. Yet 1985 witnessed the worst case of spectator violence in sports history when British soccer fans attacked Italian fans at a match in Brussels. Thirty-eight died and 400 were injured.

Evidence of a national gambling spree was all over network TV and in the betting lines published in some of our nation's most respected newspapers. Yet the point-shaving scandal at Tulane somehow shocked our collective national conscience. How soon we had forgotten the nightmares of 1951, 1961, and the 1970s. Some said the Tulane case was most shocking because drugs were involved.

Super Bowl drug revelations, the banning of Michael Ray Richardson, Baseball Commissioner Uberroth's announcement of sanctions against twenty-one known users in the Major Leagues, and revelations that fifty-seven of the top senior collegiate prospects for the NFL draft tested positively for drugs made 1986 seem like The Drug Review. However, it only made real what we already knew—that highly paid athletes, like highly paid executives, are drawn to the drug culture in America. The most frightening but less publicized item was that nearly 5.6 million high school athletes were abusing chemicals in 1985.

Also in 1985, the media, which helped keep us in the dark during the days of hero-worship, were finally ready to expose the sores that fester in the sports world. Finally, the demystification was underway.

With major boycotts of the last three Olympics now history, and with profound political events in the 1968 Games and great tragedy in 1972, no one can deny that politics are a significant part of sport. As 1985 came to a close, there was no certainty that the 1988 Games would be any different, with North Korea fighting South Korea for hosting rights.

The issue of South Africa dominated the international news throughout 1985. The horrors of apartheid, finally acknowledged by the Western world after nearly eighty years of internal oppression matched only by the Nazis, made sports contacts with South Africa virtually nonexistent.

All of these issues are addressed in *Fractured Focus*. Although the chosen articles highlight the current, they also give the reader a sense of the history of each issue and the impact it has on society. Taken as a whole, it is hoped that the book will help the reader understand the combined impact of all these issues and seek some ways to bring about change.

Fractured Focus

1

Intercollegiate Athletic Abuses

Recent revelations of the graduation rates of college athletes have only underscored what many people close to the campus scene have known for years. Universities, along with families and religious organizations, are charged with being the guardians of our nation's moral values, but the glamorization of sport has led to a near collapse of that guardianship in university athletics.

Look at 1985's revelations. The graduation rate for basketball players nationwide was 27 percent. The rate was a shocking 6 percent for Final Four participant Memphis State University, and it was alleged that no black basketball player had graduated from there in more than a decade. The University of Georgia's graduation rate for black athletes was 4 percent. Overall, 30 percent of scholarship athletes in football and basketball graduate, but only 20 percent of black athletes graduate.

Cheating within athletic departments has taken on plague-like proportions. Walter Byers, executive director of the National Collegiate Athletic Association (NCAA), stated that many good college players are making up to $20,000 a year. The nation's best "big men" were said to receive $100,000 when they signed with certain universities.

Tulane University suspended its basketball program after a point-shaving scandal was uncovered. The key player at Tulane admitted receiving $10,000 from an assistant coach on signing to attend the university in 1981. Texas Christian University suspended seven football players when they admitted to their coach that they had received substantial cash payments from boosters. The president of Clemson University resigned when he realized that he could not control his athletic department.

The use of recreational and performance-enhancing drugs was rampant on the country's campuses. A coach at Arizona State University reportedly gave some of his baseball players drugs to end their depression during a rare losing season, and a trainer at Vanderbilt University was accused of being a retail distributor of steroids to athletes throughout the southeast.

In all these areas, the greatest concern of educators should be that athletes have become primarily performers—that their education has become a secondary issue. For many years, however, the attitude of educators—from university presidents to faculty and coaches—has been most disturbing. The former president of the University of New Mexico said: "Our recruits were recruited to be athletes, not students. There was never an expectation that they'd get their ass out of bed at 8 o'clock to go to class and turn in their assignments." Such attitudes made it easy for North Carolina State University to admit Chris Washburn with a 475 college board score when the average student there has achieved a 950—or for Tulane to admit "Hot Rod" Williams with close to the minimum score.

Indeed, the scandals of 1985 were nothing new. The only difference was that there was now more to gain, so the colleges were taking more chances. Under the media microscope as never before, the Presidents' Commission of the NCAA passed a series of reforms at its New Orleans convention in June 1985. The college presidents tried to regain control of their athletic departments, which, in too many cases, were like unguided missiles.

One of the four "outside" pieces chosen for this book—"Abuses in College Athletics"—is a three-part series by Mark Asher of the *Washington Post* (16, 17, 18 June 1985), published as the aforementioned NCAA Presidents' Commission convened in New Orleans to address the question of integrity in intercollegiate sports. A roll-call vote assured the passage of nine major reforms, including the so-called death penalty. Asher interviewed college presidents, educators, coaches, and athletic directors, and the *Post* polled 192 presidents for this three-part series. The first part examines "a system gone awry." The second part presents case studies of universities that have succeeded on and off the field with their athletes. The final section deals with proposals for reform, specifically those adopted by the NCAA in 1985.

Over the past two decades, Harry Edwards has been the man most identified with the attempt to change college sport—to make it more humanized and less exploitative. His article, "The Collegiate Athletic Arms Race" (*JSSI*, vol. 8, no. 1), examines the origins and implications of the NCAA's "Proposition 48" in the context of the problems of academic exploitation of athletes and integrity in college sports and discusses how they reflect the much broader crisis in education in the United States. Edwards clearly shows that the factors that led to the adoption of Proposition 48, as well as those that made it so controversial, were "rooted in the traditions and the ongoing character of interracial relations in American sport and society." (This article might well have been placed in the chapter on racism in sport.)

Like many others, I believe that it took Harry Edwards' courage to defend the standards included in Proposition 48 so that it could get beyond the controversy and be adopted. Many applauded the NCAA for passing the 1985 reforms and Proposition 48, but a close examination reveals that these reforms were passed almost in spite of the traditional NCAA power structure. It was the active intervention of the university presidents that made the crucial difference.

George Sage is another of our nation's most prominent sports sociologists. His updated article, "The Intercollegiate Sport Cartel and Its Consequences for Athletes" (*Arena Review*, vol. 3, no. 3), demonstrates that the exploitation of athletes is virtually a natural consequence of big-time athletic programs that are protected by the NCAA, acting as a cartel.

The article by Joseph Raney, Terry Knapp, and Mark Small, if applied to many college campuses, could have an enormous impact on our knowledge of patterns of academic abuse. "Pass One for the Gipper: Student-Athletes and University Coursework" looks at the academic records of athletes at the University of Nevada–Las Vegas (UNLV) and systematically identifies ways in which athletes at that school maintain their eligibility. The article traces the credits and grade point averages transferred in, mostly from junior colleges (more than 35 percent of all credits in basketball, football, and baseball, with better than a 2.5 GPA); the patterns of course credits at UNLV (47 percent of baseball players' credits in physical education and anthropology/ethnic studies); and other factors, such as teachers being favorably disposed to athletes.

In 1978, demoralized by the problems of college sports, Jim Frey wrote "The Coming Demise of Intercollegiate Athletics" (*Arena Review*, vol. 3, no. 3). He predicted the demise of what we know as "big-time" sport, claiming that it was already underway. No one can deny that the crisis in sport is worse a half-decade later. Ironically, many of the factors that Frey predicted would lead to that demise have been embellished rather than eliminated. Although schools such as Notre Dame and the University of Washington make more than $19 million from basketball and football, fewer athletic departments are making money in the mid-1980s. Yet, like the player who believes he can beat the odds and turn pro, the losing athletic department thinks *it* will turn the big profit. Moreover, the enormous increase in TV revenues for college sports has heightened all the negative factors. Thus, although college sport may never self-destruct, we certainly can no longer view it innocently. It is a big-time business.

Abuses in College Athletics

Mark Asher
The Washington Post

He had played on a high school basketball team ranked among the best in the country, and when it was time for many big-name colleges to recruit him, his grades apparently were not all that important to the sweet-talking coaches who came calling.

In his first three years of high school, he had failed English once and world history twice and had Ds in three other English courses, including reading. His high school transcript further notes he was absent 84 days and tardy 68 other days in those years. He ranked 388th in a class of 435.

Going into his second semester of his senior year, which ends next week, he had a 1.8 grade-point average on a 4.0 scale, buoyed by courses in physical education, health, art and music. To get the required 2.0 average, qualify for a scholarship and be eligible to play at the prominent private university whose national letter of intent he signed, he needs an 88 average on a 100 scale in his final semester.

His name cannot be used because there are laws protecting confidentiality of students' grades and transcripts. Yet this transcript, one of many obtained by *The Washington Post* from three college coaches, was typical, they said.

And few coaches in America have any reason to believe the player will not achieve the grades he needs to play college basketball.

In the first semester of his senior year, like many other star athletes, he improved dramatically in his academic performance. His mainly Ds and Fs metamorphosed to an 85 in algebra, 83 in social sciences, 75 in American history and 75 in physical sciences, not to mention the 90s in physical education and music.

"All of a sudden, he saw beyond the end of his nose," insisted the coach who signed him. This athlete may very well have buckled down, but several coaches familiar with the player say more likely than not he has benefited from a system that allows its star athletes to keep advancing to the next level, even if it means fudging on grades.

From *The Washington Post*, 16, 17, and 18 June 1985. Reprinted by permission.

In a college athletic system many say has gone awry because of commercialization and the accompanying pressure to win, the nameless player in the example may be the rule, but the exception, among many players entering big-time college programs.

In a recent poll by *The Washington Post,* more than one in every three Division I college presidents said their campuses had at least some athletes who do not belong in college. One in every five presidents cited the lowering of academic standards for athletes as a problem at their schools within the past five years. "There are functional illiterates in every major college football program," said Tom Reed, football coach at North Carolina State.

The NCAA is holding a special convention starting Thursday in New Orleans to deal with eight proposals concerning the integrity and economics of college sports. According to *The Post* poll, most of the proposals will be passed overwhelmingly. Many presidents say it can't happen soon enough.

"The mood now is to act. It's moved from the debate scene to action," said Bill Friday, president of the University of North Carolina system. "In our country now, sports has taken the form of a religion. All these forces have generated enormous pressures on the schools . . . It forces institutions to do things they didn't do in the old days.

" . . . There are allegations that colleges and universities are in the entertainment business, that they mold themselves and their existence to accommodate that pressure and that demand! All of these circumstances raise questions that deal with academic requirements, recruiting abuses, scheduling abuses, impact of commercial television, ineffective sanctions, salary excesses and the ultimate abuse—gambling and cheating that we have witnessed."

"If you let the business aspects and the winning aspects get ahead of the academic aspects in your mind, you're probably into trouble," said Terry Sanford, president of Duke University, where 92 percent of varsity football and basketball players graduate. "It's absolutely true that some people have got their values wrong. It's not up to me to criticize them. But it's up to me as a member of the NCAA to support more stringent regulations, and I don't think that they're stringent enough."

Eamon Kelly, president of Tulane University, which dropped its basketball program in the wake of a point-shaving scandal two months ago, says this week's meeting "is a major step in the right direction." Yet, Kelly said, it apparently will fail to address head-on the two root problems: "commercialization, where the principal goal is satisfying the mass TV market rather than providing competitive activity for students," and "the differential in admissions standards, and I really see that as the linchpin in the entire set of problems in terms of academic performance."

To keep up with other teams, many schools—including some of the most prestigious academic institutions—have lowered admissions standards for athletes. At Tulane, for instance, admitting athletes with minimum NCAA requirements meant in some instances taking students whose combined verbal and math college board scores were 600–700 points lower than the average Tulane freshman.

Transcripts obtained by *The Washington Post* (with the proviso that the athlete's name and current school not be revealed) produce a clear pattern of the quality of high school education needed to qualify for a scholarship at a major university.

■ A multisport high school star last season whose transcript was sent to such schools as Texas, Penn State, Maryland, Purdue, UCLA and North Carolina. His college board scores were 460—the minimum 200 on the verbal portion, 260 in math. He has signed a grant-in-aid to play basketball at one of the East's more academically respected state universities.

■ A player now at a large eastern state university. Going into his final semester of high school, the player was ineligible for an athletic scholarship under NCAA rules because his overall grade-point average was below 2.0—a C. In that last senior semester, he apparently became, relatively, an academic whiz, according to his transcript; B in language skills, B in economics, B in geometry, A in independent living, A in physical education, A in personal typing. . . .

Still, Stan Morrison, basketball coach at USC, says he can justify recruiting academically deficient players.

"It's something that transcends SAT scores and grade-point averages," he said. "It's a gut feeling about a guy's environment. If I've been in a kid's home and know there are no books, no magazines or no encyclopedias, and he's at a school where the faculty emphasis is not on academics, then we'll take a chance, while giving him the environment and academic support to succeed. I don't accept it [the system], I don't condone it, but I do understand it."

Clearly, there is little or no incentive to strive for academic excellence, and so few football and basketball players graduate that Rep. James Howard (D-N.J.) recently introduced a bill that would take away the tax deduction for donations to booster clubs at schools that do not graduate 75 percent of their athletes over a five-year period.

According to the College Football Association, only four of 47 member schools (Duke, Notre Dame, Virginia and Wyoming) who reported last year and three of 53 this year graduated 75 percent or more of their players. The latest CFA survey also shows eight of 53 schools with graduation rates of less than 25 percent. In basketball, there is no clearinghouse for information on graduation rates.

The academic difficulties of players like Chris Washburn of North Carolina State and Michael Graham of Georgetown became well known within the last year. Washburn's academic deficiencies—he had 470 on his college boards—came out in court papers filed during a criminal proceeding against him for stealing a stereo from another student. Graham's situation became known when he was declared academically ineligible by his coach, John Thompson. Apparently there are many athletes with similar problems nevertheless playing, starting and starring on some of America's best teams.

The questions of academic integrity permeate all aspects of win-at-all-costs athletics. Youths are recruited in junior high school by overzealous high school coaches. In high school, many teachers and administrators look the other way in order to keep a star athlete eligible.

College coaches, some of whom parlay their players' talents into as much as $500,000 annual income, often fawn over these teen-agers. By the time the players reach college, many of them are cashing in, too, if not directly from the coaches, then through more-than-willing boosters or agents.

And if a coach has no qualms about paying players under the table, why should the players have qualms about shaving a few points? The Tulane scandal added a new element to the mix. The fixers allegedly hooked the players on cocaine first, and the combination of drugs and gambling clearly has university administrators concerned.

Memphis State University, its image endangered in recent months by a federal grand jury investigation into big-money bookmaking in its area, hired a retired FBI agent to advise the university about dealing with gambling and drugs. Charles Cavagnaro, the school's athletic director, predicted that more law enforcement officers will be hired in the future.

The latest push for reform is nothing new. Ever since the early 1900s, major reports have been issued that cited extensive problems in college sports and sought changes. Yet, over the years, many of the nation's biggest athletic programs became virtually autonomous, and college presidents—sometimes with pressure exerted by governing boards—let them exist. Coaches have been fired frequently for not winning enough games, but there have been few if any reports of college presidents and athletic directors being fired because of abysmal graduation rates for athletes.

The presidents at the University of San Francisco and Tulane dropped basketball programs because of unsavory situations within the last three years, and Oklahoma City University this year decided to drop out of NCAA Division C and join the NAIA, saying it could not compete financially aginst other major schools without cheating. Many other colleges have been embarrassed by cheating and academic scandals.

Early this year William Atchley, Clemson University president, resigned after his efforts to clean up the school's athletic program were rebuffed by the athletic director and board of trustees. Bill McLellan, the athletic director since 1971, finally was reassigned to another department to wait out a short period to retirement, but he had survived major probations in both football and basketball.

Leaders of the latest reform movement see this week's convention as merely a beginning, looking ahead to business at future conventions designed to reinforce the notion that athletes are students first. The presidents have already begun to raise the academic standards necessary for an athlete to earn a scholarship. They have also made it more difficult to stay eligible. If the rules are followed, it will be difficult for athletes "to major in eligibility," as James Wharton, president of Louisiana State University, puts it.

During the 1983 NCAA convention, after an emotional floor debate, the controversial Proposition 48, which goes into effect in August 1986, was passed. Unless amended, it will require a 700 (out of 1,600) combined score on the Scholastic Aptitude Test or a 15 (out of 36) on the American College Test and a 2.0 grade-point average (out of 4.0) in a core curriculum of 11 academic subjects to be eligible to play as a freshman. Athletes who do not qualify will be permitted a scholarship, but will lose a year's eligibility.

Many educators, including Leroy Walker, chancellor at North Carolina Central University and a former coach of the U.S. Olympic track and field team, believe that the minds of many athletes are being wasted. Walker and others say if the athlete has the incentives to score 700 on the college boards and earn a C average in a core curriculum, he will do so.

Once in college, there are ways for the nonacademically oriented to stay eligible, despite all the reforms, including a current rule that athletes must make satisfactory progress toward a specific degree.

According to a 1980 graduate who was a starting lineman for a major southern state university, even academically inclined athletes are often pushed toward easy courses that will allow them to maintain what the NCAA describes as "satisfactory progress" toward a degree.

This straight-A high school student-athlete had every intention of getting a meaningful degree, and he did. But that did not deter the coaching staff from advising him, in his first semester, to take music appreciation and fundamental education. He got a B in music appreciation, even though he said he didn't study and went to class every other week. He received an A in the education course. "The professor, as they say, was 'very, very sympathetic,' " he said. "It was taught Monday nights. We'd sleep through the whole thing because we were too exhausted from practice to stay awake."

Planning to major in zoology, he also took a zoology course with a lab and freshman English. He got a D in zoology, the only D he said he ever made in school. "That zoology course just about killed me," he said. "I missed every lab but one. There was a team meeting from 12 to 1, and the lab was at 12:30. It was impossible to make all the classes."

For many athletes, apparently it still is.

One thing Tom Reed remembers about the summer of 1983, his first as the football coach at North Carolina State, is the 45 to 50 players who had to attend summer school just to remain eligible to play that fall.

He also remembers what Chancellor Bruce Poulton told him the day he was hired to coach a team whose graduation rate had been 15 percent for the entering freshman classes of 1976, 1977 and 1978. "He told me to get things straightened out and to win," Reed said. "He said, 'You must win. You're not immune from that, either.' "

Reed will not criticize his predecessors, but says, "Going to class wasn't quite the thing to do." So, for those still cutting classes, Reed implemented Friday night study halls, from 7 p.m. to midnight. "And if I was really mad, I made it Friday night and Saturday night too," he said. "It gets their attention."

Now, fewer than 10 of his players are in summer school. However, the academic turnaround has not been matched by success on the field; the team was 3-8 each of Reed's first two seasons. But the case of the football team at N.C. State illustrates a basic theme found during a month of interviews for this series.

Rules by themselves will not improve the academic integrity of intercollegiate athletics; strong leadership is needed to accomplish that. Leaders on the nation's campuses cannot turn their heads, bask in the limelight at bowl games and expect academics to coexist with the win-at-all-costs environment that pervades big-time college sports today.

What follows is an examination of some programs and an attempt to show why some have been successful, academically and athletically, and what steps reform-minded college presidents have taken:

The Raleigh-Durham-Chapel Hill area of North Carolina could be a good place to start. There, within a 30-mile triangle, are located three members of the Atlantic Coast Conference—North Carolina State, Duke and the University of North Carolina.

A look at North Carolina State shows what can happen when standards are reduced. According to figures compiled by the *Charlotte Observer* newspaper, N.C. State ranked last in graduation rates for ACC schools for the entering freshman classes of 1976, 1977 and 1978, 12 of 80 football players and zero of 15 basketball players earning degrees. Chancellor Poulton declined a request for current statistics on the football and basketball teams, but said that 35.1 percent of all athletes graduate, compared to 35.8 percent of all N.C. State students.

The university was widely criticized last fall when it became known that Chris Washburn, a freshman basketball star, had been admitted despite his combined math-verbal score of 470 on the college boards. His weak academic background became public in a court proceeding that ended with Washburn being found guilty of stealing another student's stereo.

Nevertheless, Poulton defends the admission of Washburn, saying the 6-foot-11 player would have been admitted even if he had not been an athlete.

"The facts are that we admitted others who were not athletes, who were not any stronger [in the classroom] than Chris, and we will again this year," Poulton said. "Please understand that we have a commitment to surpass 10 percent black enrollment, and the facts are that we are looking at black students who on paper might not appear to you or a lot of others to be the kind of students we should be looking at. People who are talking about him and writing about him are doing [it] from a position of ignorance.

"I've got a file that thick on his ability. He's been tested 16 ways from heaven. He's got perfectly normal intelligence. He has the ability to be successful at this university, and there's no rational reason for him not to be here."

Both Coach Jim Valvano and Athletic Director Willis Casey declined requests for interviews for this series. Valvano said he could live with "whatever rules we have" affecting his basketball program.

Less than two decades ago, N.C. State was issuing press releases about its academic excellence. In June 1971, the university reported that 26 members of the football team, including 12 starters, had made dean's list. The next year State again reported 26 players making dean's list, "one-fourth of the entire squad." The release noted that over the past nine years, the Wolfpack led the conference in placing football players on the ACC all-academic team.

The next year, the ACC dropped its 800 rule, which tied athletic scholarships to a requirement of at least an 800 score on combined math and verbal portions of the Scholastic Aptitude Test. A year later, the school's faculty senate approved a resolution allowing athletes to be included as exceptions to general admissions policy.

N.S. State, where engineering students traditionally had trouble remaining in school, then redefined "student in good academic standing." A student had to enroll for at least 12 hours to be considered full-time. But one could drop courses until the final examination and needed only to pass half of them to remain eligible. Thus, an athlete could sign up for 12 hours, drop six, pass three and be eligible the next semester.

Both Robert Fearn, an economics professor and president of the faculty senate, and F. Joseph Hale, a professor of aeronautical engineering, said the rule was not made with athletes in mind. But it was a loophole the Wolfpack could use while winning two NCAA basketball championships and going to six bowl games in seven years. The rule was changed a few years ago, when State discovered that some regular students were taking eight years to graduate. In addition, the NCAA implemented rules that required athletes to make satisfactory progress toward a degree.

Not until Poulton became chancellor in 1981 were other substantive moves made, including a reduction in the number of athletic exceptions in admissions, an outside audit of the athletic department and drug testing.

Poulton has reduced the number of athletic exceptions from 44 in the fall of 1981, during Poulton's first year, to 33, 22 and, now, 11.

Since the NCAA enforcement program began in 1951, N.C. State has been publicly penalized four times—twice in basketball, once in football and once for all sports. Only four other schools have received more public penalties—Wichita State (seven) and Southern Methodist, Arizona and Florida State (five each).

In a survey by the NCAA Presidents' Commission, 71 percent of all member schools' chief executive officers cited boosters and alumni as a major problem in the management of intercollegiate athletics. At a university like N.C. State, the university must depend on a private foundation—in State's instance, the Wolfpack Club—to pay for scholarships and some sports facilities, because state funds are not allowed to be used for athletics.

"Trying to maintain an intercollegiate athletic program at an institution like this is an enormous task," Poulton said. "We field 26 different teams . . . [Being self-supporting] is a problem in the sense that it takes an enormous amount of money. Frankly, it's a lot easier for wealthier supporters to attempt to put leverage on a program if the program is totally dependent on wealthy supporters."

Institutional control is one of the major concerns of reform leaders. As Robert Atwell, president of the American Council on Education, noted, "The institutions that emphasize [athletics] the most put the least amount of their own dollars into it."

Perhaps that is one of the reasons Duke University, a highly selective private school in Durham, appears to have a model program, in which most athletes graduate in four years and redshirting is not allowed except in medical cases.

Although 75 percent of presidents polled say redshirting—allowing a player to sit out while still on scholarship and save a year's eligibility for future

All-Time NCAA List of Public Penalties

Wichita State	7
*Southern Methodist	5
Florida State	5
Arizona	5
West Texas State	4
Texas A&M	4
North Carolina State	4
Oklahoma	4
Auburn	4
Kansas	4
Western Kentucky	4

*Sixth penalty on appeal
Source: NCAA Enforcement Department

use—is either somewhat or very helpful to an athlete academically, Duke and Notre Dame, among others, do not permit it. They maintain that athletes should be treated as any other student. Yet, they were one-two in last year's College Football Association graduation statistics.

Duke has a $7.9 million annual budget, receives a $1.75 million annual subsidy from the university and, according to its athletic director, is the only Division I school that does not charge students for admission to athletic events. Alumni members of the school's athletic council are elected for one term only, "to keep one or two people from becoming entrenched in that position," said Terry Sanford, the university president.

"We've got a pretty good governance structure," said Sanford. "I don't think we could have anything like Tulane, simply because I have confidence in the athletic director [Tom Butters]. He's alert to these things and he has confidence in the coaches, as I do too. [But] the president's got to be the keeper of academic quality. Nobody else is going to do it.

"We've done that in a very simple, straightforward way. We've assigned an assistant director of admissions to make all of the decisions about admissions, of which there is no appeal. A coach cannot come to me and say, 'Just give me an exception on this one 7-footer who we just happen to have.' That would be so inappropriate he might even get discharged. He certainly would get reprimanded and he certainly wouldn't get any attention here."

Andy Bryant, assistant admissions director in charge of athletics, declined to give the average college board score of Duke's football and basketball players. He says the school has accepted no athlete in the past eight years with a score less than 700, and rarely less than 800. "The bottom line is whether the athlete can graduate or not," he said, "And I'm correct in approximately 92 percent of the cases."

In 20 years, only one Duke basketball player who has finished his eligibility has not graduated. "That's Kenny Dennard, and he's so tired of hearing about it, he's coming back and getting his degree," Bryant said.

Duke does not offer scholarships in nonrevenue sports—swimming, fencing and men's track and cross country. However, in the case of a world-class athlete, such as Olympic gold-medal swimmer Nancy Hogshead, Duke does give a full grant-in-aid.

In addition, Butters has dropped football games against Ohio State, Oklahoma and Arizona State in favor of prospectively more competitive games against regional opponents. It is a move saluted by such faculty members as Arnie Lewin, chairman of the school's academic council, who says of Duke's athletic policies, "It's one thing to have a policy. It's another thing to have it work, and Tom Butters has made it work. He just doesn't condone coaches who try to get exceptions for athletes."

Butters said: "Intercollegiate athletics is a viable part of a university, but no more viable than other parts. It just happens to be more visible. In this day and age, it is easy to let athletics, with the financial pressure and the greed to win, get out of perspective. And a university that allows that to occur is living on borrowed time.''

Sanford, who is retiring next month after almost 15 years as Duke's president, has drawn up a 34-page policy paper on intercollegiate athletics. ''I thought it would be helpful with a new president coming in if I put a lot of things in writing,'' he said.

''I go to all the games,'' he said, ''and I'm an enthusiastic supporter—but if I just got carried away with every little detail, I might find myself tempted to forget that this is an academic institution.''

Down U.S. 15–501 in Chapel Hill, the University of North Carolina basketball team is known nationally both for its success on the court (seven Final Four appearances and one championship for Coach Dean Smith) and in the classroom (only one basketball player who completed his eligibility has not graduated).

Smith has a rule that a player must miss one game for every class he cuts. A few seasons back, one player had 28 cuts by the start of the season; he was benched the entire season, according to Smith. Also, pressure on North Carolina coaches to win is eased because they have the next-best thing to tenure: long-term contracts.

Smith tries to keep as secret as possible the identity of players he is recruiting, ''to cut down on boosters.'' Smith remembers the time a booster tried to give one of his players some money coming out of the locker room. ''He [the player] told me who it was and that stopped that,'' Smith said. ''They know better. People are afraid . . . So I think the coach does know and can control any illegal payments.''

In addition, Smith has had a car registration program for his team for the last decade. Every player with an automobile has to let the coaching staff know the make, model and year. He believes that discourages athletes from looking for deals from unscrupulous boosters, and keeps those same boosters away from his program. ''You know how players are living and you know how their family background is,'' he said.

According to Smith, North Carolina admits 36 athletic exceptions annually for all sports. He declined to break down the number for basketball.

Smith believes schools that allow athletic exceptions would be better served by ''a rule that the lower 2 percent of your entering freshmen cannot be athletes. Then you can take anybody that you wish, using class rank, grade-point average and SAT scores, because—and I believe this—that at every school, including Ivys, most of your lowest students entering will be Division I football and basketball problems.''

Back in Raleigh, Reed doesn't have the time for such philosophical matters. With an academic file four times as big as his weightlifting performance file, he is trying to establish the proper balance between athletics and academics. "Three and eight, three and eight. Some people think I'm a bum," Reed said.

And there are rumors that he is in trouble, even though he has a five-year contract.

"There's only one group of people that count. That's the players," Reed said. "Everything else will fall into place. If it doesn't, that's okay . . . Will they give me enough time? If they don't, we're in a sorry, sorry state."

Dropping varsity basketball was not the end of the story at Tulane after the scandals in the sport there a couple of months ago. Eamon Kelly, the university president, formed a select committee on Tulane intercollegiate athletics directed—none too hopefully—toward opening a new era.

Kelly asked the committee to analyze the problems and develop recommendations for a program "under which a university of Tulane's caliber and quality can participate in Division I-A intercollegiate athletics, maintain our academic standards and see that the kind of things that happened in the basketball scandal do not happen again."

That task, Kelly said recently, "is one of the most complicated intellectual questions that any group can face." He is not optimistic that Tulane will be able to resume its basketball program soon.

"I do not want to prejudge what will be the recommendation of this committee," he said, "but I would not reinstitute Division I-A basketball unless there was a dramatic change in the national environment, and I just do not see that in the foreseeable future."

Asked to define dramatic change, Kelly said: "Where there is an end to the commercialization of collegiate athletics, elimination of the culture of win at all costs in order to appear on television and a removal of the economic incentives of intercollegiate basketball."

Kelly was describing intercollegiate sports' version of Utopia, when games are being played by students and for students. The athletes would be students first and foremost, with no double standards on admission or in the classroom.

But that is easier said than done in the broad-based NCAA, where highly selective private institutions compete on the playing fields against state universities, some with open admission policies.

When a special NCAA convention this week in New Orleans considers eight proposals dealing mainly with institutional integrity, some say the convention voters—college presidents or their selected representatives—will be dealing with symptoms, not with the problems.

"It's professional athletics as far as the schools are concerned," said Bob Piper, a former high school coach now working as a financial consultant in the Washington area. "The kids aren't getting paid, but it's a big business. I don't know what the problem is, but I do know educating their athletes isn't one of their goals."

Commercialization is cited by more than six of every 10 college presidents in a recent poll by *The Washington Post* as a major problem in intercollegiate athletics today. The difference in admissions standards among NCAA members is causing many colleges to adopt a double standard in order to compete in Division I.

This is the root of the problem: decisions concerning academic philosophies are being based on financial considerations.

"I spoke to a group of athletic directors about three years ago in Las Vegas," said John Thompson, basketball coach at Georgetown University. "The issue came up as to whether freshman should be ineligible. Most of the people in the room agreed it would be beneficial for freshmen not to be eligible, because of school adjustments and sociological adjustments.

"But when they voted, a majority of the people voted against it, because people discuss education and morality but they vote economics. It's constantly done. Moral issues and educational issues are discussed, but the vote becomes an economic [issue]. That's the real world we live in, too."

The Washington Post's poll showed that 65 percent of the college presidents who responded favor freshmen eligibility. The strongest sentiment against freshmen on varsities comes among the schools with the biggest programs. In Division I-A, 36 presidents favored freshmen eligibility and 27 opposed it. In Division I-AA, encompassing all other schools that play Division I football, 53 presidents favored freshman eligibility and only nine opposed it.

A return to freshman ineligibility likely would cause a significant deterioration of the parity that exists among schools in football and basketball. The biggest would become bigger and better, because they again could stockpile players, while the smaller schools would be less able to cope. It would increase costs and lessen the available talent pool to those schools without the tradition to attract recruits.

One of the leading proponents for declaring first-year students ineligible is Bill Friday, president of the University of North Carolina system: "It gives you a chance to really get your feet on the ground. The average SAT score of entering freshmen is just at 1,100 [at Chapel Hill]. It's the same at Raleigh, so the competition is pretty severe."

But not everyone agrees.

"Who can afford at a small school just to keep a guy around?" counters Joe Johnson, president of Grambling State University, whose school already is feeling the financial pinch of a Supreme Court decision that stripped the NCAA of its hold on college football's network television packages. "Big schools have foundations and things like that. Small-college presidents feel they can provide support services to help the kid survive."

There is likely to be a push to repeal the freshman eligibility rule at the NCAA's annual convention in January. Bruce Poulton, chancellor at North Carolina State, wanted the Presidents Commission to put freshman ineligibility on the agenda this week in New Orleans. But leaders for reform in college athletics know it is difficult to push for more than one major reform at any convention. This time, they will concentrate on uniform penalties for cheating and take-the-program-away measures for repeat offenders.

Reform leaders are hopeful that a compromise to Proposition 48 can be achieved before the January convention. Proposition 48 sets new minimum requirements for first-year eligibility based on entrance exams and a core curriculum of 11 academic subjects as of August 1986. If the compromise can be reached, they can tackle other issues, such as freshman eligibility, in January.

William Lee Atchley, who resigned after failing in his attempt to get the Clemson University trustees to give him a vote of confidence in his power struggle against athletic director Bill McLellan, says there is only one issue that matters.

"That issue is athletics versus academics," he said. "No matter what your intentions and reasons may be, what you decide today, as far as almost everybody is concerned is athletics versus academics . . .

"When you have an image problem that academics takes a back seat to athletics, you have a problem. You no longer have an institution where people with integrity want to teach, or where people with common sense and good values want to send their children to learn."

Clearly, college athletics have an image problem these days. A recent poll by the Associated Press showed that six in 10 Americans believe college sports are overemphasized and seven in 10 believe that betting on college games encourages athletes to cheat.

Perhaps that is why many presidents believe that among the most important proposals this week is one dealing with "the Principle of Institutional Control and Responsibility." It requires an annual audit, by auditors with no ties to the university, of all expenditures for a school's intercollegiate athletics programs, so the president of the university knows exactly where each dollar is going.

"They want to make sure that they don't have a ticking bomb," said Shelly Steinbach, general counsel of the American Council on Education.

In theory, passage of this proposal, combined with two others, would mean that presidents would have audits not only from their athletic departments, but all booster clubs—even those incorporated outside the university.

"It's not a bad price to pay for a little more insurance and public confidence that athletics is being run in a businesslike way," said William Muse, president of the University of Akron.

Still, some apparently don't want to know, or believe that an outside audit is a wasted expense, since they already are covered by state auditors. That is the one proposal gaining the smallest majority of the presidents in *The Washington Post*'s survey. Only 61 percent favor such a rule, compared with at least 85 percent favoring uniform penalties, sanctions on coaches, and disclosure of data on freshman athletes, on the progress of other athletes and on graduation rates.

Clearly, the financial bottom line remains among the NCAA's more controversial subjects. The dollars generated by football and basketball—and network telecasting thereof—are needed to subsidize nonrevenue and women's sports and, for many colleges, mortgages or bonds to pay for construction of new arenas and modernization of stadiums.

Some say all college sports should follow the Ivy League model, where athletes are truly students first, with scholarships awarded on a need basis, with no spring football, with the most broad-based of college sports programs. But most administrators don't believe that is a realistic approach.

Instead, some major universities are simply deemphasizing some of the nonrevenue sports, easing the pressure on football and basketball to generate huge sums of money.

"You can't disarm unilaterally, either by school or conference," said Art Padilla, associate vice president for academic affairs for the University of North Carolina system, "It's always been my contention—I may be wrong about it—that you can put five midgets with State basketball uniforms on and put five midgets with Carolina basketball uniforms on, have a game and the rivalry would still be there, just as intense. However, we have to make sure Lefty [Driesell] doesn't give you tall ringers. It's the whole question of unilateral disarmament."

Other critics say coaches should only recruit athletes who their admission offices believe can graduate. And once in school, the coach and the university should be willing to offer the academic support systems necessary to get an education. Schools like Duke, Georgetown, Virginia, Indiana, Notre Dame, North Carolina and Villanova—to name but a few—prove it can be done. Maryland, for instance, spent $220,000 on academic supports last year, according to athletic director Dick Dull.

Of course, smaller schools, trying to compete for a share of the NCAA basketball tournament pie, hardly have the resources to provide that support. Those schools must find a way to pay that price, or else compete at a lower level.

The athlete himself must be motivated to do well in the classroom. And both the coach and the athlete, as the NCAA is proposing, must be held accountable for transgressions in recruiting, such as taking cars and cash.

Washington Post Presidents Poll

Q. Would you say that many of your school's football and basketball players should not be in college, that some of them should not be, or that all of them belong in college?

Many Should Not Be	1%
Some Should Not Be	34%
All Belong	63%
Don't Know/No Opinion	3%

Q. Would you say that the commercialization of college athletics has helped major colleges, or has it been a problem?

Helped a Great Deal	7%
Helped Somewhat	5%
Major Problem	62%
Minor Problem	13%
Don't Know	12%

Q. A number of NCAA violations have involved overzealous alumni and school boosters. How would you characterize your athletic program's relations with alumni and school boosters? Would you say you have no problems, some problems or major problems?

No Problems	60%
Some Problems	38%
Major Problems	1%
Don't Know	1%

Q. As you may know, the president of Tulane University terminated varsity basketball there because of allegations of serious problems in the program. Do you approve or disapprove of his decision?

Approve	61%
Disapprove	17%
Don't Know	22%

Q. In your view, should incoming freshmen be eligible to play varsity football and basketball, or not?

Yes	65%
No	27%
Don't Know	8%

Q. In 1983, the NCAA passed Proposition 48, due to become effective in August 1986. It requires a 700 minimum SAT score, or a 15 ACT score, and 2.0 grade-point average in 11 academic subjects as a standard for first-year eligibility. How do you feel about these requirements of Proposition 48? Do you approve or disapprove of them?

Approve	59%
Disapprove	20%
Approve of Some/Disapprove of Others	15%
Don't Know	6%

Q. Does your school always completely pay the way for former athletes who come back to finish their education, or not pay their way, or doesn't your school have a policy on that?

Always Pay	22%
Does Not Pay	14%
No Policy	14%
Like Any Other Student	5%
Pays for Some	6%
Partly Pays for All	6%
Depends	6%
Don't Know	4%

Washington Post **Presidents Poll** *(continued)*

Q. How important are intercollegiate athletics at your school?	
Unimportant	2%
Important, but just Another Facet	59%
Very Important	38%
Not Sure	1%

For those who portray the athlete as often a victim, especially athletes from deprived backgrounds, Georgetown's Thompson says: "The student has to take a major responsibility, and that will correct a lot of problems . . . I've met a lot of very moral and ethical people. Some of the most moral and ethical people I've ever met have been in low-income areas. So those people know right from wrong. I'm not going to buy they don't know right from wrong. So they've got to share the responsibility."

Above all, administrators agree, college presidents must continue to take a leadership role in athletics. As Edward Weidner, chancellor at Wisconsin-Green Bay, said, "The initiative that college presidents are taking is long overdue. I just hope it's permanent."

Said Bob Atwell, president of the Washington-based American Council on Education, a leader in the push for reform of college athletics: "The sands of time are running out, and you've got to have something fairly dramatic. Whether the kind of stuff we're seeing at the June convention is dramatic enough, I don't know. It's all good stuff, but is it enough?

"When all the sands have run out, where are we? We are no longer able to sustain the myth or reality of the amateur model. We will have arrived, without deciding to do so, at professionalism."

The Collegiate Athletic Arms Race: Origins and Implications of the "Rule 48" Controversy

Harry Edwards
University of California at Berkeley

The motives behind all infractions of the amateur code are the results of commercialism. Respecting the present recruiting and subsidizing of college athletes, those who tempt young men to barter their honesty for the supposed advantages of a college course, dishonestly achieved, are the Fagins of American sport and American higher education.

The common notion that athletes in general are poorer students than nonathletes is erroneous. On the other hand, participation in sports that require very hard training and long practice hours impairs the academic standing of certain athletes . . . The causes of this condition are ascribable not to an inferior mental equipment among college athletes . . . but to the conduct, emphasis, and values of modern college sport.

This is the more unfortunate, because success in life after graduation appears to be related less to personal athletic success in college than to high academic standing. . . . It requires no tabulation of statistics to prove that the young athlete who gives himself for months, body and soul, to training under a coach for a grueling contest, staged to focus the attention of thousands of people, and upon which many thousands of dollars will be staked, will find no time or energy for any serious intellectual effort. The compromises that have to be made to keep such students in the college and to pass them through to a degree give an air of insincerity to the whole university-college regime. . . . The need today is to re-examine our educational regime with the determination to attain in greater measure the sincerity and thoroughness that is the life blood of a true university in any country at any age.

—The Carnegie Foundation for the Advancement of Teaching: Bulletin Twenty-Three—*American College Athletics*, October 24, 1929

Universities and Athletics: In Pursuit of Prestige and Fortune

Collegiate sports history is rife with recurrent scandals involving the recruitment, support, and exploitation of highly touted athletes. But in recent years, widespread media exposure of unethical and even illegal dealings in college sports programs has resulted in unprecedented concern over these problems.

Most of the attention has been focused upon National Collegiate Athletic Association (NCAA) division I football and basketball programs. Why NCAA division I rather than division II or division III programs? Why football and basketball rather than, say, water polo, fencing, badminton, or field hockey? The answer to both questions boils down—as it long has—to a single word: M-O-N-E-Y.

Today, collegiate sports programs consume more than half-a-billion dollars each year. In addition, they generate billions of dollars more for sports promoters, amateur sports governing organizations, broadcast networks, advertisers and other commercial interests, legal and illegal gambling, and for universities themselves from broadcast and gate receipts as well as from sports-motivated alumni philanthropy and legislative generosity in complying with university budget requests. In short, NCAA division I football and basketball are big business.

In 1983, sixteen post-season NCAA division I football bowl games paid $27,576,107.20 to the schools and conferences involved. And by way of illustrating how rapidly the monetary rewards for such post-season play have escalated, consider the Fiesta Bowl. The Fiesta Bowl paid two teams and their conferences 380,000 dollars in 1981, disbursed 687,000 dollars in 1982, and paid $1,701,369.76 to Fiesta Bowl participants at the end of the 1983 season.

1983 Bowl Payoffs

Bowl	Payoffs
Rose (UCLA 24, Michigan 14)	$6,615,928.00
Cotton (SMU 7, Pitt 3)	3,705,068.00
Sugar (Penn State 27, Georgia 23)	3,600,000.00
Orange (Nebraska 21, LSU 20)	3,316,673.56
Fiesta (Arizona St. 32, Oklahoma 21)	1,701,369.76
Gater (Florida St. 31, W. Virginia 12)	1,198,611.10
Liberty (Alabama 21, Illinois 15)	941,383.38
Bluebonnet (Arkansas 28, Florida 24)	600,000.00
Hall of Fame (Air Force 36, Vanderbilt 28)	909,072.74
Peach (Iowa 28, Tennessee 22)	886,005.10
Sun (No. Carolina 26, Texas 10)	800,000.00
Holiday (Ohio State 47, BYU 17)	785,670.68
Tangerine (Auburn 33, Boston College 26)	700,000.00
Independence (Wisconsin 14, Maryland 20)	600,000.00
California (Fresno St. 29, Bowling Green 28)	570,418.88

Total of $27,576,107.20 represents revenue from both gate and television rights that was dispersed to the institutions and conferences involved.

Source: *The Sporting News*, May 23, 1983, p. 50.

Also by way of comparison, in 1959 when the University of California at Berkeley won the NCAA division I basketball tournament championship, it took home 17,500 dollars as its share of the tournament purse. The 1983 NCAA division I championship basketball tournament, on the other hand, generated 20,280,385 dollars in television broadcast and gate receipts with each of the "final four" schools vying for the championship receiving 600,000 dollars on top of their regular season's gate and broadcast receipts. In 1983, the NCAA expanded its tournament roster to fifty-two teams with each of the fifty-two guaranteed 120,000 dollars for merely participating in the tournament, 290,000 dollars for each team making the "sweet sixteen," and 520,000 dollars for each team surviving to be among the "final four." The price of tickets for the three "final four" and championship games at Albuquerque, New Mexico ranged as high as 1000 dollars each with one "scalper" advertising tickets for four adjacent seats for the series at 8000 dollars (Crowl, 1984).

With such riches at stake, division I colleges and universities have developed athletic programs with multi-million dollar budgets and millions more invested in facilities and equipment (e.g., the University of Michigan with a 1983–84 academic year athletic budget of over eleven million dollars and a 100,000-seat football stadium; Stanford University with an athletic budget of 14.2 million dollars and an 86,000 seat stadium).

And it has not been just institutions that have stood to reap the rewards of big time football or basketball preeminence. Indeed, in 1983, the highest paid college and university officials in the United States were not college presidents, university chancellors, or Nobel Prize laureates but head football and basketball coaches. Successful head coaches are today rewarded with salaries in the hundreds of thousands of dollars, with fast food franchises, stocks, bonds, homes, automobiles, country club memberships, income producing television and radio shows, highly lucrative product endorsements, lecture and sports clinic opportunities and other special amenities.

If the competition for such rewards has not obliterated such traditionally ballyhooed collegiate sports ideals as educational development and building character, it has certainly relegated these concerns to a secondary, if not wholly irrelevant, status. Today indications are that the quest more than ever is not so much to provide educational opportunities or to build character as *to win*— even if it means that in the process the young men generating the sports prestige and the billions in wealth are systematically condemned to the role of "losers" in life (Hutchins Institute, 1982).

Athletes: The Price and Pressures of Participation in and Preparation for the Collegiate Athletic Wars

The caliber of collegiate division I football and basketball competition has become so advanced that there is virtually no hope of winning championships without the player who has "blue chip" athletic potential and who has dedicated a disproportionate amount of his time and energy to developing that potential—players who television sports commentator and former NCAA champion Marquette University basketball coach Al McGuire quite aptly calls "aircraft carriers" and "big guns." And indeed there is today disturbingly consistent evidence that athlete recruitment and development among major collegiate football and basketball institutions has degenerated into a spiraling "athletic arms race" wherein student-athletes are both the most strategic material and chief casualties.

The systematic exploitation of collegiate-student athletes really begins long before they ever set foot on a college campus—in grammar school or junior high. As soon as someone finds that a particular youngster can run a little faster, throw a little harder or jump a little higher than all of his peers, that kid becomes—as sportscaster Frank Gifford would say—something "really special." What this usually means is that beyond sports excellence, little else is expected of him. In some states, such as Texas, even junior high school football and basketball players are often routinely "red shirted"—held back academically for the purpose of enhancing their size, strength, and athletic skills, thereby making them more attractive products for high school recruiters. In most states, red shirting at the high school level is commonplace (Underwood, 1980).

As late as the spring of 1983, it was still the case that only twenty-five of this nation's 16,000-plus school districts had set minimum academic achievement standards as conditions of high school sports participation (Faris, 1982). Thus, by the time many "blue chip" student-athletes finish their high school sports eligibility, so little has been demanded of them academically that no one any longer even expects anything of them intellectually. Thus, *the "dumb jock" is not born; he is being systematically created.*

That minority of student-athletes who do prove themselves to be legitimate "blue chippers" and who also survive the high school academic charades, usually will gain admission to some major college or university. But the traditional promise and implied contract, "You give the school your athletic talent, the school gives you an education," turns out to be far less than an iron-clad guarantee.

A systematic rip-off begins with the granting of a four-year "athletic scholarship," technically given one year at a time under existing NCAA rules. This means that though the athlete is committed to the school for four years, the school is committed to him for only *one*. Strictly speaking, each year the athlete must earn his scholarship anew. Furthermore, nowhere in the NCAA's 335-page rule book are there specifications of the conditions under which a coach may legitimately strip a student-athlete of his scholarship. Indeed, there is not a single NCAA rule specifying any student-athlete *rights* as such—only their obligations and prohibitions.

The problem with the four-year scholarship is that it more often than not takes the average non-athlete student on a major division I college campus four-and-a-half to five-and-a-half years to complete a four-year degree. Even special provision for a fifth year of support for the athlete at the athletic director's or coach's discretion—support which few student-athletes actually receive—does little to alter this situation in the student-athlete's favor because very few division I football or basketball players complete their sports eligibility with a year or less of academic work remaining before graduation.

Already among the least-well academically prepared students entering the university, the football players at a major NCAA division I institution will put in between *forty-five* and *forty-nine* hours a week during the season preparing for, participating in, and recovering from football. If travel time is counted, the average time expended escalates to *60 hours* a week. Basketball players are close behind, putting in thirty-five to forty hours a week—fifty hours a week if travel time is included—meeting their athletic obligations while, like the football player, *being required by NCAA eligibility rules to carry a "full-time" academic load*. The results of such classroom demands upon what all too frequently are academically underprepared student-athletes, functioning in a perpetual state of fatigue, and putting in more time fulfilling their sports obligations than they would be putting in on a full-time job, are as predictable as they are inevitable for most—educational mediocrity and failure (Underwood, 1980: 40).

Even those student-athletes who are drafted by the pros soon learn that the actual realities are quite different from the rumored rewards that have fueled and motivated their athletic development. Approximately eight percent of the draft-eligible student-athletes in collegiate basketball and football are actually drafted by professional teams each year. But only *two percent* will ever sign a professional contract, thereby receiving a reprieve from the consequences of their academic underdevelopment. In the National Football League, where the average athlete will play only four-and-a-half years, according to U.S.F.L. and N.F.L. figures between seventy and eighty percent of professional football players *have no college degree*. Among athletes in the National Basketball Association, where the average playing career lasts only 3.4 years, the graduation figures are equally dismal. So before the average professional basketball or football player is twenty-nine years old, his sports career is already over and these former "big guns" face the challenges of making a living utterly unarmed educationally in our technologically sophisticated society (Sources, 1983: N.F.L. Player Registry; U.S.F.L.'s National Sports Career Management, Inc.; N.B.A. Players' Association).

And what of former collegiate "aircraft carriers" who are drafted but *not* offered professional contracts? Some degenerate into athletic "Flying Dutchmen," season after season drifting pathetically from one professional tryout to another, victims of a dream that has become a perpetual nightmare of futility and disappointment, holding to the hope of professional stardom until age and despair compel them to face the realities of life after sports. Among this group, expressions of "disengagement trauma" sometimes have been severe to the extreme—including anti-social behavior, substance abuse, "nervous break-downs" and even suicides (Richardson, 1980: 84–85).

The ninety-two percent of collegiate athletes who are draft-eligible but are not drafted must face the realities of life after sports immediately. For those able to continue in college or who are within reach of graduation, disengagement from a virtual lifetime of sports participation can be disconcerting but not necessarily devastating. Tragically, such is not the case for far too many others (McGuire, 1983; Hooker, 1983).

The former blue chipper who completes his eligibility but is not drafted, signed to a pro contract, or within reasonable reach of achieving a degree tends no longer to be perceived as a "big gun." Rather, on campus he is now seen as a "smoking gun," a potential embarrassment to the athletic department, his former coaches, and his school. Because of his academic circumstances and his failure to secure a pro contract, he constitutes a "loose cannon" on the deck, a potential source of disenchantment and dissension within the ranks of new recruits and student-athletes still having sports eligibility. There are no more fast academic fixes, no more fancy fictions about fame, fortune, and fat city forever. Now the hope all too often is that he will simply go away—the farther, the faster, the better, the more easily forgotten.

Blacks and Sport: Beyond the Myth

For decades, a contract has been struck between 17 to 19 year-old freshmen student-athletes and universities. An education in exchange for athletic performance. *The athletes have kept their part of the bargain; the universities have not.* Universities and athletic departments have gained huge gate receipts, television revenues, national visibility, potential and actual donors to university programs, and more—a result of the performances of gifted basketball and football players, the most gifted *and the most exploited* of all being disproportionately Black.

Most certainly the exploitation encountered by Black student-athletes does not just happen to them; it usually just happens to them worse. To understand why, we must understand sport's impact upon Black society, how a popular myth alleging innate race-linked Black athletic superiority and a belief in sports' "inherent" racial beneficence combine with contemporary Black socio-political circumstances and Black student-athletes' high mobility aspirations to predispose them to disproportionate and more severe victimization.

Since Jackie Robinson ostensibly shattered the color barrier in professional baseball, sports at all levels have accrued a reputation for having achieved extraordinary, if not exemplary, advances in the realm of interracial relations. To some extent, this reputation has been deliberately fostered by skilled "sports propagandists" eager to project "patriotic" views consistent with America's professed ideals of racial justice and equality of opportunity. To a much greater extent, however, the portrayal of sports as an arena of inter-racial beneficence has been spawned and propagated by less calculating observers of the sporting scene who have been simply naive and critically ignorant about the dynamics of sports as an institution and its relationship to society generally, and about the race-related realities of American sports in particular.

The sources of many misconceptions about race and sport can be traced to developments in sport which would appear on the surface to validate such ill-informed views. For instance, though Blacks constitute only 12 percent of the U.S. population, in 1983 just over 55 percent of the players in the National Football League were Black while *twenty-five* of the twenty-eight first round NFL draft choices in 1981 were Black. As for the other two major professional team sports, 74 percent of the players making National Basketball Association Rosters and 80 percent of the starters during the 1982–1983 season were Black, while Blacks comprised 18.7 percent of America's major league baseball players at the beginning of the 1983 season.

Black representation on sports honor rolls has been even more disproportionate. For example, the last ten Heisman Trophy awards have gone to Black collegiate football players. In the final rushing statistics for the 1982 NFL season, *thirty-six* of the top forty running backs were Black. In 1982, not a single White athlete was named to the first team of a major Division I All-American Basketball roster. Similarly, *21* of the 24 athletes selected for the 1982 NBA All-Star game were Black, as were 18 of the 24 selected for the 1984 All-Star game. And since 1958, Whites have won the NBA's MVP title only *3* times as opposed to 23 times for Blacks. And, of course, boxing championships in the heavier weight divisions and "most valuable player" designations in both collegiate and professional basketball have been dominated by Black athletes since the 1960s.

But a judicious interpretation of these and related figures reveals the mythical quality of sport's racially beneficent reputation and points toward conclusions quite different from what might be intuitively anticipated.

Patterns of Black opportunities in American sport are consistent with those in the society at large, and for the same reason—deeply rooted traditions of racial discrimination. I contend that racial discrimination in both sport and society is responsible for the disproportionately high presence of extremely talented Black athletes in certain sports on the one hand and the utter exclusion of Blacks from most American sports and from decision-making and authority positions in virtually all sports on the other.

It is today generally accepted in learned circles that the level of Black representation and the quality of Black performances in sports have no demonstrable relationship to race-linked genetic, biological, or physiological characteristics. Every study purporting to demonstrate such a relationship has exhibited critical deficiencies in methodological, theoretical, or conceptual design. Secondly, the factors determining caliber of sports performances are so complex and disparate as to render ludicrous any attempt to trace athletic excellence to some singular biological human feature (Edwards, 1973).

Thus, despite traditional myths and popular beliefs to the effect that Blacks are "natural" athletes and physically superior to athletes from other groups, the evidence tends to support cultural and social—not biological—explanations of Black athletic success and overrepresentation in the athletic role.

Briefly:

a) Thanks to the mass media and long-standing traditions of racial discrimination limiting Black access to the full spectrum of high prestige occupational opportunities, the Black athlete is much more visible to Black youths than, say, Black doctors or Black lawyers. Therefore, unlike the White child who sees many differential role models in the media, Black children tend to model themselves after the Black athlete—the one prevalent and positive Black success figure they are exposed to regularly year in and year out in America's White-dominated mass media (MacDonald, 1983).

b) The Black family and the Black community tend to reward athletic achievement much more and at an earlier stage of career development than any other activity. This also contributes to luring more young Blacks into sports career aspirations than the actual opportunities for sports success would warrant.

c) Because over 90 percent of American sports activities are still devoid of any significant Black presence, the overwhelming majority of aspiring Black athletes emulate established Black sports role models and see careers in only four or five sports—basketball, football, baseball, boxing, and track. The brutally competitive selective process that ensues eliminates all but the most skilled Black athletes by the time they reach the collegiate and advanced amateur ranks. The competition for available positions in sports offering opportunities to Blacks is made all the more intense because even in these sports, some positions (such as quarterback, center and middle line backer in football and catcher in baseball) are relatively closed to Blacks (Oliver, 1976).

d) And, finally, sport is seen by many Black male youths as a means of "proving" their manhood. This tends to be extraordinarily important to Blacks because the Black male in American society has been relegated institutionally to the status of "boy" for generations and systematically cut off from institutionalized mainstream routes of masculine expression (e.g., economic success, authority positions, etc.).

These factors contribute to channeling disproportionately high numbers of highly talented and motivated young Black males toward accessible positions in five American sports. By contrast, White male youths are exposed to countless role models and occupational opportunities. Thus, there is the probability that what was potentially a White "O.J." or "Dr. J." is piloting a plane, drawing up engineering plans for a bridge or skyscraper, or managing a corporation somewhere in America.

Despite the great pool of athletic talent generated in Black society, Black athletes get still less than six percent (6%) of all the athletic scholarships given out in the United States (between 10,000 and 12,000) (Coakley, 1982: pp. 262–263). And, as a result of the disproportionate emphasis placed upon developing their athletic talents from early childhood, an estimated 25–35 percent of high school Black athletes qualifying for scholarships on athletic grounds cannot accept those scholarships due to accumulated high school academic deficiencies. Many of these young men eventually end up in what is called, appropriately enough, the "slave trade"—a nation-wide phenomenon involving independent scouts (some would call them "flesh peddlers") who, for a fee (usually paid by a four-year college) search out talented but academically "high risk" Black athletes and place them in an accommodating junior college where their academic skills are further honed through participation in sports for the junior college while they accumulate grades sufficient to permit them to transfer to the sponsoring four-year school (Newman, 1978).

Of those who are eventually awarded collegiate athletic scholarships, studies indicate that as many as 65–75 percent may never graduate from college (Spivey and Jones, 1975; Talbert, 1976). Of the 25–35 percent who do eventually graduate from the schools they play for, an estimated 75 percent of them graduate either with physical education degrees or in majors specifically created for athletes and generally held in low repute (Spivey and Jones, 1975: p. 943). The problem with these "jock majors" and increasingly with the physical education major as well is that they have a very poor record as acceptable credentials in the job market—especially in this "tax revolt" era when physical education is usually among the first curriculum offerings to be eliminated. But surely, one might assume, there are ample occupational opportunities for outstanding Black former athletes within the sports world if nowhere else in the job market. Quite the contrary. To begin with, by several accounts, the overwhelming majority of Black scholarship athletes and professional athletes have *no* post-career occupational plans or formal preparation for any type of post-career employment either inside or outside of sports (Underwood, 1980: pp. 60–63). Black former scholarship athletes and professional athletes are employed less often and make less when they do have jobs than their non-athlete college peers; and Black former scholarship athletes and professional athletes are likely to switch jobs more often, to hold a wider variety of jobs, and to be less satisfied with the jobs they hold primarily because the jobs tend to be "dull," dead-end or minimally rewarding.

It is particularly tragic that sport, the realm assumed by most Black athletes to offer the greatest post-career job opportunities, probably offers the fewest.

Blacks are virtually excluded from authority and decision-making roles in all sports, while being concentrated disproportionally in the most dispersed, least powerful, most exploited and most expendable role—that of the athlete— in sports to which they do have access in numbers.

Among the 277 traditionally White division I colleges and universities participating in basketball and football, there is only one Black athletic director— Charles Harris at the University of Pennsylvania. There is only *one* Black head baseball coach—Dave Baker of Kansas State—at a traditionally White division I NCAA school. Among traditionally white colleges and universities classified as division I by the NCAA in basketball, only *12* had a Black head coach in 1983. Similarly, of some 96 NCAA division I football schools, only *two* had a Black head coach in 1983—Willie Jeffries at Wichita State University and Dennis Green at Northwestern University. This figure is made all the more glaring because between 1970 and 1980, there was a 90 percent turn-over among head football coaches at division I institutions. Yet it was still not until 1979 that Jeffries was hired, with Green being hired in 1980 at Northwestern—the university with the longest division I football losing streak in the NCAA history.

In the professional ranks, Blacks' access to non-athlete positions is even more limited than at the collegiate level. In the National Football League, there are:

- no Black owners
- no Blacks with executive administrative authority working out of the N.F.L. Commissioners office
- no Black general managers
- no Black head coaches
- no Black offensive coordinators
- no Black defensive coordinators
- only 14 Blacks (6 percent) among 225 assistant coaches on 28 teams
- only five Blacks holding executive or "front office" positions throughout the entire N.F.L.

The new United States Football League mirrors an almost identical pattern of excluding Blacks from authority and decision-making positions (Edwards, 1983, pp. 13–15).

As dismal as the six percent figure is for Black NFL assistant coaches, it appears that even grimmer statistics will hold sway in the future. As Professor J. Braddock of Johns Hopkins University found:

Whether direct or indirect, it is evident that race has traditionally been a limiting factor in the career mobility of Blacks in the National Football League. If recent trends are taken as valid indicators of Blacks future prospects in the NFL, then those prospects do not appear very bright. For example, in the 1963 season, Emlen Tunnell was appointed as an assistant coach with the New York Giants, and became the first Black to hold that position in the NFL's modern era. A decade later in 1973 Blacks comprised roughly seven percent of the assistant coaches in the NFL even though at that time Blacks comprised about thirty-six percent of the NFL players. In 1980, we find that despite a nearly twenty-eight percent increase in the number of assistant coaching positions, there has been a relative or proportionate decrease over the last seven years in the number of Blacks holding assistant coaching positions (even though the proportion of Black players had risen roughly fifty percent). The present trend, according to our model, suggests that the chances for a former Black player to become a head coach in the NFL appear to be worsening rather than improving (Braddock, 1980).

The problem of declining coaching opportunities in the professional ranks could be exacerbated by declining opportunities at lower levels which is the result of malevolent intent or racism. So, ironically, between 1954 and 1971 Blacks lost well over 2,000 coaching jobs due to school integration procedures that eliminated a number of all-Black schools in 14 southern states. Also, according to the *Statistical Abstract of the United States*, 1980 edition, while the number of people employed in "athletics and kindred fields" increased from 78,000 to 105,000 between 1972 and 1979, the proportion of Blacks in the fields dropped from 6.4 percent to 4.8 percent.

In professional baseball:

- of 913 front office positions, only 32 (and 26 of these are secretarial positions) are held by Blacks
- there are no Black-owned franchises
- of 568 scouts and recruiting personnel, only 15 are Black
- there have been only 3 Black managers over the entire history of professional baseball and only one of these currently managing in the majors.
- of the 123 coaches in major league baseball, there are only 13 Blacks and none of them is a third base coach—the individual generally considered second to the manager in authority.

In the National Basketball Association, there are:

- no Black owners
- three Black head coaches out of 23. In 1980, six of seven newly hired head coaches had previous N.B.A. head coaching experience and all were white. The seventh head coach hired, Paul Silas of the San Diego Clip-

pers, was the only Black hired and he had no previous coaching experience at all. Only one Black head coach who has ever been fired from a N.B.A. head coaching job has ever been rehired by another N.B.A. team.

- There are only four Black assistant coaches out of 23 in the N.B.A.

Among officials (referees, judges, and umpires), the figures on Black access for the most part follow the same pattern:

- In the National Basketball Association, *five* of 27 referees are Black.
- In the National Football League, only *eight* of 100 officials are Black.
- In professional baseball, only *one* out of 60 umpires is Black.

Given the tremendous power of the mass media in influencing perceptions of sports and disseminating ideological definitions, it is perhaps to be expected that the press box would be no less afflicted by the impact of racism than other authority realms in American sport. So, at the start of the 1983 season, not a single major league baseball team had a Black "play-by-play" announcer on its broadcast staff. In fact, with the exception of a few widely scattered Black sportscasters and reporters on media staff serving areas with substantial Black populations, a few Black network "color commentators" and one Black sports "anchor," Irv Cross at CBS, Blacks are conspicuously absent from the "regular assignment" roster of the sports media.

Thus, since Jackie Robinson's debut, Blacks have made virtually no progress beyond the athlete role in major American sports. And, even as athletes in these sports, Blacks often enjoy far less than total equality of opportunity. The evidence suggests, then, that in sport, America has "progressed" from a "Jim Crow" pre-Jackie Robinson era to a post-Robinson era characterized by what I would term "Mr. James Crow, Esquire"—a system whereby the traditonal inequities of interracial relationships are camouflaged and sustained through more subtle, sophisticated, exploitive and—for the sports establishment—highly profitable means.

What has not been thoroughly appreciated in America is the extent to which the overwhelming majority of all youths seeking affluence and stardom are foredoomed to fail. In the three major team sports, there are only approximately 2663 jobs for professional athletes regardless of color in a nation of 229 million people, roughly half of whom are male. This means that only *one* American male in about *54,000* is a professional football, basketball, or baseball player.

And for the average Black male, due to discrimination, the chances are considerably less of gaining such sports stardom.

It is simply not understood, even in Black society, that despite 74 percent Blacks in professional basketball, 55 percent Blacks in professional football, and 17 percent Black people in professional baseball, *there are still just over 1400 Black people (up from about 1100 before the establishment of the United States Football League) making a living as professional athletes in these three major sports today. And if one added to this the number all the Black athletes making a living as professionals in all other American sports, all the Blacks making a living in minor and semi-professional sports leagues, and all the Black trainers, coaches, and doctors making a living in professional sports, there would still be less than 2400 Black Americans making a living in professional athletics today!*

When this situation is considered in combination with the impact of the Black athlete's educational underdevelopment upon his non-sports related occupational potential, it becomes clear why so many Black athletes not only fail to achieve their expectations of life-long affluence, but they frequently fall far short of the levels often achieved by their non-athletic peers.

Despite the fact then that American basketball, boxing, football, and baseball competitions have come more and more to look like Ghana playing Nigeria, sport nonetheless looms like a fog-shrouded minefield for the overwhelming majority of Black athletes. It has been a treadmill to oblivion rather than the escalator to wealth and glory it was believed to be. There is today disturbingly consistent evidence that the Black athlete who blindly sets out to fill the shoes of Dr. J., Reggie J., Magic J., Kareem Abdul-J., or O.J. is destined to end up with "No J."—no job whatsoever that he is qualified to do in our modern, technologically sophisticated society. At the end of his sports career, he is not running or flying through airports like O.J. He is much more likely to be sweeping up airports—if he has the good fortune to land even that job.

Rule 48

It was mainly the Black athlete's tragic circumstances that prompted NCAA 1982 division I football "Coach of the Year" Joe Paterno to exclaim from the floor of the 1983 NCAA convention:

> For at least two decades we've told Black kids who bounce balls, run around tracks and catch touchdown passes that these things are ends unto themselves. We've raped them. We can't afford to do it another generation. (Paterno, 1983)

And with that statement, Coach Paterno gave impetus to the passage of NCAA's "Rule 48" which set off what probably is the most heated race-related controversy within the NCAA since the onset of widespread racial integration in major collegiate sports' programs during the 1950s and 1960s.

Put most simply, rule 48 stipulates that beginning in 1986, freshmen athletes who want to participate in sports in any of the nation's 277 division I colleges and universities must have attained a minimum score of 700 (out of 1600 possible) on the Scholastic Aptitude Test (or SAT) or a score of 15 (out of a possible 36) on the American College Test (or ACT) as well as have achieved a "C" average in eleven designated high school courses which include English, mathematics, social sciences, and physical sciences. Further, as *The N.C.A.A. News* (January 26, 1986) has stipulated, rule 48:

> . . . does not interfere with the admissions policies of any Division I institution. Nonqualifiers under this legislation may be admitted and attend class. Such a student could compete as a sophomore if he or she satisfies the satisfactory-progress rules and would have four varsity seasons starting as a sophomore if he or she continues to make satisfactory progress.
> Further, under related Proposal No. 49-B, any student who achieves at least 2.000 in all high school courses but does not meet the new terms of No. 48 can receive athletically related financial aid in his or her first year, but cannot practice or compete in intercollegiate athletics. This student would have three varsity years of participation remaining.

The outcry in response to the passage of rule 48 was immediate. The irony to many was that the most vociferous opponents of the rule were to be found among Black Civil Rights leaders and Black college presidents and educators—the very groups one might have expected to be most supportive of the action, given the historical educational neglect and athletic exploitation of the Black athlete. Their expressed concern was over those provisions of rule 48 specifying minimum test scores as a condition of sports participation, particularly the 700 score on the SAT leading the Black criticism of the NCAA's new academic standards were the National Association for Equality of Opportunity in Higher Education (or NAFEO), representing 116 traditionally Black colleges and universities; the National Alliance of Black School Educators; the Rev. Jesse Jackson, President of the People United to Serve Humanity (or Operation PUSH); Rev. Benjamin Hooks, head of the National Association for the Advancement of Colored People (NAACP); and the Rev. Joseph Lowery, President of the Southern Christian Leadership Conference (S.C.L.C.). They argue, first, that there was no Black input into the formulation of rule 48; second that the minimum SAT score requirement was arbitrary; and finally, that the SAT and ACT are racist diagnostic tests which reflect a cultural bias favoring Whites. It was their belief that the 700 SAT and 15 ACT score requirements would have disparate impact upon Black student-athletes given that 51 percent of Black students generally score less than 700 on the SAT and 72 percent score less than 15 on the ACT. And why would the majority of NCAA division I institutions vote to support a rule that would have a "disparate impact" upon participation opportunities for Black athletes? For NAFEO and its supporters, the answer was clear. As the most outspoken among the critics of rule 48, Dr. Jesse N. Stone, Jr., the president of Southern University in Baton Rouge, Louisiana, said:

> The end result of all this is the Black athlete has been too good. If it [rule 48] is followed to its logical conclusion, we say to our youngsters, 'Let the White boy win once in a while.' This has set the Black athlete back 25 or 30 years. The message is that White schools no longer want Black athletes. (Stone, 1983)

Members of the American Council on Education (ACE) committee, charged with developing rule 48, vehemently denied claims that no Blacks were involved in the process. In any event, the issue of whether or not there was Black input has always been moot insofar as the majority of Black NCAA delegates felt that their interests and views had not been represented.

I could not agree more with NAFEO, Rev. Jackson, Rev. Hooks, Rev. Lowery, *et al.* on their contention that the minimum SAT and ACT test scores are arbitrary. Neither the ACE nor the NCAA has yet provided any reasoned or logical basis for setting the minimum scores. But whereas NAFEO and others state that the scores are arbitrary and too high, I contend that they are arbitrary and so *low* as to constitute virtually no standards at all. But before presenting the details of my *concerns* about rule 48 and some proposed remedies to what I see as its deficiencies, let me explain and document the basis of my more fundamental disagreements with the NAFEO position.

One need not survey very much literature on the racist abuse of diagnostic testing in this country to appreciate the historical basis of NAFEO's concerns about rigidly applied test standards. But for NAFEO *et al.* to demand the repeal of rule 48 on grounds that its test score requirements are racist and will have a disparate impact upon Blacks was both *factually contestable* and *strategically regrettable.*

It was factually contestable on grounds that the overwhelming evidence indicates the SAT and ACT discriminate principally along socio-economic class, not race, lines. The major differences between Black and White scores occur on the math section of the SAT where cultural differences between the races would logically have the least impact—e.g., 2 + 2 = 4 whether one is Black, White, or Martian. Even on the verbal sections of these diagnostic tests, differences in Black and White scores are at least partially explained as class-related phenomena. As Dr. Mary Francis Berry, a NAFEO supporter, asserts:

> . . . A major differential (among test scores) was *not* between Black and White students, but between students from well-off families and students from poor families. The better-off the family, the higher the score—for Whites *and* Blacks. (Berry, 1982)

Dr. Norman C. Francis, President of traditionally Black Xavier University and immediate past chairman of the College Board, agrees:

> . . . The SAT is not merely a measure of potential aptitude, as many believe, but is also an achievement test which accurately measures what students have learned to that point. Most students do poorly on the test simply because they have never been taught the concepts that will help them to understand what testing and test-taking is all about. It is an educational disadvantage not an inability to learn . . . The plain truth is that students in poorer schools are never taught to deal with word problems and . . . critical analysis. The problem therefore is not with the students, or with the test, but rather with an educational system which fails to teach youngsters what they need to know. (Francis, 1983)

Rule 48, therefore, involves far more than a simple Black/White controversy, as 1981 SAT test statistics further bear out. Whereas 51 percent of the Black male students in 1981 failed to achieve at least a 700 on the combined SAT, as compared to nine percent of the Whites and 26 percent of other minorities, far more Whites (31,140) and other minorities (27,145) would have been affected than the 15,330 Blacks (*NCAA News,* January 26, 1983).

Furthermore, Black SAT scores are *rising* relative to those of Whites. So between 1981 and 1982, Blacks' verbal scores rose nine points and mathematics scores rose four points compared to a two-point gain in verbal and no gain in math for the White majority.

As to NAFEO claims that Black athletes would experience diminished access to traditionally White division I institutions in the wake of rule 48, even given the fact that *proportionately* more Blacks score below rule 48's minimum score requirements, it is highly unlikely that significant numbers of Blacks would be deprived of opportunities to attend traditional White schools on athletic scholarships. Indeed, if there is any threat of diminished Black athlete enrollment at division I schools in this regard, I submit that it would most likely involve enrollment at *traditionally Black colleges.* NCAA disciplinary records show that traditionally White institutions have led the way in amateur athletic rules infractions and in exploiting Black athletes. Why? Because they have the largest financial investment in their athletic programs and they and their athletic personnel stand to reap the greatest rewards from athletic success. With so much at stake and cavernous stadiums and pavillions to fill, it is ludicrous to presume that these schools which for so long have stretched, bent and broken rules to enroll Black athletes would now no longer want them and so would enact a rule that would diminish their access to them—all to the financial and athletic benefit of NCAA division II and division III schools which are not covered by rule 48. It is also the case that there are sufficient loopholes in rule 48 to allow any school to recruit any athlete that it really wants. Junior Colleges are not covered under the rule. So, schools could still resort to the "slave trade" to secure and develop athletes not eligible for freshman sports participation at four-year division I colleges. Further, as indicated, rule 48 allows division I schools to recruit freshmen athletes who are academically ineligible to participate and even to provide them with financial support. After several meetings with NAFEO representatives, the Rev. Jesse Jackson and others, I am strongly convinced that for many within the ranks of rule 48's detractors, it is the fiscal situation that has generated the priority concern, not educational issues. The overwhelming majority of the athletes recruited by traditionally Black division I schools—over 99 percent—are Black, score disproportionately below rule 48 minimum test score requirements, and tend to need financial support in order to attend college. However, because they have far more modest athletic budgets than traditionally White schools, traditionally Black schools are not nearly so able to provide financial support *both* for a roster of active athletes, on the one hand, and for a long roster of newly recruited athletes ineligible for athletic participation under rule 48. Traditionally Black division I schools, already at a recruiting disadvantage due to smaller budgets and less access to lucrative T.V. exposure, are placed at an even more critical recruiting disadvantage by not being able to afford even those athletes they would ordinarily be able to get.

It seems the case, then, that *the core issue in the rule 48 controversy is not racist academic standards or alleged efforts by Whites to resegregate major college sports so much as parity between Black and White institutions in the collegiate athletic arms race.* A major concern of NAFEO is equitable opportunities for Black colleges to recruit outstanding Black athletic talent and, so, to compete successfully for the monetary and other rewards generated by big-time college sports.

Strategically, there are two problems with NAFEO, NABSE, and the Black Civil Rights leaders' publicly expressed position on rule 48. First, they missed the greatest opportunity since litigation 30 years ago in Brown vs. Board of Education to make an impressive statement about quality and equality in education. Given that they had the attention of the nation, they also squandered a rare opportunity to focus and direct a national dialogue on restructuring the role and stipulating the rights of athletes in the academy. Secondly, with no real evidence to support their claims of racist motives on the part of rule 48's White supporters or of simple race bias in the rule's stipulations, the unfortunate and unintended impression they left was that they were really against all academic standards because of a belief that Black students are unable to achieve even the moderate standards established under rule 48. As one Black parent remarked, "If William Shockley or Arthur Jensen [the two leading proponents of the thesis that Blacks are intellectually inferior] had taken NAFEO's position on rule 48, we would be marching and picketing outside their offices."

Notwithstanding the rather transparent criticisms levied by rule 48's detractors, there are some real flaws in the measure relative to its proposed goals of shoring up the academic integrity of division I athletic programs. I submit, first, that the standards stipulated in rule 48 are *too low*. A score of 700 on the SAT, for example, projects less than a fifty-fifty chance of graduating from most division I schools (American Council on Education, Washington, D.C.).

Secondly, rule 48 does not address in any way the educational problems of post-enrollment college matriculation, which is where the real educational rip-off of collegiate student-athletes has occurred. Rather, it establishes standards of *high school* preparation and scholastic achievement necessary to qualify for freshman sports participation in college.

Nonetheless, I am fundamentally supportive of the NCAA action, not as a satisfactory solution to the educational problems of big-time collegiate sport but as a step—a very small and perhaps even inept step—toward dealing with these problems. More specifically, I support the NCAA's action on the grounds that rule 48 communicates to young athletes, beginning with those who are sophomores in high school, that *we expect them to develop academically as well as athletically*. This motivational aspect of rule 48 may in fact benefit those athletes with no college future more than those destined to win athletic scholarships. For instance, in California, 320,000 students each year participate in California Interscholastic Federation Athletic Programs and most undoubtedly aspire to win scholarships in their sports to division I institutions. However, only 5 percent of these students will ever participate in college sports at any level (including junior college) and the overwhelming majority will never even enroll at a four-year school (California Interscholastic Federation). If rule 48 does indeed spur greater academic seriousness among high school athletes, in the final analysis it might be the vast majority of high school student-athletes who are *not* going on to college who will benefit most from the NCAA's action—since they face the realities of life after sports in a solid state world immediately upon graduation from high school.

Further, I support rule 48 because in *not* supporting it, I would risk communicating to Black youth in particular that I, a nationally known Black educator, do not believe that they have the capacity to achieve a 700 score on the SAT, with three years to prepare for the test, under circumstances where they are given a total of 400 points simply for filling out the biographical information on the face sheets of the two sections of the test, and where they have a significant chance of scoring between 400 and 446 by a purely random marking of the test (American Council on Education). And, finally, I support the NCAA's action because it is my position that Black parents, Black educators, and the Black community must *insist* that Black children be taught and that they learn *whatever* subject matter is necessary to excel on diagnostic and all other skills tests.

I find outcries of "racism" and calls for Black boycotts of or exemptions from such tests as neither rational nor constructive long-term responses to the problem of Black students' disproportionately low test scores. Culture can be learned and taught. Socio-economic class-specific values and perspectives can be learned and taught. And this is what we should be about as Black educators—preparing our young people to meet the challenges they face on these tests, and by extension, in this society. We cannot afford to transform surmountable challenges—racial, cultural, political, economic, or whatever—into crutches, and then, like silly King Canute ordering the tides not to come in, demand that the technological and intellectual tides prevailing in the last fifth of the twentieth century be retarded or rolled back to accommodate our educational underdevelopment.

It is my position that (1) there must be diagnostic testing of student-athletes and non-athletes alike on a recurrent basis to assure skills achievement; (2) test score standards *should and must be raised* based upon the skill demands and challenges of our "solid state" world; and (3) the test standards set should be established as *post-enrollment* college matriculation goals and *not* pre-enrollment obstacles.

In the case of scholarship athletes, every institution should have the right to set its own academic enrollment standards. But there *must* be a binding corollary obligation and responsibility to develop and implement support programs sufficiently effective to enable the institutions to fulfill their implied contracts with the athletes recruited. Between 1966 and 1968, I was the organizer and leading strategist in fomenting campus boycotts and demonstrations across this country over the treatment and exploitation of the Black athlete. What came to be dubbed the "revolt of the Black athlete" culminated in the Olympic Project for Human Rights, the highlight of which was Tommie Smith and John Carlos' historic gestures atop the victory stand at the 1968 Mexico Olympics. Since that turbulent era, not much has changed relative to the exploitation of the Black athlete. And the situation may have become worse. But, today, we do have a more accurate and systematic understanding of how and why this exploitation occurs. Establishment of a "Student-Athlete's Bill of Rights," the setting of creditable academic standards and a more enlightened appreciation of the rewards as well as the potential liabilities of sports involvement could be major steps toward ameliorating this tragic situation (Farrell, 1983).

The Broader Issue of Educational Quality

For all of its divisive impact, the debate over rule 48 has illuminated a much larger nation-wide crisis involving the failure of this nation to properly educate its young, athletes and non-athletes. In 1982, the national average on the SAT dropped to 893 from 958 in 1967. Furthermore, even students who score well on diagnostic tests frequently require remedial work to handle college-level course work. From 1975 to 1980 the number of remedial math courses in public four-year colleges increased by 72 percent and now constitutes a quarter of all math courses offered by those institutions. At two-year colleges, 42 percent of math courses are below the level of college algebra (*U.S. News and World Report*, March 14, 1983).

There are also problems involving lowered standards and reduced academic expectations. According to the National Commission on Excellence in Education, in high school transcripts, credits for American history have declined by 11 percent since 1964 and by 6 percent for chemistry and 7 percent for algebra and 9 percent for French. In the same period, credits for remedial English have risen by 39 percent and driver education by 75 percent. Only 31 percent of recent high school graduates took intermediate algebra, only 16 percent took geography and only 13 took French, although these courses were offered. High school students have abandoned college preparatory and vocational education "tracks" in droves so that between 1969 and 1980 the number who chose the "general" track rose from 14 to 24 percent. About 25 percent of all credits earned by general track graduates were in physical and health education, home management, food and cooking, training for adulthood and marriage, remedial courses and for work experience outside school (*U.S. News and World Report:* 38).

Part of the problem is with our teachers, the way they are recruited, their low status, and their even lower rewards. A study conducted for the National Institute of Education, which looked at college graduates who entered teaching in the late 1970s, *found that those with the highest academic ability were much more likely to leave their jobs than those who were low achievers.* Among high-achieving students, *only 26 percent* intended to teach at age 30, as compared with approximately 60 percent of those with the lowest academic ability. In yet another study, it was found that one third of the 7000 prospective teachers who took the California State Minimum Competency test failed to meet the most basic skills requirements. And, in 1982, the average SAT score of students indicating teaching as their intended field of study ranked only 26th among average scores achieved by students declaring 29 different fields of interest.

Black colleges are themselves not blameless relative to inadequate teacher preparation. Currently, many states (over 20) require teacher candidates to pass a state licensing exam. Teacher college graduates in one state achieved a passing rate of 86 percent for White and 44 percent for Black test-takers. The two Black schools which produce the largest number of Black teacher candidates in the state had the worst passing rates, 35 percent and 16 percent, respectively (American Council on Education).

The state's Association of Black Psychologists held a press conference and denounced the tests as "instruments of European cultural imperialism" and urged Black students to "boycott" the tests. But there is really only one legitimate concern relative to such tests: Do they measure what legitimately should be taught in schools of education if teachers are to be competent?

The majority of Black students today come from schools in which Blacks predominate or from all Black public schools. It stands to reason, therefore, that much—if not most—of the failure to prepare Black youths educationally has occurred under Black educators. In the 1960s, from Oceanhill-Brownsville in New York to Watts in California, Blacks quite rightly criticized inner-city schools when White teachers and White superintendents were indifferent to the learning abilities of Black students. Many of these school systems now have a majority of Black teachers and Black superintendents and far, far too many Black students still do not learn. Can we afford to be any less critical when White incompetence is replaced by Black incompetence? Given what is at stake, the answer must be an emphatic and resounding *NO*! We must let all of our educators know that if they are not competent to do their jobs, *they have no business in our schools*. If they are competent and will not do their jobs, *we will not have them in our schools*.

But it is not sufficient to point out teacher inadequacies. For all of its modernity, education still advances on "four legs." Though formal instruction takes place in the classroom, education is the result of a cooperative and actively coordinated effort carried out between the home, the school, the community, and the larger society. The parent who does not participate in school activities, who does not attend parent-teacher conferences to review their child's academic progress, who generally shows low or no interest in school-related issues, indeed who does not know and has never even inquired as to the name of the teacher charged with instructing their child, over the years communicates to that child that education is not important. The community which undercuts the solvency of its libraries and schools through short-sighted tax policies communicates that education is unimportant. The school which emphasizes and revels in the glories of surpassing sports standards while fighting the establishment of academic standards for sports participation communicates that education doesn't matter. And, perhaps, the greatest contradictions exist relative to lagging societal support for educational advancement.

Current national policy that cuts severely into educational funding while proposing defense expenditures of 1.6 trillion dollars over a four-year period from 1982–1986 is both contradictory and shortsighted. Along with greater emphasis upon parental involvement in schools, insistence upon teacher competence, and greater academic expectations of our students, we must put more, not less, money into education. The National Center for Education Statistics estimates that the average current salary for classroom teachers is $17,644—up from $9,269 in 1971. However, in constant 1980–81 dollars, teachers have lost money, dropping from the 1971 equivalent of $20,168. The outlook for the future is equally bleak. The Center expects salaries in 1991 to have risen to

$20,113—still $55 below the 1971 mark. Education cannot attract and hold the best trained and most competent people without offering competitive salaries. Particularly in the more technologically applicable disciplines, education is suffering a severe "brain-drain." Thus, in 1981, nation-wide, half the teachers hired to teach high school math and science were not certified to teach those subjects while more than 40 states reported shortages of qualified teachers in these areas.

From the standpoint of this nation's position relative to its international competitions, American education also comes up short. The American school year is 180 days and the average student misses 20 of those, but Japan, Germany and most other industrial nations require at least 220 days a year and longer hours each day. In the Soviet Union, students from the first grade on attend school six days a week. About 35 percent of their class work is science. They take five years of arithmetic, then are introduced to algebra and geometry followed by calculus. The national minimum curriculum also calls for one year of astronomy and mechanical drawing, four years of chemistry, five years of physics, and six years of biology.

As a society, then, it is clear that we must demonstrate greater concern for and commitment to educational quality for all American youths—athletes as well as non-athletes. With adequate support and proper encouragement, I am confident that they can achieve whatever levels of performance are necessitated by the challenges they face and the expectations we set for them. In today's world, neither they nor we have any other choice.

References

Berry, Mary F.
  1982 "Investment in Education Pays Regardless of Color," *Los Angeles Times*, October 24, p. 5.
Braddock, J.H., II
  1980 "Institutional Discrimination: A Study of Managerial Recruitment in Professional Football." Report for the N.F.L. Players Association, pp. 58–59.
Coakley, Jay J.
  1982 *Sport in Society* (St. Louis: C.V. Mosby).
Crowl, John
  1984 "NCAA Has $3.09-Million Surplus After Previous Year's Loss," *The Chronicle of Higher Education,* January 18, p. 35.
Edwards, Harry
  1983 "Race In Sport: An Analysis and Some Briefly Stated Cross-Cultural Implications of the U.S. Case," in Eric Dunning and Robert Pearton, *The Sport Process* (London: E and F Spon. Ltd. Publishers), pp. 83–124.
  1973 *The Sociology of Sport* (Homewood, Ill.: Dorsey Press).

Faris, Gerald
    1982 "Schools Order Grade Levels For Athletes," *Los Angeles Times,* November 10, p. 1.
Farrell, Charles
    1983 "A Critic Sees His Protest Against Racism in Sports Vindicated After 20 Years," *The Chronicle of Higher Education,* January 26, pp. 17–20.
Francis, Norman C.
    1983 "Statement on Rule 48," Press Release. Office of the President, Xavier University, New Orleans, Louisiana, January 15.
Hooker, Rob
    1983 "For Most Black University of Florida Football Players, Getting Diploma is the Hardest Goal of All," *St. Petersburg Times,* May 12.
Hutchins Institute
    1982 "College Sports in Trouble," *Center Magazine,* January–February, pp. 13–33.
MacDonald, J. Fred
    1983 *Blacks and White T.V.* (Chicago: Nelson-Hall Publishers).
McGuire, John
    1983 "College Football: It's About Money" (Seven Part Series), *St. Louis Post-Dispatch,* September 18–25.
Newman, Edwin
    1978 "Big Money on Campus," N.B.C. Television Special Report.
Oliver, Melvin L.
    1976 "Race, Class and Family's Orientation to Mobility Through Sport," paper delivered at the Midwest Sociological Society Meetings, St. Louis, Missouri, April.
Paterno, Joe
    1983 "N.C.A.A. Toughens Academic Rules," Associated Press Wire Service, *Oakland Tribune,* January 12.
Richardson, Jack
    1980 "California Dreaming That Became A Nightmare," *Inside Sports,* May 31, pp. 84–85.
Spivey, D. and T.A. Jones
    1975 "Intercollegiate Athletic Servitude: A Case Study of the Black Illini Student-Athlete," *Social Science Quarterly,* Vol. 55, Number 4, pp. 939–947.
Stone, Dr. Jesse
    1983 "Black Colleges Threaten to Quit NCAA," *New York Times,* January 13, p. 1.
Talbert, T.M., II
    1976 The Black Athlete in the Southwest Conference: A Study of Institutionalized Racism. Doctoral Dissertation. Baylor University, Waco, Texas.
Underwood, John
    1980 "Student-Athletes: The Sham and The Shame," *Sports Illustrated,* May 19, pp. 36–73.
U.S. News and World Report
    1983 "What's Wrong With Our Teachers," March 14, pp. 37–40.

The Intercollegiate Sport Cartel and Its Consequences for Athletes

George H. Sage
University of Northern Colorado

The National Collegiate Athletic Association (NCAA) is a business conglomerate whose main function is the production of competitive sports events. Because of its unique structure, and a public image that it has fostered, the NCAA is able to exploit its major labor force—student athletes—to an extent that would be impossible in other American industries. Almost all of the rules and regulations of the NCAA benefit the management levels of the organization and are detrimental to the athletes.

This characterization of the NCAA and its activities applies most directly to the universities that sponsor "big-time" programs, i.e., the approximately 130 universities that are in Division I of the NCAA, but it applies in varying degrees to all of the institutions that hold membership in the NCAA. The focus of this article is on the "big-time" programs; my comments throughout the article should be interpreted by the reader to refer to these programs.

Growth and Development of the NCAA

The NCAA was founded in 1906[1] with a membership of about 35 colleges. Its original objective was "the regulation and supervision of college athletics throughout the United States in order that the athletic activities of the colleges and universities of the United States may be maintained on an ethical plane in keeping with the dignity and high purpose of education." The actual control of collegiate athletics was under the individual member institutions, according to the original charter. Thus, the original purpose of the NCAA was to serve in an advisory capacity to colleges (Stagg, 1946).

It was not until after World War II that the NCAA deviated from its traditional role as passive observer and consultant in the issues of collegiate sports and undertook a program designed to force member institutions to conform to the policies of the Association under pain of expulsion from membership if found in noncompliance with those policies. In effect, the NCAA made fundamental changes in its organization to the extent that it became an inspection and accreditation agency with the authority to employ sanctions against member institutions who violated its policies. The growth in the size of the personnel working in the NCAA and its power in controlling collegiate sports coincided with the increasing commercialization of college athletics after World War II (Scott, 1951). Today, the NCAA is the most powerful and prestigious organization regulating intercollegiate athletics in the United States. Over 725 colleges and universities hold active membership in this organization, and all universities which operate "big-time" athletic programs are members of this Association.[2]

Membership in the NCAA is institutional, and its legal authority comes from the colleges and universities which make up the membership and formal structure of it. NCAA rules and regulations are formulated at the annual conventions, where the institutional representatives come together to vote on policy, but the formal authority of the NCAA is highly centralized. This centralization is physically represented by the new $1.5 million dollar headquarters located in Shawnee Mission, Kansas; it is also represented by the 18-member Council which directs the Association between its conventions, and a 10-member Executive Committee which conducts daily business (*NCAA Manual, 1979-80*).

The NCAA as a Cartel

The official public posture of the NCAA is that it is organized only for the promotion of "amateur student-athletes" who participate in sports "for the educational, physical, mental, and social benefits he derives therefrom and to whom athletics is an avocation" (*NCAA Manual, 1979-80*: 9). In fact, the NCAA is a business organization which is part of the entertainment industry whose product is competitive intercollegiate sports events. Moreover, it is organized in the form of a cartel, which is an organization of independent firms which has as its aim some form of restrictive or monopolistic influence on the production and/or sale of a commodity as well as the control of wages of the labor force. Economist James V. Koch (1973: 129) has persuasively argued that the NCAA is a "business cartel composed of university-firms which have varying desires to restrict competition and maximize profits in the area of intercollegiate athletics." For example, the NCAA sets wages that can be paid the largest single group of employees in the industry, the athletes, it regulates the mobility of athletes during their career as collegiate athletes, it regulates the duration which the athletes may be employed, it pools and distributes profits of the cartel earned from such activities as televised intercollegiate athletic events, and it polices the activities of cartel members and levies penalties for infractions (Koch, 1971). Colleges and universities join the NCAA voluntarily, but if they are four-year schools with a "big-time" program, there is no other organization they can join.

There are additional ways in which the NCAA functions in a cartel-like manner. All national championships are held under its auspices—indeed, the only national collegiate championships for which individual athletes or teams may compete are those conducted by the NCAA.[3] The Association is a major negotiating agent for colleges in making TV contracts. As noted above, the NCAA *Manual* is the source of power, and members are bound by the rules and regulations in this document and adherence to such makes the big-time athletic industry openly collusive in nature.

Evidence of the commercial business nature of "big-time" university athletic programs, standing in much the same relation to commercial sports entertainment as the National Football League (NFL), the National Basketball Association (NBA), etc., is easy to document. The NCAA has a total revenue of some $49.3 million, over $43 million of which comes from money earned from sports events, i.e., basketball tournaments, television assessments, etc.: in other words, almost 80 percent of the NCAA's total revenue comes from the staging of commercial sports contests (*NCAA Annual Reports, 1985–86*).

The individual firm in collegiate athletics' is the college or university. Some 60 university-firms within the NCAA have annual working budgets of a million dollars or more, and at least 10 have budgets in excess of $4 million. (Benagh, 1976). In 1985, Notre Dame University earned $19.3 million from the football and basketball programs. The University of Washington "Huskies" netted $19.4 million, while the University of Michigan's programs brought in $16 million. (*USA Today*, 6/19/85). The formal rules and regulations governing the NCAA are found in the *Manual* and it is in this document that the NCAA unwittingly acknowledges that collegiate athletics is a business and that the athletes are wage laborers. On page nine of the current *Manual*, an amateur athlete is defined as one "who engages in a particular sport for the educational, physical, mental, and social benefits he derives therefrom. . . ." He, therefore, does not accept money for sport participation. In its Constitution, also published in the *Manual*, the NCAA declares that one of its purposes is to "comply with . . . standards of . . . amateurism." But, as incredible as it may seem, beginning on Page 17 of the *Manual* is a section on "Financial Aid," the key provision of which is: "Financial aid . . . may be awarded for any term . . . during which a student athlete is in regular attendance. . . ." So much for the NCAA as an amateur athletic agency! Let's not kid ourselves, college athletes are professionals as soon as they sign an athletic grant-in-aid. The "grant" is a work contract.

Perhaps the best sources for an accurate assessment of the nature of "big-time" collegiate sports are university presidents, athletic directors, and coaches, the persons who are most closely involved with these programs. By-and-large, they have no delusions about the programs. A report signed by the University of Southern California's President said that between 1970 and 1980, there were 330 athletes admitted who did not meet the school's minimum requirements. He said decisions were "based chiefly on athletic prowess, as judged by the Athletic Department, and without normal Admissions Office review." The former President of the University of New Mexico said: "Our recruits were recruited to be athletes, not students. There was never an expectation that they'd get their ass out of bed at 8 o'clock to go to class and turn in their assignments.

USC's Athletic Director, replying to the charge that only slightly more than half of the athletic team members graduated from USC between 1964 and 1977, said that he "didn't know of anything that says the purpose of higher education is to procure degrees." Attitudes like that make it easy for North Carolina State to admit Chris Washburn with a 475 total board score when the average incoming NC State student achieves a 950; or for Tulane to admit Hot Rod Williams with close to the minimum score. Bill Wall, who was the President of the National Association of Basketball Association of Basketball Coaches, said: "I know some coaches who couldn't stop cheating if they wanted to, Because their alumni and boosters wouldn't let them."

It is clear that a number of indicators convincingly show that the NCAA has many of the characteristics of a business, and that the official image that is promoted by the Association is largely a myth promulgated to conceal its real structure and functions. Lewis Cole (1976) noted: ". . . to consider . . . [the NCAA] as merely a regulator of intramural contests is like regarding the directors of General Motors as consultants who merely advise the company on safety precautions."

Consequences of the NCAA Cartel for College Athletes

The actual consequences of cartelized industries are varied and complex, depending upon such factors as the commodity produced and sold, the amount of the market actually under the control of the cartel, etc. But in most cases the negative consequences impact most heavily upon labor and consumers, since cartels typically restrict production and sale, through, for example, wage and price fixing. Space limitations preclude a comprehensive analysis of the consequences of the NCAA on trade restraints; instead, I shall briefly examine how cartel-wide policies of the NCAA protect and raise profits for the Association itself and for the individual university-firms while holding down costs of wages and restricting the mobility and other activities of the largest employee group in intercollegiate athletics, the athletes.

The NCAA *Manual* very specifically prescribes the payment that a collegiate athlete may be paid by any university-firm in exchange for his athletic performance. The athlete may be paid a sum not to exceed his educational expenses, i.e., tuition and fees, room and board, and required course-related books (NCAA *Manual,* 1979–80: 12). At 1986 prices, the cash value of this payment averages about $11,000; of course, the value of these educational expenses is not the same at all university-firms, and this does introduce an element of differential wages into the market.

It should be obvious who the beneficiaries are to this cartel-wide limitation on the salary that can be paid to athletes by university-firms. College athletes are caught in the clutches of the NCAA. They cannot sell their skills on the open market to the highest bidder because there is a wage limit that all cartel members observe. This works to the great disadvantage of athletes, some of whom are very highly skilled, and to the advantages of the NCAA cartel. The actual market value of many collegiate athletes is demonstrated by the salaries that are paid them when they are signed to a professional sports contract; a professional contract paying 20 times the college salary is not uncommon. The extent to which the NCAA restricts athletes' salaries is vividly illustrated in the average salaries of college athletes, about $11,000, and the salaries of professional athletes: $140,000 in the NFL, $430,000 in the NBA, $476,000 in Major League baseball, $130,000 in the NHL. Granted that the athletes in the professional leagues are more experienced and more highly skilled, on the average, than collegiate athletes, but it is likely that collegiate athletes could command a much higher salary, if they were able to sell their skills in an open market.[4]

The athletic scholarship is only one of the many regulations of the NCAA designed to reduce competition among university-firms for the athletic talent. An athlete who enrolls and participates in sports at one NCAA institution and then subsequently transfers to another university is ineligible for athletic competition at the latter institution for one full year. Requiring all transferring students to sit out one full season of competition seriously reduces the interorganizational mobility of collegiate athletes thus stabilizing the labor market within college athletics and undoubtedly saving the NCAA cartel untold dollars which might otherwise be spent by institutions competitively bidding for the most highly skilled workers. Koch (1971:252–53) has eloquently described the purpose behind the "transfer rules": " . . . the rules are most explicitly intended to prevent one well-heeled university-firm from raiding the ranks of another university-firm and hiring away its best student-athletes."

Here again it is easy to see who are the major beneficiaries to this restriction on college athletes' mobility. On the one hand the NCAA promotes and sells competition through sports but it severely restricts competition for wage labor within its own industry. Athletic directors and coaches are fond of explicating the virtues of competition, but they have formulated cartel-wide regulations to avoid competing for the employees who actually produce the product of collegiate athletics, the sports event.

Ironically, it is only these athlete-employees whose mobility is restricted. The NCAA does not apply such restrictions on others in the athletic productive process, the athletic directors and coaches. Indeed, the "jumping" of contracts by college coaches is common. Between 1975 and 1978 Washington State

University had three head football coaches leave with time remaining on their long-term contracts; each coach at another university the following year. Between 1970 and 1980, 49 of the 110 Division I basketball schools had at least three head coaches. As Paul Good (1979: 62) noted, in examining the feelings of betrayal felt by the athletes when a coach resigns after recruiting them: "Student-athletes are exhorted to demonstrate loyalty to their schools, and are penalized by losing a year's eligibility if they transfer to another school. But if the Astro-Turf looks greener on the other side to a coach, he's gone without penalty."

When one analyzes the NCAA rules and regulations that are applied to athletes from the standpoint of—who benefits?—it is readily apparent that the prime beneficiary is the NCAA and its member firms, i.e., the universities. In addition to policies limiting athletes' wages and mobility potential, there is the "Letter of Intent" regulation which prevents an athlete from further shopping for a university to attend after he has signed the "Letter"; there is the "Scholarship Limitation" policy which limits the number of grants-in-aid a university-firm may grant; and there is the recently enacted policy which makes freshmen eligible for varsity competition. The effect of these rules, and others too numerous to mention here, is to restrain competition and reduce costs among cartel members, to the disadvantage of collegiate athletes.

Summary

This article is primarily directed toward colleges and universities that maintain "big-time" programs. NCAA officialdom publicize the Association as merely an organization for the promotion of amateur sports for the educational, physical, mental, and social benefits the participants derive therefrom. Actually, though, the NCAA is organized in such a way as to have many of the structural and functional characteristics of a business cartel, hence it can be analyzed from that standpoint. Consistent with cartel organization, the NCAA restricts competition in order to further the ends of the individual members of the cartel. Cartel rules which regulate the salary of athletes and their interorganizational mobility are heavily stacked in favor of the university-firms at the considerable disadvantage to athletes. Other policies have similar consequences for the athletes.

Notes

1. The original name of the organization was the Intercollegiate Athletic Association of the United States; this name was changed to the National Collegiate Athletic Association in 1910.

2. Its only serious rival in men's athletics, the NAIA, claims as members only those colleges operating small-time programs. The NAIA has no television contract.

3. The NAIA does hold championships, but its champions are not recognized by the general public to be the "real" national champions.

4. It is not suggested that professional sports is a completely open market. Each of the professional leagues has cartel-like characteristics.

References

Benagh, J. *Making It To #1*. New York: Dodd, Mead, and Company, 1976.

Bryant, P.W. and Underwood, J. *Bear: The Hard Life and Good Times of Alabama's Coach Bryant*. Boston: Little, Brown, 1974.

Cole, L. "The NCAA: Mass Culture as Big Business." *Change*, September 1976, 8, 42–46.

Denlinger, K. and Shapiro, L. *Athletes For Sale*. New York: Thomas Y. Crowell, 1975.

Good, P. "I Feel Betrayed." *Sport*, June 1979, 68, 62–68.

Jones, R.F. "Gettin' Nowhere Fast." *Sports Illustrated*, September 19, 1977, 47, 88–102.

Kennedy, R. and Williamson, N. "Money: The Monster Threatening Sports." *Sports Illustrated*, July 17, 1978, 49, 29–88.

Koch, J.V. "The Economics of 'Big-Time' Intercollegiate Athletics." *Social Science Quarterly*, 1971, 52, 248–260.

Koch, J.V. "A Troubled Cartel: The NCAA." *Law and Contemporary Problems*, 1973, 38, 129–150.

McDermott, B. "Dunkers Are Strutting Their Stuff." *Sports Illustrated*, March 14, 1977, 46, 20–27.

McDermott, B. "After 88 Comes Zero." *Sports Illustrated*, January 28, 1974, 40.

Michener, J.A. *Sports in America*. New York: Random House, 1976.

NCAA Annual Reports, 1985–86. Shawnee Mission, Kansas, 1985.

NCAA Manual, 1979–80. Shawnee Mission, Kansas, 1979.

Rocky Mountain News, "Purdue Coach Alex Agase Is Fired." November 27, 1976, p. 107.

Rocky Mountain News, "Oregon Dismisses Coach Don Read." November 27, 1976, p. 107.

Sack, A.L. "Big Time College Football: Whose Free Ride?" *Quest*, 1977, 27, 98–96.

"Scorecard." *Sports Illustrated*, January 8, 1979, 50, 7.

Scott, H.A. *Competitive Sports in Schools and Colleges*. New York: Harper Brothers, 1951.

Stagg, Paul. *The Development of the National Collegiate Athletic Association in Relationship to Intercollegiate Athletics in the United States*, (Doctoral dissertation, New York University, 1946).

Van Dyne, L. "ABC Will Pay $118 Million to Televise College Football." *The Chronicle of Higher Education*, June 27, 1977, p. 6.

Pass One for the Gipper:
Student-Athletes and University Coursework

Joseph Raney
Terry Knapp
Mark Small
University of Nevada, Las Vegas

R ecent quantitative studies of intercollegiate athletics have challenged much of what has previously passed as sound opinion. Frey (1978), for example, surveyed alumni from a major western university and found that less than one percent (1%) of the sample reported athletics as their "most remembered experience in school"; in ranking spending priorities, the same group placed intercollegiate athletics as 11th out of 12. Frey suggested that athletics as a high priority concern among alumni may be a myth. More recently, Sigelman and Carter (1979) analyzed the relationship between financial contributions to 138 universities and their respective athletic win-loss records. They found no evidence for the view that the amount of alumni contributions is related to athletic success. Earlier, Roper and Snow (1976) noted a low correlation between ratings of academic excellence and the institution's success in football and basketball competition.

While the aforementioned studies have exposed much rumor solidified as myth, significant questions remain concerning intercollegiate athletics. A major one concerns how student-athletes survive in an academic environment. The prevailing attitude is that they do so by enrolling in selected courses which make few if any academic demands upon them. This opinion has often been the basis for media exposes of college players (*Newsweek*, 1980; *U.S. News*, 1980). It has formed the foundation for recent litigation which charged university officials with a failure to provide educational programs that would lead athletes to an academic degree (Ofari, 1979). And it has long been implicit in the proverbial humor and cynicism about "Basketweaving I, II, and III."

Despite such frequent concerns with student-athletes' curricula, a search of several reference bases yielded no previous studies which might provide an answer to how coursework by student-athletes is distributed across different academic disciplines. Earlier efforts have primarily focused on the parameters of total grade-point average (Larson, 1973), dropout rate (Stier, 1971)—or graduation status (NCAA, 1981). A general review may be found in Purdy, Eitzen, & Hufnagel, 1982.

In spite of a controversial history of nearly one hundred years (Frey,

1982), this may be the first time that anyone has systematically inspected the transcripts of student-athletes. It should be obvious that the primary value of such a description lies in its potential for encouraging the publication of comparable work done at other universities. Only by sharing such descriptions of academic/athletic relationships will social control mechanisms develop to prevent the type of scandals punctuating the last 100 years of intercollegiate athletics. Despite an apparent unwillingness to do so, university faculties must assume responsibility for the tarnished image of academe which athletic programs sometimes produce. The establishment of social controls based on data of the sort outlined below seems most compatible with the competencies and interests of academics.

The University and Athletic Program

The University of Nevada, Las Vegas is a thirty-year-old institution with an enrollment of 10,000 students, most of whom are commuters. The athletic program (Division 1A) has rapidly developed over the past fifteen years during which time it has evolved from independent status, to a candidate for the Western Athletic Conference, to its current membership in the Pacific Coast Athletic Conference. The basketball program in particular has been aggressively pursued by the recruitment of a nationally recognized coach and the gathering of substantial financial resources. The team has been PCAA regular season champions for the 1983–84 and 1984–85 seasons, and has made it as far as the final round of sixteen teams in the NCAA championship tournament. The program was on NCAA probation from 1977 to 1979. The baseball program has participated in the NCAA playoffs four times, the latest being 1984. The financially well supported football team had an 11-2 won-loss record in 1984, and went on the capture the California Bowl championship.

Sample and Data Base

The names of all male UNLV basketball ($N = 31$), football ($N = 126$), and baseball ($N = 41$) student-athletes for the 1978–79, 79–80, and 80–81 seasons were obtained from the office of the Athletic Director. The sample was reduced to a more manageable size by including all of the basketball players and randomly selecting an equivalent number of football and baseball team members. Official transcripts for these 93 student-athletes were obtained from the Registrar's Office and stored anonymously in a computer data base. The data base was a direct representation of the official transcripts with one exception: courses, credits, and grades were entered on a semester-by-semester basis and did not reflect subsequent transcript modifications. The Registrar's Office may, after the elapse of a semester or two, delete credit when it is duplicative of earlier enrollment, or when there are limits on the number of times one may earn credit under a particular course number. Thus, it is possible for a student-athlete to receive credit in a course one spring semester, to repeat it in the fall of the following academic year, and in the spring term of the second year lose the credit for the first enrollment. Given the purported academic advising of athletes on our campus, the frequency of such changes was surprising; never-theless, it should be clear that such courses *before* they are deleted provide one source of credits toward meeting minimum requirements.

Unit of Measurement

Describing the relative contribution of academic departments toward academic achievement of student-athletes requires a unit of measurement. The two dimensions of quantity and quality require representation; thus, reference to both credits earned and grades received is necessary. The product of these dimensions, termed grade-points, combines both quality and quantity, but familiarity with this measure is limited to Registrar personnel or others who work closely with transcripts. We have chosen to use the dual dimensions of credits and GPA's, but we caution the reader to examine in each instance the number of credits represented by any given GPA.

Credits Excluded from GPA

Courses taken on a pass/fail (P/F) basis do not contribute to the cumulative GPA, though they do add to the total credits student-athletes earned, and in doing so they contribute toward meeting the 24 credit between-season require-ment. The percent of total UNLV credits in the P/F category was relatively uniform across sports (Basketball, 3%; Football, 4%; Baseball, 2%); however, there were significant differences among sports as to how the P/F credits were distributed across departments. For the Basketball players, 94% of the P/F credits were earned in Physical Education, but the corresponding percentage for Football and Baseball players was only 38% and 23% respectively.

Transfer and University Credit

Total academic achievement is comprised of credits earned at UNLV and those transferred from community and junior colleges (see Table 1). A sub-stantial proportion of athletes in each sport transferred credits from other insti-tutions. Although the percentage of players transferring credit varied across

Table 1
Major Sources of Academic Support for 31 Athletes in
Each of Three Sports (1978–1981)

	Transfer		UNLV	
	GPA	Credits	GPA	Credits*
Basketball	2.41	849	1.96	1627
Football	2.73	315	2.18	2050
Baseball	2.63	616	2.48	2392

*Excludes P.F. credits.

sports (77% of the basketball players, 32% of the football, and 55% of the baseball players), the percent of total credits accounted for by transfer coursework remained fairly constant across sports, ranging from 35% for baseball, to 38% for football, and 39% for basketball.

The transfer GPA was also restricted in range, varying from 2.41 for basketball players, to 2.63 for baseball athletes, to 2.73 for football team members. It is important to bear in mind that remaining in an athletic program is based upon cumulative GPA; hence, credits transferred from a community college may represent a substantial foundation which permits an athlete to survive at the new institution for several semesters with an unacceptable (below 2.0) level of academic performance.

The UNLV GPA for each sport was lower than the transfer GPA. It ranged from a mean of 1.96 for basketball players, 2.18 for football, and 2.48 for baseball team members. This compares to a mean male UNLV GPA of 2.41 (Fall 1979). These GPA's are based on an average of 52.6, 66.5, and 76.4 earned credits for basketball, football, and baseball respectively.

Significantly, the credits showed a wide range of contact with academic departments. Both football and baseball team members had at least one course contact with all of the 34 academic departments available during this period, and basketball team members had slightly less at 85%, or 28 of the departments.

Coursework by Department

Table 2 displays coursework as a function of academic departments for each sport. These are rank ordered (for all sports combined) by percent of total credits and only the top ten departments are listed. Nevertheless, these ten departments account for 75%, 68%, and 69% of all the earned campus credits for basketball, football, and baseball respectively.

For all three categories of student-athletes, the Physical Education

Table 2
Departmental Academic Support for 31 Athletes in Each of Three Sports (1978–1981)

	Basketball		Football		Baseball	
	% of UNLV Credits		% of UNLV Credits		% of UNLV Credits	
Dept.	*Earned*	*GPA*	*Earned*	*GPA*	*Earned*	*GPA*
PE	30.1	2.69	26.5	3.26	22.6	2.86
Anthro.	17.6	2.78	6.5	2.38	1.5	2.58
English	7.6	1.63	7.3	2.01	5.8	2.20
Sociology	3.1	1.66	6.6	1.52	9.2	2.53
Finance	3.5	1.24	2.9	1.56	7.8	2.62
History	2.9	1.55	3.2	1.63	5.1	2.27
Economics	3.3	1.95	2.9	2.05	5.0	2.55
Hotel	.7	.86	5.6	2.04	3.9	2.56
Math	2.6	1.83	4.1	2.63	3.6	2.44
Communications	3.1	1.55	2.3	1.61	4.4	2.33

Department ranked first as a source of credits. It accounted for 30% of total UNLV credits for basketball players, 27% for football players, and 23% for baseball players.

It is possible to partition the credits earned in Physical Education since the department has five areas, each with its own course designations: physical education, dance, recreation, athletic training, and health. Table 3 displays the Physical Education credits and GPA for the P.E. area (such courses as Theory of Basketball, Football, or Baseball, Intercollegiate Sports, etc.) versus all other areas, i.e., dance, recreation, etc. Student athletes did enroll in the latter courses to a substantial degree; they accounted for 8% of the total credits for basketball, and 7% for both football and baseball. However, as Table 3 indicates, significant disparities appear between the GPA's attained in P.E. courses in contrast to "all others." For basketball players this amounted to as much as a grade and a half, and for football and baseball about one-half a grade.

Table 3 reveals another significant concentration of credits. For Basketball players, Anthropology accounted for 17.5% of all campus credits compared to only 6.5% for football and 1.5% for baseball. It is interesting to note that the departments of Physical Education and Anthropology account for nearly half (47.7%) of the UNLV credits earned by basketball players.

It is also possible to partition the Anthropology credits since they are comprised of Anthropology and those designated Ethnic Studies. When this is done (Table 3), the GPA for basketball players in Ethnic Studies is 2.94 which contrasts markedly with a 1.39 in Anthropology. A similar discrepancy is not noted for football or baseball, although over 5% of the campus credits earned by football players was in Ethnic Studies.

Table 3
Partitioning of GPA and Credits for Physical Education and Anthropology Coursework

	PE Total	*PE*	*All Other***
Basketball	2.69 (30.1)*	3.13 (22.2)	1.68 (7.9)
Football	3.26 (26.5)	3.41 (19.4)	2.86 (7.1)
Baseball	2.86 (22.6)	3.01 (15.7)	2.54 (6.9)

	Anthropology Total	*Anthropology*	*Ethnic Studies*
Basketball	2.78 (17.6)	1.39 (2)	2.94 (16.0)
Football	2.38 (6.5)	2.65 (1)	2.33 (5.5)
Baseball	2.58 (1.51)	2.80 (1)	2.43 (1)

*Percent of total credits earned at UNLV.
**Health, Recreation, Dance, Athletic Training.

Discussion

The long-standing view that student-athletes survive in an academic environment by enrolling in selected courses was evaluated by examining the coursework of student-athletes in three major sports at a Division 1A university. The data presented provide qualified support for this view. The range of contact with different academic units was extensive for all sports, so it could be said that student-athletes *do not* restrict their activity to specialized courses; however, significant concentrations of coursework were in evidence. Physical Education courses accounted for the largest single source of credits. They averaged about one-third of the total across all sports. The importance of P.E. credits can be demonstrated by calculating the GPA with these units subtracted. Deprived of P.E. credits, most of the basketball players and some of the football players would likely be ineligible to play or to remain enrolled as students.

One might suggest that the student-athletes enrolled in a large number of P.E. courses because they were Physical Education majors. This was not the case. Most of the basketball players had not declared any major, and only a few P.E. majors were identified among the football and baseball players. It seems much more likely that enrollment in P.E. courses is related to participation in intercollegiate athletics than to degree goals. Moreover, one cannot explain the superior performance in certain P.E. classes (e.g., Workshop in P.E.) on the bases of greater motivation, skill, or knowledge, since the student-athletes obtain significantly lower grades in other P.E. courses (e.g., health, recreation, athletic training, etc.).

The symbiotic relationship between the coaching staff and the Physical Education Department is perhaps the single best explanation for the proportion of the credits earned in P.E. Often the coaches or assistant coaches are a source of support for both athletic *and* academic survival through the P.E. courses they teach. An informal inspection of grade sheets suggests that the most frequent P.E. courses (PED 150, 151, 153 Intercollegiate Sports, PED 460 Workshop in P.E., PED 130 Conditioning, and PED 495 Field Work in P.E.) were invariably taught by intercollegiate coaches or assistant coaches.

A second concentration of credits, though only for basketball players, was Ethnic Studies. The heavy utilization of these courses may simply reflect the racial composition of the team. Although racial data are not available on the transcripts, it is widely known that during the period under study most of UNLV basketball players were black. Did they get higher grades in Ethnic Studies because of their possible familiarity with the material or because of their chosen sport? Any conclusion would be speculative at this point, but the data suggest the possibility of continued exploitation in intercollegiate athletics of racial factors outlined some years ago (Spivey & Jones, 1976). Since UNLV does not offer a major in Ethnic Studies and since neither their credit load nor their academic performance suggest that they are anthropology majors, the data remain uninterpretable. It is clear, however, that this source of credits and the P.E. coursework are critical to the academic survival of UNLV basketball players.

Transfer credits also played a significant role in maintaining eligibility. Clearly, most basketball players, with a cumulative average of only 1.96 at UNLV, and many football players (UNLV = 2.18) would not remain eligible for very long in the absence of the foundation provided by transfer coursework.

The pattern of student-athlete enrollment could be compared to other student groups, though it is not clear what such comparisons would add to the present analysis. For whatever any other group (P.E. majors, low achievers, minor sports participants, nonathletes, extracurricular students, minority persons) might do to survive in an academic environment does not modify what major sport student-athletes do to survive. A more appropriate comparison, but one not available to us, would be of participants in intercollegiate programs at other universities.

These data are limited to one university, and it may be argued that any conclusions are also necessarily limited. This is true, but the very nature of the research project prevents any one set of researchers from offering a data base that extends beyond their own institution. The Family Educational Rights and Privacy Act and its implementing regulations (AACRAO, 1976) provide for release of transcripts without written consent only to members of the institution who are determined to have a legitimate educational interest. At best this project can serve as only one answer to the question of how academic coursework is distributed. Examination of other college catalogs suggests, however, that the identified academic support provided to athletic programs may not be unique to UNLV.

Curiously, the data presented here tend to direct attention toward ethical considerations rather than scientific ones. For example, how stressful is the conflict of interest experienced by coaches who are involved in maintaining the academic eligibility of athletes? Given the existence of faculty curriculum and ethics committees, is the "studied indifference" expressed by most academics toward such built-in conflicts ethically appropriate? Does the concentration of credits in certain areas reflect the deliberate support of athletic programs by advisors and professors? Such questions have been raised before but published data of the kind reported here makes it much more difficult to ignore them.

As a final note, researchers should be prepared to confront powerful individuals within and without their institution who will attempt to use the "Buckley Amendment" to block the collection of the kinds of data presented here. We have read the amendment, its accompanying regulations, and relevant rulings and find nothing in these documents to suggest that use of student-athlete transcripts in faculty research is a violation or contrary to the intent of Congress in enacting the privacy amendment. It seems likely, however, that only action by the courts will provide the clarification necessary for such research to become routine. After such research is routinized, it will be possible to develop the social control mechanisms required in order to avoid the kinds of scandals which frequently threaten the academic/athletic relationship.

References

American Association of Collegiate Registrars and Admission Officers
    1976 *A Guide to Postsecondary Institutions for Implementation of the Family Educational Rights and Privacy Act of 1974 as Amended.* Washington, D.C.: AACRAO.

Frey, J.H.
    1982 *The Governance of Intercollegiate Athletics.* West Point, N.Y.: Leisure Press.

Frey, J.H.
    1978 "The Priority of Athletics to Alumni: Myth or Fact?" *Phi Delta Kappan,* September *60:* 63.

Larson, S.W.
    1973 "A Study of Academic Achievement of Athletics at the University of Tennessee." Educational Resources Information Center (Hereafter cited as ERIC), ED 095 803.

National Collegiate Athletic Association.
    1981 "Survey of Graduation Rates after Five Years for Males First Entering College in Fall, 1975," Shawnee Mission, Kansas: NCAA.

Newsweek
    1980 "The Shame of College Sports." September 22 *96:* 54–59.

Ofari, E.
    1979 "Basketball's Biggest Losers." *The Progressive.* April *43:* 48–49.

Purdy, D.A.
    1981 "Educational Attainment and Collegiate Athletes: Intra-Group Analysis and Comparison to the General Student Population." ERIC, ED 202 844.

Roper, L.D. & Snow, K.
    1976 "Correlation Studies of Academic Excellence and Big-Time Athletics." *International Review of Sport Sociology. 11*(3):57–69.

Sigelman, L. & Carter, R.
    1979 "Win One for the Giver? Alumni Giving and Big-Time College Sports." *Social Science Quarterly. 60*(2):284–294.

Spivey, D. & Jones, T.A.
    1975 "Intercollegiate Athletic Servitude: A Case Study." *Social Science Quarterly. 55*(4):939–947.

Stier, W.F.
    1971 "Student-Athlete Attrition among Selected Liberal Arts Colleges." ERIC, ED 058 834.

U.S. News
    1980 "Behind Scandals in Big-Time College Sports." February 11 *88:* 61–63.

The Coming Demise of Intercollegiate Athletics

James H. Frey
University of Nevada, Las Vegas

Introduction

It may seem incredulous to predict that intercollegiate athletics, in all of their modern splendor and adulation, will be suffering setbacks or even a "demise" in the future. On the surface these programs look healthy: television is pouring dollars and prime time into broadcasting college sport; alumni and booster clubs seems more fervent than ever in their vocal and financial support; stadiums and arenas are at capacity; athletes are performing in the finest fashion; and college "programs" are attracting well known individuals as coaches and administrators. Even under the cloud of Title IX and related financial exigencies, college athletic programs are flourishing. In fact, the college game is touted by some as a major folkloristic event of our culture crucial to the survival of society (Cady, 1978). It is almost sacrilegious to assert that behind the smoke screen of prosperity lie the seeds of destruction, or structural realignment, at least. Yet, as I hope to demonstrate below, this is the case.

College athletics have been severely attacked before. At the turn of the century college faculties, some alumni and even the President of the United States were clamoring for change, particularly with football, or elimination of college sport (Lucas and Smith, 1978). Familiar charges of over-exaggeration, demoralization of academic work, dishonesty, professionalism, brutality, illegal recruiting, and corruption were being leveled at college athletics in the 1890's and early 1900's (Savage, 1929). College sport was saved by the formation of the National Collegiate Athletic Association (NCAA) and by the forward pass. In the early 1950's, the college bribery scandals hit the front pages. Athletes went to jail; coaches were suspended; the integrity of the game was challenged. Today, sports critics, self-styled humanists and social philosophers challenge the character of sport, any organized sport for that matter, as demeaning to the individual and certainly not character-building or educational (Lasch, 1978; Isaacs, 1978; Scott, 1971).

Yet, these attacks have not stemmed the tide. The adherents of college athletics have been able to overcome their adversaries by adhering to the believable promulgations, whether myth or fact is irrelevant, of the moral, physical, financial and political advantages of a winning program on campuses. There are, however, a number of ideological, political and economic conditions of the environment of sport that could, in combination, spell the restructuring or, yes, even the demise of intercollegiate sport. Many of these factors have been overlooked by the writers of sport. Participants have sensed their presence but not publicly acknowledged their possible effect. Truthfully, much of what I will describe in the remainder of this article is based on speculation since empirical substantiation is not possible at this time. Reflection suggests their plausibility, however.

The Withdrawal of Ideological Support: The Source of Legitimation

Charges of corruption, winning-at-all-costs, commercialization, professionalization and dehumanization have been leveled at college athletics by scholars, journalists, players, and politicians. The impact of these accusations has been negligible up to this point. If anything, these elements have grown in intensity. However, the assertions of these opinion leaders and scholars are gaining more credibility as research and experience tell us that suggestions of corruptibility, character assassination, self-serving economics and player exploitation and discrimination bear a strong semblance of reality. The ideological underpinning of college sport begins to erode when its practices are demonstrated to be at odds with generally held beliefs. Without this valuational support, legitimacy or the acceptance of the "goodness" of the activity, is withdrawn. The real impact of the changing belief structure surrounding intercollegiate athletics will not be felt until the general public adopts the critical perspective. The withdrawal of their support is more devastating than any disenchantment with sport that comes from politicians who already suffer from lowered trust, from college professors whose view of reality has always been suspect, or from former players whose views might be connoted as "sour grapes."

There is a smattering of evidence that the general public no longer holds participation in sport as valuable. For example, a Harris study for the Perrier Company demonstrated that parents no longer hold participation in sport to be more important than fitness for their children (*Los Angeles Times*, February 9, 1979). The fitness value of many of the traditional team sports has been up for serious question (Bailey, 1978; Underwood, 1978). In fact, a strong case can be made that participation in athletics is detrimental to fitness (Edwards, 1973). The excessive attention to the gifted athlete, the rise in ticket prices, the selective exclusion of the person who cannot afford a season ticket or a booster club membership and the decline in value of the dollar also contribute to the denial of sport experiences for the general public. The result is an inability to relate to the sport except in a peripheral or distant fashion. The purportedly positive values of sport have no relevance for the average person. Since he/she cannot identify with sport from an experiential or intrinsic dimension, association exists on an extrinsic level. The moral philosophy of play is replaced by a fragile attachment based on a need for exhilarating entertainment or collective gregariousness.

The sanctimonious basis for the athletic world has been compromised by realism or the rational, pragmatic character of our times. The public is realizing that sports at all levels are operated no different than any other modern organization. The aura of altruism and heroic myth associated with the athletic world of the past is being replaced by a cynical view of the intentions and operations of the athletic world. The hypocrisy of it all is being exposed. Intercollegiate sport, and all sport for that matter, is finally in the company of all other of our institutions which have lost face and faith in the eyes of the public.

Just as the moral base of the law has been eroded by the injustices associated with the enforcement practices of white collar crime (e.g., price fixing, consumer fraud) (U.S. Chamber of Commerce, 1974), the moral base of intercollegiate athletics, which heretofore had been cemented in the educational, socialization and physical fitness values of sport, have also been eroded by hypocrisy, scandal and violence. The inherent moralism of the American people will lead to a recognition of the depravity of athletics and, as a result, will produce a withdrawal of their political and economic support.

Political Reality: Controlling Athletic Autonomy

When any social unit has political priority it means it has power to guide the outcome of decisions in its favor. It is able to procure resources necessary for its survival and growth even if it means the opposite for other units within the same system (Thompson, 1967). The power usually emanates from strong valuational or ideological support since that unit is producing a valued product. Being in this position means a social unit is autonomous. That is, it can act on its environment and even be impervious to its wishes.

For generations intercollegiate athletic programs have been able to operate from a position of political autonomy and priority.[1] The coalition of coaches, administrators and boosters represents a formidable structure of allies. The booster-alumnus provides the interconnection with the business and the political world; the coach provides the winning product and the administrator guides the athletic program through the academic maze. Since early in the century college faculties and administrations have never really made serious efforts to control intercollegiate athletics. Most presidents believed that a winning program attracted students, financial contributions and favorable legislative appropriations. Faculties were either disinterested and gave up all hope of rekindling educational goals with athletes; or, they were the athletic department's greatest fans. Students, who once controlled and operated intercollegiate athletics, willingly gave up that control when between school contests became too complex for their administration and too important to alumni.

Inattention from college presidents and faculties may become a thing of the past.[2] Even if faculties never conjure up enough fortitude to follow through on their vocal diatribes directed at athletic programs, college presidents surely will. There is already evidence that these individuals are asserting their authority in NCAA governance and rule-setting practices. It is only a matter of time for the presidents to demand even more stringent control on athletic budgets and operating practices. Reduced budget flexibility and the questioning of the educational value of athletics from supporters not affiliated with the athletic programs will force presidents to seek firmer control of their athletic departments. This will be a long up-hill battle because of the previous neglect and the administrator-booster networks' institutionalized role in athletic governance.

To get back to the faculty's role, nothing raises the cynical anger of a professor more than abuses of the educational goals of higher education by the athletic departments. Rarely, however, does the faculty member follow his verbal assault with concerted, collective action. University senates pass resolutions that are ignored; faculty leaders discuss the problem in ineffectual, informal settings; committees are created and dissolved with no result; the faculty athletic committee is either a mouthpiece of the athletic program or is easily circumvented by external booster interests. Faculty will only gain more effective support when they collectively organize (e.g., labor unions); this will give them more formidable political clout and will provide reinforcement and backing for the faculty member who has previously stood alone in his battles with the athletic department. Frankly, faculties have simply lacked the courage to tackle the athletic program. They have, in their intellectual arrogance, absolved themselves of responsibility for the academic credibility of athletics and many other extramural activities. Organizing the faculty will stimulate activism and subsequent demands for greater input and control of the athletic operations on campus. Collectivism enables the faculty to deal from a position of greater power vis-à-vis athletic interests.

In the future, intercollegiate athletic programs will be drawing increased attention from national and local governing bodies. Title IX and its regulatory demands were only the beginning. The Santini Committee looked at the NCAA and found it wanting in its enforcement proceedings. This congressional committee will be activated again by the continued rate of court actions on civil rights and product liability cases. More investigations will take place. In addition, almost every state is attempting to cut taxes. The mentality associated with this and similar tax packages can be translated into reduced appropriations to all funded agencies regardless of the amount they receive from property taxes. The political clout of the booster club in the legislature will be relegated to a lowered priority in favor of the public demand for reduced frills in education and other institutional spheres.

Socio-economic Factors

The loss of ideological support and reduced political priority have the ultimate consequences of retarding growth and increasing the uncertainty of the flow of needed economic resources, capital and labor. The resources of growth are drying up, and athletic departments are placing more emphasis on maintenance rather than growth. The result is what has been called the "stationary state" (Nisbet, 1979). There are several factors which have produced this emphasis. First, even though it may not appear to be true, stadiums have reached their saturation point, both in terms of the number being constructed and in terms of the volume of fans that are available to attend. Between 1960 and 1965 attendance at college events rose 21 percent; between 1965–1970 it was up 19 percent; it rose only 7.5 percent between 1970 and 1975 and since 1975 attendance is up 2.1 percent. The rate of attendance is declining while the costs of athletic programs, which are predominantly dependent on gate receipts, is up 60 percent since 1972 (NCAA, 1978). More fans are either staying away from games to pursue other recreational diversion or they avoid attending because of the non-availability of seats. This image of capacity can produce a significant number of "no-shows" or persons who refrain from purchasing tickets because they "believe" no seats are available. The exclusive right of season ticket holders, including corporate entities, who now take up nearly all of the seats in any stadium and arena, make it physically impossible to expand the attending audience thereby expanding the market. One school in the west has not added a new booster-season ticket holder for over two years because of the unavailability of seats in a basketball arena. These restrictions reinforce the elitist connotation of the college game plus limit the supportive "sense of community" that every institution seeks to create surrounding its athletic program. This means that college programs will have to get more money from the same number of persons.

Second, the delimitation of the tax dollar will prevent the expansion or creation of new athletic facilities on campuses. More frequently legislators will give higher priority to capital improvements that are more consistent with the educational goals of the university. Presidents and alumni will also lobby less actively for athletic appropriations because they will be fighting for favorable appropriations for other university functions.

Other more practical economic factors will make it difficult for athletic programs to maintain their current practices. First, rising liability and medical insurance rates, particularly for the football program, are forcing schools into a severe cost crunch on some programs. For example, in 1975 the University of

California paid a liability insurance premium of $437,602. In 1977, it was $1,144,000 (Gustkey, 1977). The "sue syndrome" plus the tendencies for juries to favor the plaintiff have contributed to escalation of product liability suits which cost considerable money regardless of outcome[3] (Appenzeller, 1979). Second, the energy shortage and rising energy costs can have serious effects on travel, and on stadium, or equipment utilization. If a team cannot travel, it cannot maintain the kind of schedule that gives its program the notoriety, exposure and financial guarantee it needs. Add these problems to the exigencies of Title IX regulations, even with the football loophole, and changes in traditional operations will take place.[4] Economic problems are even more significant when you consider that 81 percent of the NCAA football programs lost money in 1977 and only 30 athletic programs were in the black. Administrators claim this situation is still worse in 1986.[5]

If money is a serious problem, personnel or labor situations are even more problematic. First, college enrollments are experiencing dramatic declines. This will make fewer alumni available for political and financial support in the future. Additionally, the alumni that do exist will have fewer real dollars for peripheral contributions and expenses. Also, these alumni will be less likely to contribute because they can draw on few intimate, positive experiences with the athletic programs of their schools. Few were involved in direct participation since only a select number have the talent and skill it takes to participate in a college athletic program. It is possible that many students and future alumni will resist athletic support because they resented the preferential treatment received by athletics. They will also resent the dominance of boosters over what should be a student program designed to develop a sense of community on campus, not provide thrills for industrial, economic cadres which tend to make up booster clubs.[6]

The restriction on general operating funds available to universities from traditional sources of grants and legislative monies will force other departments of the university into the fund-raising game.[7] So, colleges of Hotel, Business, or Social Sciences will send out their appeals to alumni for support for equipment, scholarships and political influence. The alumnus only has so many dollars. Up to this point athletic departments have had a near stranglehold on the alumni support dollar. Even the departments of alumni affairs have been simply extensions of athletic departments with the alumni director usually a well-known athletic figure of the past. His major job is to coordinate alumni trips and parties associated with the college athletic contests. The future will find this person and department broadening their appeal to alumni thereby contributing to the reduced attention to athletic affairs. New York University's decision to eliminate its booster club in 1985 was a prime example of this.

Affirmative Action and Civil Rights legislation have opened the doors, to some extent, of opportunity for one of the major subgroups of athletic labor—

the Black. At one time the only avenues out of the ghetto and an existence of despair were athletics and entertainment. College coaches flocked to the playgrounds and athletic fields of American urban centers to find that diamond in the rough who would lead the team to great glories. Many were found as the reservoir was plentiful. The black and the white communities supported this association of success and athletics. However, the realities became well known. For every athlete from these circumstances who made it to either the collegiate or professional big-time, thousands did not. For those who made it, the career was short lived with few longterm benefits of money or fame. Many a "star" was back to his origination with stories of his experience but few tangible rewards. Even fame and glory had departed. Realizing this, many blacks who could have been athletes will pursue vehicles of success other than athletics. In fact, leaders of the Black community such as Jesse Jackson and Harry Edwards are openly challenging Black youth to look at alternatives to athletics, to funnel their energies to pursue careers which have a more reliable economic pay-off plus make some contribution to society. If such admonitions are taken to heart, the labor pool available for college athletics will suffer a considerable deficit. Leaders of predominantly Black universities maintain that the Black labor pool will be even more decimated.

The elite labor pool for athletics will suffer from another standpoint. There isn't a job in the world that carries the pressures, anxieties and insecurities that are found with the role of the coach. To win at all costs is a horrendous burden and the casualty list is high. One coach describes the pressure:

> If I took my boys, who are 5, 6 and 7 out to the lake on Sunday, I'd feel I was missing something. I'd know there was a kid shooting baskets in a high school gym somewhere and someone else was watching him. It's a profession where you think you can outwit other people. You get obsessed. The more successful you become the more involved you get. The more involved you get, the more you lose control of the stable things around you. It's almost a sickness.
>
> You fly 3000 miles to see some kid who doesn't even put you at the top of his list. You're away from your family, the only people who love you. You're giving blind loyalty to an institution and its fans, and you know eventually they will turn on you. There's literally a crisis every day. There's injuries. You get the pros after your kids. You got other colleges after your kids. You spend time getting them happy and keeping them in school. The games are nothing. People don't realize the price you have to pay and what the end result will probably be. (*Los Angeles Times*, July 7, 1979)

The turnover rate for coaching is significant. Only 20 percent of the basketball coaches of 1972 are coaching today. Few stay at one place more than 3–4 years. Forty-nine of the 110 Division I basketball schools had at least three coaches between 1970 and 1980. Even with a winning record a coach can experience the axe because he did not go undefeated or because one–three losses was more than expected. The result is that many with excellent qualifications as teachers, humanists and technicians of the game will use their talents in the pursuit of other occupational careers and not for the benefit of athletics. This leaves the coaching profession with a type of individual who may or may not have the best talent to work with players and be able to respond to their needs as a person. The role of coach as father confessor, moral trainer and teacher is compromised in favor of the role of coach as manager or production supervisor. It is an inevitable outcome of the trends of rationalization and specialization in college athletics.

The labor pool of athletics is also decimated by the high rate of disabling injuries which can keep a player from performing for a season or even a lifetime. It is estimated that nearly one million high school players, 70,000 college players and all of the players on the National Football league will suffer injuries in one year (Underwood, 1978). This requires additional player resources. The decline of scholarships available, the fewer number who are eligible or desire to play, and lowered skill of those available to replace the "star" make the quality of the product questionable.[8] The lowered quality of player personnel leads to lowered prospects of a winning season which, in turn, leads to lowered alumni and booster support. It truly is a vicious circle. In addition, if a team has no star to attract media attention, exposure, visibility and television revenues will be reduced.

One team will no longer dominate athletics in any sport. There are several reasons for this but the most significant is the equalization of talent. More schools are able to get that blue-chip athlete who can turn a program around or make it competitive. This is the result of two factors: the reduction in scholarships and the national, rather than regional, scope of recruiting assumed by more and more schools. While this is great for the competitive nature of the game it means that a school cannot always be a winner. If the institution cannot continuously field a decisive winner, alumni and booster support will vascillate and possibly decline. This makes it very difficult to keep up with the schools which are currently winning. The turnover rate for coaches at UCLA in the post-Wooden era exemplifies this.

The problem of maintaining the labor pool for college athletics is even further complicated by virtue of the results of a dramatic economic fact: more and more high school districts are dropping sports, particularly football. This means fewer trained athletes are available for college programs. As the tax-cutting mentality takes even greater effect, this will become a more serious problem.

Just as we have a "Poverty Establishment", there now exists a "Sport Establishment"—a network of organizations and occupations that depends on athletics as currently construed for their maintenance and survival (Frey, 1978). Therefore, more resources are required to support organizational maintenance, deflecting resources that would otherwise go to participation-oriented functions. This is a classic case of goal displacement. Who would think that athletics would become so organized that the athlete is one of the least priority in the system? Intercollegiate sports, in its cartel-like leagues and highly formalized athletic departments, are no different than IBM, General Motors or ITT. The organization is more important than any one individual or group.

As college programs become more rationalized and organized under this athletic industrial complex, the athlete, realizing that athletics are a business, will be less loyal to his team or nation. He/she will be less willing to sacrifice himself for the sake of the team. The reason for his participation is extrinsic and based on self-interest. This means higher turnover of personnel. A player will not remain at Good Ole U. for the sake of teammates and tradition. He will transfer to a school that will give him the most toward meeting his goals, e.g. professional career. As any foreman or manager will tell you, high turnover of key personnel is disruptive for productivity.

Conclusion

All of these factors are intertwined. Their impact has not been acknowledged. The environment of intercollegiate athletics is deteriorating. The supports are no longer there. They are missing not because of Title IX or another singular element but because systematic conditions which are subtle yet pervasive. It is only a matter of time before drastic changes in the intercollegiate athletic world will come.

What will these changes be? First, many will drop their most costly programs. In the past two decades, more than 50 schools have dropped football and more are contemplating such action. Second, regionalism will prevail over national identification. Schedules will be limited to competition within a limited radius. National championships may even be eliminated. Third, schools will seek aid from professional sports. Fourth, the frills of athletics (e.g., training tables, recruiting visits, travel to high school tournaments) will be eliminated. Fifth, college faculties will assume more responsibility for athletic programs and demand either greater academic credibility or severance of athletic programs from the institution. Sixth, the old coach will be replaced by the athletic administrator who is skilled in promotion and management.

Certainly a battle between athletic interests and college officials looms large on the horizon. Each camp will have to demonstrate the truth or falsity of previously held claims of "the functions of athletes on campus." Regardless of the outcome of this conflict, college athletics will change to the degree that they will remain only a strange facsimile of their previous organization and structure.

Notes

1. For a more detailed analysis of the problems institutions have in controlling their athletic departments see: James H. Frey. "College Athletics: Problems of Institutional Control," chapter in Jeffrey O. Segrave, Donald Chu, and Beverly Becker, *Sport and American Higher Education* (Champaign, IL: Human Kinetics Press, 1985); and James H. Frey, "Boosterism, Scarce Resources and Institutional Control: The Future of American Intercollegiate Athletics," *International Review of Sport Sociology* 17 (1982):53–70. Control is difficult because universities are large, complex, "loosely coupled" organizations with fragmented decision centers. Subunit autonomy of athletic departments is the result of the inability of the institutions to maintain strict organizational control and of the extraordinary ability of these departments to be part of external networks that include the political and economic elite of the surrounding community and region.

2. In fact, the inattention of presidents to athletics is a characteristic of the past. In August of 1983 the American Council on Education's (ACE) Committee on Division I Athletics began to pressure the NCAA to include in its governance structure a "board of presidents" that would have the power to veto or modify NCAA rules. In January of 1984 this proposal was defeated at the NCAA convention; in its place, the NCAA created a presidents commission with limited authority. It has the power to review NCAA policy and practice, to place items on the convention agenda, to conduct studies, and to demand a roll-call vote on any council or convention issue. In June of 1985 nearly 200 presidents attended the convention and every one of the presidents' commission proposals passed. In past years it was rare to see but a dozen presidents at NCAA conventions.

3. At this time there are over 100 helmet-related injury cases pending in court with claims totalling over $300 million.

4. It is interesting to note that many athletic directors are viewing women's sports as a possible salvation from the financial exigencies of maintaining a winning athletic program. From one standpoint transferring money to women's programs can be a justification for de-emphasizing some men's sports, including the major programs. On the other hand, accelerated women's sports can mean additional revenue producing avenues including gate receipts and women alumni-boosters. Schools must come into compliance with Title IX by September 1979. The cost of equalization is dramatized by the fact that it would cost UCLA $235,000 to be in compliance.

5. The most recent financial analysis conducted by the NCAA revealed that the average total expenses exceed the average total revenues for each category of athletic departments except for the largest entities in Division I. Even with television revenue, 40 percent of the top schools lost money in 1981. See M.H. Raiborn, *Revenue and Expense of Intercollegiate Athletic Programs: Analysis of Financial Trends and Relationships* (Shawnee Mission, KA: NCAA, 1982).

6. The expansion of alumni bodies into more encompassing "booster clubs" is probably the result of the saturation of financial and political support that was available from existing alumni. Wealthy businessmen were recruited as supporters with the argument that a winning athletic program would be good for their and the community's interest. In addition, since owning a sports team is a fanciful desire of many, booster club membership provides at least a vicarious thrill of "ownership" by virtue of a purchase of shares as embodied in the "scholarship."

7. There is considerable evidence to show that winning athletic programs do not produce fund-raising success for institutions of higher education. A successful football season may mean more money for athletics but, contrary to myth, it will not mean more funds for academic programs on campus. In fact, there is enough evidence to suggest the opposite effect or a negative correlation between athletic success and fund-raising. See the following for a review of this research: James H. Frey, "The Winning-Team Myth," CASE *Currents* 9 (January 1985):33–35.

8. This is the expected effect of the NCAA's latest provisions on the "academic progress" of athletes. Division I institutions are now required to monitor an athletes' progress toward a degree in a regular academic program. In addition, athletes will not be eligible for participation as freshman if their high school grade point average is not a 2.0 (4-point system) in a core of subjects including math and science.

References

Appenzeller, Herb. "Product Liability Litigation Continues to Escalate." *Athletic Purchasing and Facilities.* June 3, 1979, p. 17–20.

Bailey, Donald. "Sport and The Child: Physiological Consideration." pp. 103–112 in Richard A. Magill, Michael J. Ash and Frank L. Small (eds.) *Children in Sport: A Contemporary Anthology.* Champaign, Illinois: Human Kinentics, 1978.

Cady, Edward H. *The Big Game: College Sports and American Life.* Knoxville: The University of Tennessee Press, 1978.

Edwards, Harry. *Sociology of Sport.* New York: Irwin-Dorsey, 1973.

Gustkey, Earl. "Rising Insurance Rates Threaten Fun and Games." *Los Angeles Times.* July 20, 1977, III-9.

Frey, James H. "The Organization of American Amateur Sport: Efficiency to Entrophy." *American Behavioral Scientist.* February 21, 1978:361–378.

Isaacs, Neil D. *Jock Culture, U.S.A.* New York: W.W. Norton, 1978.

Lasch, Christopher. *The Culture of Narcissism.* New York: W.W. Norton, 1978.

Lucas John A. and Ronald A. Smith. *Saga of American Sport.* Philadelphia: Lea and Febiger, 1978.

"Money Is Not the Only Payoff." *Los Angeles Times,* February 9, 1979: IV-8.

"The Sports and Recreational Programs of the Nation's Universities and Colleges." National Collegiate Athletic Association Report Number Five, 1978.

Nisbet, Robert. "The Rape of Progress." *Public Opinion,* 2 (June/July), 1979:2–6.

Savage, Howard, *et al. American College Athletics.* New York: The Carnegie Foundation for the Advancement of Teaching., 1929.

Scott, Jack. *The Athletic Revolution.* New York: Free Press, 1971.

Thompson, J.D. *Organizations In Action.* New York: McGraw-Hill, 1967.

Underwood, John. "An Unfolding Tragedy." *Sports Illustrated,* 49, August 14, 1978: 69–82.

U.S. Chamber of Commerce. *White Collar Crime.* Chamber of Commerce of the United States, Washington, D.C., 1974.

2
Racism in Sports

N early four decades after Jackie Robinson broke the race barrier in professional baseball, professional sports abound in black athletes with million-dollar contracts. Michael Jordan in the 1984–85 season and Patrick Ewing in the 1985–86 season each made more than $2 million in player contracts and endorsements in their *first year*. Basketball (70 percent), football (54 percent), and baseball (23 percent) are in many ways dominated by black athletes.

Most Americans honestly believe that this is a sign of society's progress. Many people, black and white alike, believe that sports is a major racial equalizer. However, there is a great deal of evidence that little has changed since Jackie Robinson took that first courageous step. Although America has made numerous promises to its people, the promise of racial equality has been broken many times over. The articles in this chapter show how very far we still have to go.

"The Image of Intercollegiate Sports and the Civil Rights Movement," by Adolph Grundman (*Arena Review*, vol. 3, no. 3) clearly brings home the reality that, historically, race relations and intercollegiate sports parallel society in its failure to provide equal opportunity. This article is a unique look at the early days of sport and societal integration, leading up to the revolt of the black athlete in 1968. The irony is not lost in 1985. As Harry Edwards, the architect of that black revolt, has emphasized, we now need a civil rights movement *in sport* itself to overcome the exploitation of athletes.

Genetic theories explaining black athletic prowess have increased in proportion to blacks' dominance in certain sports. Of course, such theories have had to change over time. Not long ago, for example, it was believed that blacks were not supposed to be able to run long distances. There was a genetic explanation for that until Africans came to dominate long-distance races. Too many whites have conceded the physical superiority of blacks because it fits the racist image—"white brains, black brawn." Such beliefs have persisted despite a lack of scientific evidence to support genetic theories.

Donal Carlston's article, "An Environmental Explanation for Race Differences in Basketball Performance'' (*JSSI*, vol. 7, no. 2), addresses existing physiological, personality, and sociological explanations for differing skills and playing styles of blacks and whites in basketball. He offers an alternative environmental theory, hypothesizing that factors such as crowding foster the development of functional playing rules and norms, which in turn affect player development. Carlston details possible causal relationships between different aspects of the playing environment and player skills, styles, and attitudes.

Harry Edwards's article in chapter 1 examined race relations in the intercollegiate sports environment. It showed that, regardless of how qualified members of minority groups may be, they will be treated unequally. That article could easily have been included in this chapter. Edwards estimated that approximately three million black youths over age 12 place a high priority on a sports career because of the decades-old myth that sports is the way out of poverty. The result of this overemphasis on sports is that 25 to 30 percent of black high school athletes—and 15 to 20 percent of black athletes at four-year colleges—are functionally illiterate.

Instead of advancing the status of minorities, Edwards convincingly demonstrated that sports—while leading a few thousand blacks into better lives—has simultaneously substituted an impossible dream for millions of others. In doing so, it has almost ensured continuing poverty for them.

Finally, I have chosen to include the chapter entitled ''The Promised Land'' from my own book, *Broken Promises: Racism in American Sport,* to explore the extent of racism that still exists on the professional sports level. All of the negatives for blacks—especially the lost educational opportunities that result from an emphasis on eligibility rather than skill development in high school and college—seem to be forgotten by the pros who ''have it made.'' However, as Jackie Robinson proclaimed 40 years ago—''I never had it made''—the black pro today still has serious problems. He still has to be better, and he still faces positional segregation, quotas, differential treatment on and off the field, lack of enduring fame, and finally, lack of opportunities in sports when his playing days are over.

The Image of Intercollegiate Sports and the Civil Rights Movement: A Historian's View

Adolph H. Grundman
Metropolitan State College, Denver

I n the late 1960s, the American view of the relationship of sport and racism received a severe jolt. Until that time conventional wisdom held that sport treated blacks fairly and that it contributed mightily to good race relations. The *New York Times* captured the spirit of the latter ideal when it wrote that "there has been no one channel of understanding that has been better than that of sports. It has proved that most problems can be solved in the right spirit."[1] John Lardner, the sophisticated sports columnist of *Newsweek* in the 1950s, wrote that "race equality in baseball and in jazz music has done more than anything else to improve the climate for integration in America."[2] Thus, it came as a shock, in 1967, when two hundred participants to the Black Youth Conference, including some of America's foremost black collegiate athletes, voted to boycott the 1968 Olympics.[3] The essence of the protest was that blacks served as America's athletic "spear carriers" while the larger society remained insensitive to the condition of black America. *Life* magazine spoke for middle-America and conventional wisdom when it observed: "The athletic achievements of individual Negroes have been a source of great pride for all Negroes. The more young Negro athletes add to these powerful examples, the more they will do for their race."[4] Nonetheless, the organizer of the conference, sociologist Harry Edwards, emerged as a leading critic of the sport, especially as it applied to the black athlete. In 1968 Jack Olsen explored the shortcomings of sport in its treatment of black athletes in a *Sports Illustrated* series which later appeared in book form.[5] At the collegiate level Olsen described a very sordid story. His portrait of the black athlete depicted a young person poorly prepared for college, directed toward the easiest courses, and upon using up his eligibility, left with neither an education nor a degree.

The Edwards-Olsen critique and related events were an expression of the black militancy and the general re-examination of American culture that peaked in the second half of the decade. Stokely Carmichael, remember, introduced the phrase "black power" in Greenwood, Mississippi, in the summer of 1966. As blacks sought ways of influencing society, they naturally turned to the world of sports where they participated in numbers which far exceeded their proportion in American society. In fact, given the mood of the mid-1960s, it would have been strange indeed if sport had remained unaffected. Although one might dispute parts of the Edwards-Olsen indictment, their work brought a new level of sophistication to the study of sport and established the new parameters of the debate regarding blacks and sport. Yet a review of their work and other secondary literature revealed that most authors focused on exposing or detailing the racism of the sports establishment. Perhaps, because they were engaged in much needed muckraking, they avoided a full exploration of the reasons for the failure of racial integration in sport. Or, to be more exact, they simply used their examples as further proof of racism in American society. They neglected to examine the relationship of the premises of the civil rights movement and sport to the frustrations of the 1960s which is the purpose of this acticle. In fact, the integration of sports has some very close parallels to the civil rights movement.

The foundation of the civil rights movement of the 1950s was simply that all barriers to equal opportunity should be removed. As white liberal America and middle class blacks envisioned the future, blacks, without the handicap of past prejudice would enter the marketplace where they would rise or fall according to their abilities. Although industrialization, urbanization, and a technological revolution had made the individual in the marketplace or the self-made man a myth, its attraction was and remains powerful. This was especially so in the fifties when America's booming economy suggested that blacks could be propelled into the economic mainstream of American society without hurting whites. In addition, liberals shared the view that America must act, in its fashion, against racism in America. The idealistic rhetoric of World War II, the decolonization of the Third World, and the Cold War confrontation with the Soviet Union required some action on the part of the United States. This was the background to the famous school desegregation decision, *Brown v. Board of Education,* and it was also the backdrop to an important transition for the black collegiate athlete.

Prior to World War II, black competed with distinction for white colleges and universities in football, basketball, baseball, and track. Paul Robeson, Frederick "Fritz" Pollard, Fred "Duke" Slater, De Hart Hubbard, Eddie Tolan, Ralph Metcalfe, Jackie Robinson and Kenny Washington were among the notables. Nonetheless, white colleges provided spots for only a token black athlete, and, of course, in the South and Southwest there were no blacks attending white colleges or universities. As a result, black colleges provided competition for hundreds of skilled performers known only to those in the black community.[6] The galloping professionalization of collegiate sports after World War II, particularly football and basketball, made the recruitment of black athletes especially enticing. Many athletic programs saw this untapped source of talent as a shortcut to national recognition. Consequently universities outside the South were in the enviable position where they could build their athletic programs and claim that they were advancing the cause of race relations in America. The media, in turn, pointed with pride to collegiate sports (as well as professional) as a model for race relations in American society.

In the beginning the black athletes offered scholarships were selected with care. The impression given by the media was that integration would not jeopardize the mythic tradition of the scholar athlete. As in the first examples of school integration in the South the first black athletes were super-blacks who were admitted on white terms. To cite an example, the University of Illinois's J.C. Caroline received much publicity during the early 1950s as he broke many of the offensive records of the legendary Harold "Red" Grange. The media portrayed Caroline, a native of South Carolina, as a black Horatio Alger. With no steady home until the age of fourteen, Caroline's football skills were the ticket to Illinois. Although Caroline flunked two courses in his sophomore year, he was described as a serious student. The sports publicity director observed that "I never saw a boy work so hard. He hardly took time off from his books all summer." Caroline hinted at the real problem when he said: "If they would just leave you alone around exam time. I came up here to get an education. I'm not just going to play football. A man has to improve himself. The only way to do it is to get an education." In addition to stressing this interest in education, Caroline was described as a person with simple tastes and meager wants who did not smoke or drink.[7] Finally, Caroline avoided civil rights controversies. Although the campus barbershop excluded blacks, Caroline refused to join a campus organization's protest of this policy on the theory that "one person in particular is not going to stop anything like that."[8] Given this portrait of Caroline, it was not surprising and probably obligatory for a journalist to comment: "Caroline's teammates say that there is absolutely no racial prejudice on the team."[9]

Several years later Prentice Gautt, Oklahoma's first black football player was described the same way. Gautt rejected other scholarships offered to enroll at Oklahoma where his education was financed by a "group of doctors, dentists, and pharmacists." Although his football exploits received much attention, *Look* magazine did not fail to add that he was carrying a "B" average. *Look* credited Bud Wilkinson, the Oklahoma coach, with exercising "soft-spoken moral guidance." Wilkinson, in turn, thought that: "A person less fine than Prentice would not have made his contribution." In reflecting upon his career at Oklahoma, Gautt admitted that the first year had been tough, but added: "It was my fault. I held back." Again, Gautt's career has a civil right moral, since *Look* noted that the freshman team had walked out of a restaurant which refused to serve him.[10]

The Caroline-Gautt examples showed that integration in sport as in public schools was a one-way street in which it was incumbent upon blacks to demonstrate their ability to assimilate the white value system. Although 1960's revisionists rightly criticized the unfairness of their process, they forgot, because history had moved so rapidly, how enlightened the Caroline-Gautt road appeared to the fifties generation. After all, when historian Kenneth Stampp wrote in his preface to *The Peculiar Institution* that "Negroes are, after all, only white men with black skins, nothing more, nothing less," this was considered a statement of model liberal enlightenment.[11] When local black leaders sent the Carolines and Gautts to white schools it was to prove that Stampp was correct. The prestige of the universities and the eminence of the United States made it difficult to buck the one-way street to integration. After all, it was not until 1962 that James Baldwin asked "Do I really want to be integrated into a burning house?"[12]

In addition to identifying models for integration in sport, the media pointed to other civil rights victories in the athletic arena. Following the 1954 school desegregation ruling, the South responded by announcing that it would resist any measures that compromised racial segregation. For intercollegiate sports this means that some states and universities passed laws or adopted policies which prohibited competition in the South with institutions that had black players on their athletic teams. One example of the intermingling of sport and politics came in December of 1955 when the segregationist Governor of Georgia, Marvin Griffin, asked Georgia Tech to reject its Sugar Bowl bid because its opponent, the University of Pittsburgh, had a black player, Bobby Grier. Although two thousand students protested at the Georgia State capital and the *Atlanta Journal* thought the recommendation "ill considered," these reservations had little to do with civil rights or Georgia Tech's decision to remain in the Sugar Bowl. As one unhappy segregationist regent observed, principles were easily sacrificed "when there is money involved." David Rice, a Georgia Tech regent who favored Sugar Bowl participation, described Griffin's request as "ridiculous and asinine," since it would limit future bowl bids and hurt recruiting. The Georgia Board of Regents genuflected in the direction of "principle" by banning Georgia schools from future bowl bids in the South which did not follow segregation laws and customs.[13] In assessing these events the *New York Times* not only observed that the students were not motivated by principle but agreed with them that "The issue is not discrimination but a good football game." In formulating the dominant liberal position of the moment, the *Times* argued: "The test in any question of race is not one of pigmentation but of performance." In underscoring its commitment to equality of opportunity the *Times* observed that "The person who is really interested in human achievement . . . doesn't care about racial origins when he sees the results." Significantly, it was in the sports arena that the *Times* saw color blindness at its best. In its estimate of race relations it thought that at "no point has this struggle been better and more happily carried out than in the world of sport." The reason for this, the *Times* later wrote, was that this "is the one field in which individual human performance can be accurately measured." Expanding upon this idea in a subsequent editorial, the *Times* stressed the performance was the basis upon which "our whole [race] problem must eventually be solved. Judgments must be made on the basis of worth, not prejudice."[14]

From the liberal vantage point, collegiate sport seemed to mark the triumph of equalitarian ideals in American society. The refusal of some Southern schools to play racially integrated teams in the South was occasionally met be a decision of a Northern school to withdraw from a basketball tournament or cancel a Southern trip. The *New York Times,* for one, applauded these boycotts as a way of "simply making it plain that concepts that they have long discarded shall not be enforced upon them."[15] Some major football powers from the North did refuse to cancel games with Southern teams. The University of Syracuse thought it "unsportsmanlike" to refuse to play a worthy opponent. It told protesting alumni "that fielding a team dedicated to the best ideals is a good example for others to follow." When three Michigan State legislators asked the University of Michigan to cancel a game with the University of Georgia, the University of Michigan Board of Control of Intercollegiate Athletics thought it "legally, morally, and socially unjustifiable. . . ."[16] Despite these setbacks, from an integrationist point of view, collegiate sport was heading in the right direction. In 1963 the University of Kentucky announced that it would open its athletic program to all races. In 1964 Billy Jones was the first black basketball player to sign a letter of intent at the University of Maryland and the first in the Atlantic Coast Conference. When Warren McVea signed with the University of Houston, he and the university received national attention. The *New York Times,* once again, capsulized the liberal view of these events when it observed: "A few outfielders like Willie Mays, a few centers like Bill Russell, a few fullbacks like Jim Brown—who knows what tremendous champions might come out of the Southeast, with such recruits to build upon, and what miracles might be worked in better race relations?"[17] The passage of time demonstrated that black achievement in sport did not have a significant spillover effect in other aspects of American social, political, and economic life. Advancements in these areas were and are the result of hard fought political and legal action.

The fifties faith in sports as a model for race relations did not rest solely upon the belief that this was an arena where talent prevailed. Many Americans also held a romantic view of sports. They believed that sports built character and mandated good sportsmanship. Perhaps the concept of an All-American best captured the spirit of this idea. As late as 1960 *Look* prefaced the selection of its All-America football team by stating that: "Sportsmanship and good behavior carried more weight than ever. . . ." Walter Camp, Casper Whitney, and Grantland Rice, *Look* continued, "intended that the team reflect not only physical skill, but chivalry as well. The Football Writers cherish this image and intend to preserve it." The All-America players, *Look* concluded, were unselfish, avoided brutality, never violated the rules and found that "the true reward of football is the communal-effort experience, climaxed by victory or at least by the sure knowledge that their effort is complete."[18] This ideal was tested with the integration of collegiate sport and staunchly defended, especially when it was breached. In 1951, for example, when Johnny Bright, a record-breaking black back at Drake University, had his jaw broken by an illegal forearm, the Oklahoma A and M coach, J.B. Withworth, denied that his players ganged up on Bright. In the face of overwhelming photographic evidence, Withworth apologized for the offender, Wilbanks Smith, but did not discipline him. Withworth described Smith as "not the dirty type of football player. He just lost his head for a few minutes." Nine years later, to cite another example, the Syracuse football team charged that Texas players had barked racial slurs at them during the former's Cotton Bowl victory. Although the Texas coach, Darrell Royal, refused to comment, the University of Texas president, Logan Wilson, branded the charges as "irresponsible. They have damaged the reputation of this university, of a fine football team and of intercollegiate athletics generally."[19]

The fifties romantic view of sport also helped that generation to overlook the fact that racial integration in sport was limited to the superstar. In 1958, *Life* magazine predicted that: "on the basis of performance over the past season it is possible—and many coaches think it very probable that this year will see a unique All-America: every player will be a Negro." The players were Oscar Robertson, Wilt Chamberlain, Bob Boozer, Elgin Baylor, and Guy Rodgers. The *New York Times* also observed that the 1957–58 season marked the first time that more than "two Negroes" were named to the first team basketball All-America."[20] This evidence of racial progress hid another significant reality: black representation at white universities was limited to star athletes.

Another example of making much out of tokenism was the celebrated recruiting race for Wilt Chamberlain. The effort to attract Chamberlain to the University of Kansas involved an elaborate strategy headed by Coach Forrest "Phog" Allen. In explaining the intensity of this recruiting effort the KU president, Franklin D. Murphy, said that he was eager to improve racial integration in Kansas and that he had thought earlier about attracting a top Negro athlete to the campus. Coach Allen outdid Murphy by explaining that Kansas succeeded in getting Chamberlain because "we showed him how successful the Negro in Kansas was."[21] Since Kansas had fought school desegregation before the Supreme Court between 1952 and 1955, Allen's statement contained more than a little historic irony.

The record of recruiting excesses in the name of civil rights showed that the black middle class uncritically entered into this game. *Ebony* magazine, the voice of the black middle class, boasted that five black high school stars, Warren McVea, Vernon Payne, Mike Warren, Wesley Unseld, and James Dugan, were worth five million dollars. *Ebony* based this exaggerated statement of financial worth on their "firm offers of athletic grants-in-aid to attend nearly every major college in the country." Black athletes, from *Ebony*'s perspective, were symbols of racial and economic progress. The popular literature also suggested that the black middle class was also the medium between the athlete and recruiting institution. In pursuing Chamberlain, the University of Kansas utilized a black concert singer, a black publisher, and black businessman to sing the praises of KU. In recruiting Warren McVea, described as the first Negro to receive a football scholarship to a major previously all-white conference, Houston coach, Bill Yeoman, worked through the leadership of Houston's black community. All of this suggested that white institutions devoted some time to stroking the ego of the black middle class.[22]

By the end of 1967 racial integration passed another watershed. *Ebony* carried an article which reported that blacks were breaking into the schools of the "Old South." These young men were described by *Ebony* as "race pioneers." In reporting that Glen Page had died in a freakish accident at Kentucky, *Ebony* eulogized that "Page was credited with having made an outstanding contribution to race relations in Kentucky." The only sour note struck from Florida A and M's famous football coach, Jake Gaither, who noted that the Old South's new recruiting policies hurt black colleges. He added that black athletes were exploited by white schools and would be "until there is complete integration into every phase of college life."[23]

Another watershed in 1967 was the emergence of numerical superiority of blacks on the 1966–67 *Look* All-America basketball team. Six of the ten All-Americans were black and the following year eight black basketball players were named to *Look*'s top ten. The domination of basketball by blacks was not accompanied by any fanfare on behalf of race relations. Beneath this apparent color blindness lurked a concern, often expressed indirectly, about black domination of this game. This concern was expressed in several ways. For example, in the early sixties, *Look* commented upon the return of "a patterned ball-control offense, which seeks the good percentage shot, . . . the game [as] it is meant to be—one of balanced skills." *Look* also emphasized that an All-American "must be a team player." Was *Look* saying, in effect, that basketball was still played according to white principles? Whatever the answer the virtuosity of black players caused a ferment in college basketball where the blending of individualism and the team concept were more difficult than in football.[24]

In addition to style, the influx of black college stars led to a search for "white hopes." *Look*'s effusiveness over Princeton's Bill Bradley was unmatched in the history of its All-America. According to *Look:* "Bradley's skills are matched by his dedication and his team attitude. Nothing he might do with a basketball would surprise. He might even convert those few who regard the sport as anathema." Oscar Robertson, in *Look*'s opinion, was the only collegiate player to top Bradley. *Look* seemed relieved when it wrote: "Whether the Tiger nobody holds could go on to match or surpass Robertson as a pro never will be known because Bradley has rejected a career with the New York Knickerbockers to accept a Rhodes Scholarship at Oxford."[25] Bradley's appeal rested on his skill, his color, and his ability to confirm middle-class values. His play was a perfect blend of individualism and cooperation; his skills derived from "dedication" as much as natural ability; and his Rhodes Scholarship saved him from the sin of overemphasis.

It was ironic that black domination of the All-American basketball teams and the extension of scholarships to black athletes by the universities of the Old South came in 1967. After all, as discussed earlier this was also the year that some black athletes made a serious effort to boycott the Olympics.[26] The black indictment of sports surprisingly came at the very moment when black athletes seemed to have broken all intercollegiate color barriers. Significantly, this paralleled the larger civil rights movement. Black nationalism, violence in American cities, and second thoughts about integration followed or paralleled the Civil Rights Act of 1964, the Voting Rights Act of 1965, and the Supreme Court decisions ordering busing to integrate public schools. The linkage between intercollegiate sports and society seemed almost perfect. Intercollegiate sports were not merely reflecting society, they were part of it. Their failure to serve as a model of equality of opportunity and race relations was due to the fact that intercollegiate sports were closely connected with the symbols and economics of America. The belief so widely held in the early fifties and encouraged by the media that intercollegiate sports were different from the rest of society was less easily held in the late sixties. Thus, by 1968, as black and white civil rights activists advocated equality of result through affirmative action, intercollegiate sports stood as one more example of the limitations of equality of opportunity.

References

1. Editorial, *New York Times*, May 31, 1959, IV, 8.
2. John Lardner, "The Old Emancipator—1," *Newsweek*, April 2, 1956, p. 85.
3. *New York Times*, November 24, 1967, p. 8.
4. Editorial, *Life*, December 8, 1967.
5. Jack Olsen, *The Black Athlete, A Shameful Story: The Myth of Integration in American Sport* (New York: Time-Life Books, 1968). The *Sports Illustrated* series began on July 1, 1968. See also Harry Edwards, *The Revolt of the Black Athlete* (New York: The Free Press, 1969).
6. Ocania Chalk, *Black College Sport* (New York: Dodd, Mead and Company, 1976).
7. Fred Parker, "The Skinny Terror of Illinois," *Saturday Evening Post*, October 9, 1954, pp. 31, 117–120.

8. Letter to the Editor, *Saturday Evening Post,* November 27, 1954, p. 4.

9. Parker, "The Skinny Terror," p. 119.

10. "Oklahoma's Quiet Powerhouse," *Look,* October 13, 1959, pp. 54–54.

11. Kenneth M. Stampp, *The Peculiar Institution: Slavery in the Ante-Bellum South* (New York: Vintage Books, 1956), p. vii.

12. James Baldwin, *The Fire Next Time* (New York: Dell Publishing, 1962), p. 127.

13. *New York Times,* December 4, 1955, p. 1; December 3, 1955, p. 1; and December 6, 1955, p. 1.

14. Editorials, Ibid., December 4, 1955, E, p. 10; July 22, 1956, E, p. 8; and May 31, 1959, IV, p. 8.

15. Editorial, Ibid., October 6, 1956, p. 20.

16. *New York Times,* February 18, 1964, p. 20, and February 16, 1957, p. 10.

17. Ibid., May 30, 1963, p. 13; April 9, 1964, p. 37; Mickey Herskowitz, "Warren goes this away and that away," *Sports Illustrated,* November 9, 1964, pp. 48–49; and Editorial, *New York Times,* April 21, 1963, IV, p. 8.

18. Tim Cohane, "Football All-America—1960," *Look,* December 20, 1960, pp. 130–36.

19. *New York Times,* October 22, 1951, p. 28; October 23, 1951, p. 39; January 2, 1960, p. 8; and January 12, 1960, p. 24.

20. "New Look for the All-America," *Life,* March 10, 1958, p. 99, and *New York Times,* March 6, 1958, p. 34.

21. "What It Took to Get Wilt," *Life,* January 28, 1957, pp. 113–17.

22. "Athletes—500 Scholarships," *Ebony,* October, 1964, pp. 57–61; "Wilt," *Life,* p. 114; and Herskowitz, "Warren goes this away," p. 48.

23. Louie Robinson, "New Football Stars in the Old South," *Ebony,* December, 1967, pp. 75–78.

24. "Basketball All-America—1966–67," *Look,* March 21, 1967, pp. 71–75; "Basketball All-America—1967–68," *Look,* March 19, 1968, pp. 91–93; "Basketball All-America—1962–63," *Look,* March 26, 1963, pp. 109–12; and "Basketball All-America," *Look,* March 27, 1962, pp. 111–14.

25. "Basketball All-America—1964–65," *Look,* March 23, 1965, pp. 87–91.

26. This was not the first time that black athletes advocated an Olympic boycott. See Mal Whitfield, "Let's Boycott the Olympics," *Ebony,* March 1964, pp. 95–100.

An Environmental Explanation for Race Differences in Basketball Performance

Donal E. Carlston
University of Iowa

Both sportswriters (Kirkpatrick, 1968; Kane, 1971; DuPree, 1978a) and social scientists (Worthy and Markle, 1970; Jones and Hochner, 1973; Snyder and Spreitzer, 1978) have observed that systematic differences exist between the performance of white and black athletes. While the nature of the alleged differences varies from writer to writer, it is generally argued that black athletes are faster, jump higher, react more quickly, are more graceful, play with more style, or in other ways out-perform their white counterparts.

Numerous theories have been advanced to explain these performance differences (e.g., Kane, 1971, Worthy and Markle, 1970; Jones and Hochner, 1973; McPherson, 1975), but none of these provides a completely satisfactory explanation for the kinds of differences that have been suggested. The theories of social scientists often gloss over the finer details of athletics, focusing only on the most global or obvious aspects of sports performance. The theories of sports writers attend more closely to the nuances of sports, but fail to provide systematic descriptions of causal mechanisms that might underlie the observed racial differences.

The present article argues that the oft-observed racial differences in sports performance are not really racial at all, but rather, reflect the differing environments in which black and white players generally develop their skills. While similar arguments have been advanced previously (e.g., Edwards, 1973; Phillips, 1976; Greenfield, 1980) this article will attempt to present a more comprehensive theory relating differences in athletic performance to specific environmental factors that influence the development of playing skills, styles and attitudes. This theory focuses exclusively on the sport of basketball, a narrowness necessary if the discussion is to progress beyond the vague generalizations that characterize much of the literature in this area. However, while the discussion will be confined to basketball, the mechanisms and effects to be discussed may well have implications for other sports.

Racial Differences in Basketball Performance

One of the most concrete pieces of evidence that racial difference exist in basketball performance is that blacks are represented on basketball teams in much larger proportions than they are in the population at large. While blacks comprise about 11% of the U.S. population, they comprise 27% of NCAA basketball teams (Yetman and Eitzen, 1972) and over 73% of professional basketball teams in this country (Poliquin, 1981). Some writers have suggested that the proportion of black players might be even higher if teams did not have implicit racial quotas (cf. Yetman and Eitzen, 1972).

Blacks are represented in similar high proportions among those who excel at the professional level. Over a recent 13 year period, 12 of the National Basketball Association's most-valuable players were black (Edwards, 1973). In 1980, 84% of the top 25 players in the N.B.A. were black (*Street and Smith's Official Basketball Yearbook*, 180); and through the first half of the 1980–81 season, 100% of the top "assist" players, 93% of the top scorers, and 70% of the top rebounders in the N.B.A. were black (Poliquin, 1981). The general manager of The Philadelphia 76'ers states "The black athlete dominates the N.B.A. That's not an opinion, that's a fact." (quoted by Poliquin, 1981).

Analyses of professional basketball statistics further indicate the existence of performance differences between black and white players. Jones and Hochner (1973) found that black players averaged 25% more rebounds than white players, and blacks shot more often than whites relative to the number of assists they made. Finally, these researchers found that black players shot free throws with about 4% *less* accuracy than white players.

Perhaps even more interesting than these performance statistics are the unquantifiable stylistic differences that a number of observers have noted between white and black players (DuPree, 1978; Greenfield, 1980; Kirkpatrick, 1968; Novak, 1976; Wielgus & Wolff, 1980). In their remarkably uniform descriptions, the black playground player is characterized as smooth, flashy and independent, and his game is described as one of spin moves, double pumps, and slam dunks. In contrast, the white player is characterized as hard-working, precise, dull but efficient, and his game is described as one of picks and screens and the high percentage shots. As summarized by Greenfield (1980): "'White' ball, then, is the basketball of patience and method. 'Black' ball is the basketball of electric self-expression" (p. 318).

These stereotypes are widely held by basketball players, coaches and reporters (cf. Wielgus & Wolff, 1980; Jordan, 1979) although the black style is sometimes labeled "city," "playground," or "ghetto" ball and the white style is termed "noncity," "blue collar," or "midwest." Prototypic exhibitors or the "city" style of the professional level are Julius Erving, Earl Monroe, and George Gervin and prototypic exhibitors of the non-city style are John Havlicek, Dave Cowens and Bill Walton. Of course, there have also been some blacks who exhibited the non-city style (e.g., Wes Unseld) and some whites who played the city game (e.g., Pete Maravich).

The stylistic differences between black and white basketball players are important because they suggest the profound nature of the differences between these groups of athletes. It is not simply that blacks can jump higher or run faster or play better than whites. It is that blacks and whites appear to be playing two different kinds of games, as dissimilar in some respects as they are similar. Existing theories of racial differences in sports performance generally fail to recognize the broad and complex nature of these dissimilarities.

Previous Theories

A variety of theories have been proposed to explain performance differences between black and white athletes. Among others, Kane (1971) has proposed that blacks possess physiological characteristics that contribute to superior speed, reflexes and jumping ability. Writers have also proposed that personality, differences between blacks and whites may contribute to performance differences. For example, black athletes have been described as more "relaxed" (Kane, 1971) and as more "reactive" (Worthy & Markle, 1970) than white athletes. It has also been suggested that social factors contribute to an exaggerated emphasis on sports participation and excellence among black youngsters (Edwards, 1973; Michener, 1976) and to different patterns of socialization for black athletes (McPherson, 1975).

Although an exhaustive critique of these theories is not possible in this limited space, some common shortcomings will be mentioned. First, most of the theories are based on assumed differences between white and black athletes that have not been convincingly demonstrated with appropriate samples. For example, as Edwards (1973) notes in his critique, neither physiological nor personality differences have been shown to exist between the black and white populations of the United States as a whole nor between carefully selected samples of black and white athletes. Furthermore, the tremendous heterogeneity in body and personality types within each racial group contrasts markedly with the homogeneity attributed to the athletic styles of each group. In this regard, it should be noted that the "prototypical" exhibitors of city and non-city playing styles listed earlier represent a wide variety of body types and personalities, none of which can be appropriately characterized as "representative" or "typical" for their racial groups.

Second, these theories fail to provide tight linkage between the antecedents they assume and the kinds of performance differences that have been observed. For example, it is unclear how any of the physiological differences that have been described could lead black players to emphasize moves, improvisation, and "electric self-expression," to shoot free throws more poorly or to pass less often than white players. Even rebounding, which might seem to reflect physiologically-based jumping ability, is probably actually more dependent on skills such as positioning and timing (cf. Davis, 1969). It seems similarly unlikely that personality characteristics can explain more than some peripheral aspects of performance such as demeanor, coachability or aggressiveness. As Edwards (1973) observed: "It will be noted that none of the [personality] factors studied make any direct contribution to the development of actual physical skills or athletic ability" (p. 223).

It is conceivable that the improvisional and exhibitionistic styles of black basketball might reflect global personality traits, but research suggests that black athletes actually score lower on scales measuring impulsivity and exhibitionism than do white athletes (Ogilvie and Tutko, 1968). In any case, there is no evidence that players' off-court personality traits are linked in any meaningful way to their on-court playing personalities.

Similarly, many of the differences in the socialization of white and black athletes that McPherson (1975) observed are only tenuously related to athletic performance. For example, McPherson's finding that black (track) athletes come from larger, sociologically disadvantaged, matriarchically dominated families does not appear to have any direct bearing on athletic skills or styles. Even those sociological factors that might logically lead to variations in athletic style or performance have not been carefully linked to such effects. For example, the overemphasis on sports in black communities (cf. Edwards, 1973; Michener, 1976) might well lead blacks to take up basketball at a younger age, and to devote themselves more thoroughly and exclusively to the sport (see McPherson, 1975, for findings among track athletes). This increased devotion to the sport might explain the greater talent of black players, and consequently, their overrepresentation at the collegiate and professional levels, but it is unclear how it would lead to the various other stylistic and performance differences that have been observed. One might argue that because blacks devote more time to playing basketball, they develop greater facility at difficult skills such as spin moves, pump shots, and dunking the ball. But the assumption that the "expressive" moves and styles of black basketball reflect greater practice has a number of implications that do not appear to be accurate. For example, this implies that white professional players, who have devoted innumerable hours to basketball over their careers, should almost invariably exhibit more of the "black playground style" than black youngsters on the playgrounds, who are relatively new at the game. As this does not appear to be true, the assumption that greater experience with the game necessarily leads to more expressive play seems unjustified. It is similarly unclear why increased playing time would lead to poorer free throw shooting or decreased passing by black players (see Jones and Hochner, 1973). Consequently, the links between various sociological factors and observed differences between white and black basketball players remain rather tenuous.

Finally, as the preceding discussion emphasizes, none of the existing theories for race differences in athletic performance can account for more than a small portion of the differences that appear to exist. Physiological differences between whites and blacks might explain a few differences in physical talents, personality differences might relate to the expressiveness of playing styles, and sociological factors might explain the overrepresentation of blacks in upper levels of play. Consequently, a variety of different theories might be unparsimoniously combined to obtain some explanatory power. Even then, if all of these different theories were substantiated, there would still be glaring gaps in our understanding of race differences in playing styles. Why do black players at the professional level shoot free throws somewhat more poorly than do whites? Why do black players emphasize scoring over other facets of play? Why do white and black youngsters play pick-up games using different rules to govern play? Existing theories are clearly unable to provide satisfactory answers to such questions.

The objective of this article is to advance such an explanation, based on a variety of different observations and sources. These observations reflect a distillation from personal experiences and observations as a pick-up ball player, interviews with numerous players from a variety of backgrounds, and descriptions in secondary sources, including sports biographies (Auerbach & Fitzgerald, 1977; Cousy & Hirshberg, 1958; Frazier & Berkow, 1974; McPhee 1965; Russell & Branch, 1979; Wolf, 1972), other basketball books (Holzman & Lewin, 1973; Jordan, 1979; Wielgus & Wolff, 1980) and books on sports sociology (Edwards, 1973; Michener, 1976; Snyder & Spreitzer, 1978). These various sources provide a clear and consistent description of basketball in rural, suburban and inner city communities, and the resultant explanation for basketball styles has a coherence that I believe readers will find compelling. Nonetheless, until empirical evidence is collected to support these observations, this explanation must be considered speculative and preliminary.

A Theory of Environmental Influences on Player Development

Overview

Most black players learn the game of basketball under conditions differing substantially from those surrounding most developing white players. The inner city basketball courts frequented by blacks are generally crowded with large numbers of players competing for valuable playing time on the limited facilities. On these overcrowded courts, rules and norms have developed to handle the abundance of competitors, and to insure that superior players are able to practice and develop their skills. I contend that these norms subtly shape the skills and styles and attitudes of the inner city player in predictable ways.

In contrast, in the rural and suburban communities where most white players grow up, the number of available courts often exceeds the number of developing players. White players may spend countless hours practicing alone on their own driveway, or playing with a few acquaintances on one of the public courts provided in schools or parks. I will suggest that the skills players develop playing by themselves differ predictably from the skills that are developed in the press of competition. Furthermore, the rules and norms that evolve to govern competitive play in such neighborhoods take maximum advantage of these skills when players do converge for pick-up games. These rules also encourage participation by marginal players, who are needed if enough people are to be attracted to allow a game. It is hypothesized that these various rules, coupled with hours of individual practice, shape players' skills, styles and attitudes, creating the typical white playing style.

In summary, then, it is proposed that the different playing conditions in white and black communities lead to different playing rules and norms, and in turn to the different styles and abilities that observers have noted. In many ways this formulation is similar to Barker's (1960) theory of "overstaffed" and "understaffed" environments. Barker argues that overstaffed environments are characterized by social norms that discourage participation except by the most talented, and by a competitiveness that allows these talented individuals to rise to the top. Understaffed environments are characterized by norms that encourage participation and provide for a more egalitarian reward structure. The present formulation extends these ideas by describing a whole chain of causal factors, beginning with environmental pressures such as crowding, including the development of athletic skills and norms, and ending with the kinds of performance and stylistic differences that writers have observed among basketball players.

Environmental Influences

Playing Conditions

Inner City Games. The inner city provided relatively few basketball courts for a relatively large number of basketball players. The local playgrounds or schoolyards where most courts are located are spread widely through rather densely populated communities, and many of the baskets they provide are no longer usable. Yet, for a variety of social and economic reasons (cf. Michener, 1976), basketball is one of the more popular activities among inner city males, and consequently, large numbers of players converge on the available courts, hoping to get into games. This crowding leads to competition for spots on teams and provides an audience of would-be players and hangers-on to watch the games. It is common for 10 to 20 spectators to watch from the sidelines, and when the players in the ongoing game are prominent enough, audiences of 100 or more are possible (see Axthelm, 1970). Crowding, competition for playing time, and audiences are factors that vitally affect the nature of the city game.

Non-City Games. The central problem in the rural, small town and suburban communities where most whites learn their basketball, is player scarcity, rather than crowding on the courts. The proportion of middle class and rural youngsters who play basketball is relatively low, particularly in the off-season, when other sports and other diversions draw off sizeable numbers of potential players. Those hard-core devotees who maintain year-round interest in basketball are spread across numerous playground and schoolyard courts and an almost infinite number of driveway courts. Consequently, these players have difficulty rounding up enough other people to play with, and a good deal of the time they resort to solitary practice at the park or in their own driveway (see, for example, Bill Bradley's experience, described by McPhee, 1965). The scarcity of players and the hours spent practicing alone are critical in shaping the typical "white" playing style.

Player Development.

City Players. The city player learns basketball and develops his talents in the endless succession of games that characterize inner city play. Consequently, his skills are shaped in ways that reflect the demands of competition. Almost from the first time a player touches a basketball, someone else is trying to steal it, or block it, and the player needs to learn techniques to defend himself and the basketball from the ever-present defense. A player learns to dribble low, on the side away from the defender, to spin and fake, and to keep his head up, so he can see where the defense is coming from. He learns to deliver his shots and passes in a circuitous manner, keeping the ball close to the protected side of his body, so it won't be tipped away. And he learns to circumvent would-be blockers by faking them off their feet, altering shots in mid-air, and reaching around the basket so the rim and net shield off attacking hands. The moves, fakes, and pump-shots displayed by city players are thus essential components of their styles from the start, because these skills are essential in the games where these individuals learn to play.

City players also learn to accept contact as a routine part of basketball. Jostling, bumping and hacking are almost integral to basketball games, and players who develop their talents in competition naturally learn to handle a high level of such contact. Hence, the city player may be better able to maintain control of the basketball when attacked by a defender, and to learn to shoot while pressured.

Non-City Players. The non-city player develops his playing skills largely free from the press of competition. Playing alone on his driveway or at the park, he has little need to protect the basketball on his dribble or his shots. He assumes an upright posture facing the basket, dribbles high in front of his body, delivers the ball carelessly from the front, and learns a simple, straightforward shooting style that is effective as long as there is no defender. Of course, on occasions he mimics the players he has seen on television, faking and spinning and driving in for a fancy lay-up. But lacking any real defensive pressure, the player fails to make the many subtle physical adjustments that would be necessary to evade an actual defender. Consequently, these moves are unlikely to be effective in real competition, and they contribute little to the player's development.

To entertain himself in the absence of competition, the player is likely to work on his shooting form and effectiveness, consciously altering each aspect of his shot until he achieves the perfect form characteristic of great pure shooters. John McPhee (1965) describes how Bill Bradley consciously analyzed and changed each of his shots to mimic players he admired, and how his practice sessions involved systematically moving from spot to spot on the court, repeating each shot a dozen times. Similarly, former Celtic player Frank Ramsey explains how in practice he would "try to go back to the fundamentally correct way of taking each shot" and to check his technique against the ideal standard (Sharmon, 1968). Such devotion to the form and mechanics of basketball shots is most characteristic of players who spend a lot of time practicing alone.

In essence, then, the non-city player is likely to develop excellent shooting form and a repertoire of effective shots that he has taken hundreds of times before while practicing. However, he is unlikely to develop the stance or moves necessary to single-handedly defeat an aggressive defender. And he will be accustomed to taking his shots without hands in his face or body contact throwing him off balance.

In time, the non-city player will face more and more competition, and if he is to excel, he will need to develop better ball handling skills and one-on-one moves. But he is likely to always be most comfortable using his basic, upright, classic shooting form that he developed early in his playing career. Of course, given his inability to adjust and overcome a pressing defender, such a player will be most effective when he can lose the defense and get open for the kind of unencumbered shot that he's been taking his whole life. It is not surprising, then, that a style of play develops in rural and suburban communities that provides these kinds of opportunities, as discussed later in this article.

Playground Rules and Norms

When neighborhood "pick-up" basketball games are organized, it is necessary to change the "official" rules to accommodate the unique circumstances of informal competition. There are no pre-existing teams to play one another, no coach to determine who from each team gets to play, no officials to call fouls, and no clock to specify when competition is over. Furthermore, on many playing courts there is only one basket, which must be used by both competing teams, rather than two opposing baskets as found in full court basketball. To handle these circumstances, neighborhood players must adopt a special set of rules to govern play. A number of aspects of play are also governed by implicit social norms, which reflect the expectations of other players, though they are not articulated as explicit rules.

The playing rules and norms are enforced and maintained through the imposition of social sanctions against those who disregard the conventions (cf. Schachter, 1951). Among the most severe kinds of sanctions is physical violence, which sometimes involves outright assault, but more commonly is "disguised" as overly aggressive play. Such physical sanctions are most commonly applied in retaliation for violations of body contact norms. Deviant players may also be excluded from play in different ways, corresponding to the rejection or ostracism discussed by Schachter (1951) and others (e.g., Latane, 1966). Players can also be partially or "psychologically" excluded (cf. Schachter, 1951) by teammates who decline to pass them the basketball. This kind of sanction is commonly used against a player who is taking too many "bad shots." Finally, deviant players may be subjected to various kinds of verbal harassment, including threats, criticism, and ridicule.

On the more positive side, playing behavior is also shaped through positive reinforcements such as compliments and hand slapping. Through combinations of sanctions and positive reinforcements, players can shape each other's behavior, teaching and enforcing the playing rules and norms that exist in different communities.

It is here hypothesized that these rules and norms reflect the different demands of the city and non-city playing environments. In particular, crowding on city basketball courts seems to have led to a system of play that allots playing time according to ability, makes use of skills developed in competition, speeds up games, and allows superior players to dominate play. In contrast, the sparsity of players in non-city environments seems to have led to a set of rules that encourages the participation of marginal players, makes use of skills developed in solo practice, slows down games and prevents superior players from dominating other participants. These differing functions are perhaps most evident in the different systems that have developed for choosing teams in the two types of communities.

Choosing Teams

When players gather for informal, pick-up basketball games, there are no established teams to face each other. It is, therefore, necessary for participants to establish a system for determining which players will constitute each team, and which team will compete in what sequence on the neighborhood court. The systems that have evolved in America's inner cities differ fundamentally from those existing in non-city environments.

In the inner city, the central factor affecting the rules of pick-up games is the overabundance of players who would like to use the basketball court. If all the awaiting players take turns, sharing the facility equally, the playing time allotted to the best players is likely to be insufficient to allow development and maintenance of their skills. Yet the best players must be able to hone these skills in order to compete successfully for school teams, college scholarships or professional contracts. Consequently, games must be organized so that a) a large number of players can be worked in during the course of the playing day and b) the best players receive the most and the best competition. To accomplish these ends, a system has evolved in most inner city areas where the team to win a pick-up game gets to continue playing against a succession of challengers, until some other team wins (cf. Wielgus and Wolff, 1980). The challenging teams are selected by a series of "captains" who have declared their intention to challenge the winners, by calling out "I've got winners" or "I've got the next game." These claims represent an informal "take-a-number" system providing an orderly succession of captains. When each captain's turn comes up, he is allowed to choose four other players to make up his challenging team. He is given great latitude in doing so, and may include friends or players who participated in the preceding game or players waiting to play (including those who have only just arrived at the court).

The captain must choose a team strong enough to beat the reigning winners, however, or he will be quickly defeated and find himself sitting on the sidelines, possibly waiting half the day for another opportunity to play. Consequently, the captains are under considerable pressure to put together the best possible groups of players for their challenge. A certain amount of politicking takes place on the sidelines as captains try to attract star players to their team, using their priority ("I've got the next game") or their other players ("We've got Wilt; we can't lose") as bargaining chips, and players try to get on the best team they can, using friendship or reputation to close the deal. The challengers then take their turns on the court, trying to dethrone the champions so that they can continue to play, defending against other challenging teams still in line.

These rules encourage the survival of the fittest, with the strongest players coalescing into a team that may hold the court all afternoon, intermediate players being regularly chosen to fill out challenging teams, and weak players sitting out most of the games or enjoying, at best, a few futile minutes of play before being vanquished. The end result of this system is that players generally enjoy playing time proportional to their abilities. The star players, who are most likely to eventually graduate from the playground to organized competition, are most likely to be chosen by the captains. The stars are also able to offer their services to a team that is already strong, and thus to win and hold the court. Yet the system has enough flux so that precocious youngsters can maneuver themselves onto teams and into games, where they may play for some time (if they don't hurt the team too much), accumulating valuable experience against the best players in the neighborhood. . . .

The central pressure that non-city rules must deal with is not over-crowding but under-manning. As previously noted, it is difficult to get enough players assembled for a basketball game in many communities, particularly at certain times of the year. Consequently, teams are often rounded out by inviting younger brothers or occasional players to join the game, or by soliciting participants from baseball games or other activities going on in the area. Inclusion of such players results in wide variations in the skill levels of those involved in the game. Yet the game must be made appealing to players of marginal ability or they abandon the game for other activities. The rules of the non-city game have consequently evolved in a way that encourages and facilitates participation by marginal players.

For example, teams are generally organized so that they are of roughly equal strength. Initially players may appoint two captains who take turns choosing their teammates, may divide the players by mutual agreement, or may shoot free throws until enough players make the shot to constitute a team. If the adopted system produces teams that clearly differ in talent level, trades will often be made to redress the imbalance. In fact, trades may be made *during* the game if it becomes evident that one team is much stronger than the other. In any case, when the game is over, if one team has won by a wide margin, players will generally re-assign participants to make two new, more evenly balanced teams.

When games are over, any players who have been waiting on the sideline join the next game automatically. If too many players are waiting (a fairly rare occurrence), then free throw shooting is often used to determine who gets to play and who must sit out. This procedure is fairly time consuming, but the speed of the proceedings is of little concern in non-city environments. Often when new players show up who wish to get in a game, some of the marginal players who were playing drop out on their own accord. In any case, the new arrivals have priority over those players who have just lost a game or those who have played several games previously. Someone who is waiting cannot be made to sit out indefinitely while the same players play over and over again, as sometimes happens in city games when a captain chooses those from the losing squad to fill out his team. (This norm does not always apply, however, when an uninvited player stumbles upon a "private" game that players have organized in advance.)

The new players in the game are generally divided up by mutual agreement or by free-throw shooting, or new teams are made up altogether. The implicit objective is to divide the better players between the two teams, so that they can guard each other, and neither team is put at a strong disadvantage. Players voluntarily match up against opponents of about the same height and ability, so that marginal players are not overwhelmed by superior ones. And to a large extent, the non-city rules serve to minimize the domination of the better players while allowing the lesser players to become more involved. . . .

Shooting and Passing Norms

In the city game, scoring baskets is of paramount importance both to the team and to the individual who scores. The basket brings the team one-point closer to winning the game and keeping possession of the court. A score also enhances a player's reputation, and makes him a more attractive choice for future teams.

Since scoring baskets assumes such importance in the city game, most players are inclined to attempt to score first, and to pass only if their moves are stymied or if they can make an eye-opening assist to another player who is in scoring position. A "hot" shooter is generally permitted to take the ball and score on as many consecutive occasions as possible (and in half-court games the occasions really are consecutive, since the offense remains an offense until stopped). Players who shoot at every opportunity are rarely criticized unless they repeatedly take too long in trying to out-maneuver their defender, or take too many "bad shots." Good shots and bad shots are defined in terms of the normative styles of the neighborhood. In the inner city a good shot is any shot in which a player has achieved proficiency. It doesn't matter if the shooter is 35 feet from the basket, if he is tightly guarded, if he is off-balance or even if he misses the basket, as long as the shot is one which he frequently makes. A "bad shot" is one clearly beyond the capabilities of a player. However, this definition is a fairly stringent one, so that shooting does not seem to provoke much criticism in the inner city.

In fact, inner city players may be criticized for *not* shooting under some circumstances. Particularly when the ball is rebounded in close proximity to the basket, players are expected to shoot it back up so that teammates who have moved to rebounding positions have an opportunity to tip in the basket. Passing or dribbling the ball away from the basket is a waste of time which frustrates potential rebounders. In general, routine passing to players who are not in scoring position is discouraged as wasted effort, and players who do not create scoring opportunities by shooting or making assists are unlikely to be passed the ball with any regularity.

In non-city basketball games, shooting and scoring are generally of less importance than in the city. Players rarely need to impress others with their shooting skills in order to play and the game score rarely determines who gets to continue and who must sit out. Passing the ball is made necessary by several rules (including the in-bound rule and the take-back rule in the half-court game) and by the need to keep marginal players involved and happy with the game. Furthermore, a good deal of passing is ordinarily necessary to set up non-city players for the kinds of wide-open shots they have learned during hours of solitary practice. Consequently, non-city players learn to first look for the pass, and only secondarily for the shot. A good deal of routine passing generally occurs as players work the ball around, keeping everyone involved and trying to set up a wide-open shot. Of course, these efforts are interrupted and wasted if the recipient of a pass decides to loft up a "bad" shot. Not surprisingly then, the non-city norms concerning shooting are stricter and more often enforced than those in the inner city.

A "good shot" is generally defined not only as one at which the player is proficient (as in the city), but also as one that is taken on-balance, with good form, and without defensive pressure. In short, the good shot is one that is taken under approximately the same conditions that non-city players encounter in practicing alone. The definition also incorporates the emphasis on good, consistent shooting form which players develop from hours of working alone, trying to shape their shots into classical form. Even when taking "good" shots, non-city players may be criticized for shooting too much, and passing too little. Routine passing is viewed as an important part of the game, and a "gunner" who fails to pass the ball to others is likely to be rebuked.

Picks and Screens

An inner city player is generally expected to score without a great deal of help from his teammates. Having developed his skills in the press of competition, the city player has presumably learned how to dribble, drive and shoot while protecting the basketball from outstretched defensive hands. He is expected to have the spins and moves necessary to single-handedly lose his defender and free himself for a shot. And if a defender is able to stay with the would-be shooter, the shooter is expected to fake or jump or double-pump to get the shot off anyway. In this context, picks and screens are unnecessary and possibly counterproductive. Screens intended to free a player to receive the ball are often wasted since the ball handler is more likely to look for driving room than for an open man. Picks set for the ball handler himself may simply bring an extra defender into position to help defend against a shot. Often an inner city ballhandler will wave other players away from his side of the court altogether, so that he can take his defender to the basket one-on-one. Hence, inner city norms do not generally require players to pick or screen for their teammates.

Picks and screens are far more important in the non-city game. Without some assistance from their teammates, non-city players would have difficulty freeing themselves for the kind of shots they are used to and which are required by the non-city norms. Therefore, players are expected to help each other out on offense more than would be expected in the inner city.

Calling Fouls and Physical Contact

In pick-up games, players must call fouls themselves, since there are no officials to do so. Although circumstances conspire to make the inner city game quite physical, the rules and norms do much to inhibit foul calling. Among the factors contributing to the physical nature of the inner city contest are the necessity for players to win if they wish to continue playing, and the no-take-back rule (in half-court), which tends to pack players together in the high contact zone under the basket. However, the norms generally discourage players from calling fouls unless they have the ball and are in the act of shooting. Even then, if a player does call a foul, no foul shots are awarded, and the offended player simply gets the ball back. Consequently, if a player is fouled, but does not lose possession of the basketball, nothing is gained by calling the foul. If a player in the act of shooting calls a foul, and the basket goes in, the basket is disallowed, contrary to "official" basketball rules. Furthermore, a player must call the foul immediately, without seeing whether he made it or not. Hence, most players refrain from calling shooting fouls unless the contact is so severe that the shot has little chance of scoring. It is the offended player's decision whether to jeopardize the basket by calling a foul, and calls by other players (including the offender) are generally discouraged. This combination of forces and rules makes inner city basketball a high contact sport.

The passing and screening game favored in non-city environments spreads players across the court, reducing the number of people crowded into the high contact zone under the basket, and consequently, reducing contact. Additionally, the non-city rules discourage physical contact. Players may call fouls anytime they feel they have been physically offended, whether or not they had the basketball or were in the act of shooting. If a player calls "foul" on a shooting attempt, the basket goes in, the score is counted and the foul call is nullified. If the basket misses, the player who fouled generally receives possession of the basketball, although players will occasionally agree to shoot free throws on shooting fouls. Fouls may be called voluntarily by the offending player, or sometimes even by uninvolved players, practices frowned upon in most city games. The circumstances and norms on non-city courts thus tend to reduce the amount of fouling and contact that occurs.

The different rules and norms concerning physical contact are understandable consequences of the different environmental pressures in the different kinds of communities. First, games tend to be slower if a number of fouls are called, and thus the non-city rules slow down the game while the more stringent city criteria for foul calling speed it up. Second, the non-city rules serve to protect players from contact which could disrupt dribbling and shooting skills learned in the absence of defensive pressure, while city players presumably need less protection, having developed their skills in the heat of competition. Third, the non-city rules reduce the advantage held by large, physical and well-skilled players by preventing them from pushing less talented participants around, while the city rules give the better players more latitude. Finally, the non-city rules help to reduce excessive fouling and conflicts which could alienate potential players, a concern not shared on overcrowded city courts.

Effects of the Playing Environment on Player Development

The ways in which players are shaped by community playing rules and norms, and other aspects of the playing environment, are summarized and elaborated in the following sections.

Playing Skills

Inner city players develop their skills in the press of competition, learning to protect their shots and dribbles from defenders. They are expected by their peers to score without a great deal of assistance from their teammates in the way of passes, picks or screens. They are also expected to shrug off the incidental contact that occurs as they maneuver and launch their shot, and the rules discourage them from calling fouls when they are hindered. They often must challenge better players who hold the court by virtue of previous wins, and must therefore attempt their moves and shots against superior defenders. All of these factors demand and foster the moves and skills generally characterized as "one-on-one" basketball. Players who compete successfully in this environment during their formative years are likely to be superior at the one-on-one game.

On the other hand, non-city players develop their skills in a considerably different milieu. They spend a considerable proportion of their time practicing shots without defensive pressure. When they do find or organize games, the norms prescribe a passing and screening style of play that allows the same kinds of unimpeded shots that have been learned in solitary practice. The rules discourage tight defensive pressure since players can call fouls for the slightest interference. And shooting norms prescribe that shots be taken on-balance, with good form, and only in the absence of defensive pressure. These various pressures impede the development of one-on-one basketball and the various feints and moves necessary to single-handedly defeat the defense. However, they foster the development of pure shooting skills, and the ability to consistently hit the wide-open jump shot.

The different demands made by the inner city and non-city playground environments thus affect the kinds of skills that players in those environments develop. The frequent observation that blacks have better one-on-one moves while whites are better pure shooters (e.g., Axthelm, 1970) can be readily understood in terms of factors in the playing environment, without resort to physiological, personality or societal explanations. The statistical superiority of white professional ball players at free-throw shooting (Jones & Hochner, 1973) also makes sense, since the free throw is exactly the kind of unimpeded shot that non-city white players spend their formative years developing.

The superiority of black professionals at rebounding (Jones & Hochner, 1973) is also consistent with the nature of inner city play. In half-court basketball, no-take-back rules place considerable emphasis on rebounding, since players from either team can score off a rebound. The area under the basket becomes congested and players are forced to learn positioning, timing and jumping to compete for the basketball. Even in full-court play, rebounding is an important means for a player to gain offensive possession of the basketball, since the likelihood of receiving a pass from a teammate is relatively low. And finally, the physical nature of the city game is ideal preparation for the physical nature of college or professional play under the basket, where a player must venture if he is to rebound effectively. White professionals who have grown up in non-city environments are less likely to have been exposed to no-take-back basketball, highly physical play, or the necessity of rebounding. Consequently, they are less likely to have developed the various skills comprising that ability.

Team Style of Play

Black basketball has been described as more individualistic and less team oriented than white basketball (e.g., DuPree, 1978). In fact, there are a number of aspects of inner city basketball that tend to emphasize shooting and scoring rather than more team oriented activities like passing and screening. The previous section described the superior development of one-on-one skills among inner city players—skills that reduce the need for passing and screening to free an offensive player. In addition, inner city shooting norms pressure players to look for the shot first, and to take any shot they feel they can make with regularity. Make-and-take rules emphasize shooting by allowing players to run off a series of baskets and possibly to win a game, without the defense ever getting possession. And the need to impress the team captains, who are prone to choosing good scorers for their teams, forces players to take shooting opportunities when they arise.

In contrast, the non-city environment where most white players learn the game places more emphasis on passing and screening. As discussed in the preceding section, non-city players are more likely to require good passes and screens to free themselves for the shot. Non-city shooting norms pressure players to look for the pass first, and to shoot only under narrowly prescribed conditions. Shooting and other norms require players to make routine passes and to set picks and screens for their teammates. Non-city rules require inbound passes between baskets and take-back passes between misses. And the sparsity of players makes shooting and scoring less important than in the city, since players do not need to win or impress others in order to continue playing; but it makes passing more important, since marginal players must be kept involved in the game.

One would expect these pressures to dispose non-city players to make relatively more passes between shots than city players do. A good indication of such tendencies would be the ratio of shots to passes attempted by individual players from each environment. Jones and Hochner (1973) have calculated that white professional players do take fewer shots relative to the number of assists they make than do black professionals. While this is consistent with expectation, it must be interpreted cautiously, since assists are a rather special kind of pass (namely, one that leads directly to a score) and may not reflect the amount of routine passing players engage in.

Individual Styles of Play

Inner City Players. It is commonly claimed that black basketball players play with more style, flair, finesse, and flamboyance than do white basketball players. To some extent these observations about individual styles of play probably reflect the greater facility that inner city blacks have at one-on-one moves, as discussed earlier. The ability to feint, spin, pump and engage in similar gymnastics are clearly essential to the individualistic city game, and contribute to the apparent "style" of inner city players. But descriptions of black basketball suggest an emphasis on dunks, steals, blocked shots and other spectacular plays that may go beyond the simple components of one-on-one play.

One important aspect of the inner city playing environment may help to explain this emphasis on dramatic play: the presence of an audience. As mentioned earlier, it is not unusual for inner city pick-up games to attract audiences of 10 to 20 people. These audiences can become highly involved in the games, and are particularly appreciative (as are audiences everywhere) of spectacular plays, such as dunks, reverse lay-ups, blocked shots and so on. While the crowd's cheers and comments provide substantial reinforcement for such activities, the contribution which these plays make to one's reputation is even more important in the inner city. In his book, *The City Game,* Peter Axthelm states:

> In its own way, a reputation in the parks is as definable as a scoring average in the N.B.A. Street ballplayers develop their own elaborate word-of-mouth system. One spectacular performance or one backwards, twisting stuff shot may be the seed of an athlete's reputation. If he can repeat it a few times in a park where the competition is tough, the word goes out that he may be something special. Then there will be challenges from more established players, and a man who can withstand them may earn a "neighborhood rep." The process continues in an expanding series of confrontations, until the best athletes have emerged. Perhaps a dozen men at a given time may enjoy "city-wide reps," guaranteeing them attention and respect in any playground they may visit. (p. 199)

The "rep" which a player develops is more important in determining whether he will be chosen for a street captain's team than any other single factor. A player with a strong reputation can get into the best games on the best courts against the best competition, while lesser players must sit and hope to be chosen.

Under these circumstances, players are likely to attempt dramatic plays in an effort to enhance their reputations. Solid position defense doesn't build a reputation, but blocking a few shots or stealing a few balls will. Making routine passes won't help a reputation, but making dramatic assists might. And taking simple lay-ups won't impress anyone, but flying slam dunks should. Greenfield (1980) states:

> The moves that begin as tactics for scoring soon become calling cards. You don't just lay the ball in for an uncontested basket; you take the ball in both hands, leap as high as you can, and slam the ball through the loop. When you jump in the air, fake a shot, bring the ball back to your body, and throw up a shot, all without coming back down, you have proven your worth in incontestable fashion. (p. 310)

Consequently, the inner city player is more likely to attempt flamboyant moves and shots in pick-up games during his development years, and is more likely to ultimately incorporate these into his repertoire of skills as a player.

Non-City Players. Of course, non-city players may occasionally attempt dramatic plays too. But these efforts differ in several critical respects. First, the level of reinforcement is lower for such activities in the non-city environment; there are rarely audiences for pick-up games, and one's playing time is not contingent upon one's reputation. Second, the non-city shooting norms dictate against flamboyant shots: since the team has worked collectively to free a player for an open shot that shot is supposed to be taken while open and on-balance. A player who eschews the open jumper to try a spinning reverse lay-up is likely to be criticized if the shot misses. Third, the non-city environment provides numerous opportunities to try spectacular shots *outside* of competition. A player who wishes to show his friends that he can do pump shots or dunk shots can do so during the long intervals between games. However, such moves, made in the absence of competitive pressure, are unlikely to generalize to game situations. Fourth, the non-city norms discourage players from dominating the marginal players who have been recruited to fill out the teams. Consequently, it would be bad form for a player to repeatedly block a lesser player's shots or to steal the ball from him. All things considered, then, the pressures of the non-city playground environment do more to discourage flamboyant play than to encourage it.

Playing Attitudes

It would be surprising if the different character of the inner city and non-city basketball environments didn't produce different attitudes towards the game. Some such attitudinal differences are readily predictable from the observations made in earlier sections. For example, non-city players are likely to develop more team-oriented attitudes towards basketball, while inner city players are likely to be more individualistic. Inner city players are likely to view shooting as the most important aspect of the game, while non-city players are more likely to emphasize passing and other skills. However, there are other attitudinal differences that are less readily discerned from the preceding sections.

For example, an inner city player is more likely to view basketball as a personal battle against the opponent he is matched up with. The one-on-one style of play makes each player personally responsible if this man scores; there are no zone defenses in inner city basketball, and "switching" men when a player is screened is not very common. So if a player drives past his defender for a score, the defender is embarrassed in front of the watching crowd, and may feel a need to get back somehow. Inner city product Walt Frazier (in Frazier and Berkow, 1974) says "I get close to angry when my man scores on me. So that's my motivation on defense. I take my man's basket personally. I can play passive defense until he starts scoring. Then I start picking him up right away to show him that I'm the man" (p. 49). In this light, steals, for which Frazier was famous, or blocked shots are not only flamboyant plays, but are emphatic public retaliation against one's opponent. Another form of retaliation is discussed by Kirkpatrick (1968):

> Get back is instant playground reprisal. If a man exhibits his best move and scores on a negligent opponent, all hands yell "get back get back" at the defender, whereupon, he must immediately try to get back at the opponent

who just took him. Promptly, with what is often a spectacular retaliatory move of his own, the second man usually does get back. (p. 7)

In the inner city, then, the one-on-one nature of the game, the crowd pressure, and the importance of winning may all contribute to make the game an intensely personal struggle between opponents. The objective is not simply to play well, not simply to win, but to beat your man: to show that you are better than he is.

In the non-city environment, basketball assumes more recreational proportions: A player need not out-shine his opponent to have a successful performance. This recreational attitude is probably fostered by three factors. First, there is no crowd to cope with, so both pride (for good plays) and shame (for bad ones) are tempered. Second, the team-oriented offenses of the non-city spread the responsibility for any score across several players. Switching is expected on defense (and even zone defenses are used with some frequency), so that no single defensive player is entirely to blame for an opponent's score. Finally, games are generally less intense and less important, since they do not determine future playing time.

The peculiar circumstances of the non-city basketball environment also lead to certain characteristic attitudes regarding shooting form, practice and warm-ups. As noted earlier, a substantial portion of non-city players' basketball time is spent practicing shots alone. During this time, players commonly work on their shooting form, adjusting hand and arm positions, body movements and shooting rhythm until every shot feels just right. One consequence of these efforts is that non-city players often come to believe that shooting is a matter of mechanisms, and that for a successful performance, the bodily "machine" needs to be properly tuned, aligned and warmed-up. This "mechanical" attitude underlies the norm requiring that shots be taken on-balance and with proper shooting form. It also underlies the considerable emphasis that non-city players place on shooting practice and game warm-ups, which can be viewed as efforts to tune the "machine" properly. The shooting ritual which Bill Bradley engaged in prior to every game is an exaggerated example of this emphasis.

The shooting slumps that players inevitably experience are therefore explained in terms of some poorly understood mechanical malfunction, and a variety of elaborate superstitions exist about the kinds of factors that might be responsible. Some non-city players believe that tying sneakers improperly, failing to wear knee pads, or having the wrong pre-game meal can upset their delicate mechanical balance. A common set of superstitions deal with mental attitude and its possible effect on performance. Many non-city players engage in a kind of intense, studied concentration prior to games in an effort to "psych up" for the forthcoming contest. Non-city norms discourage levity, irrelevant chatter or anything else that might interfere with the delicate bodily gears. The resultant locker room atmosphere has been described by some as a dreadful combination of fear, purpose and gloom.

The inner city player is more likely to try to keep his composure ("cool") and self-confidence prior to games, viewing the game itself as a contest between players. There is less emphasis on "psyching-up" or "concentrating" intensely (although perhaps, more emphasis on "psyching-out" or rattling the opponent). And, of course, inner city players often view individual shooting practice as irrelevant to game situations, and thus a waste of time. So inner city attitudes towards several aspects of preparation differ somewhat from non-city attitudes.

Conclusions

This analysis suggests that players' skills, styles, and attitudes are a coherent reaction to the circumstances under which they learn to play basketball. The formulation thus provides a parsimonious explanation for apparent differences between white and black basketball players, without resorting to indefensible claims regarding physiological or personality differences. The formulation does have some limitations, however, which are spelled out below.

First, although the descriptions of inner city and non-city basketball provided here are based on extensive reading, interviews and observation, there is clearly a need for empirical research to establish their objective validity and generality. I am hopeful that this article will stimulate such studies into the relationships among player backgrounds, styles, abilities and attitudes. I suspect that such research will show my characterizations of inner city and non-city basketball to be prototypes, approximated to different degrees in different communities and in different regions of the country. For example, different kinds of "non-city" locales (rural, small town, suburb) seem likely to vary in playing systems and styles, with crowded suburbs adopting something between the city and non-city styles of play.

Second, the kinds of playing differences that have been described are most likely to be observed at the neighborhood level. College and professional players may have had their styles refined and their attitudes mellowed by years of coaching. Nonetheless, some residual influences are likely to persist, and professional player Darryl Dawkins may be correct when he observes that "Coaching has a little bit to do with your style, but not as much as you might think. It's all in your background" (quoted in DuPree, 1978).

Third, it is unclear how the present formulation, which deals exclusively with basketball, relates to possible performance differences among athletes in other sports. Novak (1976) suggests that the "black athletic style" is most pronounced in sports activities that are closely related to basketball, possibly reflecting carry-over effects among black athletes who played this sport at some point in their lives. It is also possible that careful analyses of other sports (e.g., sandlot baseball) would reveal some of the same kinds of mechanisms discussed here. Finally, it may be that the differences observed in many sports are illusory, reflecting stereotypical generalizations from basketball or naive interpretations of the prevalence of blacks in particular playing positions (as detailed in Edwards' 1973 analysis of racial "stacking"). In any case, the present account argues that racial differences in basketball are a function of factors specific to the basketball environment, suggesting that great care must be taken in generalizing to other sports.

Finally, it may be valuable to highlight several implications of the present analysis. The differing norms and expectations that city and non-city basketball players bring to the court with them can explain a good deal of the conflict and self-segregation that occurs when players meet on common courts, such as a college gym. These differences also relate to the tension that sometimes exists between players from one background and coaches from another. For example, Bill Spivey, an inner city player who ultimately quit his college team, stated: "Cats from the street have their own rhythm when they play. It's not a matter of somebody setting you up and you shooting. You *feel* the shot. When a coach holds you back, you lose the feel and it isn't fun anymore" (quoted in Greenfield, 180). Our analysis suggests that the roots of such conflicts may be more cultural than racial.

This analysis also has broader implications, beyond simply the explanation of athletic styles. It illustrates the complex interrelationships between man's environment and his behavior. Understanding these interrelationships is important to theorists and researchers in such domains as anthropology, sociology and psychology. Perhaps in a small way, this analysis contributes to those efforts.

References

Auerbach, A. & Fitzgerald, J.A.
    1977, *Auerbach: An Autobiography.* (New York: G.P. Putnam's Sons).
Axthelm, P.
    1970, *The City Game.* (New York: Harper and Row Publishers, Inc.).
Barker, R.G.
    1960, "Ecology and Motivation," in M.R. Jones (ed.), *Nebraska Symposium on Motivation.* (Lincoln: University of Nebraska Press).
Cousy, B. (As told to Al Hirshberg)
    1958, *Basketball Is My Life.* (New York: Lowell Pratt & Company).
Davis, Ruban M.
    1969, *Aggressive Basketball.* (West Nyack, NY: Parke Publishing Company, Inc.).
DuPree, D.
    1978a, "It's a Stylish Game They Play," *Los Angeles Times*, Feb. 24.

1978b, "Each Team Does It With Style," *Los Angeles Times*, Feb. 28.

Edwards, H.
1973, *Sociology of Sport*. (Homewood, IL: The Dorsey Press).

Frazier, W. & Berkow, I.
1974, *Rockin' Steady*. (New York: Warner Brooks, Inc.).

Greenfield, J.
1980, "The Black and White Truth About Basketball: A Skin-Deep Theory of Style," in Stubbs & Barnet (eds.), *The Little, Brown Reader*, 2nd ed. (Boston: Little, Brown).

Holzman, R. & Lewin, L.
1973, *Holzman's Basketball: Winning Strategy and Tactics*. (New York: Warner Books, Inc.).

Jones, J.M. & Hochner, A.R.
1973, "Racial Differences in Sports Activities: A Look at the Self-Paced Versus Reactive Hypothesis," *Journal of Personality and Social Psychology*, vol. 27, pp. 86–95.

Jordan, P.
1979, *Chase the Game*. (New York: Dodd, Mead & Company).

Kane, M.
1971, "An Assessment of Black Is Best," *Sports Illustrated*, Jan. 18.

Kirkpatrick, C.
1968, "A Place in the Big City Sun," *Sports Illustrated*, Aug. 5.

Latane, B. (ed.)
1966, "Studies in Social Comparison," *Journal of Experimental Psychology*, Supplement 1.

Loy, J.W. & McElvogue, J.R.
1970, "Racial Segregation in American Sport," *International Review of Sport Sociology*, vol. 5.

McPhee, J.
1965, *A Sense of Where You Are: A Profile of Princeton's Bill Bradley*. (New York: Bantam Pathfinder Editions).

McPherson, B.D.
1975, "The Segregation by Playing Position Hypothesis in Sport: An Alternative Hypothesis," *Social Science Quarterly*, vol. 55, pp. 960–966.

Michener, J.A.
1976, *Sports in America*. (Greenwich, CT: Fawcett Publications, Inc.).

Novak, M.
1976, *The Joy of Sports: End Zones, Bases, Baskets, Balls and the Consecration of the American Spirit*. (New York: Basic Books, Inc.).

Ogilvie, B. & Tutko, T.A.
1968, "Psychological Consistencies Within the Personalities of High Level Competitors," *Journal of the American Medical Association*, October.

Phillips, J.C.
1976, "Toward an Explanation of Racial Variations in Top-Level Sports Participation, *International Review of Sport Sociology*, vol. 11, pp. 39–53.

Poliquin, B.
1981, "Trouble . . . With a Capital T: Empty Seats Put NBA in a BIND," *The Sporting News*, Feb. 21.

Russell, B. & Branch, T.
  1979, Second Wind: The Memoirs of an Opinionated Man. (New York: Random House).
Schachter, S.
  1951, "Deviation, Rejection and Communication," *Journal of Abnormal and Social Psychology*, vol. 46, p. 190–207.
Sharmon, B.
  1968, *Sharmon on Basketball Shooting.* (Englewood Cliffs, NJ: Prentice-Hall, Inc.).
Snyder, E.E. & Spreitzer, E.
  1978, *Social Aspects of Sport.* (Englewood Cliffs, NJ: Prentice-Hall, Inc.).
Street and Smith's Official Basketball Yearbook 1980–81.
  1980, (New York: Conde Nast Publications Inc.), Oct.
Tate, L.
  1975, "Tatelines: Studies Show Blacks' Jumping Advantages," *The Champaign News Gazette*, March 24.
Wielgus, C., Jr., & Wolff, A.
  1980, *The In-Your-Face Basketball Book.* (New York: Everest House Publishers).
Wolf, D.
  1972, *Foul! the Connie Hawkins Story.* (New York: Holt, Rinehart & Winston).
Worthy, M. & Markle, A.
  1970, "Racial Differences in Reactive Versus Self-Paced Sports Activities," *Journal of Personality and Social Psychology*, vol. 16, pp. 439–443.
Yetman, N. & Eitzen, S.
  1972, "Black Americans in Sports: Unequal Opportunity for Equal Ability," *Civil Rights Digest*, vol. 5, pp. 20–34.

The Promised Land

Richard E. Lapchick
Northeastern University

Those among the approximately 11,999 out of 12,000 who didn't make it to the pros have received heavy doses of reality therapy. However, there is still that one. And in the pros it is assumed that the black athlete is finally on nearly equal footing with white athletes. He is there because of his talent.

The pro athlete is financially rich. He does not face the discrimination he knew in high school or college. Perhaps a coaching career looms ahead, or a front-office job will follow after he finishes playing. In any event, if he is exceptional, he will be remembered in the minds of fans and the media.

You can't argue about the money. Agents, players associations, and free agency have resulted in annual incomes that make up for the years of toiling for little or nothing in colleges and in minor leagues.

The racial integration of baseball, basketball, and football has been remarkable. Owners realized that there was an enormous black market that had been untapped prior to the arrival of Jackie Robinson at Ebbets Field in 1947. Movement was slow at first as the waters were tested. The NBA and NFL were integrated in 1950. Ten years after the barriers fell in Brooklyn, the major leagues had only eighteen blacks. The NFL was only 14 percent black and the NBA only 5 to 7 percent. However, the complexion of America's three major sports was very different three decades later when 23 percent of major league baseball players, 54 percent of NFL players, and 70 percent of NBA players were black.

There is certainly no other professional area where blacks occupy such high percentages of the totals.

And blacks have broken into other sports. They are, of course, dominant in boxing and track and field.

Althea Gibson astonished the tennis world when she beat Darlene Hard for the 1957 Wimbledon crown. Arthur Ashe won the U.S. Open in 1968 when he overwhelmed Tom Okker. Leslie Allen captured headlines in 1980 when

From Richard Lapchick, *Broken Promises* (New York: St. Martin's Press), 1984. Reprinted by permission.

she became the first black woman since Gibson to win a major tournament. 1983 brought forth two African-born tennis stars for the first time. Blacks have been represented at the top levels of tennis for all three of our integrated sports decades. However, fewer than two stars per decade is hardly dominance.

Pete Brown became the first black man to win a Professional Golf Association (PGA) event when he won the 1964 Waco Turner Open. Charlie Sifford, the first black on the PGA tour, had won the Long Beach Open in 1957 and the Alameda Open in 1960 but the PGA made both events "unofficial." However, Brown was an official winner at last in 1964 when public pressure made it impossible to deny black golfers any longer. Yet, victories for black golfers, like black tennis players, have not been common in the last three decades. Calvin Peete is a new phenomenon.

Barriers fell quickly in the big three sports. In 1966, Emmett Ashford became a major league umpire after a twenty-two-year career. In April 1966, Red Auerbach named Bill Russell as the first black coach in any of sports' big leagues. (John McLendon was hired to coach the Cleveland Pipers in the American Basketball Association in 1961.)

The civil rights movement, the acknowledgment of black athletic talent, and the owner's vision of a black market have indeed opened the doors in the last thirty years. No matter how far to the right America swings in the 1980s, it is difficult to imagine a decrease in black participation in baseball, football, and basketball. However, increasing racism could easily further delay black emergence in other sports.

Blacks have access to basketball courts, and some parks that can be used as baseball diamonds and football fields. However, they have little or no use of golf, tennis, swimming, and ice-skating facilities. For the most part, these facilities are in the suburbs and are expensive. Also, the socializing that exists almost as part of these sports will further inhibit the acceptance of blacks. Such relationships in country club sports are part of the package. They are not a part of baseball, football, or basketball.

If blacks do use role models to determine what athletic direction they might choose, the choices are surely broader in the big three sports. Black youth will be motivated by the breadth of the examples they see. Five star tennis players in three decades and even fewer golfers do not compare with the 70 percent black NBA. The choices are clear.

So the question becomes how good are the options for the black athlete in baseball, football, and basketball? Is he treated equally in each sport? Is he viewed as the equal of his white counterparts by coaches, the front office, and the fans? Is he paid the same? Are the stereotypes applied to him earlier in his career still assumed by whites? Does he face quotas? Is he limited to playing certain positions because of stacking? Must he perform better than whites in order to stay on the team? Does his fame endure after his playing career? Will he become a coach in the pros or join the front office of his team? Will he be out on the street when his sports career is terminated?

Any serious assessment shows what a short distance we have traveled. To be sure, the numbers of black players have dramatically increased and many have become wealthy. However, what has benefited those few has helped perpetuate the tragedy of so many blacks who reach for the ring only to crash back to the real world without skills. And even those few face racial discrimination in the pros, day after day.

For the black superstars, life *is* secure. Their salaries are equal to white stars. Black superstars have come a long way since 1966 when Frank Robinson, the Most Valuable Player (MVP) in the American League, was offered only two speaking engagements and one TV commercial. (By comparison Carl Yastrzemski, the white 1967 winner, estimated that his extra income resulting from the MVP award was $150,000 to $200,000.) In 1982, Reggie Jackson was supposed to have made $750,000 in endorsements and speaking engagements. In 1985, Patrick Ewing received more than $1 million for a shoe endorsement.

It is more difficult to tell if salary equality and income from endorsements apply across the board since teams do not reveal the salaries of all their players. Likewise, companies rarely announce the value of the endorsement packages. Irwin Weiner, a well-known agent for ballplayers, said, "When I go in with a fringe player who's white, I can squeeze out a little more money."

Information of salary differences between blacks and whites has been very difficult to obtain. However, David Meggyesy, the National Football League Players Association Western Regional Director, did a preliminary analysis based on the 1982 NFL season that gives us a clear picture that whites do earn significantly higher incomes than blacks. League-wide, whites averaged $100,730 while blacks averaged only $91,980.

It made no difference whether you played offense or defense or started or were a backup. White offensive players earned an average of $4,970 more than black offensive players. The biggest difference was on defense, where whites took in $11,100 more than blacks ($97,100 to $86,000).

White starters overall made $121,050 compared to $112,880 for black starters. On offense they earned $4,500 more and on defense a very significant $14,960 more than their black counterparts.

White offensive backups received an average of $87,290 in contrast to the $78,630 for black offensive backups—an $8,666 differential. White defensive backups made $5,060 more than black defensive backups.

While Meggyesy's preliminary study has yet to go into the causal relationships of these figures, his memo to the NFLPA's Board of Player Representatives in May of 1983 went to the heart of the matter:

> Consistent with this historical pattern of racial discrimination, a similar pattern exists today regarding players salaries. Simply put, in the NFL, black professional football players earn less than their white counterparts. Numerous theories have been presented as to why racial discrimination exists in the NFL. These theories are beside the point; the real issue is that racial discrimination does exist, and that it must be eliminated.

It would appear then that, at least in football, the salary differential is great below the superstar level. A case could be made that the black superstar has not only been allowed to make big money both in salary and commercials, but that it is to the advantage of the owners for this to happen. Reggie and O.J. seem to be everywhere. Such special cases are then used to anesthetize the public. In fact, the big changes in these areas affect only the most visible blacks.

There still are situations where black pros, even when they are superstars, are viewed differently from whites. Some blacks are accused by white team-mates, management, and fans of being lazy—of dogging it.

Wayne Simpson is a case in point. In 1981, everyone was talking about the sensational start of Fernanco Valenzuela. Forgotten was the year of the then twenty-one-year-old Simpson in 1970. He won 10 straight and 13 of his first 14 games for the Cincinnati Reds. Among his victories was a one-hitter. He was an All Star at twenty-one. However, over the next nine years he averaged only 4 wins a year, complaining of incessant pain in his arm. Team doctors said nothing was wrong. Sparky Anderson, the Red's manager, was quoted as saying "Simpson's problem is mental." Another black man dogging it.

But Simpson kept on pitching with pain by taking cortisone shots. Then in May 1978, under a doctor's observation, Wayne Simpson tried to throw a few pitches. His hand grew cold, white, and numb. The doctor called for an emergency operation to prevent the loss of the hand. Simpson had four bypass operations in the next year and still has almost total disability in his right hand.

When he was finally examined by doctors who had no stake in keeping him in the game, it was revealed by Simpson that "over the course of my pitching career, I had rubbed out an entire artery." Referring to his two sons, Simpson told Ira Berkow, "when the time comes, I'd be crazy not to tell my two boys that sports isn't nearly as glamorous as it seems." It was a hard way to learn. He is still learning. He had to sue to attempt to get workmen's compensation from the teams he pitched for. As of the writing of Berkow's article he had not received it.

Houston's star pitcher, J. R. Richard, may be the worst victim yet. He was in the midst of his best season in 1980 with a 10–4 record, 119 strikeouts, and a league-leading 1.80 ERA. He had struck out more than 600 batters in his previous two seasons. He had not missed a turn in the starting rotation in five years. His highest ERA in those five years was 3.11. He had won 20, 18, 18, and 18 in his last four full seasons. There were few if any better pitchers in baseball.

In June 17, Richard complained of "deadness" in his arm and sat out until June 28, when he was knocked out by Cincinnati after only 3½ innings. The media attack began. It alleged that Richard was lazy, a loafer. But he pitched better on July 3 (six innings, three hits, two runs) and in the All-Star Game, which he started (two innings, one hit, three strikeouts). Then he lasted only three innings against Atlanta on July 14. The media attack intensified even as Richard went on the disabled list. Hospital tests discovered a clot but doctors said he could pitch under supervision. Then he had a stroke during his first workout and nearly died.

The critics were silenced. Enos Cabell, the Astros third baseman, told Bill Nack of *Sports Illustrated* that the criticism would not have come down if Richard had been white. "We always knew we had to be better. There is a difference." Carolyn Richard, J.R.'s wife, lamented to Nack, "Black and big, a big star. . . . Other guys had problems on the Astros. Ken Forsch [a white pitcher] was out a whole half of a season. [Nolan] Ryan hasn't been pitching to his ability. I've never seen a player dragged through the mud like this. It's something we'll never forget. Never."

Charlie Sanders of the Detroit Lions was chosen as the tight end on the NFL's "team of the seventies." He had been selected for the Pro Bowl seven times and caught 336 passes in ten years. He hurt his knee on a preseason play in 1976 but continued to play on the advice of team physicians. On the game day, doctors had to wire his knee, shoot it with electrical charges, and have his leg heavily wrapped. The pain was enormous, but he played. The media printed stories saying coaches thought Sanders was a hypochondriac. In November 1977, he went to see a specialist in Toronto, who performed an arthroscopy to discover that the bone "was completely rotted out."

Sanders asked Ira Berkow of the *New York Times*, "Why wasn't I given an arthroscopy earlier, or why did people refuse to believe I was in such pain? I don't know." He discovered that Lions physicians had withheld medical information from him. One of the Lions' physicians told Berkow, "Sometimes it's not good to tell a patient everything . . . you wind up scaring the patient needlessly." Unlike the Astros, the Lions have not apologized. In fact, they appealed a workmen's compensation award to Sanders of $32,500 cash plus $156 per week for the injury, but the award was settled out of court and Sanders was hired as a part-time community relations worker for the Lions.

These are the cases of black superstars. Grumbling about average black pros is incessant. The difference is that the average black pro who grumbles can be let go.

There has been considerable publicity given to athletes taking drugs in pro sports. NBA executives, for example, estimate that 40 to 75 percent of the players use cocaine and 10 percent use free base, a heightened form of cocaine. A five-day binge on free base can cost between $2,000 to $12,000. Whites are too smart for that, according to the image projected by the press. The junkies are black.

It didn't seem to surprise anyone when Pete Rozelle suspended four players—all blacks—prior to the 1983 season for cocaine use. Yet no one believed that Pete Johnson, Ross Browner, E.J. Junior, and Greg Stremrick were the only users in the NFL. The drug-related convictions of Kansas City baseball stars after the 1983 season shocked many. The revelations from the 1985 drug trials in Pittsburgh did so even more. Yet we knew there were many others.

Simon Gourdine, the former NBA deputy commissioner, wondered whether the furor caused by the drug revelations was racially motivated. He told Jane Gross of the *New York Times*, "if someone chose to, they could have concluded that 100 percent of the black players were involved with drugs. Anytime there are social problems like drugs or alcohol, the perception is that it's black players involved. That concerns me." The size of the fine and then the suspension of LA Dodger reliever Steve Howe—a white—gave hope that Gourdine's projection is not totally accurate.

In September 1983, the NBA and the NBA Players Association took a strong stand on drugs. Starting at the end of 1983, any player known to be distributing or using drugs would be banned from the NBA. With an estimated 75 percent of the players using drugs, it will be difficult to see how this ruling will be effectively and equally enforced. However, if it works, it could be the model for other leagues. And cleaning up the players' acts would also help countless youth who see them as role models.

When it comes to taking out aggression through sport, there is a difference for black athletes. The white athlete can act out his aggressive impulses against other whites or blacks. The black athlete can do the same with other blacks. However, he approaches a dangerous line when he considers hitting a white man. He knows the price could be too high and may have to further repress these feelings.

Many stories have been told of the restraint displayed by Jackie Robinson when he broke into baseball. He turned the other cheek so often that some men thought him saintly. Larry Doby, the American League's first black, told Jack Olsen what it was like in those days:

> When I think of things the way they were, I wonder how we did it. I remember sliding into second base and the fielder spitting chewing tobacco juice in my face and just walked away. I walked away. They'd shout at you: "You dirty black so and so." I didn't have a fight until 1957. Charlie Neal had one in Brooklyn about the same time. I guess we celebrated our independence.

During the same era, Bill Russell's white high school coach in Oakland told his all-black team to keep cool since, "the second there's any trouble everyone is going to blame you, whether it's your fault or not. You'll be guilty . . . and everyone will claim it's a riot."

While there has been a change in the black athlete's freedom to defend himself, distinctions still exist.

Incidents of black versus other blacks or Latins on the playing fields were treated disinterestedly. On August 22, 1965, for example, Dodger John Roseboro, one of the league's first prominent black catchers, was seriously injured when the star pitcher of the Giants, Juan Marichal, hit him over the head with a bat, causing serious injury. Roseboro sued for $110,000 but settled for $7,500 out of court.

In a case of comparable brutality, Los Angeles Laker forward Kermit Washington, a six-eight black man, was involved in a fight with two white Houston players. It broke out between Washington and seven-foot Keven Kunnert in a December 9, 1977 game. Washington then hit six-eight Rudy Tomjanovich so hard that he broke his jaw and fractured his skull. Tomjanovich sued the Lakers and received $3.3 million, $600,000 more than his lawyers requested! The Lakers appealed, and prior to a decision, an out-of-court settlement was reached for an undisclosed but presumably lesser amount. Still, that type of fine has to have a numbing effect on future fights. But one wonders why Roseboro got $7,500 and Tomjanovich $3.3 million.

One could argue that Roseboro was not hurt as seriously as Tomjanovich, who missed the remainder of the 1977–78 season. However, he returned the following year to average 19 points. That was *prior* to the jury's staggering award, so there was little doubt about permanent damage totally ruining his career. Was there any thought in the minds of the jurors that a black man who viciously hit a white man in public must pay dearly for his sins? Was the ruling to make other blacks return to "turn-the-other cheek" to survive?

Kareem Abdul-Jabbar went a long way toward answering this question in *Giant Steps*, his autobiography. Kareem witnessed the fight and saw it as Washington, enraged by Kunnert's punching him, swinging wildly in self-defense at the oncoming Tomjanovich. Kareem was restraining Kunnert, and Tomjanovich, coming from behind, was trying to do the same with Washington.

Kareem discussed the NBA's response. Kunnert was not disciplined at all. Washington was fined $10,000 and suspended without pay for 26 games. "What that said to me, and to all black players in the league, was that if somebody white punches you out, you play defense and hope that the refs will try and stop it at some point. If not, just realize that the NBA needs white players to keep the white fans interested and the arenas filled and the networks on the line. Count on no support from the people who run this business."

Washington was told that the league owners forced Jack Kent Cooke, the owner of the Lakers, to trade him, as they would not tolerate Kareem and Washington on the same team. Kareem had hurt Kent Benson, a white rookie center, earlier in the season. Kareem noted, "Here were two extremely powerful black men who had both severely beaten white players, and the owners wanted us separated because they would not have us intimidating the rest of the league. That's hard to prove and easy to deny, but I fully believe it."

Much of this is a matter of speculation. Other questions in the three major sports are not so open to speculation. One is the matter of quotas, which continue despite denials. Another related issue is that of the need for blacks to perform better than whites to remain in the pros.

As we've seen, NBA management denied quotas existed when Bill Russell first exposed them in the 1960s. They were denied again in 1980 when the league took action against Ted Stepien, the new owner in Cleveland who proclaimed, "I think the Cavs have too many blacks, ten of eleven. You need a blend of white and black. I think that draws and I think that's a better team." He sent black star Campy Russell as a gift to the Knicks. He dumped black guard Foots Walker, who was third in the league in assists. He obtained undistinguished whites Mike Bratz and Roger Phegley in trades. He offered his budding superstar Mike Mitchell (black) to San Antonio for Mark Olberding (white). In only his second year, Mitchell had averaged 22.2, shot 52 percent, and led the team in blocked shots. Olberding averaged 10.5, his best in five seasons. But San Antonio reportedly nixed the deal because Olberding was their only white starter.

Ironically, Mitchell eventually went to San Antonio for Ron Brewer and Reggie Johnson, two blacks, while Olberding ended up in Chicago along with Dave Corzine in the Artis Gilmore trade. In spite of losing two white regulars, San Antonio managed to begin the 1982–83 preseason with five white players on the squad.

No matter how badly coach Stan Albech's management might have wanted white starters, the fact is that the five whites had a combined career-game average of only 6 points per game each, compared to the nearly 14-point average of the seven blacks on the preseason roster. The likes of Mike Bratz, Paul Griffin, Roger Phegley, or Rich Yonaker were not ready to shake up the NBA. The career of Rich Yonaker is a case in point. He was drafted in 1980 in the third round after averaging 3.7, 5.7, 6.8, and 5.9 during his four-year collegiate career at North Carolina. His NBA average for 1981–82 was 3.3, yet he was still on the 1982–83 preseason roster. None of this should be surprising since San Antonio is one of only four cities cited in the 1980 census as showing an increase in the percentage of whites since 1970. Its black population was less than 5 percent.

Joel Axelson, the director of operations for the NBA, objects and calls the charge of quotas in the NBA "total garbage." He told Gary Meyers of the *Daily News*, "I never heard of a personnel decision made on the basis of black or white. They don't make decisions on that basis—99 percent of the clubs are looking for people to win games."

However, Lenny Wilkens, who was one of the very few black pro coaches in all pro sports, said, "The unwritten rule is that there should be a minimum of three white players on each team." Larry Fleischer, the counsel to the NBA Players Association, as reported by *Sport* at the end of 1978, said simply,

"There are a number of players in the NBA who are on teams not because of their ability but because they are white."

Is there a system in the 70 percent black NBA to regulate the number of whites per team? In spite of the denials, the twenty-three official preseason team rosters submitted prior to the 1982–83 season reveal some convincing evidence. Fourteen of the twenty-three teams listed at least a 25 percent white roster. The nine exceptions included Atlanta, San Francisco, Houston, New York, Philadelphia, and Washington—all of which have large black populations, running from 25 up to 61 percent. Still, most sought whites in the draft since crowds are predominantly white. The nine teams with the most whites include Boston, Dallas, Denver, Phoenix, Portland, San Antonio, and Seattle.

It is even more interesting to look at the 1982 college draft. Fifteen whites were chosen in the first three rounds and selected in the official *NBA Register* as "promising newcomers." Of those fifteen, twelve or 80 percent were chosen by eight of the nine teams who did not have at least a 25 percent white roster. New York, Philadelphia, Washington, and Kansas City took two whites each in the first three rounds. A glance at the statistics of these newcomers makes one wonder if the teams were selecting for increased strength or for adding players who might join the already existing pool of marginal white players in the NBA. Four of the fifteen had career averages below 10 points per game including one drafted by Houston who had a college-career average of 3.0! Only four of the fifteen averaged more than 14 points per game. Utah selected Mark Eaton early in the fourth round after he averaged 1.8 points per game at UCLA, where he played a total of forty-one minutes in his senior year.

Is it plausible that this is an accident? If it is, how else can you explain that Seattle, which has a high percentage of whites on its basketball, baseball, and football franchises, drafted Bill Hanzlick of Notre Dame in the first round in 1980? Hanzlick averaged 4.1, 3.7, 8.7, and 7.5 in his four years of college basketball. Seattle has one of the smallest black populations (46,755) of all the major U.S. cities. It needs white players and it gets them.

Quotas aside, there is no way to argue against the charge that blacks must perform better than whites to remain in the NBA. Front-office people deny this, but candid white sports personalities do not. Al McGuire noted, "If a white and black player are equal, I think the white player would get the edge in time played and pictures in the program." Former Knick white superstar Dave DeBusschere said simply, "The white guy has a better opportunity." The numbers don't lie. All figures that follow come from the 1982–83 official *NBA Register*.

To be sure, there are genuine white stars like Larry Bird, Alvin Adams, Bill Walton, Dan Issel, Jack Sikma, Scott Wedman, Kiki Vandeweghe, Kelly Tripuka, and Tom Chambers. There are other fine white players like Paul Westphal, Tom Owens, Swen Nater, Billy Paultz, Ernie Grunfeld, Mark

Olberding, Rick Robey, Chris Ford, Bobby Jones, Steve Mix, Kevin Grevey, Mitch Kupchak, Dave Robisch, Kyle Macy, Kevin McHale, Kent Benson, Mike O'Koren, Jim Paxson, Jeff Ruland, and Kurt Rambis, among others.

But a look at who the NBA teams carry is revealing. Of the four whites on the preseason roster of the 1982 champion Lakers, three had career averages under 7 points. This was true of both whites listed by Golden State. Five of the six shown on Portland's roster averaged under 5 points per game. Five of the six whites for Dallas had career averages of less than 9. Statistics like this hold throughout the NBA with only a handful of exceptions like Boston, Denver, San Diego, and Philadelphia.

In fact, New York, Utah, Denver, San Diego, and Philadelphia were the only teams in 1981–82 whose white players had collective career-scoring averages greater than their black teammates. The average career-scoring average for whites in the league is 9.3. For blacks, it is 11.1. As Enos Cabell said about baseball, "There *is* a difference."

And blacks dominate the top of the league. There were only four whites among the twenty-four chosen for the 1982 NBA All-Star Game. In 1981–82, nine of the top ten scorers were black as were eight of the top ten in rebounds and field-goal percentage. The top ten in assists were all black. In 1980–81, blacks held the top ten positions in scoring, field-goal percentage, and assists. In 1979–80, blacks had nine of the ten top positions in scoring, field-goal percentage, and blocked shots plus a clean sweep again in assists.

The prospect is bleak for owners who might want whiter teams. Only 27 percent of the first-round draft choices in the 1970s were white. Of the fifty Associated Press first-team All-American selections in the 1970s, only thirteen were white.

So as more blacks come into the league, owners have to retain the marginal white ballplayers in order to maintain the desired percentage of whites. Black athletes have claimed that this was the case for many years. It is no different today.

In spite of the fact that blacks in the league outnumber whites by almost three to one, white players with five years' experience in the NBA and who averaged under 8 points per game actually outnumber blacks in the same category by nineteen to sixteen. Black veterans averaging more than 8 points outnumber whites in the same category by seventy-two to twenty-eight. Measured on a statistical basis, marginal whites have a better chance of becoming "veterans" than marginal blacks by almost four to one.

Sports critics agree that the reason quotas are most frequently mentioned in basketball is that positional segregation in a five-man game that is almost seventy percent black is impossible. While the guard position in college is overwhelmingly white dominated, no position in the NBA is. Height in basketball is the key determinant. The whole range of a player's skills are on display when he is on the court. Without the ability to control the number of blacks by making them compete for the same positions, it is suggested that the same has been accomplished in basketball through quotas.

However, the fans apparently believe that there has not been enough control. While attendance in baseball, football, and hockey has soared since 1976, it has declined in basketball. Baseball sold 8 million more tickets in 1980 than in 1976 (up 26 percent); the NFL sold 2.3 million more in 1980 than in 1976 (a 21 percent increase); 2 million more hockey tickets were sold during the 1979–80 season than in 1976–77 (up 24 percent). But the NBA tickets sales for 1980–81 were down by 8 percent over the previous year and were less than they were in 1976–77. The frustration of fans with player strikes reduced attendance in baseball in 1981 and football in 1982–83. But race seemed to be a primary factor in the NBA.

A fan at a football game can hardly tell who is black and who is white under all that gear. But the fan can be virtually certain that the quarterback, Mr. All-America, is white. In baseball, the players are so spread out on the field that a racist fan would not feel overwhelmed by hordes of blacks.

But in basketball there is no way to hide black bodies glistening with sweat. Ten could be concentrated in a twelve-square-foot area. *That* is too much for some.

A survey of Philadelphia fans during the 1980–81 season confirmed this. Philadelphia had the best record in the NBA and had Julius Erving, the league's most exciting player. But the survey was taken by the Philadelphia *Daily News* because the 76ers were bringing in only 55 percent of their capacity and ranked only ninth in total attendance. Fifty-seven percent of 955 responses agreed that "a white audience won't pay to watch black athletes." Julius Erving agreed. "I would like to say that race is not involved, but that would be naive."

The Celtics have always had at least one white superstar. Now it is Larry Bird. The Celtics sold out 95 percent of their seats, compared to 57 percent in Philadelphia. The teams were fierce rivals and had nearly identical records. Yet, on a percentage basis, the Celtics outdrew the 76ers by almost 40 percent. Knowing the formula, they made Larry Bird the highest-paid player in the NBA and made Kevin McHale the fourth highest-paid player prior to the 1983–84 season. As outstanding as McHale is, he is not the NBA's fourth-best player. Bird is close to the best.

With the exceptions of Los Angeles, which won the 1982 NBA championship, and Milwaukee, which won its divisional title, all the league teams that had an average attendance of more than 70 percent of capacity had at least three whites on the team. You couldn't buy a Knick ticket in New York when it had white superstars Bill Bradley and Dave DeBusschere to blend with Walt Frazier, Earl Monroe, and Willis Reed. With an up-and-coming young, but all-black team, the Knicks could draw only 63.4 percent of capacity in 1980–81. It did not seem coincidental that the Knicks chose white players in the second and third rounds of the 1982 draft.

If you are among those who agree that the NBA needs a quota system since it is "too black," then look at major league baseball, which has the smallest percentage of blacks of the three major sports. All figures are taken from the 1983 *Who's Who in Baseball*.

Only 19 percent of major league players are black Americans—a decline from the 1960s. If you include black Latin Americans, then blacks make up a total of 23 percent. Are black baseball players evenly distributed through a quota system? Twenty-two of the twenty-six teams in the majors had seven or less blacks (nineteen teams if you include black Latins). The number seven is 23 percent. Is it an accident that more than 75 percent of basketball and baseball teams conform to the overall percentage? It would seem hard to believe that the distribution of blacks and whites could be so if it occurred by chance.

Statistics would seem to show that blacks in baseball have to perform even better than those in basketball vis-a-vis their white teammates. Let's take a close look.

A veteran is defined as anyone who has played in the majors for five years. All figures are career averages. While the percentage of black veterans (seventy-nine) to white veterans (sixty-eight) is higher, a black has to be better than the white to last that long. Only 21 percent of black veterans had career batting averages below .261 while 46 percent of whites did. Only 4 percent of black vets hit below .240 compared to 17 percent of the whites. Sixty-six percent of black veterans had lifetime averages above .270 in contrast to the twenty-seven percent of whites who hit that well. Forty-four percent of black veterans had better than a .281 lifetime average juxtaposed to only fifteen percent of whites.

The figures hold steady if you include all players in the 1983 *Who's Who in Baseball* with more than 100 at bats. Ten percent of the blacks hit above .300 compared to only two percent of the whites. Forty percent of the blacks batted .281 or better while only fourteen percent of the whites did. Sixty percent of the blacks had career averages above .270 while seventy-five percent of the whites had career averages below that.

Any realistic analysis must conclude that blacks outperform whites in baseball *by far*. It goes on—black Latin American ballplayers also outperform white Latin Americans. Only 4 percent of the black Latins have career averages below .241 while 31 percent of the white Latins do. As Hispanic markets open up, the recruitment of Latin American ballplayers increases. But once again, the color of their skin plays a part in their chances to have a lengthy career.

The story for pitchers is the same. Nearly twice as many blacks as whites have career records above .600 (18 percent versus 10 percent). Twenty-nine percent of black pitchers in the league had more than 100 career victories versus only seventeen percent of the white pitchers.

In terms of the pitcher's career earned-run averages (ERAs), considerably more blacks than whites (30 percent to 20 percent) have ERAs below 3.20. Almost three times as many whites as blacks (31 percent versus 11.7 percent) have ERAs greater than 4.01. Whereas 16 percent of white pitchers have career ERAs greater than 4.41, no blacks do. Consistently, black pitchers have lower ERAs. They are better, and they have to be, for it is next to impossible for black pitchers to play major league baseball *unless* they are excellent black pitchers.

Do blacks dominate in baseball as they do in basketball? The answer is clearly yes, especially considering that barely one out of five players in baseball is black, including black Latins. In 1983, half of the top twenty hitters in the National League and American League were black. Among home run leaders, five of eleven were black, as were six of the ten leaders in runs batted in and runs scored. Eight of the ten leaders in hits were black.

Unlike basketball, the chances of becoming "whiter" are excellent. According to a 1978 study by James Curtis and John Loy, the percentage of blacks in baseball went from 10 percent in 1960 to 16 percent in 1968 and 27 percent in 1975. However, only 19 percent were black Americans in 1983, rising to 23 percent if black Latin Americans are included.

The number of minor league teams has decreased rapidly in the 1970s as college baseball has taken up more of their role. By 1982 the number of leagues has declined from fifty-nine in 1949 to seventeen while the number of players in the minors had declined from 9,000 in 1949 to only 3,300. In 1970, blacks used to make up 30 to 40 percent of the players in the minor leagues. By 1975, the minors were only 15 percent black. This reflected several things. First, since many of those blacks who sign contracts are more talented than whites, they move up to the majors faster. Second, some more are going to college on scholarships. A third, less tangible factor may reflect racial tensions in big cities. Most scouts are whites who may not only dislike blacks generally but are also reluctant to go see blacks play in the inner cities.

But don't look to the colleges with any hope of seeing more blacks playing baseball. While more black baseball players are going to college, the numbers are still small. In 1979 and 1980 combined, only one black made the *Sporting News* baseball All-American team. Since the proportions of college players selected in the baseball draft has risen from 40 percent in 1971 to 67 percent in 1982, the prospects for blacks going to the majors is even dimmer.

Not much has been said about professional football. Are there quotas? Are blacks also outperforming whites there? It is harder to tell since football as played in the NFL is almost totally segregated by position.

I was living in Denver when the Broncos drafted Marlin Briscoe from the University of Omaha in the late 1960s. He was drafted as a defensive back in spite of the fact that he was a star quarterback in college. Injuries compelled the Broncos to play him at quarterback. He passed for 3 touchdowns in his first game. The following week he was on the bench watching the woeful Broncos fall behind 14–0. He was sent in and they won 21–14. He didn't play in the next game. When the regular was injured, Briscoe started and passed for four TDs in a victory. That was their last win but in two of the final three losses Briscoe passed for more than 200 yards. In his five starts he did this four times. At the end of the season, Briscoe was released and never played quarterback again. That was my first introduction to the word "stacking," or segregation by position.

Is it true now in the NFL? Using the twenty-eight NFL 1983 team media guides, the statistics are overwhelming. On offense, 99 percent of the quarterbacks were white; 97 percent of the centers, 77 percent of the guards, and 68 percent of the tackles were white.

The patterns are more pronounced today than they were in 1968 when a white player told Jack Olsen:

> It's not very complicated to figure out. The play starts right in the cluster. . . . Those three guys and the quarterback are it. It doesn't make a damn bit of difference what the other seven players do; if anybody in that tight little cluster screws up, that's it. The play is dead. Now, how can white coaches, with all their built-in prejudice about the Negro, assign positions like that to the black men?

On the other hand, 88 percent of the running backs and 77 percent of the wide receivers were black.

Sociologist Jonathan Brower did a survey of coaches and asked them how they would characterize the three positions dominated by whites. They used the following words: intelligence, leadership, emotional control, decision making, and technique.

The defensive position that shows the most meaningful statistical difference by race is cornerback (92 percent black). The words used by coaches for the black-controlled positions of running back, wide receiver, and cornerback were: strength, quickness, and instinct.

There are no black coaches in the NFL. If the white coaches hold traditional racial beliefs, then player assignments could easily be made according to race. [Table 1] was compiled from veterans listed in the 1983 media guides and demonstrates the patterns.

A 1975 study of NFL players by Eitzen and Sanford shows that as their careers developed from high school to college to the pros, blacks were increasingly underrepresented in control positions. Not only stereotyping by coaches,

Table 1

Position	Whites by Percentage	Blacks by Percentage
Offense		
Quarterback	99	1
Running back	12	88
Wide receiver	23	77
Center	97	3
Guard	77	23
Tight end	52	48
Tackle	68	32
Kicker	98	2
Kick-off returner	18	82
Defense		
Cornerback	8	92
Safety	43	57
Linebacker	53	47
Defensive end	31	69
Defensive tackle	47	53

but also self-selection by some black athletes who assess their chances of success exacerbate the problem of positional segregation. As black athletes mature and see what happens to the Marlin Briscoes, they may choose to change positions.

Lee Ballinger, in *In Your Face*, elaborated on what happens in football. In 1974, Joe Gilliam was named as starting quarterback for the Pittsburgh Steelers. He led them to a 4–0–1 record and first place in the AFC Central Division. Gilliam was benched because the Steelers were "weak offensively." The facts that their points-per-game average was better than 75 percent of the teams in the NFL and that they were in first place in the division were irrelevant. What was relevant was that Joe Gilliam was black.

In 1976, James Harris became the NFC's leading passer after never being given the opportunity to play quarterback for Buffalo. After helping to win twenty of the twenty-four games he started and being named Most Valuable Player in the Pro Bowl, James Harris was traded for future draft choices.

Such examples have to teach black high school quarterbacks that they should try out for other positions. Actually, Briscoe, Gilliam, and Harris were fortunate. Most black college quarterbacks drafted by the NFL are switched to other positions without ever getting the chance to prove themselves at their natural position. This is not to say it is impossible for a black to make it at quarterback; however, it is very unlikely as the 99 percent white figure shows.

The offensive team is clearly the most visible in the minds of fans. It is interesting to note that of the twelve of twenty-eight NFL teams with a majority of blacks, eight had more total whites on offense than blacks. Sixty-five percent of the whites in the NFL play offense; fifty-six percent of the offensive players are white while sixty-two percent of the defensive players are black. Do the clubs do this for fans who want to recognize more white faces?

Baseball has its own positional segregation. The pitcher and the catcher are central to every play of the game. Of the fifty-eight catchers listed in the 1983 *Who's Who in Baseball,* none were black Americans. Seven percent were Latins. Only 6.6 percent of the 296 pitchers were black. Another 7 percent were Latins. It should not be surprising that these pivotal "thinking positions" are held mostly by whites. The people who cover second base, shortstop, and third base are also considered to be in thinking positions. Blacks make up 21 percent of second basemen, 11 percent of shortstops, and 9 percent of third basemen.

However, first basemen and outfielders mainly react to other players. Outfielders need quickness and instinct. Not as much skill and training is considered necessary to hold these positions as the others. Eighty-four percent of all blacks listed as offensive players were either first basemen (19 percent) or outfielders (65 percent). In spite of being outnumbered in the league by almost five to one, blacks have numerical superiority over whites in the outfield (seventy to sixty-eight).

The positional segregation has gotten worse over time. In 1960, there were 5.6 times as many black outfielders as pitchers; in 1970 there were 6.7 times as many. By 1980, it stood at 8.8 times as many black outfielders as pitchers. The total percentage of black pitchers and catchers had declined since the late 1960s.

According to *Who's Who in Baseball* for 1983, the positional breakdown is as follows:

Position	Whites by Percentage	Blacks by Percentage	Latins by Percentage
Pitcher	86	6.6	7
Catcher	93	0	7
1B	55	38	7
2B	65	21	14
3B	82	5	13
SS	73	11	16
Outfield	45	46	9

Sports sociologists have written at length on the question of why positional segregation exists in baseball. James Curtis and John Loy have done some of the best work in the early 1970s. But their studies were done when the overall proportions of blacks to whites were substantially increasing. However, now the overall proportion is at best stabilized. The sport is no longer "opening up." It never opened up at the central positions. According to Harry Edwards, management did not want to yield these positions to blacks because of the high degree of leadership responsibilities and outcome control associated with them. Denials of racism are made by both general managers and social scientists.

The search for white superstars will be most intense in any sport such as basketball where the numbers of blacks are highest. The perennial search for the Great White Hope in boxing is also well known. White promoter Bob Arum has been mining white South African fighters in his efforts to find one. Black promoter Don King reportedly said: "I'd run through the jungle and fight a lion with a switch to get a good white fighter." South African Gerrie Coetzee proved to be inept in his first two WBA title shots, then won in an unprecedented third try late in 1983. Many believed Gerry Cooney to be the man— before he fought Larry Holmes.

In 1978, Calvin Griffith, the owner of the Minnesota Twins, shocked everyone when he spoke to a Lions Club in Waseca, Minnesota: "I'll tell you why we came to Minnesota in 1961. It was when I found out you had only 15,000 blacks here. Black people don't go to ball games, but they'll fill up a rassling ring and put up such a chant it'll scare you to death. . . . We came here because you've got good, hard-working white people here." Many understood what Griffith was saying. Whites understood he wanted to make more money. Blacks understood he was a racist. Rod Carew was the star of the Twins. He has been baseball's most consistent hitter for twelve seasons in a row, with a .300 or better average and a .333 lifetime average. Although Griffith later apologized and said the statements were taken out of context, Carew said, "I refuse to be a slave on his plantation and play for a bigot." He was traded to California.

It is no small irony that after Jackie Robinson blacks were let into sports largely to increase attendance. Thirty years later they are being restricted again because it is perceived that they are hurting attendance. How far back the pendulum will swing is open to question.

Professional black athletes are sophisticated enough to know that they will face the same pressures in sports that other blacks will face in society. At least they take comfort from the money they have made and from their fame that will endure over time. When their careers are over they think they can, perhaps, approach the general manager for a job coaching or in the front office. Perhaps.

I remember the day my father was elected to the Basketball Hall of Fame. It was one of the happiest days of his life. There was no reason to doubt he would be selected, yet the fact of election was nevertheless a proud moment, and my father went to the ceremony with joy.

When Bill Russell followed Bob Douglas as the second black man elected to the Hall, he refused to go the induction because of the racism in the sport. It made one think. That was 1974. Blacks were already dominating basketball and yet there were only two black men in the Hall of Fame. Abe Saperstein, the white owner of the Harlem Globetrotters, went in before Bob Douglas.

I assumed that the controversy created by Bill Russell would move more blacks into the Hall quickly. Between 1974–80, twenty-two whites and five blacks were chosen. That made a total of 102 whites and 7 blacks. The other blacks were Elgin Baylor, Tarzan Cooper, Wilt Chamberlain, Oscar Robertson, and John McLendon. Amazingly, McLendon was chosen as a "contributor" and not as a coach. He won 522 college games, was the first to win three consecutive national titles (NAIA, 1957, 1958, and 1959), and was the first black pro coach. The NBA is 70 percent black. The Basketball Hall of Fame is 94 percent white.

Emlen Tunnell, the great New York Giant defensive back, was the first black elected to the Football Hall of Fame in 1967. Willie Davis, defensive end for Green Bay in the 1960s, was the fifteenth black chosen in 1981. George Blanda, the ageless quarterback and place kicker, was also enshrined in 1981. He was the ninety-fifth white. The NFL is 54 percent black. The Pro Football Hall of Fame is 86 percent white.

The National Baseball Hall of Fame is in Cooperstown, New York. Jackie Robinson was appropriately the first black inducted. That was in 1962. Eighty-six whites preceded him. His induction didn't exactly open the floodgates for blacks. Up to 1981, the only modern-class blacks chosen have been Robinson, Roy Campanella, Roberto Clemente, Ernie Banks, Willie Mays, and Bob Gibson. The Baseball Writers of America select those chosen few. In 1979, twenty-three members voted against Willie Mays, who hit 660 home runs, had 3,283 hits, and played in twenty-four All-Star Games. Nine blacks have also been chosen from the Negro Leagues in separate elections and are housed in a separate (but equal?) room. Baseball is 23 percent black; the Baseball Hall of Fame is 91 percent white if you include the Negro League stars, 96 percent if you don't.

Who knows sports better than the athletes who play it? It is natural to think that one could transmit the skills and knowledge accumulated over the course of many years in playing to young players. Many athletes have dreamed of this. Black athletes have also dreamed of it. They want to become managers and coaches.

That dream had barely begun when Olsen interviewed Larry Doby in

1968. The number of blacks in the major leagues had only just started to rise. Doby, of course, was the first black allowed into the American League. In 1968, he hoped to be the first black manager. He said. "Wouldn't it be a shame if baseball waited until the ball park is burned down before it stepped in and did the right thing." In 1968 Jim Gilliam of the Dodgers was the only black coach. There were no black managers and only a handful of blacks in the front offices. Many whites thought having blacks in such positions would be bad for publicity. Others thought blacks weren't smart enough. Many didn't want blacks to be in charge of whites.

Doby added, "Black athletes are cattle. They're raised, fed, sold and killed. Baseball moved me toward the front of the bus, and it let me ride there as long I could run. And then it told me to get off at the back door."

Doby was suddenly hired as a coach by Cleveland after the article appeared. Was he hired to prove he was wrong or to co-opt him? It must have hurt when Frank Robinson was hired by Cleveland in late 1974 to manage the team for which Doby was coach. There was a lot of talk about which black man would be chosen as the first black manager. Speculation centered largely on Gilliam, Doby, and Hank Aaron. White writers wrote for years and at length about which blacks might be qualified to manage while white owners hired white manager after white manager.

So Robinson managed Cleveland in 1975, 1976, and then was fired in early 1977. Under his guidance, the Indians had their best two-season record in ten years. Yet he was let go early in the next year. The image of a black boss was just too tough. Before he was canned, Robinson had a highly publicized argument with Gaylord Perry, his white pitching star. The next day a sign was hung at the ballpark: "Sickle Cell Anemia: White Man's Hope."

Larry Doby was finally hired to manage the White Sox for the tail end of the 1978 season. It was hardly a real chance.

Henry Aaron seemed certain to be the next black named as manager in 1978 when the incumbent manager of the Atlanta Braves was fired during the season. After all, he had just broken Babe Ruth's all-time home-run record in spite of death threats, racial harassment, and the need for police protection. It seemed that some whites couldn't stand to see a black break the greatest record of the greatest white superstar of all time. But Aaron seemed the natural choice to become manager. In fact, he was traded to Milwaukee. He told Phil Musick, his biographer:

> The owners seem to have gotten together and decided that certain men—certain white men—should be hired and rehired no matter what kind of failures they've been . . . as soon as they're fired by one owner, they're hired by another.
>
> Baseball is no different than stagnant water. The Negro has progressed no further than the field. Until we crack that area, there is no real hope for black

kids coming into sports. We're greats on the field for twenty years, then they're finished with us.

Late in 1980 Maury Wills, the former great Dodger shortstop, was hired by Seattle. Frank Robinson came back when the Giants hired him for the 1981 season. 1981 marked the first time two black managers were working simultaneously. When they met for the first time in 1981, the *New York Times* duly recorded it as an historic event. It was good that they did because Wills was fired only 24 games into the season.

It should be noted that Wills and Robinson were the only two of twenty-six major-league managers with Hall of Fame credentials. If you are black, you have to be better. If you are black and want to manage, you better have been a superstar. Robinson was one of twenty-six managers in 1983.

There were some 123 coaches in the major leagues in 1983. Of the 123, 110 were white.

Opportunities for blacks as managers in the minor leagues and in college are even fewer. Kansas State was the only Division I school with a black manager in 1983. Front-office jobs are just as scarce.

There were three black coaches leading NBA teams as the 1982–83 season began. Paul Silas was in his third year at San Diego and was the only black NBA coach with a losing record. Lenny Wilkens had coached for ten years and was in Seattle. He had a winning percentage of .541. That was the fourth best record of anyone in the NBA with a tenure of five years or more. Al Attles had coached for thirteen years and had a .531 winning percentage. That was the sixth-best coaching record in the NBA. Once again, blacks had to be better. Both Silas and Attles left at the end of the season. The hiring of K. C. Jones by Boston left two black NBA coaches at the start of the 1983–84 season.

Look at the graveyard of black NBA coaches. Bill Russell was the first coach in 1966. In his two reigns with Boston and Seattle his record was 367–249 for a .595 percentage. Those black coaches with bad records never got a second chance. They include Earl Lloyd in Detroit and Elgin Baylor in Utah. In fact, Wilkens is the only black to lose with one team and be hired elsewhere. Yet many whites like Larry Brown, Gene Shue, Dick Motta, Conny Fitzsimmons, Tom Nissalke, and Kevin Loughery were instantly rehired after failures.

What about other black coaches? Ray Scott was fired by Detroit in one year after he was named coach of the year. He had a .523 percentage. K. C. Jones was fired by Baltimore a year after he led them to the NBA finals. His three-year record was 148–91, for a .629 percentage. It took almost a decade for him to be hired again when he joined the Celtics in 1983. The Celtics have been by far the most consistent in hiring black coaches with Russell, Tom Sanders, and K.C. Jones. While this would seem to contradict Boston's emphasis on white players, in fact it may show that in this case race plays no real part.

In Willis Reed's first year of coaching the Knicks, they rose above .500 and made the playoffs for the first time in four years. He was fired after fourteen games in his second season. Reed told the *Sunday Daily News:*

> To be let go without a shot, though, is very disappointing. If you don't do the job, that's different. But when you do and show signs of continued improvement, that makes it hard to take. . . . It's really tough on a black coach. I do believe some of what happened to me was racial. But that's something you learn to live with because you must cope with it every day.

When he couldn't get another pro job, he took an unpaid assistant-coaching job with St. John's in 1980–81, then accepted the job at Creighton. But still no NBA. Even if blacks *are* better, they still might not make it. The winning percentages of Scott, Jones, and Reed were .523, .620, and .510, respectively. Nine of the twenty white head coaches at the helm when the 1982–83 season started had *worse* records than any of these.

The 1982–83 NBA guide showed only four of the thirty-six assistant coaches as black. The percentages go down when you discuss black college coaches.

The situation in football is even worse. A report commissioned by the NFL Players Association was released late in 1980. It revealed that there were no black head football coaches and only 10 black assistant coaches out of 225 in the NFL. In 1983, there were still no black head coaches while 27 out of 269 assistants were black. The NFL is 54 percent black. Ninety percent of its coaches are white.

Dr. Braddock, who headed the Johns Hopkins research team studying race as a factor in the NFL, reported:

> Whether direct or indirect, it is evident from our data that race has been a limiting factor in the career mobility of blacks. If recent trends are taken as valid indicators of blacks' future prospects in the NFL, then these prospects do not appear to be very bright.

No research team was really needed to recognize that fact for pro football. College football, however, is in a self-congratulatory mood these days after Wichita and Northwestern became the first major colleges to hire black head coaches. College baseball had only one black as head coach at a major college (Kansas State) at this writing. While some acknowledge these hirings as a beginning, the percentages are still dismal.

The following chart shows the coaching breakdown in the three major professional sports at the close of 1985:

	Head Coaches			Assistant Coaches*		
	Black	*White*	*% White*	*Black*	*White*	*% White*
Baseball	0	26	100%	13**	123	90%
Basketball	3	21	84%	4	32	89%
Football	0	28	100%	27	242	90%
Totals	3	74	96%	44	397	90%

*Figures for assistant coaches for the close of the 1983 baseball season and the start of the 1983 football and 1982–83 basketball seasons.

**Includes Latins.

The executives and members of the front offices in charge of professional sports in America are whiter than white. All the information that follows has been derived from the 1980 publications of the individual teams in all three sports.

A black man, Simon P. Gourdine, the former NBA deputy commissioner, didn't become the commissioner although no one doubted his talents. Gourdine himself said, "If sports ever has a black commissioner, it will be in the NBA." Note he did not say *when*, he said *if.* No black man has been president, or vice-president, or . . . Gourdine is no longer with the NBA. He was not replaced with another black as some had expected.

Cecil Watkins, also black, was the NBA's assistant supervisor of officials. Watkins is now referee development administrator, too, but it should come as no surprise that there are few black NBA referees (five of the twenty-seven total) for Watkins to supervise. Or that there are only eight blacks out of a hundred in the NFL and only one in major league baseball. Comments made by ex-umpire Art Williams, now a bus driver in California, were readily ignored. As reported by *Sporting News* in 1978, he was disgruntled after he was let go by the National League. After all, he had to deal with Al Barlich, consultant to the National League on umpires and not with sympathetic Cecil Watkins. Williams said, "They're letting me go because I'm black. They're bringing up another black umpire and they don't want to have two when the American League doesn't have any. I'll never work for Barlich again. . . ."

So the NBA had two blacks in the thirteen posts in the NBA league office in 1982. Progress? Perhaps, but it is certainly not a great leap forward for blacks. Look around the NBA. Wayne Embry was vice-president of the Milwaukee Bucks. Arnold Pinkney was an executive in Cleveland. Al Attles was not only the coach of Golden State but was also sports' first black general manager. Progress? The NBA's great leap forward is like Chairman Mao's—an abject failure. These were the totals! There were 121 whites listed as executives (presidents, vice-presidents, board chairmen, general managers, etc.). Embry, Attles, and Pinkney were the only three blacks. That was a total of 2.4 percent in 1982.

There were 300 people listed as administration and staff for NBA teams in that season. Larry Doby, unable to manage in the major leagues, was the Nets' director of community relations. Will Robinson held the same post in Detroit. Wayne Scales was Portland's director of promotions. There were only nine others in the rest of the league. Fourteen NBA teams had no blacks listed as administration/staff. Zero! The league had 12 of 399 or a total of 4 percent.

Segregation applied even to the sportscasters (chosen by management). If you live in New York you have seen Butch Beard doing the Knick games; in Chicago you have seen Norm Van Lier and Kenny Mac; in Washington it has been James Brown; and in Portland Steve Jones. In nineteen of the twenty-three NBA cities there were no black sportscasters. Of the fifty-five sportscasters, five, or 9 percent, were black. Perhaps this represents progress compared, for instance, to the 4 percent of the nation's newspaper writers who are black. But it does not when compared to the black percentage in the NBA.

Of the total of 544 listed in all categories combined, 29 were black. That's 5.3 percent, less than half the proportion of blacks nationwide when the proportion of blacks in the NBA is some 650 percent greater than the national proportion.

The NBA is probably trying to balance its image as an all-black league by overwhelming us with white faces in other sections of their media guides. Maybe they are even hiding some black faces in lesser positions to do this.

What about the NFL, which is not perceived as all-black and has no such image difficulties? Buddy Young was director of player relations for the NFL Office until his tragic death late in 1983. He was replaced by Mel Blount in 1984. Paul "Tank" Younger (San Diego) and Bobby Mitchell (Washington) were assistant general managers for their respective teams. They were the only 2 executives out of 117 working for NFL teams. That's .016 percent in the NFL, which was 54 percent black in 1983.

There were 452 people listed as administration/staff for NFL teams. The following black men were listed as scouts for their teams: Rosey Brown (Giants), Dick Daniels (Washington), Bob Hill (New Orleans), Lawrence McCutcheon (Rams), Ralph Goldston (Seattle), Bobby Grier (New England), Otis Taylor (Kansas City), Charles Garcia (Denver), Clyde Powers (Baltimore), Milt Davis and Elbert Dubenion (Miami). Paul Warfield was director of player relations for Cleveland. Frank Gilliam had the same post for the Vikings. Darryl Stingley was executive director of player personnel for New England while Bill Nunn, Jr. (Pittsburgh) and Jackie Graves (Philadelphia) were assistant directors of player personnel. Ronnie Barnes was head trainer for the Giants; Sid Brooks was equipment manager for San Diego; Willie Alexander was a career consultant for Houston; Claudia Smith was director of public affairs for New England; and Ted Chappelle was director of security for Cleveland. Only thirteen others were listed as assistants, receptionists, or secretaries. That is 32 of 452, making a total of only 6.6 percent for blacks—barely one-tenth of the number in the league. Of the twenty-eight teams surveyed in 1983, nine had no blacks in this category of administration/ staff; ten others had only one black; six others had only two. The LA Rams with four out of fifty had the most.

Combining all categories of executive, head and assistant coaches, and administration/staff, as listed in the 1983 team media guides, there were 879 posts, 61 (6.5 percent) of which were held by blacks. It was a stark picture for future employment prospects for ex-black football players.

If black professional athletes entertain any ideas of staying on with their teams after their playing days end, they should look elsewhere. The door is shut tight for blacks. Very tight.

What are the "retired" black athletes going to do? What are their marketable skills? Roscoe Brown, president of Bronx Community College, estimates that only 20 percent of the NBA players have college degrees. Less than 16 percent of major league baseball players have degrees. The NFL Players Association 1982 survey showed 67 percent of their players did not receive degrees. The employment records of former athletes is hardly encouraging.

Everything is compounded for the retiring black athlete. It doesn't matter whether you are Bill Russell, Jackie Robinson, Bob Gibson, Hank Aaron, Ron Leflore, or Tony Oliva, all of whom wrote books when they retired. A black player out of uniform looks like any other black to most whites. A cop might back off once he sees the driver's license, but until then any athlete is just another black face.

There are, of course, extreme examples of what happens to former pro athletes who suddenly find themselves facing double- instead of triple-figure incomes. Bill Robinzine chose to take his own life. A small but growing number have had to turn to crime. Broke, with no professional training, former star running back Mercury Morris began dealing drugs. Prison is now his home.

Morris was among the one in nearly 12,000 who made it to the pros. Many of the others who "made it" soon will join the 11,999 who didn't. Back on the streets, they will have to decide what they will do. For most, the options are slim. Corporations no longer need to hire blacks to fill quotas. The Equal Employment Opportunity Act, introduced in Congress with the approval of the Reagan administration, would prohibit the use of quotas to increase the hiring or school enrollment of women and minorities.

Team owners use blacks just as corporations use them in factories. Maximize their utility and then discard them. In the meanwhile, the athlete has devoted most of his life developing the skills necessary to become a pro player. Because of that, he is not likely to become a surgeon, a lawyer, or an intellectual leader. When his career is over, his standard of living is likely to decline.

If sports are ever to live up to their promise of harbingers of racial change, then the press must tell us about the fates of all those who have fallen as well as those have risen. And we must learn about the deeds, and not just the statistics, of multifaceted men like Paul Robeson, Bill Russell, and Kareem Abdul-Jabbar if blacks are to avoid the trap of a life of playing sports alone as youth and being forced to work as unskilled labor forevermore. Everyone needs a role model to help draw out and build his natural talents. When poverty makes success seem a far-distant goal, children need so much more than a helmet, a glove, a bat, or a ball. Creatively used, sports can help the process of total education. Tragically, the truth is that for blacks today, even considering the important exceptions, sports helps to mire most blacks in the quicksands of ignorance that only perpetuates their poverty.

3
Women in Sport

The denial of equality to women in sport comes as no surprise to those who recognize that sport is a reflection of society. In fact, with the sexual role expectations our society has imposed on both men and women, it might be expected that women would face an even more difficult road in sport than in other areas they might choose to pursue. Social expectations of the demure, fragile woman who wants a home, a white picket fence, and two children are in stark contrast to the image of a woman who is exploring and asserting herself through competitive activities in the world of sport.

Title IX of the Educational Amendments Act of 1972—which called for more equalization between men's and women's sports—and the women's movement have brought about dramatic changes in the number of women competing at all levels of sport. Between 1970 and 1980, the number of women who competed in high school sports increased by 500 percent. The 1984 Olympics had women superstars—Mary Lou Retton, Mary Decker (Slaney), Evelyn Ashford, Cheryl Miller, and Joan Benoit. Gains for women at the college level were so great that the National Collegiate Athletic Association (NCAA), which did not have women's sports in 1970, crushed the 800-member Association for Intercollegiate Athletics for Women (AIAW) to gain control. This was the same NCAA that not only didn't support Title IX but actively opposed it. In spite of all the gains, however, there is still a great void in the second half of the 1980s regarding women in the structure of sports administration and equal spending on women's athletics.

From the time of its founding, one of the issues that ARENA was committed to addressing was the inequality of women in sport. Five of the twenty-six issues of *Arena Review* were devoted to this topic (no other topic was covered more than twice), and numerous related articles appeared in the *Journal of Sport and Social Issues* (*JSSI*). It was difficult for me to choose among the many fine articles that have appeared on the subject.

Mary Bell's article, "Role Conflict of Women as Athletes in the United States" (*Arena Review*, vol. 4, no. 1), examines the image that has been socially acceptable for women in American sports. Bell maintains that the traditional role expectation for the "ideal woman" is that she be a loving homemaker, not a person who strives for competition. She is not expected to display characteristics that are admired in male athletes and that make them successful. Bell concludes that the women's movement and the resultant changes in the status of women, coupled with increased sports competition, have hastened the acceptance of women's participation in competitive sport. Still, Bell sees the perpetuation of role conflict for a generation while American society moves through a social transformation regarding the status of women. As a case in point, she cites a survey showing that 65 percent of a group of college women nonathletes responded affirmatively to the question, "Do you feel there is a stigma attached to women's participation in sports?" Even more telling was the fact that 56 percent of women basketball players and 50 percent of women track athletes also answered affirmatively.

Judy Jensen's "Women's Collegiate Athletics: Incidents in the Struggle for Influence and Control" (*Arena Review*, vol. 4, no. 2) illuminates the history of the struggle for control of women's sport. As a vehicle for the discussion, she traces the debate between opposing philosophies: sports for all women versus sports competition for elite women athletes. Dr. Jensen concludes that physical educators have been politicized and are now the leaders of the women's movement in sport. Ironically, she seems to consider that the rise of the Association of Intercollegiate Athletics for Women (AIAW) has been, in part, a culmination of this movement.

Donna Lopiano, who has been a president of the AIAW and is currently a director of women's athletic programs at a major university, is a pioneer in the area of women's participation in collegiate athletics. Her article, "A Political Analysis of the Possibility of Impact Alternatives for the Accomplishment of Feminist Objectives Within American Intercollegiate Sport" (*Arena Review*, vol. 8, no. 2), lays out a plan for change in the male-dominated sport structure. She examines the demise of the AIAW and the power structure of the NCAA and concludes that women must become part of that power structure before they can change it. That push for power—not only at the level of the NCAA, but in the corporate world, in academe, and in the political power structure—is part of the long road ahead for women in our society. Strong feminist analysis of women in sport will help further the process.

Role Conflict of Women as Athletes in the United States

Mary M. Bell
Northern Illinois University

Although women in the United States have a long history of participation in sports and athletics, there has not been widespread acceptance of women and girls as serious competitors within our culture. As this situation changes because of the great upsurge of numbers of women who participate, women will continue to find both subtle and overt expressions of disapproval. Some of this will be stated publicly, as was done when Olga Connolly, a women discus thrower who had competed in the Olympic Games five times, was chosen to carry the United States flag in the opening ceremonies at the 1972 Munich Games. Russell Knipp, a United States weight-lifter, said, "The flag-bearer ought to be a man, a strong man, a warrior. A woman's place is in the home" (Gilbert and Williamson, 1973).

Some of the disapproval will not be expressed verbally, but the impact can have a great effect. Recently, a college freshman was discussing her budding career in sports and her participation in high school. She said, rather sadly, that her parents had rarely seen her compete. Then she added, "When I was growing up, we always went to the high school football games when my older brother was on the team. He never started and usually played only a couple of minutes. When I got to high school, I always played a good percentage of the time and frequently started, but the family almost never came to watch." She dropped off the intercollegiate squad before the end of the semester.

Many young women face a conflict in wanting to participate in athletics as a serious competitor and in trying to live up to the expectations of society as they grow to adult women. This could be defined as an inter-role conflict.

The role upon which inter-role conflict is predicted concentrates on the study of real-life behavior as it is displayed in genuine on-going social situations. This includes such problems as the processes and phases of socialization, interdependencies among individuals, characteristics and organization of social positions, processes of conformity and sanctioning, and specialization of performance. The theory stresses the social determinism of behavior through the influence of immediate or past external situations. These influences include the framework of demands and rules, the behavior of others as it aids or hinders and rewards or punishes the person, the various roles that an individual plays, and the person's own understanding and reaction to these factors (Biddle and Thomas, 1966:17).

The expectations or evaluative standards applied to an individual occupying a role might be specified in terms of behavior (what the individual should do), especially the direction (what he/she should do or should not do), and the intensity (what he/she must do, ought to do, might possibly do, etc.) of these expected behaviors as opposed to expectations defined in terms of attributes (what the individual should be, what achievements should be attained). The expectations may also be characterized in terms of rights (what the individual may expect from others) versus duties (what others may expect from him/her) (Gullahorn and Gullahorn, 1969:418).

Because of the plurality of roles most people occupy, there is a certain endemic potential for role conflict inherent in the lives of all persons. These roles involve different patterns of behavior. The differences have to be adjusted by an ordering or allocation of the claims of the different role expectations to which the person is subject. This allocating occurs by distribution, by time and place, and by priority. There is always a variety of activities which have their appropriate time and place and appropriate partners and groups. The allocative ordering by a person is often delicately balanced. Any serious alteration in one role may encroach on others and thus, necessitate a whole series of adjustments (Parsons, 1966:275). In addition to a conflict caused by a person's occupying two or more roles, a conflict may occur from within the same role. This type of conflict would be called intra-role conflict, as opposed to the inter-role conflict. This discussion will be limited to the conflict which some women experience in trying to become serious athletes while being feminine members of the society within the United States. It will not deal with other inter-role conflicts such as students or wage-earners.

Role Expectations

In order for a woman to experience a conflict, she must perceive the role expectations of athlete and of woman as having incompatible obligations. Thus, some woman either will not develop a conflict or will have a relatively easy time in arranging priorities to fulfill the claims of the two role expectations. One of the factors which may affect whether or not a woman athlete perceives a conflict in the two role expectations is how legitimately she views the role expectations to be. A legitimate expectation is one which the individual feels others have a right to hold, and an illegitimate expectation is one which the individual does not feel others have a right to hold. Gross, McEachern and Mason (1966:288) have given the term "perceived obligation" to the expectations which one views as legitimate and the term "perceived pressure" to the expectations which one views as illegitimate. Thus, a woman athlete who perceives that the traditional role expectations for her as a female are legitimate may be more susceptible to role conflicts than one who does not.

The role expectations of a female include the perceptions of what females do and what females like to do. This consists of a complex of behavior considered characteristic of or appropriate to females (Hartley, 1966:354). Linton (1945), an anthropologist and early contributor to the role theory, stated that "the division of the society's members into age-sex categories is, perhaps, the feature of greatest importance for establishing the participation of the individual in culture" (Linton, 1945:63). He gives seven age-sex categories which are universally recognized: infant, boy, girl, adult male, adult female, old male, old female. Linton believed that pre-pubertal boys and girls are very similar in strength and activity and would be quite capable of participating in nearly all of the same culture patterns. The fact that there is a universal distinction is due to training the boy for his role as a man and the girl for her role as a woman (Linton, 1945:66).

Mead's (1971) study of primitive societies, the Arapesh, Mundugumor and Tchambuli, would seem to indicate that sex-role behavior is learned rather than of a biological nature. The Arapesh were cooperative and unaggressive with little differences between sexes, while both sexes of the Mundugumor were ruthless, aggressive, violent and undisciplined. In the Tchambuli, a genuine reversal of the sex attitudes as perceived within the United States was found, with the woman the dominant, impersonal managing partner and the man the less responsible and emotionally dependent person. Mead concluded that traits such as aggressiveness and passivity cannot be considered to be sex-linked and stressed the malleability of the human organism and the importance of cultural conditioning (Mead, 1971:376).

A series of observations and studies was done at the Endocrine Clinic at Johns Hopkins University with hermaphrodites. The researchers concluded that gender role is more related to assigned sex in child-rearing than to chromosomal sex (Hampson, 1965:125). Studies of sex identification in children gave some support to this theory. In 1972, Lewis reported that mothers had started to move their sons away from physical contact by six months and by thirteen months, boys were exploratory and autonomous in their behavior than were girls. One-year-old girls were encouraged to spend significantly more time touching and staying near their mothers than boys were (Lewis, 1972:56–57). Rabban (1950) studied children in two diverse social groups, working-class and middle-class families. He found that three-year-old boys and girls of both groups showed incomplete recognition of sex differences and, as a group, were unaware of any appropriateness of sex-typed toys. The fourth and fifth years were periods of growth in clarification of sex role for boys of the working-class families, while the sixth year was particularly significant for boys of the middle class. Girls from the working-class families accepted the sex-appropriate pattern by six years of age, but the girls from the middle class did not fully acquiesce to the definition of appropriate sex patterning even by the eighth year, when all other groups had accepted the social expectations (Rabban, 1950:141).

Tuddenham (1951) reported a study concerning popularity among elementary school children in grades 1, 3 and 5. He concluded that athletic competence, daring and leadership constituted the cardinal sources of prestige for boys (Tuddenham, 1951:269). A different situation existed for girls. Traits denoting quietness, sedateness and unassertiveness were valued more among girls than boys, and outgoing, dominant, aggressive qualities were valued less (Tuddenham, 1951:272). Kagan and Moss (1960) did a longitudinal study which compared the dependency behavior of young children with their behavior patterns as adults. The results indicated that while the passive and dependent behaviors were quite stable and consistent for the women, this was not true for the men. The comparison of dependency behavior of the boys at the ages of six to ten did not indicate a stable behavior pattern for the same boys as adults. Kagan and Moss suggested that environmental disapproval and punishment of dependent behavior in young males led to inhibition of these traits. They further theorized that social acceptance of passive and dependent behavior in females would be expected to result in a greater stability for women (Kagan and Moss, 1960:591).

Oglesby (1978) discussed the psychological damage which can occur when people try to place themselves in stereotyped gender roles in which they do not feel comfortable. She indicated that the period when males suffer the greatest alienation through denial of self is during childhood when the child's orientation is influenced by traits such as dependency which are considered feminine. Adolescence and adulthood, however, are the times when women suffer the greatest damage since these are periods when patterns and values center around masculine principles (Oglesby, 1978:80).

In a study reported in 1970 (Broverman, and others), 79 trained psychologists, psychiatrists, or social workers (46 men and 33 women) were asked to describe the behavior of mature, healthy, socially competent adults. The 79 subjects were divided into three groups. One group was asked to describe adult men, another adult women, and the last was asked to describe adults. A comparison of the descriptions indicated a close resemblance between adults and adult men and a different standard for adult women. Broverman, and others, indicated that "healthy women are perceived as significantly less healthy by adult standards" (Broverman, and others, 1970:5). The authors concluded that the double standard for adult men and women probably stems from the fact that many women have made a good adjustment to the environment. They have been systematically trained to fulfill the social role of women. Women have been put in the position of having to decide whether or not to exhibit traits considered desirable for men and adults, and have their femininity questioned, i.e., be deviant as women, or live in a prescribed manner and live as second-class citizens (Broverman, and others, 1970:6).

In a 1971 study (Peterson, and others), college women were asked to evaluate paintings, with half of the women believing that the artist was a man and the other half thinking the artist was a woman. A significant sex–painting interaction was found, with technique of the artist rated more highly by those students believing the artist to be a man (Peterson, and others, 1971:118). The authors attributed this result to a concept of Allport (1954) that the group of people who feel themselves to be the target of prejudice tend to accept the attitudes of the dominant majority. This phenomenon has been called the identification with the aggressor (Allport, 1954:150).

The reports of research findings lend support to the concept that the role expectations for a woman are culturally determined. But little evidence of how or why this happens has been presented. Linton (1945) stated that the most outstanding and most continuously operative of an individual's psychic needs is an emotional response from other people. It is this need for a favorable response which provides the main stimulus to socially acceptable behavior. Individuals abide by the mores of their culture quite as much because they desire approval as because they fear punishment (Linton, 1945:7–8). The desire for emotional response from others is so universal and so strong that some social scientists have regarded it as instinctive.

Linton's second psychic need is security of a long duration. This is explained as people are in constant need of reassurance. His last psychic need is that of novelty of experience which he felt was a much less compulsive need (Linton, 1945:9).

Although these psychic needs hold for both sexes, in the United States, achievement has been stressed for men and interpersonal relations for women. The pre-pubertal girl had a bisexual rearing in that achievement was stressed, particularly in the academic area, but the emphasis changes at puberty. The cultural definition of successful femininity requires interpersonal success, especially with males. For the boy, there is a comparable pressure to achieve athletically or academically or vocationally.

Because little girls are often less impulsive and physically aggressive and less sexually active than little boys, they tend to get into less trouble. As a result, they are not as apt to see parents and teachers as people who thwart impulses. To the extent that girls are not separated from their parents as sources of support and nurturance, they are not forced to develop internal controls and an independent feeling of self. In addition, girls are permitted to remain dependent and infantile longer than boys because the dependency, fears, and affection-seeking that are normal in early childhood for both boys and girls are defined as feminine in older children. Girls are not pressed by society's definition of ''sissy'' to become independent as early as boys. And, more than boys, they will continue for an extended period of their lives to value the self through the appraisal of others. This means, in a very pervasive and significant way, that girls and women will continue to have a great need for approval from others and that their behavior will be guided by fear of rejection and loss of love.

The healthy adolescent girl accepts her femininity, takes pleasure in being desired and courted, and is acutely aware of the physical changes in her appearance. Because she is still responding to others, she values these changes because they are a means of securing love. The sexuality of the adolescent girl is combined with the pleasures of dating. Dating can be considered the testing ground for one's desirability as a woman, and the girl is ready to fall in love again and again because each relationship reassures her of her desirability (Bardwick, and others, 1970:6–9).

Role Expectation in Sport

Since the United States has established sport as male territory, the adolescent girl athlete is often subject to rejection and alienation, often from those of whom she most needs the approval. Michener was confounded by the desire of many girls and women to participate in the sporting world as cheerleaders and members of pom pom units rather than as athletes. A woman from South Carolina explained that "there is hardly a real mother in this nation who would not prefer to see her daughter dressed in a cute outfit, attracting boys and being the most popular girl in her class and maybe marrying a football star after she graduates, rather than growing big muscles and looking like a man in some sports" (Michener, 1976:142).

There is little evidence that sports participation tends to masculinize the behavior of girls. The traits that are necessary for success in competitive athletics—aggressiveness, tough-mindedness, dominance, self-confidence, and the willingness to take risks—often correspond to traits that are admirable in males. Yet these same qualities are often necessary for the female to be successful (Harris, 1971:1). It seems amusing that people worry that too much physical activity for women will tend to masculinize women, when little concern was expressed for pioneer women who kept house, helped run a farm, beat laundry in a cold stream, carried water and did various other types of physical exertion; as long as it was within her role in the family, it seemed appropriate (Albright, 1971:56).

Metheny (1972) developed some principles which she feels govern the socially sanctioned image of feminine sports competition for college women in the United States:

1. It is not appropriate for women to engage in contests in which:
   the resistance of the opponent is overcome by bodily contact;
   the resistance of a heavy object is overcome by direct application of body force;

the body is projected into or through space over long distances or for extended periods of time.

2. It may be appropriate for women identified in the lower levels of socioeconomic status to engage in contests in which:

   the resistance of an object of moderate weight is overcome by direct application of force; the body is projected into or through space over moderate distances or for relatively short periods of time.

3. It is wholly appropriate for women identified with the more favored levels of socioeconomic status to engage in contests in which:

   the resistance of a light object is overcome with a light implement;
   the body is projected into or through space in aesthetically pleasing patterns;
   the velocity and maneuverability of the body is increased by the use of some manufactured device;
   a spatial barrier prevents bodily contact with the opponent in face-to-face forms of competition. (Metheny, 1972:285)

The girl or woman who enjoys golf, swimming or tennis will feel much less pressure to give up sports than the girl who loves basketball or softball. When the mother of Billie Jean King ended Billie Jean's football career at age ten, Billie Jean asked her father what she could do. He suggested golf, swimming or tennis (King, 1974:25).

There is nothing incongruous about women participating in sports being physically attractive, yet the prevailing sentiment among female adolescents who are likely to be the most prestigious is that females who indulge regularly in sports programs are oddballs. This seems to be particularly true of the more active team games (Sherif, 1972:132).

The lack of sporting news about females may have contributed to these attitudes. Because the feats of outstanding women athletes are briefly, and sometimes bizarrely, reported, there are few role models. Girls at all levels of play are deprived of the genuine satisfaction of seeing their athletic accomplishments publicized. Boys are bombarded with daily stories about how much fun male athletes are having, how skillful, important and admired they are. The suggestion is made that playing games, and playing them well, is an exciting and popular thing to do. Girls have few such models and seldom receive such messages advertising athletics (Gilbert and Williamson, 1973:96).

At about age thirteen is the time when boys go through a real apprenticeship in violence, and girls begin to drop out of rough games. Girls are forbidden to venture, to compete physically, to extend the limits of the possible and to assert themselves above other people. Boys learn what it is to confront another, to dare to climb higher, to force an opponent's shoulders to the ground, to assert one's sovereignty over the world in general (deBeauvoir, 1957:330).

With the changing status of women and an increase in sports participation by girls and women, the societal pressure against women athletes should decrease. However, changing the cultural pattern is a slow process. According to Komarovsky (1953), a sacrifice of two generations is necessary to make a transition from one social system to another (Komarovsky, 1953:74). Thus, it seems apparent that many girls and women will continue to develop an inter-role conflict as they follow their inclination to participate in competitive sports. There are three alternatives open to these girls and women who have an inter-role conflict. The first would be to accept the responsibility for the decision and decide either to pursue athletics regardless of the sanctions of society, or to drop sports and accept the feminine role in our society as she perceives it. The second alternative would be to delay the decision; the last would be to reject the responsibility of the decision.

Considering role conflict situations in general, the majority of women could be expected to pick the three alternatives in the following order: postponing the decision, rejecting the responsibility by referring the decision to others; and making the decision would be last. Generally, postponing a decision is the least punitive response in a role conflict situation. If the girl or young woman can evade pressure and continue to delay, the conditions might improve so that she may never have to make a decision. If she follows the second alternative, she may let her parents decide for her. Or it may be that peer pressure is strong enough that she acquiesces to what her friends do. In some cases, a coach may talk to her and her family and make the decision. In these cases, she does not carry the responsibility for the decision and develop guilt feelings (Gullahorn and Gullahorn, 1968:428).

If, however, the girl chooses the alternative of making the decision for herself, the majority will probably accept the cultural role and not compete in sports in a serious way. The nature of competition demands not only sacrifices, but discomfort and pain. Most people find it impossible to accept the mental and physical distress inherent in athletics unless their motivation is extremely high. Only the girls who are strong enough to erect an emotional barrier to the criticism and discouragement from those around them can maintain enough courage and motivation to continue participation. There is no way of knowing how many thousands of girls and women would be playing and competing if there were not so many obstacles for them to overcome (Neal and Tutko, 1975:12).

Faced with the conflict between what she is and what she is expected to be, an ambitious, competitive, athletic girl sometimes responds by becoming defensively aggressive and masculine in attitude. Resenting the restrictions placed upon her, she reacts by mimicking the only success models around, men. Unfortunately for her, there are few popular athletic heroines for her to emulate (Boslooper and Hayes, 1973:23).

Some girls, particularly if given parental support or outside encouragement, will be able to adjust the claims of each of the role expectations in such a way that they feel little or no conflict. They will be able to display appropriate behavior in both athletic and social situations and not feel uncomfortable that one is infringing upon the other. However, women athletes find themselves in a rather select group; they often must fend for themselves in a not-too-accepting environment. According to Gullahorn and Gullahorn (1969), individuals who occupy statuses subject to recurring role conflicts are likely to be lonely people (Gullahorn and Gullahorn, 1969:429).

Anthropologist Linton (1945) wrote that when two fundamentally incompatible statuses converge upon the same individual, the situation makes for high tragedy. He stated that such conflicts rarely arise in primary societies or in larger social groupings which have existed for a long time and developed well-integrated cultures. But they may be fairly frequent in the post–World-War-II United States, where the system of statuses and roles in breaking down and a new system has not yet emerged. An individual is compelled to make choices but can feel no certainty that he has chosen correctly and that the reciprocal behavior of others will be that which he anticipated (Linton, 1945:80–82).

Snyder and Kivlin (1977) reported that college women competing in national tournaments were asked: "Do you feel there is a stigma attached to your sport?" The four groups of tournament competitors responded as follows:

Sport	*% Responding Affirmatively*
Basketball	56
Track	50
Swimming and Diving	40
Gymnastics	31

A group of college women non-athletes were asked: "Do you feel there is a stigma attached to women's participation in sports?" Sixty-five percent of these women answered affirmatively (Snyder and Kivlin, 1977:23).

It is not surprising that so many women have dropped out of sports participation as they enter the adult feminine status. However, they simply escape one conflict to find themselves in another. They may be compared to the young woman who went sailing with a man who so obviously enjoyed the role of protector that she told him she did not know how to sail; as it turned out, neither did he. They got into a tough spot and she was torn between a desire to take charge of the boat and a fear of letting him know that she had lied (Komarovsky, 1953:79). Hayes (1973), author of *The Femininity Game*, wrote that "feminine woman—in the traditional sense—is the portrait of a loser. To win at the femininity game, she must lose at all other games. . . . Women must get into the game and learn to compete on their own, instead of competing vicariously through men" (Hayes, 1973:7).

In a recent study, Sage and Laudermilk (1979) questioned college women intercollegiate athletes about role conflict relating to the role of the female and female athlete. Forty-three percent of the athletes responded that they had experienced role conflict of a moderate, great or very great degree. The women who had participated in the less socially approved sports of softball, basketball, volleyball, field hockey and track and field had experienced significantly greater role conflict (45% vs. 34%) than the women competing in the socially approved sports of tennis, golf, swimming and gymnastics. The findings may be somewhat biased by a sample of women who chose to stay in sport because they had not experienced role conflict and because women who had experienced such conflict had already withdrawn from sport participation. However, the findings suggest that the social cost of sport participation has been reduced through a broadening definition of sex role behavior (Sage and Laudermilk, 1979:93).

As women begin to participate in sports in far greater numbers than ever before, the traditional concept of women's role may be affected. In the United States, athletics are used extensively in teaching attitudes to teach that achievement and success are desirable, that they are worth the necessary self-discipline. Better athletic programs will develop more assertive females, women with confidence who value personal achievement and have a strong sense of identity. That would benefit everyone (Gilbert and Williamson, 1973:68).

Bibliography

Albright, Tenley E. Which sports for girls? In Dorothy Harris (Ed.). *D.G.W.S. Research Reports: Women in sports.* Washington, D.C.: American Association for Health, Physical Education and Recreation, 1971.

Allport, Gordon W. *The nature of prejudice.* Cambridge: Addison-Wesley, 1954.

Bardwick, Judith; Douvan, Elizabeth; Horner, Matina; and Gutman, David. *Feminine personality and conflict.* Belmont, Calif.: Wadsworth, 1970.

Biddle, Bruce, and Thomas, Edwin. *Role theory: Concepts and research.* New York: John Wiley and Sons, 1966.

Boslooper, Thomas, and Hayes, Marcia. *The femininity game.* New York: Stein & Day, 1973.

Broverman, Inge; Broverman, Donald; Clarkson, Frank; Rosenkrantz, Paul; and Vogel, Susan. Sex role stereotypes and clinical judgments of mental health. *Journal of Consulting and Clinical Psychology,* Feb., 1970, 34(1), 1–7.

deBeauvoir, Simone. *The second sex.* New York: Alfred Knopf, 1957.

Gilbert, Bill, and Williamson, Nancy. Sport is unfair to women. *Sports Illustrated,* May 23, 1973.

Gross, Neal; McEachern, Alexander; and Mason, Ward. Role conflict and its resolution. In Bruce Biddle and Edwin Thomas (Eds.). *Role theory: Concepts and research.* New York: John Wiley and Sons, 1966.

Gullahorn, John, and Gullahorn, Jeanne. Role conflict and its resolution. In Dwight G. Dean (Ed.). *Dynamic social psychology.* New York: Random House, 1969.

Hampson, John L. Determinants of psychosexual orientation. In Frank A. Beach (Ed.). *Sex and behavior.* New York: John Wiley and Sons, 1965.

Harris, Dorothy. The sportswoman in our society. *D.G.W.S. Research Reports: Women in sports.* Washington, D.C.: American Association for Health, Physical Education and Recreation, 1971.

Hartley, Ruth E. A developmental view of female sex-role identification. In Bruce Biddle and Edwin Thomas (Eds.). *Role theory: Concepts and research.* New York: John Wiley and Sons, 1966.

Hayes, Marcia. *The sportswoman*, 1973, 1(3), 7.

Kagan, Jerome, and Moss, Howard. The stability of passive and dependent behavior from childhood through adulthood. *Child Development*, 1960, 31, 577–591.

King, Billie Jean. *Billie Jean.* New York: Harper & Row, 1974.

Komarovsky, Mirra. *Women in the modern world.* Boston: Little, Brown, 1953.

Lewis, Michael. Culture and gender roles—there's no unisex in the nursery. *Psychology Today*, May, 1972, 54–57.

Linton, Ralph. *The cultural background of personality.* New York: Appleton-Century-Crofts, 1945.

Mead, Margaret. Sex and temperament. In Nancy Reeves (Ed.). *Womankind, beyond the stereotypes.* Chicago: Aldine-Atherton, 1971.

Metheny, Eleanor. Symbolic forms of movement: The feminine image in sports. In Marie Hart (Ed.). *Sport in the socio-cultural process.* Dubuque: William C. Brown, 1972.

Michener, James A. *Sports in America.* New York: Random House, 1976.

Neal, Patsy, and Tutko, Thomas. *Coaching girls and women.* Boston: Allyn and Bacon, 1975.

Oglesby, Carole A. *Women and sport: From myth to reality.* Philadelphia: Lea and Febiger, 1978.

Parsons, Talcott. Role conflict and the genesis of deviance. In Bruce Biddle and Edwin Thomas (Eds.). *Role theory: Concepts and research.* New York: John Wiley and Sons, 1966.

Peterson, Gail; Kiesler, Sara; and Goldberg, Philip. Evaluation of the performance of women as a function of their sex, achievement, and personal history. *Journal of Personality and Social Psychology*, 1971, 19, 114–118.

Rabban, Meyer. Sex-role identification in young children in two diverse social groups. *Genetic Psychology Monographs*, 1950, 42, 81–158.

Sage, George H., and Laudermilk, Sheryl. The female athlete and role conflict. *Research Quarterly*, 1979, 50, 88–96.

Sherif, Carolyn Wood. Females in the competitive process. In Dorothy Harris (Ed.). *Women and sport: A national research conference*, University Park: Pennsylvania State University Press, 1972.

Snyder, Eldon E., and Kivlin, Joseph E. Perceptions of the sex role among female athletes and non-athletes. *Adolescence*, 1977, 12, 23–29.

Tuddenham, Read. Studies in reputation III, correlates of popularity between elementary school children. *Journal of Educational Psychology*, May, 1951, 42, 257–276.

Women's Collegiate Athletics: Incidents in the Struggle for Influence and Control

Judy Jensen
State University of New York College at Brockport

Conflicting Sports Philosophies

In 1899, a group of women physical education teachers compiled the first standardized set of basketball rules for girls and women.[1] In 1972, the Association for Intercollegiate Athletics for Women sponsored the first national collegiate basketball championship. It had taken seventy-three years of turmoil and challenge to reach the point where women physical educators, basketball, intercollegiate athletics and national championships could be mentioned companionably in a single sentence. The years were filled with stress for women physical educators as they struggled to determine and impose appropriate standards of control on "inter-competition." The pages which follow will focus on selected events and trends during this struggle, with particular emphasis on the conservative and nearly obstructive efforts of women physical educators as they sought to contain college athletics.

Sensitive from the moment sports emerged in their programs to their social implications and to their potential as "threats" to the healthful purposes of physical activities, physical educators—at least those whose views were heard in professional meetings and literature—asserted strict control over the selection of sports and the manner in which they would be played. They counseled for physical examinations, limitations on the strenuousness of activities, conservative dress, women-only audiences, restricted travel, a friendly spirit among opponents, leadership by women, and separate rules.[2] Lucille Eaton Hill (1903) of Wellesley College, Massachusetts, proclaimed health, beauty and moderation as program ideals. Intramurals involving class teams were preferred for they insured "a larger number of entries in the sport and less danger from over-excitement than inter-scholastic matches, where a school furnishes but one team and more intense nervous strain accompanies the keener competition" (1903:12).

From the first, then, women physical educators put a firm hand to the controls of sport in college programs. These women dominated professional literature and the organizations which were developed to control college sports. Spears and Swanson (1978) pointed out the impact of that domination:

. . . by carefully controlling the type of activity, by supervising all matches, and by planning types of activities which were different from the men's, the women physical educators were able to provide opportunities for many women to pursue sport in acceptable surroundings and to enjoy the new games of the period. (1978:186)

These efforts, as Gerber indicated, separated women's collegiate sport from "the larger social milieu" (1974:48). Accordingly, Gerber contended, collegiate sport developed in a relatively unified, controlled pattern across the country, governed as it was by the women physical educators with no external interference" (1974:48).

Controversy reigned, nonetheless. As with most new phenomena, there was a tendency to experiment with a variety of forms of collegiate sport. Intercollegiate basketball play began in 1896. The number of basketball games played between colleges increased steadily into the mid-1920s. But then a combination of events nearly eliminated the intercollegiate contest.

Tracing its origin back to the basketball rules committee in 1899, a women's athletic committee of the American Physical Education Association (APEA) was formed in 1917 to guide the growth of sports for girls and women. The National Association for Girls and Women in Sport (NAGWS) and the Association for Intercollegiate Athletics for Women (AIAW) are its modern descendents. "Sport for all" has been the credo of the various committees and associations. That point of view served to minimize attention to the specialized few who might be selected for intercollegiate competition. In effect, the highly (or potentially) skilled women was not central to the plans of the physical educator; she was used instead as a model of performance or assistant instructor to help the lesser in ability in physical education classes.

A none-too-subtle form of peer pressure was employed by women physical educators to keep the flock together. Mabel Lee's two volumes of memories (1977, 1978) contain vivid accounts of an "old girls" system in action. Lee, the first woman president of the APEA, was a leading proponent of sport for the masses rather than for the elite few. Her many leadership roles provided opportunities to share her views with colleagues. She described nuances of persuasion throughout her autobiography. In addition, women leaders such as Lee were, typically, directors of women's physical training departments. Their students, in turn, carried forth the beliefs of their mentors,[3] including their strong positions regarding appropriate forms of sport and competition. Further, directors convened annual meetings which served as forums to reinforce the views of the more-outspoken and strong-willed leaders. Competition was controlled by commandant, not by law.

Conflict Within and Without

The skilled woman athlete had to turn to other outlets than physical education for opportunities to enhance and test her performance. Women swimmers had been registered by the Amateur Athletic Union (AAU) in 1914 (*New York Times*, November 2, 1916). That organization had initiated the supervision in order to provide responsible direction for a group which desired competition, but not to impose itself on women's sports. Shortly thereafter, Harry Stewart (1916), an advocate of athletics for girls, reported research data in his effort to inject substantive evidence into the controversy over appropriate forms of competition. If his research was not convincing, his subsequent actions were certainly provocative. In 1922, not only did the AAU vote to take over amateur competition, but the organization also sent a group of women under the guidance of Stewart to an international track and field meet in Paris. The women on the Athletic Committee of the APEA were incensed and withdrew from any cooperative ventures with the AAU, seeking instead to expand their own sphere of influence in girls' and women's sports. The battle lines of an enduring feud were drawn and the women wasted little time in mounting an attack.

In April, 1923, the physical educators joined representatives of health professions and other organizations who had interests in girls' athletics to form the Women's Division of the National Amateur Athletic Federation (NAAF) to promote the best interests of girls and women in sport.

> The Women's Division of the National Amateur Athletic Federation of America believes in the spirit of play for its own sake, and works for the promotion of physical activity for the largest possible proportion of persons in any given group, in forms suitable to individual needs and capacities, under leadership and environmental conditions that foster health, physical efficiency and the development of good citizenship. (Women's Division, 1930:3)

Of course, it was no accident that the Women's Division was organized within a year after the AAU had made its commitment to the fostering of women's athletics. The Women's Athletic Committee of the APEA quickly supported the platform of the Division and those two organizations joined the battle to standardize sport participation in the best interests of girls and women—and in juxtaposition to promoters of competition. The actions and words of the women's groups were often interpreted to be opposed to competitive athletics. Though neither group ever professed such a position, their pronouncements would not have been interpreted as negatively if individual members had not, at every opportunity, condemned competition so strongly.

Subsequently, the AAU and women's groups confronted each other over various issues. In 1929, the Women's Division, primarily under the urging of women physical educators, sought to eliminate the participation of women in the Olympic Games. An alternative proposed instead was festivals of dancing, music, singing, mass sports and conferences (Non-Olympic Rule, *New York Times*, January 6, 1929). Despite these proposals, women did participate in the 1932 Olympic Games in Los Angeles. Though the women's groups did not alter the Olympic situation, the rising tide of intercollegiate competition was stemmed. Such competition was nearly eliminated by the late 1920's and dissolved into the play-day form preferred by the Women's Division in the 1930's. It is impossible to determine conclusively that the women's groups were primarily responsible for these events, but there can be little doubt of their influence on many school programs (Jensen, 1972).

Years later, the lingering strains between the national amateur organization and the women's athletic committee's successor, the National Section on Women's Athletics (NSWA) were evident in the writings of Roxy Andersen (1952, 1953), who was a track and field commissioner for women in the AAU.

To begin with, our school system presents a highly organized solid front against the participation of girls in competitive athletics. The graduating woman physical educationist is thoroughly imbued with the fixation that competitive sport is harmful to women and in consequence they must be protected from this contamination at all costs. (1952:17)

To the predictable horror of the NSWA, Andersen (1952) suggested that the skilled woman athlete needed to be pitted against men athletes during training sessions in order to improve her skills. By 1953, Andersen was more conciliatory:

The hard, cold fact is that there just isn't any program of competitive athletics for girls in the schools governed by NSWA mandate and *there never will be unless* the AAU can make certain concessions to the NSWA point of view. (1953:14)

In the 1960's, Andersen chaired an AAU study of the effects of athletic competition on girls and women (Amateur Athletic Union of the United States, n.d.). Clearly, one of the intentions of the study was to answer the critics of women's athletic competition. By 1963, the AAU and the Division for Girls and Women's Sports (DGWS), successor to the NSWA, were cooperating to develop basketball rules for the woman participant.

To conclude this sequence of events, it is interesting to note that the DGWS joined the United States Olympic Development Committee in November, 1963, to sponsor the first of five national sport institutes for the improvement of sport skills for all girls (Jernigan, 1963). By its participation, the DGWS indicated the institute met its standards for sport and gave tacit approval to Olympic participation.

Women's athletic activity, during the four decades of rivalry (1920's–1960's) between the women's groups and the AAU, had not been void of other, equally significant, events. Field hockey and lacrosse stand out as team sports which were "allowable exceptions" to many of the standards for women's athletic competition. Organized into national associations in 1922 and 1933, respectively, the two sports were formed on a club basis and depended heavily on college graduates, college students and women in physical education for players, coaches and officials. There were national tournaments, all-star teams, several games played per day and considerable travel (even international tours) associated with both sports. In addition, the DGWS standard which opposed participation on a college team and an outside team during a season did not seem to apply to field hockey and lacrosse. Women physical educators seemingly did not question these activities. The two sports were acceptable extra-curricular activities for students and faculty alike.

The women interested in controlling competitive athletics, meanwhile, had not united behind a single banner to set forth a position. For example, women physical educators through the National Section on Women's Athletics in 1937, formulated an elaborate set of standards for girls' and women's sports ("Standards in Athletics for Girls and Women," 1937). The sports day, or college team versus college team form of competition was condoned. The Women's Division of the National Amateur Athletic Federation, proponents of the play day, thought the NSWA was too liberal. The two groups, which had been brought together by their common concern for healthful and appropriate sport, were divided irrevocably by this designation of a different form of competition and the promulgation of a formal set of standards by NSWA. Concurrent with the intensification of the rivalry between the Division and NSWA was the growing financial difficulty of the Division, a concern which led to merger discussions between the Division and the American Association for Health, Physical Education, and Recreation (AAHPER)—*not* the latter's section on women's athletics. The Division and AAHPER merged in June, 1940, though there is no evidence that the interests of the Division were perpetuated in any fashion after the agreement to join. In effect, NSWA became the standard bearer, and its more moderate position on competition was a portent of events to come.

Championships Foster Organizations

The leadership in women's physical education, especially directors of college women's physical education programs, was tested in 1941 by a proposal from

Gladys Palmer and her staff at The Ohio State University for a national inter-collegiate golf tournament. Palmer and her colleagues did seek the approval of the Midwest and National Associations of Directors of Physical Education for College Women for the golf event. (The NSWA was not consulted, demon-strating, in this instance, the voluntary nature of its standards and the reality of its influence on actual practice.) The Directors found the tournament "inad-visable" (Resolutions, 1941).

Despite the disapproval of its peers, the Ohio State University staff carried on with the tournament. The event proved to be the stepping stone for the eventual development of the Association for Intercollegiate Athletics for Women. It is particularly worth noting that the Ohio State staff had the pre-science to recognize the need for such an organization with the initiation of that first championship event. The staff proposed that a women's national col-legiate athletic association be developed. Thirty years later, the association was a reality.

After the Second World War, the golf tournament became an annual event with its reestablishment in 1946. First, in 1956, to oversee its development, there was a Tripartite Golf Committee, composed of members from the NSWA, the National Directors and the Athletic and Recreation Federation of College Women. A Tripartite Committee, interested in more than golf, fol-lowed in 1957. In succession came the National Joint Committee on Extra-mural Sports for College Women (1958), Commission on Intercollegiate Sports for Women (1966), Commission on Intercollegiate Athletics for Women (1967), and finally, the Association for Intercollegiate Athletics for Women (1972).

Companion to this seemingly endless chain of governing bodies was the inevitable attention to the justification and/or limitation of women's athletic competition. In a most comprehensive analysis of women's sport. Metheny (1965) suggested that women participants made conscious choices of both their activities and the intensity of their participation. Though evidence indicates that others had considerable influence on those choices, Metheny's (1965) analysis did delineate socially approved characteristics of sports for women.

> Strength and bodily contact are de-emphasized in favor of skill and grace; force is applied to weightless objects with lightweight implements; and veloc-ity is attained by use of manufactured devices. And there is no serious com-petition in which women are matched against men. (1965:55)

As Metheny was analyzing sport participation, Ley and Jernigan (1962) and Scott and Ulrich (1966) were preparing their colleagues for changes on behalf of the Division for Girls' and Women's Sports. The tone of their remarks indicated a major shift of emphasis: "If the DGWS is to grow and re-main an influential women's sports organization, it cannot be completely bound by the traditions and thinking of the past fifty years" (Ley and Jernigan, 1962:57). As the DGWS assumed responsibility for women's intercollegiate competition, a structure for national championships was developed by the Division's Commission on Intercollegiate Sports for Women. The Commission took charge of all aspects of major tournaments in "an attempt to place responsibility for the direction of intercollegiate competition for women in one nationally visible structure so that all concerned will know where to seek assistance" (Scott and Ulrich, 1966:76). The highly skilled performer became the focus of attention. In further contrast to previous times, the women physical educators leading the trend toward championships did not rely on support from research to develop the new model for competition. Scott (1970) observed that "so far as we are able to determine there is no research evidence that would negate our offering intercollegiate programs for women" (1970:26). Conservation appeared to take the backseat as these women took the initiative. Where lack of evidence to support or reject an endeavor inhibited progress in the 1920's, it was considered a signal to proceed in the 1960's. The nature of society and general developments in education were supportive of change. The medical profession, also, was less likely to allow social attitudes to influence medical facts. Most significant of all, however, was the threat by the National Collegiate Athletic Association, the dominant force in men's athletics, to offer championships for women. One standard endured from the 1890's: women would not tolerate leadership of their athletic programs by men. As the women's alternative became a reality, Aldrich (1974), a leading physical educator, optimistically commented that "the quality of the programs should enhance the lives of the participants, and society should benefit from girls and women in sports" (1974:71). The new movement was founded on immutable ideals.

Proving that an organization cannot please all the people any of the time, the decisions of DGWS were criticized by Kenyon (1969) for being anti-men, separatist, out of step with their times, and maternalistic. Lambert (1969), head of women's physical education at Oregon State University, criticized the move toward tournament competition:

> Personally, I do not think the world needs a substantial increase in highly aggressive, competitive, tough-minded women. I prefer physical education to give us efficient, graceful, healthy women who have sufficient skill in a variety of areas to pursue with interest a lifetime of physical activities for pleasure and for health. . . . (1969:75)

Current Events and Consequences

Concurrent with the change in sanctioned forms of competition came questions. According to the handbook of the AIAW (1978), "the organization maintains an educational and philosophical association" (1978:1) with both

NAGWS (National Association for Girls and Women in Sport) and AAHPER (American Alliance for Health, Physical Education, and Recreation). Will that symbiotic relationship survive the withdrawal of AIAW from the NAGWS when their formal affiliation no longer exists in the 1980's? Was women's physical education to be separated from women's athletics?

The competence of women physical educators to handle the new responsibilities in athletics was a matter of concern to Ley (1974), nearly a decade after she had been a leader in the change to the new concept of competition.

> In our experience, we find our students are returning from sports camp with the latest techniques and strategies. Meanwhile, the knowledge possessed by our women coaches, who have been busy going to summer school to earn advanced degrees to be able to retain their jobs, is less than that of the team members. (1974:31)

Never having valued or promoted high-level performance and, consequently, having neither prepared nor rewarded coaches to care for the skilled athlete, there did not appear to be a support system for a varsity program in physical education. As a result, women physical educators "are uncomfortable with the changes and find it difficult to reconcile them with concepts previously learned" (Gerber, 1974:1). Social change had preceded preparation for its arrival.

As the men had done before them, women began to organize separate athletic departments in their schools (or to join the men's department). Consequently, the coaches were not always members of the physical education faculty. Even in cases of shared appointments, an individual was typically hired for her coaching competence. Interest in and time for teaching were sources of agitation between the "teaching faculty" and the "coaching staff." Under these circumstances, coaches' jobs depended upon success, and success was typically determined by the won-loss record.

In women's programs, this pattern of separate organization was not totally without precedent. Form the earliest days of sport on campus, the non-instructional programs for women were the responsibility of an association of students, usually a women's recreation association. Intramurals and extramurals were planned by the association. Though under the firm guidance of a faculty advisor from physical education, these activities were peripheral, extracurricular, done without pay or workload credit. In recent times, partially as a product of that earlier organizational structure, the physical education department has tended to lose its grip on the athletic program which typically was housed in and grew from the recreation association.

Coaches, needless to say, banded together for a voice in the athletic area. Athletics were governed by the campus student affairs offices rather than academic administrators. The college president, predictably, designated the athletic director as the voting representative of the institution. The athletic director, as a result of this network of responsibility, was not representing the interests of physical education. Purposes of the two domains differed sharply.

The differences are reflected in other ways. At traditional physical education conventions, young women are noticeably absent. Their loyalties reside with their coaching responsibilities. They are more likely to attend a clinic to enhance their coaching skills than a scholarly conference where the subject matter is increasingly remote from their responsibilities. This era of specialization has divided physical educator from coach, just as physical education itself has become divided into special interest groups. Perhaps there will be some reconciliation as the theorists' and researchers' work is translated for the benefit of practitioners. That time, however, does not seem close at hand.

While the AIAW evolved in some measure to keep the National Collegiate Athletic Association from controlling women's athletic programs, the "evils" of the men's programs, so often cited through the years, were not avoided by the women.

> Originally, we said we would learn from the mistakes the men made and yet, at present, we seem to be rushing headlong down the same primrose path. I am appalled that our desire is only to have what men have: to copy what the men do: I blame the extreme feminists to a large extent. (Ley, 1974:68)

Ironically, the once-conservative physical educators had become standard bearers for the modern women's movement. As a result of a series of laws which affected higher education, women in the work setting and educational opportunity, it was not possible to impose some of the limitations on intercollegiate programs which might have been preferred. Edicts against recruiting athletes, for example, fell victim to the equal opportunity concept. Size of program and funding were guided by implications stemming from Title IX of the Education Amendments Act of 1972. It may have been inevitable, then, that the AIAW would become both the product and producer of liberation and change (Oglesby, 1974:64). It is an odd twist of fate, since women physical educators had been so reluctant to use sport as a model for social change.

Prospectus

Lou Jean Moyer (1977) looked to the future and foresaw the unavoidable necessity of growth and change.

> So where is women's sports headed? Probably toward professionalism, toward excesses, and toward acceptance by our society as a worthy activity for women. We, as educators, will like some aspects and dislike others, but

women will participate, get recognition, and enjoy the freedom of sport participation more than ever before in the history of our country. (1977:52)

Just as the story began, women's intercollegiate athletics are opening new avenues of endeavor and women physical educators are trying to determine how to cope with them. This time, however, it seems that athletics have the upper hand in the struggle. Perhaps they always did.

Notes

1. Though college women were participating in other sports, basketball was chosen as a focus because of its central role in the emergence of controlled competition and intercollegiate sport.

2. For a thorough analysis of the development of standards see Ethel Kesler, "The History of Standards Governing Extramural Competition for Girls and Women from 1932–1953," unpublished master's thesis, Wellesley College, 1953, or Judith Lee Jensen, "The Development of Standards for Women's Athletics and Their Influence on Basketball Competition in the State of New York," unpublished Ph.D. dissertation, The Ohio State University, 1972.

3. Sex segregated departments both validated differences and provided necessary support systems. The author admits to having been socialized under these conditions. Perhaps the turning point came the day a student asked why girls couldn't play fullcourt basketball. Calling upon available research and experience, there seemed to be no reason to restrict movement to half a court in basketball while field hockey players roamed up and down a one-hundred-yard field.

References

A.A.U. delegates differ. The *New York Times,* November 2, 1916, 14.

Aldrich, A. "Reflective thoughts" in *Women's athletics: Coping with controversy.* Washington: American Association for Health, Physical Education, and Recreation, 1974.

Amateur Athletic Union of the United States. *A.A.U. study of effect of athletic competition on girls and women.* New York: Amateur Athletic Union, n.d.

Andersen, R. Don't blame our girls. *The Amateur Athlete,* 1952, *23,* 17.

Andersen, R. Reconciliation. *The Amateur Athlete,* 1953, *24,* 14.

Association for Intercollegiate Athletics for Women. *AIAW handbook, 1978–1979.* Washington: American Alliance for Health, Physical Education, and Recreation, 1978.

Gerber, E., et al. *The American woman in sport.* Reading, Mass.: Addison-Wesley Publishing Company, 1974.

Hill, L.E. *Athletics and out-door sports for women.* New York: The Macmillan Company, 1903.

Jensen, J.L. "The development of standards for women's athletes and their influence on basketball competition in the state of New York," unpublished doctoral dissertation, The Ohio State University, 1972.

Jernigan, S.S. The national institute on girls' sports. *Journal of Health, Physical Education, and Recreation*, 1963, *34*, 8.

Kenyon, G.S. "Explaining sport involvement, with special reference to women" in *Sports and dance in our culture*. Proceedings of the Fall Conference, Eastern Association for Physical Education of College Women, Lake Placid, New York, 1969.

Lambert, C. Pros and cons of intercollegiate athletic competition for women: A middle of the road position paper. *Journal of Health, Physical Education, and Recreation*, 1969, *40*, 75, 77–78.

Lee, M. *Memories of a bloomer girl, 1894–1924*. Washington: American Alliance for Health, Physical Education, and Recreation, 1977.

Lee, M. *Memories beyond bloomers, 1924–1954*. Washington: American Alliance for Health, Physical Education, and Recreation, 1978.

Ley, K. "The changing scene in physical education and athletics" in *The changing scene*. Proceedings of the Annual Fall Conference of the Eastern Association for Physical Education of College Women, Chicopee, Mass., 1974.

Ley, K., & Jernigan, S.S. The roots and the trees. *Journal of Health, Physical Education, and Recreation*, 1962, *33*, 34–36, 57.

Metheny, E. *Connotations of movement in sport and dance*. Dubuque, Iowa: Wm. C. Brown, 1965.

Moyer, L.J. "Women's athletics—what is our future? *Journal of Physical Education and Recreation*, 1977, *48*, 52, 54.

Non-Olympic rule adopted by women. The *New York Times*, January 6, 1929, 4.

Oglesby, C. "Future directions and issues" in *Women's athletics: Coping with controversy*. Washington: American Association for Health, Physical Education, and Recreation, 1974.

Resolutions adopted by the National Association of Directors of Physical Education for College Women, April 29, 1941. In archives of National Association for Physical Education of College Women, University of Illinois.

Scott, P.M. "Intercollegiate sports for women: Present problems and future directions" in *Sports programs for college women*. Washington: American Association for Health, Physical Education, and Recreation, 1970.

Scott, P.M. & Ulrich, C. Commission on intercollegiate sports for women. *Journal of Health, Physical Education, and Recreation*, 1966, *37*, 10, 76.

Spears, B., & Swanson, R.A. *History of sport and physical activity in the United States*. Dubuque, Iowa: Wm. C. Brown, 1978.

Standards in athletics for girls and women. *Research Quarterly*, 1937, 8, 17–72.

Stewart, H.E. The effect on the heart rate and blood pressure of vigorous athletics for girls. *American Physical Education Review*, 1916, *21*, 369–375.

Women's Division, National Amateur Athletic Federation. *Women and athletics*. New York: A.S. Barnes and Company, 1930.

A Political Analysis of the Possibility of Impact Alternatives for the Accomplishment of Feminist Objectives Within American Intercollegiate Sport

Donna A. Lopiano
The University of Texas at Austin

Introduction

Over the past months I have been asked about the role women will play in intercollegiate athletics and more specifically, the role they will play within NCAA. My honest response has been, "I don't know." I don't know whether we know enough yet of this new environment for women's athletics. Although unsure of how best to attack the future, I have developed a plan of sorts, a starting point. Its purpose is to find a place and to create a strategy for dealing with the new realities we are facing and will face.

As with any design for change, one must begin with some assumptions about the nature of reality upon which the design is constructed. The discussion of feminist objectives within intercollegiate sport will therefore begin with my basic assumptions about that reality.

Assumptions

First, the central focus of analysis of the reality we face must be from a "radical" feminist perspective. When I say "radical feminist," I am agreeing with the view that the central issue is male supremacy in the power structure, and perhaps more precisely, male *value* supremacy. With the demise of AIAW's role in intercollegiate sport, almost total control of all organizational structures associated with the development, control and conduct of women's intercollegiate sports rest with a 95 percent male decision-maker system. The value system associated with and promulgated by the NCAA and its con-

An earlier version of this article was presented at the 1982 Women as Leaders in Physical Education Workshop, "Feminism and Sport: Connections and Directions," sponsored by the Department of Physical Education and Dance, University of Iowa.

ference and member institutions supports the commercial enterprise of sport and the economic value of the athlete. I have no problem with the former, but the latter is a 180 degree turn away from values associated with women-centered or feminist sport.

However, it must also be noted that "liberal" feminism's primary focus on the need to work within the system and to debunk mythical sex differences associated with athletic performance should not be discarded. Such reformist efforts are necessary but not primary. These brushfire myths have been initiated by and perpetuated by the male power structure for the sole purpose of confusing, fatiguing and disorienting those women seeking to change that system.

The second assumption is that the connecting force, the glue holding the male dominated sport system together is economic—money. Any plan must therefore attend to defining reality as a socio-economic construct.

Third, the starting point for any feminist strategy, potentially the most powerful tool of change depending on how it is used, is knowledge.

Fourth, any *political* analysis and assessment of options, any plan, must include:

1. A definition of feminist goals and objectives.

2. A realistic critique of past efforts and use of the lessons of history.

3. A critical analysis of the operable male hierarchy: What is the nature of the male power structure? How does it work? Where are we in it?

4. A description of the tools of power, the mechanisms of change that the system itself tells us must be used—and a consideration of other methods or tools which are available. What are they? Can they be used?

5. An identification of individuals and groups of women who must participate in feminist strategies, and the strengths and limitations of those groups.

6. A clear understanding of the probable reaction of the male power structure to feminist strategies.

7. The development of a definitive agenda of process and content for every feminist sub-system or sub-group operating within the system. Yes, we need a grand plan, an overall direction, but it must include the translation of ideas into easy to understand, narrowly defined actions . . . moving from the what and why to the "how to" for individuals with specific occupations and frames of interest in the sport system.

8. The inclusion of a built-in steering mechanism which constantly reevaluates, refines, and possibly redirects the implementation of feminist strategies at all levels.

Finally, no feminist strategy should lose sight of the fact that the majority of women and a not so small group of men in sport have traditionally *RE-JECTED* the supremacy of the male sport value system. There has been and must continue to be a clear rejection of such values *as primary* and an agreement on a value priority which is "feminist" or *"non-gender based."* Such a value priority must be equally applicable to men and women in that it is exploitive of neither.

Let me make one small but important point with regard to our perspective on values. Some feminists argue that we must create a new feminist value system to replace a dominant male value system in sport. I do not subscribe to this view. I believe that feminist values exist and that they are simply oppressed. The male values which we find abhorrent or unacceptable exist and will continue to do so. They will not disappear. In fact, participant exploitive values in sport will constantly tug against any effort to push them down the priority ranking. The real battle is a constant effort to deny supremacy to abhorrent values.

The Plan

This last assumption goes hand in hand with the first step of the development of "The Plan"—What do we want to do? Instead of talking about the need to describe women-centered or feminist sport, please allow me to posit what it is:

1. *All men and women should have the opportunity to explore their physical selves,* to test their abilities and limits over the broadest range and levels of self-chosen physical activities.

2. Sport should be a "means" by which one gets to know oneself, not an end in and of itself. The participant exploits the possibilities of sport, not vice versa. That does not mean that *sport* cannot be exploited, but I am saying that participants *must* not be exploited.

3. The participant's access to the knowledge and ultimate possibilities of sport—their exposure to coaches, their use of sporting equipment, their ability to compete against those of equal or greater skill—should not be limited by gender or race or socio-economic class distinctions. If this appears to be a simple explanation, it is. Sport involves nothing more than propelling an object through space or overcoming the resistance of a mass with various measures of performance (time, distance, accuracy, efficiency, weight or qualitative estimates of grace or aesthetic values) being used to evaluate progress or levels of achievement. The performer, the

spectator, the coach and various other actors or observers bring their own values to a quintessentially meaningless human activity.

Access to a self-chosen sport activity is one problem, one item on the feminist agenda. It will always be a constant problem. The other side of the coin, the second and more critical problem is the primacy of the feminist value system which should be attached to sport. I have defined that value as allowing the *individual* to know his or her physical self in terms of strength, speed, reaction time and, depending on the context of performance, his or her physiological and psychological response to physical stress and to others who are also participating as integral or ancillary elements of the sport experience. Men and women *value* the opportunity to know themselves in such ways. Let me suggest to you that these so-called "feminist" values are inherent in the nature of sport—a given. They are simply not emphasized as primary or most important.

As with most important human pursuits, activities like sport which are valued, have a tendency to become institutionalized, to become highly organized within a social system. They then attract an overlay of values which are important to the society as a whole. It is a given that society's dominant public institutions will inevitably seek to exploit any human activity which is valued—to make money, to retain power, to exercise power over others. No feminist agenda can realistically overcome that cement-encased reality of societal tendency. There will be a constant pull or struggle for the primacy of values between those preferred by the individual and those preferred by the larger society in which the individual exists.

The only alternative therefore, the task before us, is to focus the feminist agenda on allowing the participant to retain control over the meaning of sport to him and her, to retain the primacy of the self-knowledge values and thus resist the exploitive tendencies of the society-at-large.

As another sidelight, I would suggest to you that the fact that much of American amateur sport resides in the institution of education creates a unique leverage. Our society has permitted education in general and higher education in particular to have a degree of license not tolerated in law, politics or economics, to have a vastly different value primacy in many instances. Therefore, sport in education can be a very practical and potentially more profitable focus for feminist intentions.

So let me add a #4 to our description of women-centered feminist sport:

4. The retention of an athlete's right to resist and prevent participant exploitation.

Let me digress once again. The Association for Intercollegiate Athletics for Women (AIAW) was a creation *of women* in sport and physical education, *for women* in sport who desired to explore the potential of their bodies. Whatever might be said in retrospect regarding AIAW's embrace of athletic scholarships or similar trappings of the male athletics establishment, one thing must be acknowledged: AIAW started with and ended with a definitive statement of goals and purposes which was peculiarly "feminist" and which was rejected almost in total by those women and men supporting the male NCAA model.

AIAW's value priorities were:

1. Sport as educational—a "means" to knowing oneself
2. Protection from participant exploitation (athletes' rights)
3. Increase number (level and type) of sport options
4. Increase quality (skill) of sport opportunity
5. Debunk "myths" via visibility of strong, highly skilled female athlete
6. Create capable female leadership
7. Provide current and future career opportunities for women
8. Attack racial exploitation

One example of the struggle concerning participant exploitation is scholarships. AIAW was forced by law to permit the awarding of athletic scholarships to female athletes. Scholarships in the men's model have always been a form of economic exploitation, the establishment of a minimum wage at poverty or below-poverty level for athletes who were directly responsible for making millions of dollars for educational institutions.

It always amazed me that female athletes didn't earn anything for their institutions, and yet, not only did they receive athletic scholarships, but they were also allowed by AIAW to receive more than their male counterparts in the NCAA. Where male recipients were not permitted to work or receive need-based aid in excess of an artificially low limit, women were permitted to do both. While it can be argued that both the AIAW and NCAA sought to economically exploit their athletes, because of the lack of any profit in women's athletics, that argument simply does not hold as much water with regard to AIAW. If anything should be indicative of being on the right track, total male rejection of the AIAW value system is a sign which cannot be ignored.

Whether or not AIAW would have succeeded in resisting athlete exploitation in particular, we'll never know. As the AIAW model developed, those pressures to exploit indeed increased. Whether the resistance of exploitation can be accomplished in the already developed male model in which women now find themselves, is a more important and worthwhile question. I would suggest that this anti-exploitive feminist direction in sport is very on point within the greater context of radical feminism as previously defined: resistance and cessation of male dominance and exploitation of females.

One more digression is required to avoid an interpretation that this feminist direction in sport is too narrow. I find three things very troublesome about the feminist movement:

1. We readily acknowledge that women are having a hard time identifying themselves as feminists. At the same time, everyone I hear defines feminism in an exclusionary manner—on one hand acknowledging that women shouldn't be excluded but immediately following such statements with reaching for academic or theoretical purity of definition which is inherently exclusionary. If we want a basketball coach to be a feminist, to identify with oppression or exploitation of women, we must frame our charge of her responsibility as a woman within her self-chosen area of interest. We must make feminism meaningful. Over 50 percent of our population is female. No narrow interpretation of feminism will permit us to acquire sufficient numbers to overthrow the male establishment. We're fine at finding generals or defining ourselves as generals. We are less successful in recruiting privates, the people who have to hold the line in the trenches when it really counts.

2. We are in a power struggle. Why any feminist would deny the validity of participation in a highly competitive activity that produces strong women who are able to resist oppression or have the guts to uphold principle is beyond me. Sport *itself* is not "bad." The values that men have brought to it and inserted as "primary" are an anathema. Don't discard the baby (sport) with the bath water (exploitive values).

3. To say that reformists cannot be revolutionaries is a self-defeating requirement. The exclusion of any method of change by any one or more individuals is to put all the eggs into one basket and is to give the opposition an easy victory. We need martyrs, revolutionaries, reformists, separatists—anyone that is willing to change the system. The revolutionary makes the reformist more effective, and the martyr makes the revolutionary appear reasonable. Every change strategy must be used. Operating as an athletic director I can use reformist strategies. When I go home I can help female athletes overthrow the system by helping them take legal action against it.

A Look at the Past

We now have a feminist agenda for sport. The next step is to examine the lessons of history. What have women's past actions in sport or in the larger women's movement taught us?

1. By accident or design, women who have been co-opted by the system or at the very least have been participants in a male dominated system (really,

all of us) have had an opportunity to be reformist and at times, even revolutionary. The male sport system has been susceptible to error, especially in terms of doing the right thing for the wrong reason and not realizing what they have done until it is too late.

It is my basic belief that it is only a matter of time before women who have joined the male supremacy construct will find that they have been duped. Sometimes it is that kind of experience which wakes people up and makes them change direction. Never completely write off a woman in power. There will come a time when they will participate as feminists and/or help the feminist cause.

2. The demise of AIAW was inevitable—anything valued by women *and*—not "*or*"—threatening to the dominant power structure will eventually be taken over or destroyed. Everything that AIAW stood for was a threat, an opposite, to existing male practice. While a separatist structure is ultimately more effective and preferable in sport for women, once it becomes effective it is too threatening and must be stopped. In sport, after this AIAW-NCAA battle, it will be quite a while before a separatist national women's sport governance structure will be permitted to exist again. It was a stage of change—not a failure.

3. The tools of change promulgated and promoted by the male system have limited usefulness for women. Traditionally those tools are:

   - money—the system can mobilize more than you can
   - position or status—there are more men in positions of power than women
   - social influence—women aren't allowed in the men's room
   - knowledge—men can successfully attack the credibility of and motive for the use of knowledge—they can deny that truth is truth and get away with it.

That is not to say that these tools cannot be effectively used for short-term goals. They have been assigned, however, for small "non-system treatening" reformist goals. There cannot be a dependence on any one of these tools or solely on all of them. Other tools must be identified.

4. Low keyed, low profile, low visibility tactics are more likely to be successful than high visibility, public controversy issues. When you come out of the forest and lose the protection of the trees, you're a much easier target to hit. When you step out of behind the scenes politics, you have to exist in a high risk arena regarding gains vs. potential losses. Do as much as you can under the table before you lay your cards on top. In other words, be armed with knowledge and have a well planned strategy before attempting change.

5. The male power structure utilizes progressive tactics whenever frontal attacks fail. It specializes in wearing out the opposition with brushfires and "divide and conquer" techniques. Women have not used either very well if at all in the past. We must begin to use them.

6. There is an inherent danger in using the "feminist" label or any label which in and of itself creates heightened sensitivity to change or a defensive reaction to the possibility of change. I wish to make it clear that I am not talking about a policy of "denial." I am talking about an insistence on using non-gender based terms whenever we're in enemy territory or on unsophisticated ground. Allowing the opposition to focus on a label puts you in a "defensive" rather than offensive position and draws attention away from central issues.

These lessons from women's past sport experience are admittedly limited by my own ten years of personal experience in sport politics.

Current Male Hierarchy

Having reviewed some history lessons in women's sports and having outlined some of the plan, let's move to task #3: our need to understand and be able to describe the male intercollegiate sport power structure. I'd like to focus on the dominant national governance construct, the NCAA, which is very similar to conference and individual institutional constructs where total male control is the rule.

This might also be a good time to mention that although this exercise is primarily concerned with intercollegiate sport, the steps in the development of "The Plan" are applicable to all levels of sport, within and outside of educational institutions.

As I mentioned before, attentiveness to the socioeconomic context of the male intercollegiate sport power structure is essential. National athletic governance organizations have three primary functions:

1. to sponsor national championships
2. to promulgate and enforce a system of rules and regulations which ensures the participation of bona fide students and guarantees "fair" competition
3. to act as an agent to obtain both visibility and money for its members.[1]

All of these functions must be viewed first and foremost in an economic context. By providing national championships, the NCAA provides its member institutions with a measure of the success of their athletic programs. This measure, a national ranking for instance, is used to attract spectators (and spectator income), and alumni and friends' donations. It gives schools ammunition which makes it easier and less expensive to recruit blue-chip athletes. It enables institutions to sell their own product on the marketplace (to radio and local TV) in addition to the NCAA's formal agency or middleman assistance. More directly, if there are championship profits, participating institutions may receive a split and the NCAA retains its share of such income (especially from the TV sale of such events) and uses that income to provide across the board member services which have significant value but for which there is no or a minimal below-cost charge.

The second function, promulgation and enforcement of rules and regulations, must be viewed as a double-edged economic sword. First, rules and regulations limit the cost of "playing at" athletics to the institution. It keeps the number of scholarships down and establishes a ceiling on the value of salaries to individual athletes (the athletic scholarship) to below minimum wage, poverty levels and in doing so, is a serious economically exploitive device affecting athletes. Rules limit material benefits to athletes, the cost of recruiting and the number of games that can be played in a season (reduces travel costs, etc.). The transfer rule ties an athlete to an institution for four years, thus limiting the amount an institution has to spend each year to recruit.

On the other side of the coin, the *enforcement* of rules has negative economic consequences. The NCAA penalty system is directly and indirectly economic in nature. Sanctioning a Division I institution by limiting or prohibiting TV appearances can be a $300,000–$500,000 per appearance loss. TV and/or post-season play prohibitions also limit visibility. Loss of such exposure may be the equivalent of losing a million dollar national advertising campaign that puts the name of the institution on the lips of millions of prospective athletes and viewers, affects alumni identification with and contributions to an institution and in the case of smaller institutions, may affect enrollment and the life blood income therefrom.[2]

It is this economic sanction power together with "selective enforcement" which gives the NCAA power hierarchy, not its individual members, almost total control of the organization and its members. In such a system, even those schools which would be willing to support a feminist direction do not have the guts to depart from the party line and risk investigation/economic sanction.

In addition, the NCAA rules system is so complex and ambiguous that few, if any, members believe they haven't committed a violation. The hierarchy's power of interpretation and arbitrary creation of legislation which can circumvent normal legislative process, goes virtually unchallenged for these same reasons.

The third function, commercial agency, is an obvious controlling force. The NCAA football TV package alone will bring in over $250 million in the next four years. Although million-dollar-a-year guarantees to the major Division I powers provide a visible economic control mechanism, this money also finances the NCAA's championship reimbursement; economic services where all Division I, II and III members participating in national championships receive cold cash outlays in the form of travel and possibly per diem reimbursement. Few members, especially in economic hard times, are willing to buck the system and risk losing such benefits.

The NCAA's economic control over its members provides the most pervasive insulation to change. The resulting NCAA environment has not only bred a membership that has become increasingly dependent on the NCAA for economic reasons, but one that is effectively resistant to change. Why bother to chase philosophical windmills as long as big brother takes care of me? Revolution of the masses is difficult if not impossible in good economic times. The economic health of sport is best when the society's economy is at a low ebb and citizens seek entertainment distractions to run away from a depressive reality.

The NCAA has also successfully insulated itself from infiltration by the opposition. Its ruling hierarchy is virtually closed to unscreened, disloyal activists.

COUNCIL
appoints
NOMINATING COMMITTEE
produces
Single slate
(one candidate per office)
for
membership "vote"
to select
COUNCIL
AND OTHER POWERFUL LEGISLATIVE UNITS

The ruling class is self-perpetuating. Even if women were successful in gaining a two candidate elective system, the NCAA staff control of information (knowledge) and excessive agenda volumes would inhibit change agency efforts.

To make matters worse, women have been relegated to 16 percent representation on the NCAA Council, and from 18–24 percent membership on other important NCAA structures—not even enough to block a two-thirds vote. The institutional or member vote via one faculty representative from each member institution is 95 percent male.

As was seen in the AIAW-NCAA controversy, the NCAA's awesome economic power has virtually closed the marketplace to competing governance structures. No other organization has the financial base to compete against

NCAA benefits. The NAIA is allowed to exist at a subsistence level as long as it agrees to limit its program to those programs of no or little economic value.

This, incidentally, is what the NCAA thought AIAW's role should be. The College Football Association (CFA) challenged the NCAA on the issue of the right of individual institutions to televise intercollegiate football game. While they won on the issue of monopoly, these CFA members must still belong to the NCAA for the governance of all intercollegiate sports, including football. In a very real sense, the NCAA provides men's athletics with the necessary facade of educational purpose.

In addition, this athletic governance construct has circumvented the possibility of individual institution protest or the lobby pressures of chief executive officers. No one institution can leave the NCAA without suffering competitively, losing traditional opponents or suffering economic losses. There is no other organization to join. There is no option but the NCAA.

Likewise, chief executive officers are powerless—at least they have been to date. Politically, a wrong move in athletics can mean the demise of a CEO as a result of public wrath and the alumni dollars. It is no accident that the average job span of Division I CEO's and head football coaches is identical—three years. The external value system of the public is dictatorial. In the case of intercollegiate sport, a winning team supersedes any notion of educational value being primary. Few are willing to change the status quo for fear *any* change would damage a winning football team.

This rigidly controlled male construct is duplicated in the smaller athletic conferences and on individual campuses. These male dominated systems have consumed separate women's structures at a deadly pace. The strength of male supremacy in the intercollegiate sport context is awesome. Frontal assaults are, in my opinion, suicidal. Other methods of attack are feasible but their potential effectiveness is yet to be determined and the magnitude of change will most certainly be incremental over a long period of time.

Tools for Change

Now that we have an idea of what we are facing, what tools can we use for our assault on the system? If outright elimination of the system is impossible, can the strength of the system be diminished so that it will be more susceptible to change? Can we hurt the NCAA economically? Unlikely. Can its value system be touched? I say yes—slowly—with great difficulty, probably through actions under the guise of another color, but yes. As I've said before, the removal of athlete exploitation as a primary NCAA value is the feminist challenge. In the past, the NCAA system has shown signs that it will trade off or flex under the criticism of educators but only if there is an assurance that members will retain its economic benefits.

I believe we can count on women to utilize the male recommended tools of change:

- ascending to positions of status and potential power
- controlling some money
- exercising influence in social settings
- using knowledge

Of course, those women embracing the men's model who have compromised or sold out in the AIAW battle will be the first to move in those arenas. That is good. We can patiently wait for the birth of their feminist consciences or at the very least, a helpful reaction because they've been treated unfairly. There will be a time and place when these women will assist in the pursuit of feminist objectives.

As stated previously, I have been disappointed with the lack of effectiveness in using the tool of knowledge in at least a frontal attack sense. I firmly believe we, especially women in academe, need to provide information that we can feed into the power structure through men with selfish interests, strange bedfellows, for the purpose of starting brushfires which will diffuse the current concentrated attention and opposition to anything related to feminist interests. It is basic to a changed structure that women begin to use these tools of divide and conquer and knowledge. It is no accident that a primary tool of control over NCAA members is the withholding of knowledge. It would be most helpful for academics to concentrate on providing politically useful information. It is up to feminist politicians in sport to tell the researcher what type of knowledge we need. Those of us involved in the sport establishment must frame the appropriate questions.

Consciousness-raising tools also need to be considered—but not utilized in a frontal attack sense. But before I speak about that in detail, let me put the last piece of "The Plan" before you.

There are two things that I feel must be done: (1) recruitment of the masses—primarily women but also some men; and (2) the establishment of a steering mechanism to direct the feminist movement in sport from a grass-roots level.

In the past, our small numbers of women generals have been very successful when (1) the opposition has chosen to fight on their narrow battlefield and with their weapons, or (2) when the opposition has defined its issues in such a way as to incite the anger or opposition of the female masses. As soon as the male establishment utilized divide and conquer tactics or tactics like brushfires which prevented the generals from having the time to educate and organize the masses, we lost.

Highly visible frontal attacks are too threatening to be effective. We must therefore work behind the scenes to do the things that must be done. We must

(1) attend to the need to educate the masses to the feminist movement in sport in a very methodical way . . . so the privates are there and ready when the fighting comes down to the trenches and (2) start the process of distracting the opposition through the use of brushfires, diverting their attention from these troublesome women.

With regard to the steering mechanism, we need to establish an underground charged with accomplishing the following:

1. Organizing a network within each of the sub-systems operating in the larger sport system with a narrow agenda for each sub-system, one that is meaningful and "lays the value groundwork," one that defines a woman's responsibility to other women within and congruent with her occupational context (coaches, faculty representatives, administrators, chief executive officers, etc.)

2. Precipitating, in a "catalyst" rather than "direct active" sense, the distracting brushfires and encouraging other guerrilla tactics

3. Setting priorities for slow, calculated value change as opposed to demanding "quantum leaps": determining the agenda for all sport system legislation in addition to the sub-system feminist agenda

4. Deciding when, and for what, the underground should surface

5. Directing the acquisition of knowledge packages to support these efforts

6. Maintaining alliances with the large women's movement in general and similar undergrounds in other fields for the purpose of sharing advice, tactics and providing essential support when feasible—especially when the "generals" without the masses can achieve progress.

In closing, women in collegiate sport must recognize that AIAW was a construct that allowed women to operate from a position of power. Its political significance lay in the fact that for ten years, women controlled the development of their own progress—at least at a national level. Whatever positive thing may be gained for women's sport within the NCAA structure, women looking back in search of lessons from history must recognize that such gains were achieved at a tremendous cost, a return to male supremacy over women in sport.

Although I, and many others, would prefer operating from a position of power via the re-establishment of AIAW, a separatist structure, the solution of the court was not the one we are seeking.

We must prepare for a new reality. Quite honestly, I am almost looking forward to going underground for a while. It has been a long and tiring ten years. In a way, it would be nice to have the time to play and not always to be the so very visible target for the opposition. Having the time to think and to try to increase the sensitivity of those great numbers of women in sport who have not yet defined the basic problem of male dominance and exploitation, nor in any way have identified themselves as feminists, will be functional. We must repair our ranks and create strong soldiers. I think that women in sport need this time and need "The Plan."

Notes

1. This article was written prior to the Supreme Court ruling that NCAA's control of televised intercollegiate football is a violation of antitrust law.

2. The Supreme Court's ruling voided the last two years of the NCAA's football contracts with three television networks, contracts worth about $140 million. The authority of NCAA to impose television sanctions in football on the member institutions is questionable. For more general discussion of the issues raised by the Supreme Court ruling, the reader is referred to the July 1984 issues of the *Chronicle of Higher Education*.

4
Youth Sports

Games provide a way for children to grow up. For decades, we looked at youth sport as an ideal way to structure our children's games. We thought that winning and losing, competition, and camaraderie among teammates would help prepare our children for adult life.

Youth sport has become an enormous enterprise in America. Thirty million school-age youngsters play, 4.5 million coaches guide them, 1.5 million people administer the programs, and up to 100 million parents and relatives become involved in one way or another. Children compete in twenty-five different sports. There are 4-year-olds in hockey leagues and 6-year-olds in mini-bike national championships. With so many activities involved, the enterprise has become very complex.

To witness this complexity, one simply has to go to the nearest Little League or Youth Soccer game. Some parents scream for their child to make "the big play," regardless of whether or not the team does well. The coach, not understanding the values of children but knowing how pro and college coaches work, adopts "the win comes first" models. The children, once thought to receive unmixed blessings from participation, often become victims of that participation.

According to studies, the desire to be a "star" seems to be implanted in children by adults; it is not inherent in young athletes. Some parents want to live vicariously through their sons and daughters, and some coaches have yet other ideas and motives. The effects on children from families with a sound economic base differ from the effects on children who are raised in poverty and are taught to believe that participation in sports may be the only way out of that poverty. The effects are especially devastating on these poor children, who may spend their youth and relinquish their educational opportunities to "escape" unaware of the 12,000 to 1 odds against making it to the pros. (This is discussed further in other chapters.)

Many of our nation's leaders contend that sports prepare our youth—implying *all* of our nation's youth—for successful adulthood in whatever careers they choose. Critics contend, however, that emphasis on sport maintains class status by teaching "appropriate corporate values" to white kids while preparing minorities to remain perpetually an underclass in society.

Kareem Abdul-Jabbar epitomizes the athlete who coped successfully with all the pressures on youth in sport and became a great player and a well-balanced adult. The lead article in this chapter is an excerpt from his book, *Giant Steps* (Bantam Books). The rich material could have been included in the chapters on race and college sport, but because it focuses on Kareem's youth and ends up with his choice of college, I felt it was most appropriate in this chapter on youth. Although the other articles in this book are academic or journalistic in style and Kareem's is not, this single, powerful piece could be the most important work in the collection.

Gai Berlage's article, "Are Children's Competitive Team Sports Teaching Corporate Values?" (*Arena Review*, vol. 6, no. 1), examines elite youth hockey and soccer programs. Through interviews and questionnaires, she found that parents whose children play these two sports are hoping to instill values in their children that will lead to success in the corporate world.

The families studied were overwhelmingly white and middle class. This fact begs for a study geared toward youth basketball and, perhaps, football. Studies of black high school players, for example, have tended to show that the application of sports values in education has dropped with the increasing emphasis on eligibility rather than education.

Still Berlage's results are fascinating. She shows the degree to which families sacrifice their regular lifestyles (dinner hours, vacations, and other family activities) so that their children can compete. The children, age 11–12, had already played 4 to 5 years in organized sports and the fathers hoped that their 11-year-olds would go on to play in high school and in college. The acceptance of the coach as authority figure was universal, thus facilitating acceptance of other authority figures in the future.

The role of the coach in youth sport programs is the subject of concern for Bennett J. Lombardo's article, "The Behavior of Youth Sport Coaches: Crisis on the Bench" (*Arena Review*, vol. 6. no. 1). Lombardo maintains that coaches at this level are unprepared to deal with children, whose desires are primarily for friendship, enjoyment, playing time, and socialization. This is in sharp contrast to the coaches' reasons for participating—generally, winning and developing proficient motor performance. These conflicting goals result in changing motivations for the children, who come to rely on the adult coach while spending an inordinate amount of time on the playing field. One consequence is that the coach's influence eventually extends far beyond the sport itself.

Lombardo analyzes the reasons why the backgrounds of many of the 4.5 million youth sport coaches can be a negative factor for the children they coach. These reasons include a lack of even rudimentary knowledge of the emotional, psychological, social, and physical needs of children and the fact that youth coaches take their leads from adult (college or pro) models, which stress winning over all.

Lombardo concludes with a plan to better prepare youth coaches for their important role with up to 30 million of our nation's young people. Among the things too many coaches are unprepared to recognize are symptoms of "burn-out" and special situations that make young people more prone to injuries, with life-long effects. The burnout syndrome has recently been examined more thoroughly after it was found that a tennis star like Andrea Jaeger was unable to continue her career into adulthood. Also, injuries in young athletes, such as broken bones, can disrupt their growth plate development and affect the length of their arms, legs, and so forth.

Bill Bruns and Tom Tutko helped open the nation's eyes to the potential psychological stress involved in participation in youth sport. This stress can come from fear of injury, from having to demonstrate one's talent before significant others, and from the pressure to win. These authors argue force-fully that one of the aims of youth sport should be to help youngsters "learn to deal with these anxieties in a productive way." Their article, "Dealing with the Emotions of Childhood Sports" (*Arena Review*, vol. 2, no. 1; adapted for the book *Winning Is Everything and Other American Myths*), examines the major areas that can produce stress and provides important suggestions on how parents can best help their children cope.

Excerpt from *Giant Steps*

Kareem Abdul-Jabbar
Peter Knobler

The basketball team went undefeated through the entire '62–63 season. By midwinter I had all the confidence I could handle on the court. Some wins were routine, some hard-fought, and as our reputation developed, other teams came gunning for us. Coach Donohue was emphatic about our not hot-dogging, and as the center of attention, I had to be very careful when to allow my emotion to show in my play. It would have been simple to stuff over everybody, growl at and intimidate our opponents. But, because I was so clearly better than most of the people I was playing against, it seemed unpleasant to shove it in their faces. I had absorbed too much abuse from aggressive strangers to feel comfortable embarrassing anyone else.

But, boy, embarrass me and you were in a world of trouble. There was a lot of fancy maneuvering in those games, and if anyone went out of his way to show me up, then he was going to get his shots thrown off the court or take three straight dunks through his face. I'd dribble the length of the floor and jam it. All Coach Donohue had to do to motivate me was to get me to remember some time I'd been made to look bad in the past. Nasty tongue that he had, he could pick the exact moment we needed some fire and light one under me with a few choice recollections from freshman year. He could make me go nuts. I never quite realized what he was doing; all I knew was that I didn't want to look bad in front of Coach Donohue.

I was an innocent, the kind of idealistic teenager who wants to live in a world where things run the way they should. I was offended by bad calls, or by no calls at all, which is how the officials decided to even things out. I had developed into not only a giant—there were huge guys playing basketball even then, Swede Holbrook types—but an agile and fluid ballplayer. I knew it, they knew it.

But they must have felt I had an unfair advantage because they let me get beat to shit. But I was cool; I didn't complain. I tried to transcend them, to play over their heads.

We clinched the CHSAA Manhattan division by beating defending champions LaSalle at home and met them again in the city championship semifinals. Val Reid gave me the official elbow in the mouth, cut me up until I was tasting my own blood, but we went on and whipped them and then won it all. I got very excited when we finally took the title, but the exhilaration faded within a day. The best awards are the ones you don't expect, and we had peaked too soon. It was good to be city champs, but the feeling after the final was more relief than triumph.

Coach Donohue let me make the rounds when I was chosen to each of the newspapers' All-City teams, and each writer asked the same obvious questions and gawked and made the same cute jokes, the journalistic equivalent of "How's the weather up there?" Was this all there was?

Mr. Donohue was also Power's baseball coach and encouraged me to come out for the team. I had been a pretty good Little League outfielder and pitcher, but by high school I just wasn't interested. My studies had fallen off during basketball season because of the time demands and the pressure. While I would have loved to have played baseball just for fun, winning was running in my blood like a drug, and I didn't want to need that fix all springtime too. . . .

The real world closed in on me real fast when I returned for eleventh grade. On September 15, 1963, while I was attending mass with my mother, the Sixteenth Street Baptist Church in Birmingham, Alabama, was bombed by white folks. Four little black girls were killed. As I watched the ineffectual moral outrage of the black southern preachers, the cold coverage of the white media, and the posturings of the John F. Kennedy White House, my whole view of the world fell into place. My faith was exploded like church rubble, my anger was shrapnel. I would gladly have killed whoever killed those girls by myself. Those red-necked cracker bastards should all die, but I knew in my gut that they would get away with it, that nobody cared about black people except black people, that we needed vigilance and protection. We were alone in a world more hostile than I had been led to believe. Forget about equality by assimilation, harmony through brotherhood, freedom through justice. If they had their way, we'd all be dead. Johnny Harrison, my abandonment at St. Jude's, the trip to North Carolina—these weren't isolated incidents; this was the way the world worked, and I had better get used to it. We had no allies. The government couldn't care less; behind the pious pronouncements from Washington and the local law-enforcement communiques, it was obvious that the identity of the killers was common knowledge, and no white folks were talking. Until thirty years before that, they'd been lynching black people in Alabama; did anyone really expect the state troopers to set the dogs on a few rambunctious good ol' boys who just blew a couple of blacks up? Who's to say they weren't involved already? The liberals had money but no power, and it wasn't their ass on the line, so how far could you trust them. God certainly wasn't stepping in; they'd just bombed His house! . . .

Power was overflowing with white kids and, while they were mostly just acceptable, they weren't bastards. The teachers weren't venal, only unenlightened. There was some discussion of current events, but it was academic and carefully distant. While I was connecting directly with Birmingham and Bull Connor and billy clubs, no one else seemed to be taking anything personally, as if nothing were really in one's own control. Power was an institution run on misplaced faith—in God, the government, the administration, the faculty— and, though I couldn't articulate it at the time, the school encouraged a terrible sense of futility. As a student, if you were looking for inspiration, advice, or action, you had to trust in a tight Chain of Command with you at the bottom. Your life was taken out of your hands. You were the last one approached, and you were never consulted, you were told.

They weren't telling me what I wanted to hear. At Power it was more important to march in the Columbus Day parade than to demonstrate for equal rights. At first I spoke up in class, created opportunities to discuss what was important to me. But nobody really wanted to get into it, and soon I simply kept my ideas to myself and started the long walk through high school.

Junior year is dead center, all the way in and halfway out, and the scramble for college was on. My grades were good and my education was important to me, so I started talking to Coach Donohue about where I might go from here. Letters from colleges and universities had begun arriving in ninth grade and by junior year there was a deluge, all correspondence handled by Mr. Donohue. He received everything that came for me at school, and all mail on academic letterhead that showed up at my house was forwarded to him unopened. High school was getting old, and I was always after the coach about my future.

"Lew, don't worry," he'd tell me, "you can go to any school you want to."

"Did Harvard write me a letter?" I'd ask. I never saw any of the mail; it was like getting love letters and not being able to read them.

"Don't bother about who's written the letters," Mr. Donohue would say. "Any school you want to go to, you can go to."

For a while I was excited and proud—I can go to college anywhere!—but soon even that faded. I still had two years of high school to sit through.

The basketball team continued undefeated. Thirty straight, thirty-five, forty. The team was solid, good shooting, tight defense. I enjoyed rebounding even more than scoring, demonstrating with every snatch, with every rejection, that I was not one of these Negroes who was going to be pushed around. We went out to win each game, and we had some scares. Mr. Donohue was teaching us and cajoling us, but mostly he kept on our backs, and practices were, if anything, more intense because he had to maintain our motivation. He didn't want us taking anything for granted.

But one winter afternoon we were ragged. We were at home against St. Helena's, a Catholic high school from the Bronx, and though we were definitely out of their league and should have been whipping them by twenty, minimum, we were sluggish and only up by six at the half. I was playing badly, one of those lousy games when for no good reason nothing goes right and there doesn't seem to be much you can do about it. I may have been keyed up for our next game, against DeMatha, one of the best high school teams in the country, two days ahead down in Maryland. They were excellent, and we'd have to be tough to beat them. So maybe St. Helena's was an annoyance, and I was trying to ignore them as one might walk through a cloud of flies.

We trooped out the east end of the gym, down the drafty stairwell to the next landing. There was a big crowd, as usual, and you could hear the subdued buzzing as students stretched and wondered at the boring game. I ducked my head to get inside the locker room and again as the team was ushered into Mr. Donohue's office. Outside it was getting dark, and our heat started to fog over the grilled windows as the team stood around, some of us sitting on the beat-up wooden chairs and filing cabinets in the close little room. I sat, weary and distracted, as the coach closed the door with his left hand and the latch snapped.

Mr. Donohue was in a rage, storming from wall to wall. We're terrible, we don't deserve to win this or any other game, we're asleep, we're a disgrace. And then he pointed at me.

"And you! You go out there and you don't hustle. You don't move. You don't do any of the things you're supposed to do. You're acting just like a nigger!"

No! I looked up at him, my eyes burning. The word jumped at me like lasers. He couldn't have. I knew this man; he didn't say that. Donohue kept berating me, then moved on to the rest of the squad.

I don't remember the rest of the game. We won, and I'm told I played well. When I got back to the locker room, before I could strip off my uniform and be scorched or soothed by a shower, Donohue called me into his office alone.

"See," he said happily, "it worked! My strategy worked. I knew that if I used that word, it'd shock you into a good second half. And it did." He kept talking, about DeMatha and determination and playing up to my potential, but I just sat there watching my sweat drip onto the dust balls. I knew what he'd been trying to get at. He meant I'd been playing lazy and slow, like something and someone I didn't want to be. But was that what he thought of blacks? Was I shiftless, too, couldn't be trusted with the game? Didn't I smile enough fo' de fans? Should I be twirling the basketball like an ol' watermelon? Mr. Donohue! I sat in his office wondering, Am I here all alone?

We had to leave for Maryland right after the game, but when I hurried home to pack I told my parents. My father was upset; my mother was livid. I wanted to leave Power that day. Talked about transferring to the Hill School over the weekend, or tossing it all in and going to George Washington High School in the neighborhood and just partying until college. But I couldn't transfer without my parents' permission and without losing a year of eligibility, and though my mother was outraged, she didn't want me being left back a year, or spending two more semesters playing basketball when I could be on my way to college. I was trapped. No apology was acceptable, no moment at Power tolerable, yet I was faced with another year and a half before I could get out.

Word traveled fast. In the Power hallways everyone was talking about what Mr. Donohue called Lew. It was 1964, and black people weren't above using the term, but usually as a fraternal symbol and never in front of white folks. It had never intruded here where I spent so many hours, so many days. How could I live with it every day? Usually we'd joke about the names the coach called us. Not this time. I never said anything more about it to the coach. What could I say?

We went down and beat DeMatha and everybody else they threw at us. We won the city championship for the second straight year and were voted the number one Catholic high school team in the country. I made All-City and All-American again. Only a year to go. . . .

I felt strange heading back to high school that fall of 1964. . . . The Power team continued undefeated; classes were just classes; I'd seen my name in print enough so that the thrill of publicity had been blunted, and I wasn't talking to the press because all they would have wanted was, Where are you going to college? and I just didn't know.

It is always nice to be in demand, but I didn't have a lot of respect for the people who wanted me, and that took the edge off the adulation. My summer of blackness had made me even more wary of strangers, and most of the new people I would have to be meeting were white. I maintained my school friendships, and once in a while I would go downtown and party with some white people Kelly knew, but for the most part I wasn't very interested in meeting strangers, especially white strangers. I spent the autumn studying where I could be next year at this time. I was looking forward, nothing to be learned from looking around. Though I was quite literally pondering my future, my life was effectively on hold. . . .

I wanted to play good, winning basketball at an institution that treated its athletes with an element of dignity, under a coach whom I could respect. I wasn't looking to turn anyone's program around, to save anything or anybody. I didn't want to be the first black athlete at a school, or the last. And I wanted someplace that was fun. I was looking to get out of the house and stay out. . . .

As national champions, Power was the team everyone in the Catholic leagues keyed on. Teams who tried to run with us, we outran; teams who tried to shut us down, we either beat with outside shooting or got the ball in to me for the easy two. We hadn't lost since the end of my freshman year, though we'd had some close calls, and most games we played with the good intensity high schoolers give to their closed universe. Coach Donohue stayed on our backs, though he had become just a little gun-shy with me, and we kept on winning. . . .

What can a teenager really tell about a school from a letter full of superlatives and a four-color brochure? It's amazing to me that high school kids manage to make their choices at all; what it comes down to is a close analytical reading of advertising copy. I read what was presented, looked at the standings, asked around, and finally narrowed the field. My final four were distilled to the University of Michigan, Columbia, St. John's, and UCLA.

Michigan was a large school in an industrial state with a developing black presence. The university was placed in an urban setting without being grim, and there were plenty of black guys to hang around with. The perks that were hinted at sounded promising, and with Cazzie Russell making a lot of noise, the basketball program was in full swing. I had a good time on my visit there and thought about Michigan hard.

Columbia was New York. My father had gone to Juilliard and I kind of liked the continuity of our both being taught in and by the city. I could live near the campus which, at 116th Street and Broadway, was within walking distance of Harlem and only a subway ride from every jazz club I'd ever had to leave early. It was Ivy League and had that aura of hip, horn-rimmed cool—the Miles Davis of the education world—that would have told everyone, without their asking, that not only was this guy big but he was smart. I could see myself ambling the campus in a tweed jacket with suede elbow patches, puffing thoughtfully on my pipe, humming "Straight, No Chaser" on my way to sociology class.

Unfortunately, the Columbia basketball program wasn't happening. They'd had losing seasons several years running but were beginning a new push. They recruited intensely, and their effort paid off nicely when Haywood Dotson and Jim McMillan chose Columbia a year later, but, much as I loved the idea of living the New York life, I finally decided to add my assets to a winner.

St. John's did a lot of winning, largely because of its coach, Joe Lapchick. I'd known his son, Richie, at Donohue's camp, and since I liked Richie I had to like his father. Joe Lapchick had played for the original Celtics and coached the Knicks and St. John's, and won everywhere he'd been. He knew basketball inside and out, fundamentals, strategy, the psychology of winning; his teams were adaptable and aggressive and smart. And he was an honorable man, I could just tell. He liked young people and set a hell of an example. There was a unique charisma about Coach Lapchick that I responded to the first time we met.

After a very short while, meeting with even the limited number of recruiters Coach Donohue permitted access to me. I became quite adept at intuiting out the phonies, the guys who had dollar signs or championship rings spinning in their eyes. Everyone I met with talked about how their concerns were for me and my education and my progress, but I knew quickly who was jive; it was someting in the tone of voice—overstated authority or an air of desperation—and in the muscles at the side of the mouth that would pinch when I asked them about black players. But Coach Lapchick had obviously given some serious thought to me personally. He was the first man to put in words for me how the world alienates tall people. They expect more from a giant, he told me; they scale up their demands. You are larger than life and therefore less affected by it, as if it took more noise to get your attention or more pain to hurt you.

Joe was from New York, six feet five inches tall, a son of immigrants, and in his neighborhood full of newly arrived, rather diminutive people from Czechoslovakia, Yugoslavia, and southeastern Europe, he was a freak. "I'd go places," he told me, "and people would stare and say, 'Look, a gypsy!'" He proved right away that not only was his heart in the right place but he and I had the kind of simpatico I truly needed.

There were other good reasons for me to go to St. John's. By scoring well on a daylong, statewide scholastic examination, I had won a New York State Scholarship, so that was $265 a month the state would give me on top of my basketball scholarship—I would have my own cash at last. Sonny Dove, whom I had played against in high school and become friends with, was at St. John's, so I would have immediate connections and no problems making friends. Johnny Graham was there on a music scholarship, and lots of black kids from Manhattan and Brooklyn went to St. John's, so I could definitely hang out.

But there were debits. St. John's was a Catholic school and I had had enough Catholic school. My mother, so close, would have kept after me about church and studies and just about everything else. In fact, St. John's was so close that I could have lived at home, which was not at all what I had in mind. That was one argument I would rather not have. Maybe I should just go far away.

Ultimately, St. John's eliminated itself. Coach Lapchick turned sixty-five, the school's mandatory retirement age. I had the sense that he would have liked to stay on, that basketball was in some way not only his pleasure but his sustenance, but he had been in college ball for almost twenty years and wouldn't fight the rule that retired him. He did go out in glory, however, winning both the Madison Square Garden Holiday Festival over Christmas and, that spring in his final game, the National Invitational Tournament.

But I had considered St. John's because of Coach Lapchick, and without him the school lost much of its appeal. Then I went and visited the University of California at Los Angeles, and that settled that.

UCLA was gorgeous. They showed me a twenty-minute walk I'd have across campus to my classes, and I saw that, if I wanted, I could stroll the whole way on fresh green grass. It was sunny and warm and open, and I couldn't imagine why anyone would willingly live anywhere else. Seemed like it was always springtime there, people in shorts moving from class to class like a fashion model parade, more pretty girls within arm's reach than I'd see all summer cruising the walkways of Central Park. Did I have to go back to the guys at Power? Couldn't I just stay here now?

I was shown around campus by Edgar Lacy, who was a starting forward on the UCLA team. I had met Edgar my sophomore year when we were both high school All-Americans and made one of those thirty-second, "And now on our big stage" group appearances on *The Ed Sullivan Show*. We had become friends then, and as Edgar pointed out the sights and laughed when I gawked at the ladies, he also gave me the lowdown on what UCLA was really like. The campus was cool; black guys hang together but the whites were okay; there was no problem in that area. Things were made comfortable for you—there were ways of finding more than the bare necessities of life—but not palatial. And you *would* work on your game.

The basketball inducements were not to be ignored, either. UCLA had just won the national championship for the second time in a row. The players themselves had become campus heroes. Pauley Pavilion, a mammoth new athletic arena that could hold 13,000 screaming Bruin fans, had already been erected and was standing there waiting for its convocation.

The construction of Pauley Pavilion had uprooted the athletic department from its old haunts and temporarily relocated it in one of a series of Quonset huts that occupied the campus like a bivouac. The buildings were drab affairs not made any more attractive by even the slightest attempt to decorate them, and what was impressive about the place was the complete ordinariness of it all—national champions tucked among the file cabinets. If there was some price in accomplishments around here, I thought as I looked at the cubicles, it certainly wasn't external.

But most of all, what UCLA offered was John Wooden. Coach Wooden's office was about the size of a walk-in closet. I was brought in, and there was this very quaint-looking midwesterner, gray hair with a part almost in the middle of his head, glasses on. I'd heard a lot about this man and his basketball wisdom, but he surely did look like he belonged in a one-room schoolhouse. He stood up, shook my hand, and invited me to sit down.

He was quiet, which was a relief because so was I. I am a great believer in my own snap judgments, and I am quick to find major fault in minor offenses, particularly in strangers who need me, but I found myself liking Mr. Wooden right away. He was calm, in no hurry to impress me with his knowledge or his power. He could have made me cool my heels, or jumped up and been my buddy, but he clearly worked on his own terms, and I appreciated that in the first few moments we met. His suit jacket was hanging from a peg on the wall, and he was working in shirt-sleeves, casual but not far from decorum. He called me Lewis, and that decision endeared him to me even more; it was at once formal, my full name—We are gentlemen here—and respectful. I was no baby Lewie. Lewis. I liked that.

There was a plainspokenness to Mr. Wooden, a distance from cynicism that my own teenage idealism responded to, and rather than gloss over the possible conflicts that might dissuade a recruit from deciding on the school, he told me what they expected from people at UCLA.

"We expect our boys to work hard and do well with their schoolwork," he told me in his flat yet not uninviting midwestern twang, "and I know you do have good grades so that should not be a problem for you. We expect you to be at practice on time and work hard while you're there. We do not expect our boys to present any disciplinary problems, but, again, we know you're not that kind of young man, and I don't expect you will have any difficulty here at UCLA.

"You've seen the campus. Do you have any questions?"

"I like the campus very much," I told him, "and I am very impressed with UCLA's basketball program."

"That's all very good," Coach Wooden said, "but I am impressed by your grades. You could do very well here as a student, whether you were an athlete or not. That is important. We work very hard to have our boys get through and earn their degrees. I hope all my student-athletes can achieve that. It is to both our benefits; your being a good student will keep you eligible to play in our basketball program, and your degree will be of value to you for the rest of your life."

I made a point of talking with all the coaches who recruited me about topics other than basketball. These were men, one of whom might have a profound effect on the course of my life, and I wanted to be as certain as I could that, basketball aside, I did not misjudge them. Again, Coach Wooden came through as a well-read, genuinely caring man. People would always tell me that they cared about me, but I felt Mr. Wooden really meant it. I came out of his office knowing I was going to UCLA.

Are Children's Competitive Team Sports Teaching Corporate Values?

Gai Ingham Berlage
Iona College

Since World War II children's play has been transformed from informal games to highly organized sporting events. Adults now organize and direct most sports programs for children from Little League baseball to youth soccer. Today these programs mirror professional teams. Each team has a coach, a manager, uniforms and an official schedule. Scoreboards, official league standings, tournaments now determine success. Trophies and newspaper coverage signify winners. The play ethic associated with children's games of playing to have fun, to relax, to let off steam has shifted to teaching skills, to developing character, to developing scholarship winners and professionals. Children's sports resemble more and more training grounds for the adult world and for business than games for fun. Beisser, for example, sees sports as a useful bridge between child play and adult work.

> Work has already lost many of its traditional characteristics and so has play. Play has become increasingly transformed into organized sports, and sports, in turn, increasingly resemble work in the arduous practice and preparation they require, in the intense involvement of coaches and athletes in the spirit of work. . . . (1973:94–95)

Today, sports may serve to socialize children in values, attitudes and behavior suited to corporate jobs. Several organizational studies on women in corporations suggest this. They cite women's lack of experience with team sports as one reason why they have not been more successful in the corporate world. Harragan, for example, discusses the similarities between the corporate group and the competitive sport team. She explains why men's participation in team sports socialized them for the corporate world.

Excerpt from paper, "Are Children's Competitive Team Sports Socializing Agents for Corporate America?" presented at North American Society for the Sociology of Sport, 2nd Annual Meeting, Forth Worth, Texas, November 12–15, 1981.

The traditional boy's games are far from pointless childish pursuits. They are training grounds for life, preparation for adult imperatives of working with others, practical education for the discipline of business. The most popular games of baseball, football, and basketball are all team sports, and a structured, organized team is a well-defined social unit. . . . each player knows exactly what his duties are and how they dovetail into operations of the rest of the team . . . and each player knows that he has to perform smoothly and cooperatively with the others if he wants to retain his place on the team. If there's a conflict between individual glory and the greater glory of the team, then personal virtuosity must be sacrificed. (1977:50)

Various sociologists such as Edwards, Page and Schafer have commented on the role of sports as a socializing agent for American society.

. . . the social world of sport, although clearly distinguishable, is an inseparable part of the larger society; its cultural characteristics reflect the more inclusive culture and in turn, help to shape society's standards and style of life. (Page, 1973:35)

However, traditional American values as expressed in the Protestant Ethic may have changed to what Whyte in the 1950s called the "social ethic." The social ethic according to Whyte could also be called an organization or bureaucratic ethic. The social ethic has three main propositions: "a belief in the group as a source of creativity; a belief in 'belongingness' as the ultimate need of the individual; and a belief in the application of science to achieve the belongingness" (1957:7).

Scott and Hart in 1979 state that a new "organizational imperative" has replaced the Protestant Ethic of the past.

The organizational imperative, while originally a subset within the context of the overarching social value system, has now become the dominant force in the homogenization of organizational America, displacing the more individualistic values of the past. (52)

Margolis in her study of corporate managers in one community also emphasizes how corporate values are affecting the whole community and not just those employed by the corporation. "Giant corporations appear to be setting the style and dictating the terms of life for those they do not employ almost as much as they do for those in their pay" (1979:267).

Today American cultural values have become more and more oriented to a corporate economy and the values of children's organized team sports may reflect these changes. Competitive team sports may have become socializing agents for corporate America.

This research was designed to explore the question: Are the values of children's competitive team sports programs similar to corporate values?

Method

Data was based on examining the organization of children's soccer and ice hockey organizations in the Connecticut and New York metropolitan area. Information is based on observations, interviews and responses to questionnaires from 222 fathers with sons on soccer and ice hockey travel teams.

The reason why questionnaires were distributed to fathers of elite or travel team players was that it was felt that if the values of competitive team sports are similar to corporate values that they would be most salient at the highest levels of competition.

The hockey sample consisted of fathers who had sons competing in the Pee Wee Level Division III Connecticut State Tournament. The Pee Wee division is comprised of boys ages 11 through 12 years. All fathers of participants were asked to fill out questionnaires. No one refused to participate. However, some boys' fathers were deceased, divorced or unable to attend the tournament and therefore, responses were collected from 107 fathers.

The soccer sample consisted of fathers who had sons competing in a local Connecticut soccer tournament. Teams were drawn from communities in New York and Connecticut which are part of the New York metropolitan area. The teams were comprised of boys ages 11 through 12 years. As with the hockey sample, all fathers of participants were asked to fill out the questionnaires. 115 fathers completed questionnaires.

Although the fathers represent all educational and occupational levels, the majority would be classified as middle class. This is probably the result of two factors: one the nature of the socio-economic backgrounds of people living in the New York metropolitan area and in Connecticut and two, the high cost of participating on a travel team. Similar research should be conducted with a more working class population.

Results

Fathers' of soccer travel team players were asked to check off the three attributes that sports develop that they thought would be most important for a youth to develop to be successful in business. The most important attributes according to these fathers were teamwork and self-discipline. 67% of the fathers selected teamwork and 62%, self-discipline from the list of ten items.

Hockey fathers were also asked to list the three attributes that sports develop that they considered the most important. The words for business were not included. Teamwork was listed by 71% of the fathers and self-discipline by 61%.

Teamwork was a central theme of the fathers. No one spoke of making a star, but rather that the group effort was more important. This value is congruent with Whyte's notions about the "social ethic." Whyte stated: "The man of the future, as junior executives see him, is not the individualist, but the man who works through others for others" (1957:21).

Whyte also stresses the importance of self-discipline in the "new" corporate ethic.

> As organization men see it, through an extension of the group spirit, through educating people to sublimate their egos, organizations can rid themselves of the tyrants and create a harmonious atmosphere in which the group will bring out the best in everyone. (1957:54).

The top two values that the majority of fathers considered important for their sons to learn from playing on a team (teamwork and self-discipline) are the same two that Maccoby describes as central to the new corporate top executive.

> The new corporate top executive . . . is a team player whose center is the corporation. . . . Thus he thinks in terms of which is good for the company, hardly separating that from what is good for himself. . . . He has succeeded in submerging his ego and gaining strength from his exercise in self-control. (1977:41)

The new leader of corporate America according to Maccoby is not the jungle-fighter, industrialist of the past who was driven to build and preside over empires but rather the man who is a good team organizer (1977, p. 24).

Coaches, too, want dedicated team players, not individualistic stars. Players that don't conform and don't submit to practice schedules, team assignments and who don't get along with team members are dispensable. No one is indispensable. If the youth isn't totally dedicated to the team effort, he can be replaced.

As the coach emphasizes the need for the child to totally commit himself to the team and to be loyal and dedicated to the team, so does the corporation. As Whyte states: "Social ethic (corporate ethic) rationalizes the organization's demands for fealty and gives those who offer it wholeheartedly a sense of dedication in doing so" (1957:6).

As corporations demand total commitment to the organization on the part of the worker, travel team coaches constantly stress the importance of the child's total commitment to the team. Practices and games take precedence over family dinner hours, family activities and other social events. As with the corporate man, the company comes first and dominates his life, the team comes to dominate the child's. As wives and children learn that the husband often has to work late or travel on business trips and misses family and school occasions and they have to mold their schedule around the husband, the family also molds their schedule around the travel team player. Many parents of travel team players for both hockey and soccer reported that the child's participation interfered with dinner, vacations, family activities and even with school.

84% of soccer fathers said soccer interfered with dinner hours. 46% said it interfered with family vacations, 77% said it disrupted family activities and 16% even said it interfered with school.

Hockey fathers reported similar accounts. 80% said hockey interfered with dinner hours, 44% with family vacations, 72% with family activities and 28% with school.

One may wonder why parents let their children's sports interfere with family activities. But the reasons are similar to why company men let the corporation interfere with their family life. Being on a travel team is prestige conferring for the child and his family. As social prestige for the father revolves around this work, for the child social prestige at school and in the community often is a product of his sports participation (Gordon, 1981; Coleman, 1961). As families often bask in the reflected status of the corporate husband, parents bask in the reflected status of having an athletic son or daughter.

Another reason parents may want their child to participate on the travel team is that they may see this participation as the first step toward an amateur sports career. For example, in the hockey sample 94% of the fathers hoped that their sons would play high school hockey and 86% college hockey. For soccer fathers, it was 99% for high school soccer and 95% for college soccer.

If one doesn't allow his son or daughter to meet his or her commitment to the team, some other parent will and their child will be dropped. Control by the coach is maintained much the same way a boss maintains control in a corporation, one can be fired or let go.

In interviews with parents, parents would often comment on how they planned family activities on weekends around the child's travel games. Several commented on how they took their sons to visit relatives out of state and how they had asked the coaches' permission. No one expressed the idea that family trips even at Thanksgiving or Christmas took precedence over travel games.

The coach as boss, mentor and arbitrator of values has become a dominant figure in the eyes of his team and their parents. A child learns that loyalty and devotion to the team is important and he becomes proud to be associated with and known as a member of a particular team. Team membership becomes a part of his self-identity. Commitment and loyalty to a team is similar to loyalty to a company.

As a child knows that a coach's command is to be obeyed, so does a corporate person know that the order of a superior is to be obeyed. At an early age, these team players learn to accept an authoritarian structure and to learn that a team is not a democratic organization. Even parents, as was noted before, grant and accept the coach's authority since it is the coach who determines who plays, how long one plays and what position.

As Al Rosen has stated about organized youth sports, "Organized sports are not democratic nor should they be. They teach respect for authority, discipline, and the individual's role in a group activity" (1967:26).

The emphasis on teamwork, obedience, and dispensability in sports are some of the same values that Scott and Hart speak of when they discuss the changes in American values from that of the Protestant Ethic to that of the "organizational ethic or imperative." The change in values has been "from innate human nature to malleability, from individualism to obedience; from indispensability to dispensability; from community to specialization; from spontaneity to planning; from voluntarism to paternalism" (1979:53).

These changing values are evident in business as well as team sports. The concept that athletes are made not born is widely accepted today. The malleability of the individual or athlete is what training is all about. Good training, good coaches, hard work and dedication make a winning player and winning team.

At earlier and earlier ages youth in sports are asked to specialize not only in a particular sport but in a particular position. By age 8 in both ice hockey and soccer, travel team players are designated as defensemen or forwards. These positions become more and more fixed as the youth move up through the league.

Specialization by boys is evident in both the hockey and soccer samples. In the hockey sample, the mean age that boys started playing in an organized program was age 6½. These boys by Pee Wee level, ages 11–12, had been playing an average of 4½ to 5½ years. They were already veterans on the ice. In order to further perfect their skills, 70% of the fathers planned on sending their sons to summer hockey camp.

For soccer, the findings were similar except that soccer has both a Fall and Spring season in the Connecticut and New York area. So soccer youth have more months of organized play than do hockey players. Still 45% of fathers of soccer players planned on sending their sons to summer soccer camp. The mean age that boys began playing organized soccer was 7 years.

"Sport is ideologically bolstered by the performance principle, a principle which suggests that athletes are recruited and maintained on the basis of their merits" (Ingham, 1975:363).

American businesses or corporations also operate on the "performance principle." Both the businessman and the athlete must play by the rules to win whether it be winning a game or an economic profit. However, the ideal and the reality are not always synonymous. The ideology is to play by the rules.

However, as Brower states when discussing the professionalization of organized youth sports, the reality of the situation is:

> using all "reasonable" tactics to win. Getting away with undetected rule infractions and taking advantage of an umpire's mistake has become institutionalized as "part of the game." (1979:44–45)

Business tactics also include being shrewd and taking advantage of a competitive situation. The rules can be bent if one makes a profit, the belief being that if you don't take advantage of the situation, the competition will.

Competition in business and in youth sports sometimes gives rise to politics. Ideally, the selection process for making the team is based purely on performance. For the majority of youth this is probably the case, however, favoritism sometimes exists whether it be the coach's child or that of a large contributor. Favoritism also exists at times in business with "the boss's son." The expression "It's not what you know, but who you know" although not the case most of the time, has some basis in reality.

When fathers were asked if the selection process for travel teams was based on skills, politics and skills, or politics, 39% of the soccer fathers and 51% of the hockey fathers said politics and skills.

One hockey father made this rather pessimistic comment about what he thought youth learned from competitive hockey.

> We think that instead of providing a focus for development and happiness during the important years between eight and twelve, youth hockey quickly became a harbinger of events that probably would occur in adult life. (Politics, the best man doesn't always get the job, etc.)

On the whole, fathers held positive attitudes toward competitive youth sports. The majority of both hockey and soccer fathers believed that their son's playing competitive sports would be an advantage to their child in later years in a business career. 93% of hockey fathers and 88% of soccer fathers believed that a boy has an advantage in business if he has played competitive sports. When fathers were asked why they thought sports were important, the majority emphasized teamwork, competitiveness and tenacity.

Fathers' beliefs that sports foster values and skills that are important in the business world are supported by testimonials of famous Americans and even sociologists. The following examples are found in Tutko and Bruns' book, *Winning Is Everything*.

Sociologist David Riesman: "The road to the board room leads through the locker room." (1976:41)

Gerald Ford: "Broadly speaking, outside of a national character and an educated society, there are few things more important to a country's growth and well-being than competitive athletics." (1976:42)

All the evidence seems to point to the fact that children's competitive team sports are socializing agents for corporate America. From testimonials to corporate studies, athletes are shown to have advantages in business careers.

The research in this study of children's soccer and ice hockey associations supports the view that the attitudes, values and skills inculcated in the training of team athletes more and more mirrors the corporate structure, its values and ethic. From observations and interviews, it appears that parents and coaches accept and want their children to be socialized in these values. These values are now seen as basic to American society.

References

Beisser, Arnold
    1973 "Modern Man and Sports," pp. 85–86 in J. Talamini and C.H. Page (ed.), *Sport and Society: An Anthology*. Boston: Little, Brown.

Brower, Jonathan
    1979 "The Professionalization of Organized Youth Sport: Social Psychological Impacts and Outcomes." *Annals, AAPSS*, 45:39–46.

Coleman, James
    1961 *The Adolescent Society*. New York: Free Press.

Gordon C. Wayne
    1981 *The Social System of High School*. Glencoe, Ill.: Free Press.

Harragan, Betty
    1977 *Games Mother Never Taught You: Corporate Gamesmanship for Women*. New York: Rawson.

Ingham, Alan
    1975 "Occupational Subcultures in the Work World of Sport," pp. 337–389 in D. Ball and J. Loy (ed.), *Sport and Social Order: Contributions to the Sociology of Sport*. Reading, Mass.: Addison-Wesley.

Maccoby, Michael
    1977 *The Gamesman: The New Corporate Leaders*. New York: Simon and Schuster.

Margolis, Diane
    1979 *The Managers: Corporate Life in America*. New York: Wm. Morrow.

Page, Charles
    1973 "Pervasive Sociological Themes in the Study of Sport," pp. 14–37 in J. Talamini and C.H. Page (ed.), *Sport and Society: An Anthology*. Boston: Little, Brown.

Rosen, Al
    1967 *Baseball and Your Boy*. New York: World.

Scott, William and Hart, David
    1979 *Organizational America*. Boston: Houghton Mifflin.

Tutko, Thomas and Bruns, William
    1976 *Winning Is Everything and Other American Myths*. New York: Macmillan.

Whyte, William H., Jr.
    1957 *The Organization Man*. Garden City, N.Y.: Doubleday Anchor.

The Behavior of Youth Sport Coaches: Crisis on the Bench

Bennett J. Lombardo
Rhode Island College

Recent estimates have placed the number of American boys and girls, 6–16 years of age, participating in agency-sponsored and school sports programs as high as thirty million (Martens, 1978). While the lay public is elated about such involvement, the consequences of participation in organized sport depend upon several factors, including the organizational nature of such programs, the adult supervision, and the personal characteristics of the athlete.

The critical variable in organized sport is the quality of the adult leadership. While authorities consistently emphasize the centrality of the coach in this experience (Smoll and Smith, 1981; Feltz, 1978; Coleman, 1974), there is a scarcity of information regarding coaching behavior, especially in the nonschool setting. Questions related to the competence of the coaches in youth leagues remain unresolved. This article will attempt to address this issue, specifically, the behavior of youth sport coaches.

An overwhelming majority of the approximately 4.5 million youth sport coaches (Simon, 1979) are not prepared for the often highly charged, pressurized arena of organized sport, however unselfish and well-intentioned their motives may be. Aside from a history of participation and/or a strong interest in the activity itself, little is known about the qualifications of volunteer coaches. Yet, many leagues are totally dependent upon volunteers and, short of being a convicted felon, all are welcomed! In most cases, each of these volunteers, whatever their preparation, is given full discretionary power in the organization and administration of the activities of the team. In effect, the youth league coach is the major determinant of the youth league experience, often the young athlete's first.

Surprisingly, while participation continues to increase dramatically, there is little that can be stated about coaching behavior with confidence, and even less attention has been devoted to its analysis. Recent literature has noted the powerful impact youth sport programs and coaches have on the participants (Coleman, 1974; Feltz, 1978; Purdy et al., 1981). Several investigators have indicated that many youngsters spend an inordinate amount of their free time practicing and competing under the tutelage of the adult leader (Burke and Straub, 1976; Gould and Martens, 1979; Gould, 1981). Smoll and Smith (1981) believe that the coach's influence extends well beyond the playing field and into other aspects of the athlete's life. While the sport experience becomes increasingly important to the athlete and continues to be an effective vehicle of socialization, the significant adult in this process has consistently been overlooked as a viable topic of study.

Evidence of a crisis on the bench can be ascertained upon the realization that there seems to be serious conflicts between the coaches' and players' reasons for participation in sports. It has been noted that, while adult leaders expressed much concern for winning and proficient motor performance, the young athletes were more concerned with enjoyment, socialization, playing time, and the development of friendships (Moriarty and Olafson, 1975; Thomas, 1978; Weinberg, 1981). Analysis which contrasted participants with non-participants in sport have suggested that the actual outcomes attributed to the sports experience may be more negative than positive. For example, Kistler (1957), Richardson (1962), and Mantel and Vander Velden (1974) all reported that boys and young men who participated in organized sports were less concerned about sportsmanship and placed greater emphasis on skill and victory than non-participants. Webb (1969) found that athletes were more likely to experience increased professionalization and decreased interest in fairness.

The crisis in youth sports related to coaching behavior has been heightened by the meager data related to this problem which has typically been replete with speculation and characterized by unsupported rhetoric. A promising trend has been the application of descriptive research techniques to the study of youth sports. These systematic observation investigations have attempted to generate a data base related specifically to the objective, observable, and recordable behaviors of coaching personnel. Smith et al. (1977), who developed the Coaching Behavior Assessment System, have spearheaded the description of coaching behavior in naturalistic settings. The voluminous work of Smith, Smoll et al. (1977, 1978, 1981) not only has provided profiles of the behavior of coaches, but also has resulted in the development and implementation of training programs to enhance the player-coach relationship. Smoll and Smith (1981) suggested methods of intervention which might improve the athletic experience for the youngsters involved. Chelladurai and Saleh (1980) designed the Leadership Scale for Sports (LSS), to assist in the determination of the most salient dimensions of coaching. Their work with LSS holds much potential for the future study of coaching behavior and the enhancement of youth sports. A recent study by Lombardo et al. (1982) provides descriptive data relative to the quantity and quality of interaction of coaches during competition, employing a simple, three category system, including the classification of verbal and nonverbal behaviors. An analysis of the data revealed that:

1) Positive interaction between coaches and players occurred at a rate several times greater than negative or critical interaction. 2) Of all observed behaviors, 27 percent took the form of interaction with or directed to one athlete. 3) Coaches rarely engaged in behaviors unrelated to the action or playing field. 4) There were countless opportunities for the attainment of other objectives in addition to winning and the demonstration of skills (e.g., affective and cognitive outcomes), as demonstrated by the high ratio of positive, supportive, and encouraging behaviors to negative interaction (positive or negative interaction) between players and coaches accounted for a small percentage of the total behaviors recorded. 5) The interaction was overwhelmingly direct, and typically initiated by the coach. and 6) The most prevalent behavior manifested by the coaching personnel observed can be described as instruction, information-giving, demonstration, and commands (i.e., 22 percent of all recorded behaviors). Lombardo et al. concluded that coaches behaved in a manner which placed greatest value on playing as directed and obedience, indicating a primacy on performance and winning. Dubois (1980) reported similar results, and concluded that coaches were socializing their young athletes into a "product" rather than "process" competitive orientation because of the emphasis on winning.

Why is there a crisis on the bench? Why does the mere presence of adults change the games children play? Why do coaches feel such a need to be totally in control, even to the extent that they deny enjoyment and total involvement in the game? The crisis is most evident when adults urge youngsters to produce, win, to act like "big-leaguers," rather than acting their age and enjoying the experience of playing. There are numerous factors which shape coaching behavior and have resulted in this crisis. Among these factors are: 1) The alarmingly general ignorance of the emotional, social, mental, and physical characteristics and needs of youngsters. The typical youth league coach fails or refuses to recognize the vast difference in needs and motives between the big-leaguers and little-leaguers. 2) The coach's perception of the coaching role in youth sports related to his/her experiences in competitive athletics, and the concomitant contact with adult models. Unless major interventions are undertaken by trained individuals, familiar with the needs and capabilities of young athletes, the volunteer coach, normally a product of similar organized sports, will continue to imitate, mindlessly, the behavior of those coaches he/she played for. 3) The media-projected image of the coach (i.e.,the professional coaching model) in American society is also a major factor in this process. Since the media's investment in professional sport and their broadcasts is calculated in the millions, this should come as no surprise. As a result of this monetary commitment, the professional level of sport receives by far the most media coverage. The professional coach, with his/her livelihood continually (and probably logically) assumes the autocratic leadership style, thereby controlling all phases of the game. Youth league coaches seemingly model their behavior so as to be congruent with that of the most visible model, that is, the major league coach. Youth league coaches have great difficulty differentiating their need to emulate the professional coach from the needs of the young athlete, who requires patience, acceptance, and much more sensitivity. Each of these factors is a source of models of behavior for the individual youth sport coach as well as vehicles for socialization into the role of the coach. Each factor has contributed to the present crisis in youth sports.

The proponents of formal sport programs for children set forth extremely optimistic statements about the consequences of participation. It is time to move beyond rhetoric. The dismantling of the vast network of organized sport is neither suggested nor desirable. Youth sports should continue to grow and flourish in the coming years. Yet, supporters of such programs must redesign sport programs in order to insure that the effects on the participants are positive. There is no better place to start reconstructing formal sport programs than by examining the behavior of the volunteer coaches. The following interventions are suggested.

1) Provide educational programs for coaches in order to develop an understanding of the values of physical activity and competition beyond mere product outcomes. The development of a strong, positive self-image, enhanced self-esteem, increased self-confidence, and the maintenance of the athlete's initially high interest for the activity are among the many desirable process objectives to be strived for. Snyder (1970) suggested that the development of positive character and personality traits would be more likely to occur if the sport experience was characterized by a strong personal commitment, voluntary participation, and expressive relationship with those in the sport setting. Since it can be assumed that most sports involvement by youngsters is voluntary and normally intiated because of a personal commitment and interest in the activity, expressive relationships seem to be the missing element within the context of the sport experience. To resolve the present crisis, therefore, players must be provided with more freedom within the context of the game, encouraged to be spontaneous and "playful," and given opportunities for meaningful input into their games. Lombardo et al. (1982) found that interaction between players and coaches was characterized by its individual nature (i.e., 27 percent of all behaviors were directed to one athlete), indicating that the opportunities for the development of expressive outlets are numerous. If coaches would also provide opportunities for such expressive contacts between and among the players, the difference in values and objectives which presently exists between participants and adults might be minimized, if not eliminated. Smoll, Smith, and Curtis (1978) provide an excellent paradigm of such a training program, with their Coach Effectiveness Training Program, which includes a model and specific guidelines for implementing such training. 2) Provide training programs which will alert adult leaders to the participants' capabilities and needs, at the various stages of development as well as emphasizing the implications for

the coach's behavior. Adult leaders and coaches would do well to model their programs along the lines suggested by youngsters in their sandlot games. Coakley's analysis provides excellent direction for such modifications (Coakley, 1980). 3) Coaches must be instructed how best to relate to their players and how their behavior influences their athletes. It should not be assumed that the well-meaning, volunteer coach is ready to lead children. Smoll and Smith (1981) have designed such a program, including specific guidelines. 4) Youth leagues should provide coaches with feedback, derived and based on observation research methods, about their coaching behavior. Leaders of organized sport should establish desired objectives in terms of the coach's behavior prior to the season, in addition to the expectation of victory and improved motor skill. The Change Agent Research (CAR) Project, outlined by Moriarty, Guilmette, and Ragab (1977), has been field tested with positive results. and 5) Parents must become more actively involved in this meaningful youth pastime, at levels other than as spectators. It is suggested here that the educational process be extended to parents as well. Prior to the season, and as a prerequisite for involvement of their children, parents should be informed of the specific objectives of the youth league and the standards of behavior expected of the coaching personnel. Parents, as well as coaches, have been conditioned to accept the professional model of coaching as the standard for all levels of sport. Parents need to be made aware of the appropriate coaching behavior for their youngsters and what steps to take if such behavior does not materialize. As such, parents must be encouraged to become monitors and astute observers of the athletic experience if changes are to be effected. In effect, the parents could assist greatly in the transformation of organized sport from a product-oriented system to an emphasis on process outcomes, with their children being the direct beneficiaries of such change.

With the number of youngsters participating in sport increasing each year, it is imperative that action be taken to insure that such athletic endeavors make positive contributions. It is important that changes be instituted primarily at the level of the adult supervisor. The adults entrusted with the major part of the formative years of so many young people must be competent and adequately prepared to enhance the psychological and physical consequences of the participants in sport. In order to resolve the present crisis on the bench, modifications must be undertaken by all concerned, especially trained professionals, who as a group have chosen the passive role of sideline observers. It is not enough to sit back and criticize. It is time to act in the manner professionals know best: by providing training, providing leadership and by speaking out at every opportunity.

References

Burke, E.J. and Straub, W.F. "Focus Control and Other Psycho-Social Parameters in Successful American Age Group Swimmers." Paper presented at The International Congress of Physical Activity Sciences. Quebec City, Quebec, Canada, 1976.

Chelladurai, P. and Saleh, S.D. "Dimensions of Leader Behavior in Sports: Development of a Leadership Scale." *Journal of Sport Psychology.* 2(1):34–45, 1980.

Coakley, J. "Improving Organized Youth Sport Programs: What We Can Learn from Children." *Colorado Journal of Health, Physical Education, Recreation, and Dance.* 7(1):11–13, Fall, 1980.

Coleman, J.S. *Youth: Transition to Adulthood.* Chicago: University of Chicago Press, 1974.

Dubois, P.E. "The Youth Sport Coach as an Agent of Socialization: An Exploratory Study." Paper presented at The Convention of the Eastern District Association of AAHPERD. Lancaster, Pennsylvania, 1980.

Feltz, D. "Athletics in the Status System of Female Adolescents." *Review of Sport and Leisure.* 3:98–108, 1978.

Gould, D. "The Role of the Physical Educator in Non-School Youth Sports." *The Physical Educator.* 38:99–104, May, 1981.

Gould, D. and Martens, R. "Attitudes of Volunteer Coaches Toward Significant Youth Sports Issues." *Research Quarterly.* 50:369–380, 1979.

Kistler, J. "Attitudes Expressed About Behavior Demonstrated in Certain Specific Situations Occurring in Sports." *Proceedings of the Annual Meeting of the National College Physical Education Association.* Washington, D.C., 1957.

Lombardo, B.J., Faraone, N. and Pothier, D. "The Behavior of Youth League Coaches." Paper Presented at the Convention of the Eastern District Association of AAHPERD. McAfee, New Jersey, 1982.

Mantel, R.L. and Vander Velden, L. "The Relationship Between the Professionalization of Attitude Toward Play of PreAdolescent Boys and Participation in Organized Sport." In Sage, G., ed., *Sport and American Society.* Reading, Massachusetts: Addison-Wesley Publishing Company, Inc., 1974.

Martens, R. *Joy and Sadness in Children's Sports.* Champaign, Illinois: Human Kinetics, 1978.

Moriarty, D., Guilmette, A. and Ragab, M. "Change Agent Research: An Organized Process for Reorganizing Organizations." *Journal of Physical Education and Recreation.* 48:42–44, February, 1977.

Moriarty, D. and Olafson, G. "Change Agent Research for Windsor Aquatic Club." ED 104 874, 1975.

Purdy, D.A., Haufler, S.E. and Eitzen, D.S. "Stress Among Child Athletes: Perceptions by Parents, Coaches, and Athletes." *Journal of Sport Behavior.* 4(1):32–44, 1981.

Richardson, D. "Ethical Conduct in Sport Situations." *Proceedings of the Annual Meeting of the National College Physical Education Association.* Washington, D.C., 98–104, 1962.

Simon, J.A. "America's Attitudes Toward Youth Sports." *The Physical Educator.* 36:186–190, December, 1979.

Smoll, F.L. and Smith, R.E. "Preparation of Youth Sport Coaches: An Educational Application of Sport Psychology." *The Physical Educator.* 38(2):85–94, May, 1981.

Smoll, F.L., Smith, R.E., and Curtis, B. "Behavioral Guidelines for Youth Sports." *Journal of Physical Education and Recreation.* 49:46–47, March, 1978.

Smith, R.E., Smoll, F.L., and Hunt, E. "A System for the Behavioral Assessment of Athletic Coaches." *Research Quarterly.* 48(2):401–407, March, 1977.

Snyder, E. "Aspects of Socialization in Sports and Physical Education." *Quest.* June, 1970, pp. 1–7.

Thomas, J.R. "Is Winning Essential to the Success of Youth Sports Contests?" *Journal of Physical Education and Recreation.* 49:42–43, March, 1978.

Webb, H. "Professionalization of Attitudes Toward Play Among Adolescents." In Kenyon, G.S., ed., *Aspects of Contemporary Sport Sociology.* North Palm Beach, Florida: The Athletic Institute, 1969.

Weinberg, M.J. "Why Kids Play or Do Not Play Organized Sports." *The Physical Educator.* 38:71–76, May, 1981.

Dealing with the Emotions of Childhood Sports

Bill Bruns
Tom Tutko
San Jose State University

There was a newspaper cartoon a few years ago that could serve as the epithet for nearly every youngster in organized, competitive sports. A little boy is playing the outfield and circling under a fly ball. "If I catch the ball," he says, "the manager will love me, my friends will think I'm great, my parents will adore me, and I'll be a hero." Then his buoyant spirits darken. "But if I miss the ball, the manager won't like me, the kids will make fun of me, my parents won't let me in the house, and I'll be a dud."

The ball finally comes down, hits the boy's outstretched glove—and bounces out. In the final panel we see him trudging off the field, shoulders slumped and head bowed. "Six years old," he says, "and already a failure."

Most parents look upon competitive sports as an activity that will offer good exercise and companionship for their child while providing valuable lessons in competition, teamwork, dedication, and self-discipline. They think their own feelings and reactions have no real effect on their child. If the child also makes it through the season without being seriously injured, the parents will consider the entire venture a success. "Isn't it great that Johnny could play?"

This rosy viewpoint, however, overlooks—even dismisses—the crucial psychological effects of sports, from how the child handles personal failure and defeat to the way he copes with a lack of ability and sitting on the bench. Competitive sports are not a succession of unspoiled pleasures for the young athlete. The fear of injury can create a great deal of anxiety, let alone the painful aspects of contact sports like football and hockey. Demonstrating one's talent before teammates, parents, coaches, and spectators adds further stress—especially when the adults involved have expectations that far exceed the child's physical and psychological maturity. The pressure to win poses additional tension by making the average little athlete constantly fearful of failure, if not on a personal level then as part of a team. Add the differing circumstances of competition, such as a championship game or the final set of a crucial tennis match, and it is easy to see how athletes can be a continual source of anxiety, even for the most talented players. One of the goals of sports participation should be to have the youngster learn to deal with these anxieties in a productive way. But this takes sympathetic, reassuring parents and coaches.

My critics often say, "How can something like winning and losing affect our children? It's good that they compete, even if they lose and shed a few tears." This ignores the fact that many adults, let alone ten-year-old quarterbacks, are unable to handle personal setbacks in sports. In addition, child's play is not the equivalent of adult's play. Games are the child's way of growing up, of developing his personality. If the child fails or suffers sharp disappointments, it can have a strong impact on his emerging psyche, unless he is supported by his coach and his parents.

One reason why the psychological impact of childhood sports is consistently glossed over is that many parents have a tendency to overlook anything that might be a symptom. Or they alter the symptom in their heads. If, for example, they see their child crying after a loss they tend to think that it's good for the child to learn about adversity and fighting back. Conversely, the child may hide the fact that he cried after losing the game—for fear of being ridiculed by his father—or that he was injured, for fear of having to miss the next game.

On a deeper level, the child may come home from a game and seem relatively sullen and sad. He doesn't say anything but goes to his room and stays there for an hour. He may have lost the game, he may have been a substitute and didn't get a chance to play, he may have played poorly and is depressed even though the team won. Instead of discussing it with the child and helping him deal with his disappointment, the parents will say, "Aw, he's okay. It's just one of those things. It's only Little League." What if the same thing happened to the husband who didn't get the big contract or the promotion or who got chewed out by the boss? How would he feel if his wife just shrugged her shoulders and told him, "That's okay, dear, it's just your job. It's only a passing thing"?

The same proportional pressures affect the young athlete, and parents must respond in a corresponding manner. There's relatively little difference, theoretically, between being a Little Leaguer and being a major league baseball player. We build stadiums for our children, manicure their diamonds, enforce the rules, keep statistics and standings, pick All-Star teams, and send them to the play-offs. These same early pressures exist in Pop Warner football, where players are "drafted," study game films, memorize plays, and sometimes travel out of state for road games or "bowl" appearances. In neither sport is losing a laughing matter.

Following are the major areas that can produce emotional stress in a childhood sport, and some thoughts on how parents can best help their children cope.

Nearly every parent has been faced with the awkward, sometimes distressing situation of having their child in tears after losing the crucial baseball game or important tennis match. What the youngster needs more than anything is emotional support. He needs somebody to put an arm around him and say, "Johnny, that's alright. That was a tough game. I know how you feel." There's no magic liniment that parents can rub in to ease the hurt. Sometimes, however, just having the parents there watching the game and being around afterwards will be all that's necessary. The most destructive thing a parent can do is punish the child for losing, either verbally or physically. Losing is painful enough; there is no need to heap more misery on the child by indulging in the "I told you so" game: "I told you that you weren't practicing hard enough. I told you that you would lose if you didn't start going to bed early. I told you they would beat you if you didn't listen to the coach." These are common means of parents' adding to an already painful situation. No child wants to hear such statements, when he is already hurting from the sting of a defeat. It is a poor way for the parents to establish superiority. In fact, it is possible that they are undermining the opportunity to establish greater communication and rapport with their child. Equally cruel is for parents to use this approach when dealing with a youngster's minor injury—"Brush it off, it's not that bad." Well, you can't deny feeling miserable. If you could brush off disappointment and personal conflicts, mental health would be no problem.

Parents should instead emphasize more positive approaches, based on the understanding that every mature person must learn to adjust to failure. A person doesn't have to be happy or content to lose, but the fact remains that everybody fails in something sooner or later. The question is how to adjust, and there's no better place to learn this than in sports, where everything happens so fast that it can be forgotten in a short period of time.

Parents (and coaches) should keep certain things in mind when faced by a child who has lost or failed in sports.

Don't ignore him or give him the silent treatment. Let him know that it's painful, and that you understand how it feels to lose. But remind him that winning and losing are a part of life and that a loss is not the end of the world. One of the beauties of sports is that you can play again tomorrow, or in another week; it's sad today but tomorrow it will be a little different.

Don't give the child the impression that he is personally a failure. Losing doesn't mean that he is a lesser person. He may have worked and hustled and been just as talented as the winner, but society says that someone has to win and someone has to lose, no matter how fine the line between them may be.

Be understanding, but realistic. Don't let the child make excuses, and don't try to make him feel better by offering him excuses. Remember that the opponent was simply better *today*, if not yesterday or next week.

Instead of looking upon failure as a complete, dismal blackout, parents should talk from a positive, encouraging standpoint: "What did you learn from this game? What information did you pick up that can help you later?" Losing, in fact, may be more valuable to a person's growth than winning—*if* the losing is seen in its proper perspective and you lost while giving your best. It may be that you don't learn too much from winning; there's less of an adjustment, and it can obscure personal faults. But losing may provide a more realistic appraisal of what's going on. It forces a person to rethink what he is doing: "Maybe I'm not as good as I thought I was. I'd better find out what I'm doing wrong."

Emphasize the philosophy that the true test of an individual's competitiveness is his ability to handle defeat maturely. Praise the youngster who can lose gracefully and with courage. In terms of personal growth, that should be seen as a form of winning. Former UCLA basketball player Tommy Curtis remembered that when he was fourteen his team lost a game, and he was so down on himself that he "cried like a baby" and walked twenty-one miles home. His mother told him, "You won't have control over what happens most of the time, but you will have the opportunity to dictate how you react."

The parents should be concerned about what losing means to the child, not to them. Some parents, for instance, will interpret the child's failure as a rejection of them. This may be true in some cases, but mostly it's a case where the child simply did not succeed. Parents who feel rejected by the child's failure will proceed to punish the child, as if to retaliate for what the child has done to them.

Defeat should never be such a crushing matter that it ruins the weekend. The child must know that if he loses, or has a bad game or performs poorly, he can still come in the front door and his parents are going to be happy to see him. Regardless of the outcome, be it a baseball game or a swimming meet, the parents and child should be able to communicate in a pleasant way. The child is in trouble when the outcome becomes a significant factor in the eyes of the parents.

After a loss, parents should rarely evaluate performance, but rather should reward physical involvement: the effort, working hard, putting in the time and sticking with it. If the child performed his best or worked up to his potential, he shouldn't have to apologize or feel guilty about losing. The key concern should be: did he still have fun playing the game? Did he enjoy himself?

Parents and young athletes alike should realize that it is entirely possible to gain and maintain self-respect—and still lose—by admitting, "This is the best I can do." Just to say "Let's face it—I'm less talented" is a healthy form of adjustment. "I can still figure out math and play the piano; I just don't have as much talent in this one sport." Unfortunately, the American culture has built so much guilt into losing that the person who tries to make a healthy adjustment to it—like cracking jokes in the midst of a losing streak—is thought to be a lousy competitor, if not a little crazy. We incorporate this fatalistic feeling into the fiber of the child's personality as he's growing up. The child should be free to take honest pride in winning. But he should also be allowed to learn to cope with defeat.

The Substitute

Another prevailing myth in sports is that a hardworking substitute will come out of the experience with a stronger character. On the contrary, unless a child is extremely mature or unless he gets a great deal of support from his parents, being a substitute will affect him adversely. I have only known of one preadolescent competitor who was content being a substitute, and that was because he had been rejected by a number of other groups and so didn't mind being a substitute, just as long as he belonged. He was also extremely awkward so just being kept on the team was satisfying.

We don't give much thought to the poor little guy on the bench, his disillusionment and his sense of futility. Dr. Bill Hammer and I conducted a study that showed that the athlete who suffers the most, and often loses his motivation, is the substitute. The reality he faces is that things rarely get any better during the season. For one thing, he doesn't get a chance to improve his skills; those who play all the time keep drawing further ahead of him. He grows progressively more disillusioned and more isolated, especially on a winning team, where he is frustrated at not being able to contribute. On a losing team, ironically, the substitute can always cling to the hope of playing, while feeling, "I can play better than those guys."

Another painful aspect of being a substitute is the fact that the child's presence on the bench is an obvious sign of his being somewhat inferior. If he were more talented, he would be on the first string. He must face this embarrassment not only with his peers, who are clearly aware of it, but with his parents as well. If, in addition, he is highly competitive, being on the bench can serve as a personal letdown, because he has not attained goals he may have set. He may appear somewhat depressed during the season because of this. To add to the problem, this depression may carry over to other phases of his life. For example, he may begin to do poorly in school, particularly if school is not that important to him. There may be a tendency to avoid his friends, especially those who are on the first string, simply because they may ask sensitive questions or poke fun at his practicing with the scrubs. If he is also quizzed by his parents as to why he is not starting, or if they begin to push him to practice more, the problem becomes even greater.

To make matters worse, as sociologist Dr. Jon Brower observed after studying a North Hollywood, California, baseball program (boys ages eight to fourteen) for nearly a year: "It is the poor players who get the brunt of the coaches' displeasure and thus suffer the most. Like most young competitors, their athletic involvement constitutes a major part of their lives; they have fewer alternative activities than adults and thus if they are poor players they define themselves as defective human beings.''

There are several important ways in which parents can help their child effectively handle the role of a substitute. It is vital that they let their child know that they are not judging him as a person based on his playing ability, and that they love him because of the kind of person he is. Unfortunately, many parents respond as if it were a personal insult that their child is a substitute, no matter how uncoordinated he might be. This simply compounds the child's guilt and misery.

If the child comes home and is obviously disappointed, it is extremely important to empathize with him. If he says, ''I didn't get a chance to play again today,'' the parent shouldn't tell him, ''Well, the other kids are better than you'' or ''Life is like that, it's tough.'' The parent should say something like, ''It must embarrass you not to play, and I know how the feeling is. You kinda feel left out. If I were sitting on the bench it would hurt my feelings, too. But I'm really proud of you the way you're sticking it out.'' Sometimes the parent doesn't have to say anything; he can just pat the youngster on the back or be a good listener. The parent should also make an effort to see that the child gets a chance to play in some way, such as in a pickup game after work once a week with some of the other youngsters who aren't playing. Or the parent could offer to help the child improve by throwing extra batting practice or taking him out to the basketball court and working on his shooting.

Parents can help preempt the problem before the season even begins by telling the child, ''Everybody has different abilities and different talents. That's part of the game. You may not get the chance to play as much as you might want to, but we're happy that you want to go out for the team. No matter what happens, we're behind you.'' Don't discourage the child by being derogatory; don't destroy his motivation. The valuable part is that he wants to take part, he wants to give the sport a try, even though the odds may be against his playing very much. That is why the process—the trying—must be rewarded, rather than waiting until he does well, which may be improbable.

Once again, that old nemesis—the emphasis on winning—is what leads to most of the substitute problems on a childhood sports level. For example, there was a Pop Warner football coach in Los Angeles who used only his best players in one particularly close, important game. The team still lost, and afterwards the coach was confronted by a group of angry parents whose youngsters had not played. The coach was later quoted in *Los Angeles* magazine, in which he defended his position and criticized the parents. ''That's not what Pop Warner is all about. The kids want to win, too, and if you play everybody and keep losing, it's demoralizing. The point about all these organized sports for kids is, if you can't have fun, forget it.'' Yes, but fun for whom—the coach and the twenty-two starters? What about the other eleven boys on the bench, one-third of the team? Isn't it demoralizing for them to keep coming out to practices and to the games but seldom getting to play? A letter to the *Miami Herald* from the mother of a Little League football player presented a poignant protest in this regard. She wrote that her son's coach screamed at referees, screamed into the faces of the boys, and, worst of all, allowed only twelve of his eighteen players to play. "The other boys sat on the bench for the second week in a row, not being allowed in for even one play," she said. "These are eleven-year-olds who give up every night of the week to practice, come home late, tired, dirty, hungry, but with the thought it will be worth it when they play on Saturday."

I will discuss in more detail later why every childhood sports league should require the coach to play every youngster in every game, and more than just token appearances. Some league officials and coaches might be surprised to learn that most parents could be in favor of having all the players see as much action as possible. In 1974 I surveyed one hundred parents and coaches in a San Jose Little League, and the overwhelming majority of parents preferred to have their youngsters play regularly for a loser than ride the bench for a winner. A similar study of Pop Warner football players in the Colorado-New Mexico area showed that almost three-quarters of them would rather see action with a losing team than sit on the bench with a winner.

Peer Group Troubles

Parents are sometimes faced with a situation where the other players are giving their child a rough time because of his clumsiness or general ineptitude. They ridicule him and taunt him, and he doesn't know how to respond. The most important thing here is for the child to know that his parents are concerned about him. They should talk to him about his feelings and let him know that they understand. They should ask him why he thinks the other players give him such a rough time. Perhaps the child's personality is contributing to the problem; he may be an alibier or a constant complainer, or he may be insulting to the other players. If the parents have a good relationship with the coach, they could ask him to provide an insight into what is happening, since he sees the interplay going on during a game or at practice. The parents should let the coach know they're concerned. Is there anything they can do? What might change the situation? Sometimes the parents can ease the tension by inviting the whole team over to the house for hamburgers. The other ballplayers may realize that Fenwick isn't such a bad kid after all; they might like him a little bit more. Above all, however, the child needs to know he at least has his parents behind him. He needs to know they support him.

Fear of Getting Hurt

Many children have the very natural fear of getting hurt when they take up a sport that has repeated physical contact or is fraught with potential dangers. For instance, every Pop Warner team has the littly guy who doesn't like to get hit, who's not very aggressive, but whose father is going to make him a football player. Young hockey players everywhere are afraid to scuffle for the puck amidst flailing sticks or to be knocked against the boards by an aggressive opponent. In individual sports, the athlete must overcome similar fears while learning to ski the downhill or dive from the ten-meter platform or perform on the balance beam in gymnastics.

Children in these situations need emotional support. They need to know that their parents and the coach understand their fears and will not reject them if they cry or back away from danger. One of the recurring problems in baseball, for example, is how to relax the player who is terrified of coming up to the plate against a fast pitcher, especially one with control problems. A mother once asked me for advice on how to cope with this dilemma, which involved her baseball-crazy husband and their young son, who was just starting Little League and was terribly "gun-shy" up at the plate, jumping away from every pitch. The father was a pushy, tough-minded person whose "solution" was to take his son out to the baseball field and make him stand at home plate with a bat while he hit him with baseballs. "It's gonna make him tough," he told his wife. "This is the only way he'll learn to stand in there." Obviously this was crazy behavior. Trying to browbeat bravery into a youngster only reinforces and increases his existing fears. But this was typical, albeit to the extreme, of the insensitive approaches taken by many parents and coaches in trying to calm the fears of young athletes. They try to either shame the child—"Don't be a sissy"—or provide false hopes—"Don't be afraid, it's not going to hurt you." The latter is make-believe thinking. I mean, there's no denying the fact that getting hit by a hardball is painful, sometimes even injurious.

What the adult should do is talk to the youngster about fear and recognize the fact that the child is afraid. Just discussing the problem will help alleviate worries: "I know what it's like to get hit by the ball. It hurts. I wish it didn't have to be a part of the game. But really, it happens very seldom. If you're alert up there, you can jump out of the way almost every time. The pitcher is *trying* to get the ball over the plate—he's not aiming at you—so just concentrate on hitting the ball." When the youngster is first learning how to hit, the adults should use a softball or a whiffle ball so that the youngster knows he won't be hurt if he stands in at the plate. He should be allowed to gain confidence in his ability to hit the ball before he moves up to a hardball and faster speeds. The youngster who knows he can hit the ball, or at least make repeated contact, will soon have the confidence to concentrate on hitting rather than on his fear of getting hurt.

The Child Who Wants to Quit

In most highly competitive and involved families, the pressure on young athletes is not only to win, but not to quit, especially if they have talent and a "future" in the sport. In such families it is difficult, if not impossible, for the child to go up to his parents and say, "I've decided to quit." His parents just aren't going to accept that decision gracefully, no matter how long the child might have suffered, enduring a sport he no longer enjoyed while trying to get up enough courage to face condemnation by his parents. Competitive parents will almost always take a strong stand—"If you start something you have to see it through"—and will argue that quitters never learn to face the real world. To drop out of football, especially, is to admit an unmanly weakness.

However, as Dr. Bryant Cratty writes in *Children and Youth in Competitive Sports:* "There is no data which indicates that a child who is not willing to endure the physical rigors of sports is likely to fail in tasks involving intellectual or artistic persistence. . . . Indeed, if the child has personality traits that do not suit him for competitive sports, he may be suited for participation in activities which may result in more worthwhile contributions to himself and to others. In other areas he may display competencies which may endure into adulthood more than do sports skills."

If the parents and the child wage long, heated arguments over the question of continued participation in a sport, the child can never win. Even if the parents finally give in, the child will be left with so much guilt that he will wish he were back on the team. Instead of producing such a confrontation, parents should allow a reevaluation time to sit down with the child and discuss in a positive way why he wants to quit. Since most families consider quitting a form of losing, the parents should remember all the ramifications. The child needs support, not a browbeating, and the parents need to explore his reasons, not simply dismiss him as a quitter. For example, is the coach riding him too hard? Does he resent being on the bench most of the time? Does he feel left out? Do the other players make fun of him? Is he embarrassed because his friends are on the first team and he's a substitute? If he's a starter, why has his interest in the sport diminished? Perhaps the child is hurting physically but he doesn't want to admit it and this is his indirect way of doing it. Maybe he never really wanted to participate in the first place, despite having good talent, but he didn't want to disappoint his parents, or he's afraid of what his friends will think.

Parents will never know these things until they talk to their child. The child may, in fact, be going through such a painful experience that the decision to quit may be entirely reasonable. But if the parents persist in forcing him to finish out the season, they can expect to create more problems and produce deep-seated negative attitudes. For the child it may be like developing school phobia; he has to go to the ball field and it's going to be very painful. He will find ways to fudge. He will play so poorly and show such obvious disinterest that he should have stayed home anyway. His reaction will be, "If I'm playing just to please my parents, then I'll just go through the motions." The parents, in fact, are teaching him to slough off.

Many times the pressures on a young athlete can build up to such a point that the youngster indirectly, but very purposely, takes his frustrations out on his parents. I've had athletes tell me that they purposely played poorly because they wanted to be thrown off the team; they couldn't take the conflict with their father any longer. I knew of an outstanding high school pitcher who started on the mound in the championship game. The stands were filled with scouts and he knew his father was there, a smart-ass, cocky type who was loudly arrogant about his son's ability. The boy proceeded to throw the first ten pitches nowhere near the plate—in the dirt, into the backstop. He later admitted to his school counselor that he did it intentionally to pay back his father, because his hurt was so deep and so great and he had carried it for so long.

Another example occurred in the San Jose area, where the father was a former wrestler and his son was wrestling on the high school team. The father would get so engrossed that he would literally become his son during a match, going through all the motions, the empathy, the agony, as he watched from the stands. Then came a crucial qualifying match for the state championships. Late in the match the son got in a tough spot and pulled some blunder, and there in this silent gym the father lost control of himself. He started shouting instructions at the top of his lungs and putting his son down. When the boy finally got loose he walked over to his corner, pulled on his sweat pants, and left the ring. He never wrestled again.

The decision to drop out of a sport may not come until the season is over, and the reasons may surprise those parents who fail to realize that organized sports are not the ultimate joy of childhood for many youngsters. I knew one boy who played on two winning Pop Warner teams, but he realized that he was never going to be that good, so why continue to go out and sit on the bench? He quit because he liked other things and it seemed sensible to shift his focus of attention; playing football was a chore, like carrying out the garbage.

I once talked to a father who had wrestled his son to learn to compete and to be successful. So he talked Jimmy into going out for the junior high basketball team. The coach was just out of college and he had the players come in every day for a rough, two-hour practice. He really put them through the grinder, but they won their league and Jimmy was one of the leading scorers. His father told me about this in a very proud fashion, and the implication was "It's wonderful that my boy had this sports experience." Then he admitted, "I asked Jimmy, 'Well, how did you like basketball? Are you looking forward to next year?' And he said, 'Well, Dad, I'm not going out next year.' When I asked him why, he said, 'Jeez, that's a lot of work and it took all my time. I always had to stay after school for practice and I couldn't play with my friends, or watch TV.' "

Clearly these things were more important to the boy than playing basketball all winter. Many parents would argue that since he had athletic ability, he should have been forced to compete. But look at it from the child's point of view; he went to school and he did his work; he was entitled to his free time. Forcing him to compete would be unfair.

Perceptive parents can usually sense ahead of time when a sport is beginning to affect their child in a negative way, and can help the child wrestle with the problem before it leads to a confrontation over quitting.

For example, the child who starts discovering that a sport just isn't fun anymore will reveal a number of symptoms. He will find it hard to concentrate on the sport. He will cease to speak excitedly about what he is doing, and will lose his eagerness to go to practice. He may even feign sickness or act hurt in order to get out of going. If he's a substitute or has been playing poorly, he may try to avoid his friends who do play—and who used to be his close pals. He may no longer even want to participate informally with his brothers or his father. He begins to find fault with his teammates and tries to blame the coach for whatever problems he is having in the sport. If he plays poorly he may go home and hide in his room. If you try to talk about practice, and it happens that he has just been benched, instead of telling you he may begin to cry. In severe cases there might be anxiety symptoms such as fidgeting and nail biting or even nausea and nightmares, all associated with participation in sports—and affected to a large degree by the amount of pressure being exerted on the home front.

If the parents created the situation in the first place, by strongly encouraging the child to sign up for the sport, they will only compound the problem by trying to ignore these emotional symptoms. Again, what the parents must do is talk to the child at some length about his participation. If the symptoms persist, or a number of them intensify, then the parents should even encourage the child to withdraw. At the least, they should always leave the door open for the child to make that decision on his own, and without guilt.

5
Violence

With each passing year, the world is further exposed to the harsh reality and consequences of excessive violence in sport. Sport participants and spectators alike have suffered serious bodily harm; even death has resulted from sports violence in its most severe form. Athletes die in boxing rings, on high school football fields, in automobile races, and while participating in many other forms of athletic competition. Soccer riots in Latin America and Africa are buried in small summary paragraphs in our morning newspapers, and deaths that may have resulted from these riots are viewed as isolated incidents or aberrations.

However, the soccer riot that occurred on May 29, 1985, in Brussels made the Western world sit up and take notice. The aftermath of violence initiated by English spectators when they attacked Italian fans left 38 dead and nearly 400 spectators injured. As a consequence of this tragedy, British soccer teams were banned from the Continent.

American spectators have never been quite so violent. When sport violence does occur in the United States, it is most often fueled by alcohol. As the city of Pittsburgh "celebrated" the 1971 World Series triumph of their beloved Pirates, two people were killed and twelve women were raped. The 1984 World Series win by the Detroit Tigers was marked by significant drunken behavior; six police vehicles were destroyed or damaged, several stores and businesses were ransacked, and sixteen people were seriously hurt. A month before the Series, five fans were arrested when they joined a bench-clearing brawl between the San Diego Padres and the Atlanta Braves.

Despite these incidents and others like them, mass spectator violence in the United States and Canada has never reached the destructive level of soccer riots in Europe and Latin America, in which hundreds of spectators have been killed. Nevertheless, the 1985 soccer riot in Brussels increased fears that such violence could happen in North America, largely because the incidence of spectator violence has been increasing at such an alarming rate.

The riot in Brussels also forced the media, as well as the public, to view sports violence as a building phenomenon leading to potential catastrophe for individuals and groups. For example, more than 300,000 football-related injuries are treated annually in hospital emergency rooms. In the National Football League, an average of 1,600 players annually are forced to miss at least two games because of serious injuries. According to Rick Horrow, one of the nation's experts on sports violence, a professional football player's life expectancy is significantly lower than that of most men because of the physically debilitating nature of that sport.

Violence, including fights, is very much a part of professional ice hockey. Baseball, despite its status as a noncontact sport, has more bench-clearing brawls than any other sport. Basketball players have become more aggressive as the pressures to succeed have become stronger. With all this, Horrow sees a dramatic increase in the potential for excessively violent conduct during actual competition.

Michael Smith helps us understand different types of violence in his article, "Sports Violence: A Definition" (*Arena Review*, vol. 5, no. 1). He presents a typology that includes body contact, which occurs according to the official rules of a given sport; borderline violences, which are "assaults which though prohibited by the formal rules of sport, occur continuously" and are accepted; quasi-criminal violence, which violates formal and informal rules and usually results in very serious injury; and finally, criminal violence, which is so serious that it is immediately handled by legal authorities.

John Schneider and Stan Eitzen examine violence in the four major sports in America, comparing incidents of normative violence (blocking in football, body-checking in hockey, sliding hard in baseball, deliberate fouls in basketball) with illegitimate violence. Their article, "The Structure of Sport and Participant Violence" (*Arena Review*, vol. 7, no. 3), examines the prevailing theories regarding reasons for the occurrence of illegitimate violence. They then discuss specific factors that account for variance in the amount of illegitimate violence, such as the aforementioned high number of bench-clearing brawls in baseball as compared to the few that occur in football, which is generally considered the most normatively violent sport. Schneider and Eitzen treat the structures of the specific sports as factors that can affect the level of violence in those sports.

Many scholars have concluded that so long as society is increasingly violent, so long as a significant segment of the population is unemployed, and so long as nationalism or regionalism prevails at athletic contests, violence will continue, regardless of any preventive measures. Such conclusions do not augur well for the future of sport.

Sports Violence: A Definition

Michael D. Smith
York University

> No rules or practice of any game whatever can make that lawful which is unlawful by the law of the land; and the law of the land says you shall not do that which is likely to cause the death of another. For instance, no persons can by agreement go out to fight with deadly weapons, doing by agreement what the law says shall not be done, and thus shelter themselves from the consequences of their acts. Therefore, in one way you need not concern yourself with the rules of football.
> —Hechter, 1977:44

These were Lord Justice Bramwell's instructions to the jury during the 1878 British court case, *Regina v. Bradshaw*. A soccer player was accused of manslaughter after he charged, collided with and killed an opposing player in a game played under "association rules." The defendant was acquitted, but the judge's pronouncement has been often cited of late, usually by those who wish to make the point that sport should not be exempt from the laws that govern our behavior elsewhere.

But the fact is that sports violence has always been viewed as "different" in the public eye and has always enjoyed a certain immunity from criminal charges, in somewhat the same ways as sports in general have enjoyed special exemptions from laws governing labor relations and the restriction of economic competition. Except for isolated cases, until the mid-1970's, the courts showed a marked reluctance to touch even the most outrageous incidents of sport-related bloodletting; and legal experts still flounder in their attempts to determine what should constitute violence in sport. Despite the emergence of sports violence as a "social problem" in the last few years, athletes in many sports still get standing ovations for what would send an alley thug to jail *post-haste*. One-time National Football League linebacker, Mike Curtis, noted for both his ferocity and his candor, put it bluntly some years ago in a single, much-quoted sentence: "I play football because it is the only place where you can hit people and get away with it" (*Globe and Mail*, July 31, 1970:24).

Sports Violence and the Law

There is a host of reasons for this indisputable fact. First, most players seem to be reluctant to bring criminal charges against another player. Based on a mail survey of professional athletes in three major sports, Horrow (1980) concludes that professional athletes, in particular, tend to believe: (a) that player disputes are best settled privately and personally on the field of play; (b) that team management does not appreciate "troublemakers" and "clubhouse lawyers," and contract difficulties or worse probably await an athlete who turns to the law for justice; (c) that the sheer disruptiveness of litigation can ruin careers. And so on.

Second, writes Horrow, from the point of view of the law, many officials are reluctant to prosecute sports violence because they believe: (a) that they have more important things to do, like prosecuting "real" criminals; (b) that the leagues themselves can more efficiently and effectively control player violence; (c) that civil law proceedings are better suited than criminal for dealing with an injured player's grievances; (d) that most lawyers do not have the expertise to handle sports violence cases; (e) that it is almost impossible to get a guilty verdict anyway. And so on.

There are other, more elaborate legal reasons for the near-immunity from criminal prosecution and conviction given performers who engage in all but the most unmistakably criminal violence during athletic contests (Kuhlman, 1975). The "community subgroup rationale" is the recognition that law enforcement authorities tolerate certain illegal activities conducted by members of a definable group, because the illegal activities are widespread in the group and because group members look upon them less seriously than does society in general. This rationale usually arises in connection with the issue of differential law enforcement for racial minorities. For instance, in some predominantly black precincts in U.S. cities, police rarely make an arrest for felonious assault involving family members and neighbors, even though such assaults are frequent. Police in these precincts tend to define domestic violence as mere "disturbances," whereas officers in other districts are more inclined to define them as genuine assaults. It may be that certain assaultive practices in sport are looked upon with the same benevolent tolerance.

The "continuing relationship rationale" applies in assault cases where offender and victim have a continuing relationship. Legal authorities may wish to avoid further straining the relationship by prosecuting one party. Husbands and wives may wish to continue living together; neighbors may have to; athletes typically compete against each other at regular intervals. Criminal prosecution in sport could exacerbate already-present hostility to the point where league harmony is threatened. The 1976 prosecutions on various assault charges of three Philadelphia Flyers hockey players caused considerable strain between the Philadelphia and Toronto Maple Leafs hockey clubs and even a public squabble between the Philadelphia District Attorney and the Ontario Attorney-General (*Toronto Star*, April 22, 1976). The assumption underlying this rationale is that society has an interest in maintaining such social relationships.

Finally, certain assaultive practices in sports, though technically illegal both under the law of the land and of the sport in question, are accepted by sports people and legal authorities as "part of the game." In some sports, this is attributed simply to longstanding custom; in others, elaborate explanations have been constructed. Hockey fisticuffs provide a good example of the latter. Apologists claim these are safety-valves for aggressive impulses (usually described as "frustration") which inevitably accumulate owing to the speed, body contact, the very nature of the game. Because this aggression must be vented, the argument goes, if not one way then another, prohibiting fist-fighting would result in an increase of more vicious and dangerous illegal use of the stick. Since fist-fighting is considered legitimate, it is not thought of as "violence" (Smith, 1979). Belief in the inevitability of violence in hockey is so entrenched that one of the judges in the famous Ted Green–Wayne Maki affair (a stick-swinging duel during a game in Ottawa that nearly resulted in Green's death) concluded that the game "can't be played without what normally are called assaults" (*New York Times*, September 4, 1970:31).

A typology of violence that fails to take these perspectives into consideration does "violence" to what most people, not to mention criminal justice systems, regard as violence.

A Typology of Sports Violence

I shall categorize sports violence into four types, ranging roughly on a scale of legitimacy, from greater to lesser, both in the public perception and under law. Parts of this scheme are based on one reported by Kuhlman (1975) in the *Wisconsin Law Review*. In fact, legal scholars have dealt with the question, what is sports violence? more thoroughly than anyone else, and I shall pay considerable attention to what they have written.

Body Contact

This category of sports violence comprises all significant body contact performed according to the official rules of a given sport: tackles, blocks, body-checks, collisions, legal blows of all kinds. This contact is inherent in sports such as boxing, wrestling, ice hockey, rugby, lacrosse, football, and to lesser degrees in soccer, basketball, water polo, team handball and the like. It is taken for granted that when one participates in these activities, one automatically accepts the inevitability of contact, the probability of minor bodily injury, and the possibility of serious injury. In legal terms, players are said to "consent" to receive such blows. On occasion, death results and a court case ensues. If the defense shows that the defendant could not have foreseen that his actions would cause death, hence did not behave recklessly or negligently, he is found not guilty. This is not as simple as it sounds, of course. Richard Horrow (1980) takes more than fifty pages to explain the complexities of "consent," "foreseeability" and related arguments in his book on sports violence and the criminal law.

In 1895, Robert Fitzsimmons engaged in a public boxing exhibition with his sparring mate, Riordan, in Syracuse, New York. Riordan was knocked unconscious by a punch to the head and died five hours later. Fitzsimmons was indicted for manslaughter. The judge instructed the jury as follows:

> . . . if the rules of the game and the practices of the game are reasonable, are consented to by all engaged, are not likely to induce serious injury, or to end life, if then, as a result of the game, an accident happens, it is excusable homicide. . . . (Hechter, 1977:443).

Fitzsimmons was acquitted. But what is noteworthy about the case is that the rules of the sport were taken into account in determining criminal liability, a precedent directly contrary to that established in *Regina v. Bradshaw*. It is the Fitzsimmons ruling that has more or less held ever since.

Legal, or "normal," body contact becomes of interest as violence, in my view, when it develops, or as some might prefer, degenerates into "brutality." A rising toll of injuries and deaths, followed by public expressions of alarm, then demands for reform typically signal this condition. An "intrinsically brutal" sport like boxing always hovers not far from this point; for this reason, boxing is almost everywhere regulated by government. When body contact assumes an importance far out of proportion to that required to play the game—when viciousness and ferocity are publicly extolled as virtues, when inflicting pain and punishing opponents are systematized as strategy—a stage of brutality can be said to have been reached. These practices may strain the formal rules of sport but do not necessarily violate them.

Of course, such practices are not new. The history of football in medieval Britain, for example, is largely an intermittent chronicle of edicts issued by state and local authorities banning the game because of its bloody and riotous nature. . . .

In 1893, public indignation against alleged brutality in American college football, smoldering for some time, erupted across the country. A campaign led by the *Saturday Evening Post* and *The Nation* caused several institutions to drop the game, including Harvard, one of the first schools to play it on a regular intercollegiate basis. . . .

Anti-football sentiment swept the country again in 1905. . . . A Chicago newspaper published a compilation for the 1905 season showing eighteen players dead, eleven from high schools and three from colleges, and 159 more-or-less serious injuries. President Theodore Roosevelt called representatives of Yale, Harvard and Princeton to the White House and threatened to ban the game unless its brutality was eliminated. Stormed Teddy "Rough Rider" Roosevelt: "Brutality and foul play should receive the same summary punishment given to a man who cheats at cards" (Stagg, 1927:253).

Inflicting pain as a legal, if unsportsmanlike, strategy seems to have grown to new proportions in the last few years with the unprecedented commercialization of sport. North American football still offers perhaps the best example. In a *Sports Illustrated* investigation of "football brutality," one interviewed player, the notorious Doug Plank, a defensive back for the Chicago Bears (self-described as "an excellent example of a player who plays within the rules"), reveals the dubious philosophy behind some of his actions (Underwood, 1978: 34–35):

> Opposing players complain about my hits. They complain to me. But I don't really feel I'm at fault if there is no penalty called.
>
> [Last year] there was a wide receiver who'd been trying to come down on me all day, throwing [himself] around my legs. There was one play in particular—a play that was almost over, and that I had had no part in—where he went out of his way to go for me. I started to think, "I wonder how he would like it if I started throwing at *his* knees." On a kickoff return, I realized that once I had my man blocked I was pretty much free to do whatever I wanted . . . so I found out where the wide receiver was [and] came running up behind him. He was the contain man. He didn't see me coming. Just as he was turning inside to face the ball-carrier—it was completely legal—I blindsided him and knocked him on the ground. He got up and said, "Before the game's over I'm going to knock out one of your knees." What can you say to that? I made sure I kept my eyes on him the rest of the game.

Borderline Violence

In this category are assaults which, though prohibited by the formal rules of a sport, occur routinely and are more or less accepted by league officials, players and fans. To wit: the hockey fistfight, late hitting in football, high tackling in soccer, the baseball brushback pitch, basketball "body language," the sometimes-vicious elbowing and bumping that takes place in track and road races. These practices are tolerated and justified on a number of grounds, most of which boil down to some version of the "nature of the game" argument. Serious injuries do not often occur, but when they do they are usually dismissed as unfortunate accidents. Borderline violence is essentially the province of referees, umpires and other immediate game officials; higher league officials and law-enforcement authorities seldom become involved. Penalties for this sort of violence never exceed suspension from the game being played, plus perhaps a fine.

Essentially, legal officials seem to feel that applying criminal statutes regarding crimes of violence to borderline cases in sport would be ineffective or inappropriate: ineffective because the seriousness of the penalties provided by the law are widely regarded within and outside the sports community as out of proportion to the seriousness of the illegal acts. Binder (1975:237) observes of criminal law in general: "When a criminal conviction is not supported by the moral judgment of the community, the overall effectiveness of the criminal sanction is diminished."

Quasi-Criminal Violence

Quasi-criminal violence is that which violates not only the formal rules of a given sport but to a significant degree, informal norms of player conduct. It usually results, or could have resulted, in serious injury, which is probably what brings it to the attention of the top league officials and which generates public outrage in some quarters; this in turn puts pressure on legal authorities to become involved. Penalties for quasi-criminal violence usually go beyond the contest in question and range from several-game suspensions to lifetime bans, depending upon the sport. Civil legal proceedings increasingly follow. Criminal proceedings, rare in the past, are occurring more frequently, but convictions remain few and far between.

Many high publicized episodes of this nature have occurred over the years. One of the first in sport's modern era took place in baseball during a 1965 game between the San Francisco Giants and the Los Angeles Dodgers. Giant batter, Juan Marichal, felled Dodger catcher, John Roseboro, with his bat following an acrimonious verbal exchange. Roseboro sustained considerable injury; Marichal was fined $7,500 by the league and suspended for eight games. Roseboro filed a $110,000 civil suit for damages against Marichal and the San Francisco club, which reportedly was settled out of court for $7,500 (Kuhlman, 1975).

A decade and a half later (inflation being what is it), Houston Rocket basketball player, Rudy Tomjanovich, was awarded a whopping 3.3 million dollars for injuries received from a devastating punch thrown by Kermit Washington of the Los Angeles Lakers during a 1977 game. Tomjanovich suffered a broken jaw, broken nose, a puncture of the brain cavity and a torn tear duct and was, not surprisingly, out for the season (*Toronto Sun*, August 23, 1979:67).

Criminal Violence

This category consists of violence so serious and obviously outside the boundaries of what could be considered "part of the game" that it is handled from the outset by the law. Death is often involved, as in the 1973 Paul Smithers case, which received world-wide publicity. Smithers, a seventeen-year-old black hockey player, was convicted of manslaughter after killing another boy in a fight in a Toronto arena parking lot following a game (Runfola, 1974). Typically, such incidents, though closely tied to game events, take place prior to or after the game itself. On the extreme fringe of this category are assaults and homicides only incidentally taking place in a sports setting.

Conclusion

What is or is not called violence is not a trivial matter. The extent to which a behavior is perceived as violence has a great deal to do with what people are willing to do about it. As philosopher Robert Audi (1974:38) puts it in his essay, "Violence, Legal Sanctions and the Law": "Misnaming the disease can lead to the use of the wrong medicine or none at all." I think we are close to being able to say with some clarity what sports violence is. Perhaps soon, we shall know with assurance what to do about it.

References

Audi, Robert. "Violence, Legal Sanctions and the Law." *Reason and Violence*, ed. Sherman M. Stanage. Totowa, N.J.: Littlefield Adams, 1974.

Binder, Richard L. "The Consent Defense: Sports, Violence, and the Criminal Law." *American Criminal Law Review*, XIII (1975), 235–48.

Davis, Parke H. *Football: The American Intercollegiate Game*. New York, Charles Scribner's Sons, 1911.

Elias, Norbert, and Eric Dunning. "Folk Football in Mediaeval and Early Modern Britain." *The Sociology of Sport*, ed. Eric Dunning. London: Frank Cass and Co., Ltd., 1971.

Globe and Mail (Toronto), July 31, 1970.

Hechter, William. "The Criminal Law and Violence in Sports." *The Criminal Law Quarterly*, XIX (1977), 425–53.

Horrow, Richard B. *Sports Violence: The Interaction Between Private Law-Making and the Criminal Law*. Arlington, Virginia: Carrollton Press, 1980.

Kuhlman, Walter. "Violence in Professional Sports." *Wisconsin Law Review*, III (1975), 771–90.

New York Times, September 4, 1970.

Runfola, Ross T. "He Is a Hockey Player, 17, Black and Convicted of Manslaughter." *New York Times*, October 17, 1974, pp. 2–3.

Smith, Michael D. "Hockey Violence: A Test of the Violent Subculture Hypothesis." *Social Problems*, XXVII (1979), 235–47.

Stagg, Amos A. *Touchdown!* New York: Longmans, Green and Co., 1927.

Toronto Star, April 22, 1976.

Toronto Sun, August 23, 1979.

Underwood, John. "An Unfolding Tragedy." *Sports Illustrated*, August 14, 21, 28, 1978.

The Structure of Sport and Participant Violence

John Schneider
D. Stanley Eitzen
Colorado State University

Player violence in sport is of two types. There is normative violence where it is a part of the game to aggress against the opponent. Examples of normative violence are bodychecking in hockey, blocking and tackling in football, and legitimately sliding hard into a fielder in baseball. Although approved by coaches, peers, and spectators as part of the sport, normative violence can result in injury (Underwood, 1979). Illegitimate violence also occurs in the major American sports. This type of behavior involves the intentional use of force to harm the opponent outside the rules of a sport. Examples of this type of violence are "late hits" in football, "high sticking" in hockey, and fighting. The distinction between legitimate and illegitimate violence is often blurred, however. Some coaches and players may incorporate illegitimate means to intimidate, incapacitate, and exploit opponents with the tacit or even explicit approval of fans and participants.

The purpose of this article is twofold: first, to examine both types of violence, illustrating the prevalence of normative violence in the four major American team sports; and second, our goal is to explain why the incidence of illegitimate violence varies by type of sport. In doing so, we will focus on the structure of sport as the explanatory variable. This emphasis differs from the current theories on player violence.

I. Explanations for Illegitimate Violence

The explanations of player violence vary greatly. There are six theories used to explain violence in sport. . . . Any one of these theoretical approaches may be considered useful in explaining a small portion of violence behavior among participants in a number of sports. But do these theories, alone or in combination, address the issue of participant violence across all sports? If not, are there new ideas that might add to the understanding of this phenomenon across the sports spectrum? The following section reviews each of these theories.

The Violence in Sport Mirrors the Violence Found in Society. The argument is commonly made that sport, like other institutions, is a microcosm of society; that sport simply reflects the prevailing ideologies, values, and behaviors extant in the larger society (Smith, 1979; Eitzen, 1981; Eitzen and Sage, 1982; Edwards and Rackages, 1977; and Smith, 1974). Thus, the investigation of violence in sport must begin with the assumption that sport does not occur in a vacuum but is shaped by the history, culture, and distribution of power in society. We must understand that American society has been and continues to manifest and glorify violence. Several points require emphasis:

Violence has occurred throughout American history. . . .

The U.S. ranks higher than other western industrial societies in the proportion of violent crimes (Graham and Gurr, 1979:303).

The amount of violence in the media is staggering. . . . By the time the average child is 14 he or she has witnessed 11,000 television murders.

There are cultural norms that support violence. . . .

The incidence of spouse abuse and child abuse is high. . . .

Capitalist society creates conditions where workers are exploited, alienated, and treated as commodities (Sugden, 1981), increasing the likelihood of violence.

Military strength, even in times of peace, is a very high priority, as evidenced by the Reagan Administration's commitment to spend in excess of $1 trillion for defense over a five-year period.

Violence as the Result of Economic Incentives. Another explanation for player violence rests on the assumption that commercialization and economic incentives influence how athletes perform. Gregory Stone (1955) has made the case that sport is comprised of "play" and "dis-play." The element of play refers to the participants' personal concern with the dynamics of the activity; the element of display refers to action that symbolically represents the dynamics of the activity for the expressed purpose of making it more amusing to the spectators. When sport become commercialized, the element of dis-play becomes increasingly important so that spectator interests can be maintained at the levels necessary to stage profitable events (Coakley, 1981). Edwards and Rackages (1977) have added to this commercial aspect with their assertion that recent economic developments have been a major contributing factor to the intensification of competitiveness. The demise of the World Football League and the American Basketball Association, for example, left the National Football League and the National Basketball Association as monopolies with considerably fewer player opportunities. This constriction of opportunity could possibly be a major factor in the increase of on-the-field sports violence (Edwards and Rackages, 1977). The play, dis-play model formulated by Stone (1955) does not suggest that skill and finesse are unimportant when a sport becomes entertainment. But skill and finesse in sport have become overshadowed by what Furst (1971) has described as heroic action. When this value transformation takes place, athletes may tend to emphasize actions of daring and courage, which may often take some form of violence. This phenomenon is illustrated by Jerry Kramer's description of his pre-game feelings about the opponents he used to face as an offensive lineman for the Green Bay Packers:

> I've started day-dreaming about Merlin Olsen. I see myself breaking his leg, or knocking him unconscious and then I see myself knocking out a couple of other guys and then I see us scoring a touchdown and always . . . I see myself as the hero. (1968)

Commercialization can change the entire context in which a sporting event takes place. Attention is now focused on the outcome of the event, not on the meaning of the sport experience. Moreover, a "victory at all costs" attitude seems to be a result of commercial productivity.

The Influence of Crowd Behavior on Player Violence. The literature on participant violence in sport is also filled with references pertaining to the influence of spectators upon athletes' performances (Thirer, 1981; Coakley, 1981; Hatfield, 1973; Smith, 1973; Pilz, 1979). The assumption, based on collective behavior theory (Blumer, 1959), is that as spectators become more rowdy and vocal, the participants will become more violent. Fans' encouragement for violence, overall crowd noise, spectator aggression towards players, and game-related tension on the field are all factors that increase the possibility for player aggression.

Genetic Causation for Player Aggression. A fourth existing theory which might explain why players aggress argues that athletes have a genetic predisposition to do so. The Drive-Discharge Hypothesis maintains that aggression is an innate drive in all human beings. This aggressive drive is "somewhat responsive to the environment which acts to generate aggressive pressure on every individual and in society itself" (Brown and Davies, 1978). The assumption is that tension is cumulative within individuals and must be released before it erupts in violence. This tension can grow collectively in society as well. Thus, the Drive-Discharge theory predicts an inverse relationship between the presence of war and aggressive or war-like sports. Sipes (1973) has stated that the probability of war can be reduced, according to this model, by increasing the incidence of alternative behavior similar to warfare (such as combative sports). . . .

Sipes (1973) has suggested, alternatively, that individual aggressive behavior is primarily learned. Utilizing the "Culture Pattern Model" of human aggression, Sipes predicted different levels of aggressive behavior for different cultures. More important, Sipes has argued that the intensity and configuration of aggression is affected predominantly by cultural characteristics. Contrary to the Drive-Discharge Hypothesis, the Culture Pattern Model posits that "behavior patterns and value systems relative to war and warlike sports tend to overlap and support each other's presence" (Sipes, 1973:65). Therefore, periods of intense war activity should be accompanied by less intense sports activity.

Sipes' evidence supports the Culture Pattern Model of human aggression. "Rather than being functional alternatives, war and combative sports activities in a society appear to be components of a broader culture pattern" (Sipes, 1973:80). Therefore, aggression appears to be a learned, rather than instinctive behavior.

Learning Theory and Player Aggression. Yet another existing theory about why athletes aggress is forwarded by the social learning theorists. Social Learning Theory suggests that individuals are influenced by exposure to aggressive models, especially if their subsequent behavior is reinforced (Bandura and Walters, 1963a and 1963b). The concept of aggression is defined as "any sequence of behavior, the goal response to which is the injury of the person toward whom it is directed" (Dollard, et al., 1939). A number of sports sociologists and psychologists have discussed the social learning theory in their work on sports violence (Silva, 1978; Cataldi, 1978; Thirer, 1981; Smith, 1974; Goldstein, 1982). Berkowitz (1964) has demonstrated that adults respond with increased aggression after observing a violent model. The research findings supporting these beliefs deal severe blows to the belief that violence in sport is innate. The idea that athletes have a genetic tendency to aggress lacks any solid empirical support (Coakley, 1978).

There are, however, some serious drawbacks to the learning model. Michael Smith (1974) has outlined what he considers to be a number of severe limitations to the learning theory. Among these limitations are: (1) most of the research is based on the responses of young children, and it remains an open question whether some of the findings can be generalized to older children and adults; (2) much of the imitation of aggression via the media seems to apply to "novel" behaviors; (3) it is unclear how long-lasting the effects are of exposure to aggressive models; and (4) Sears (1965) has concluded that the responses imitated in the Bandura experiments are simple and easily recognized, and that more complex behavior may not be learned by modelling (Smith, 1974).

Psychological Stress and Player Violence. Jay Coakley (1978, 1980) has attempted to draw an analogy between a prison setting and player training camps. In this view the repressive aspects of training camp settings reflect many of the same characteristics as a prison setting, which may, in turn, promote player violence. Using the original work of criminologist Gresham Sykes (1971), Coakley has illustrated how training camp settings parallel prison settings. For example, both training camps and prisons promote: (1) the deprivation of liberty: a threat to moral worth; (2) the deprivation of autonomy: a threat to adulthood; (3) the deprivation of security: a threat to physical well-being; (4) the deprivation of heterosexual relationships: a threat to masculinity; and (5) the deprivation of material goods: a threat to person adequacy (Coakley, 1978).

As players respond collectively to these five threats, a social system develops where violent behavior comes to be defined as the normative means for establishing status among peers, maintaining self-esteem, and protecting one's physical well-being. Coakley admits that there are obvious differences between prisons and training camps. A central similarity, though, is that the subjective meanings of the deprivations experienced in prison are akin to the meanings of the deprivations experienced by the athlete (1978). Resorting to violent action is perhaps the primary method used by athletes to cope with widespread deprivations.

Each one of these theoretical perspectives provides some general understanding of why illegitimate violence occurs among players. But according to them, the amount of illegitimate violence should be constant across sports. But it is not. The theories are not very helpful because they do not treat violence as a variable. They omit the sport specific factors that account for the variance. The remaindser of this article examines the structure of sport as an independent variable.

II. The Structure of Sport and Player Violence

We have thus far outlined the six major theoretical perspectives that are currently being utilized to understand why participant violence occurs. Aside from some generalities, the insights of sociology are missing from these theories. Sociological research has been negligent in attempting to identify why sports violence exists. During the past ten years, sociologists have investigated illegitimate violence among sports participants, but *only* in contact sports such as football and hockey (Smith, 1974, 1978, 1979; Coakley, 1978, 1981; Vaz, 1974). Since violence also occurs in baseball and basketball, we should examine each of the four major North American sports. This will permit us to view illegitimate violence as a variable, affected by the characteristics inherent in the structure of each sport.

There are four structural characteristics common to these four sports that will help us understand this phenomenon. We would hypothesize that participant violence in sport is related to: (1) the amount of scoring in each sport; (2) the amount of body contact allowed within the rules of each sport; (3) the amount of retaliatory power players have in each sport; and (4) whether the structure of the sport has high or low rewards throughout the game. These four characteristics of the structure of sport work *in combination* to help explain why illegitimate violence by participants exists. These variables work together simultaneously, not individually. A discussion of how each of these structural characteristics are manifested in each sport will clarify the argument.

Scoring: The Lower the Scoring, the Greater the Potential for Illegitimate Violence. The amount of scoring in a contest could be linked to violent participant behavior. The basic assumption is that if a high score is obtained in a contest, violent behavior will be lessened because an outlet for frustration and aggression has been obtained. Conversely, if scoring in a contest is low, frustration levels among participants will elevate because the outlet for frustration is not available. Moreover, in low scoring sports tension is heightened by the fear of making a crucial error leading to failure. Freischlag and Schmidke (1978) have stated that whether the game is high or low in scoring will have a direct effect on the amount of pent-up tension among participants.

This hypothesis would seem to be valid. Although we do not have the data to support this argument, bench-clearing brawl behavior seems to occur more frequently in hockey and baseball, which have very low scores, than in football and basketball, where scoring for the most part is higher.

Scoring frequency may explain participant violence rather than total scoring, but we think not. For example, on many occasions the frequency of scoring in hockey or baseball is much higher than the frequency of scoring in football, yet baseball and hockey contests are constantly reporting fights. Even in situations where the scoring frequency is identical between baseball or hockey (3–2) and football (21–14), baseball or hockey still appears to have more situations involving player violence. It would be useful if we had data on incidents of violence by sport as well as the frequency relative to the score in each contest. Assuming that our contention is correct that the amount of scoring is more strongly correlated with illegitimate violence, this is explained by the symbolic importance players attach to the number of points given for a score. If so, then high scoring would tend to decrease the pent-up frustration on the part of players. That football and basketball reward a score with more points than do hockey or baseball would seem to be a valuable insight into why these sports may have a lower frequency of illegitimate violence than baseball and hockey.

Body Contact: The Greater the Normative Body Contact, the Lower the Amount of Illegitimate Violence. The amount of legal body contact between players in different sports varies greatly. We hypothesize that there is an inverse relationship between the amount of legitimate body contact allowed and the amount of illegitimate violence found in each sport. As the amount of legitimate body contact increases, the amount of illegitimate violence decreases. Conversely, if legitimate body contact is virtually nonexistent within the structure of the game, we would expect to see high amounts of illegitimate violence among players.

In football, contact between players is simply part of the game. The ability to "move bodies" and "stick" an opponent are ingredients that are mandatory if a team is to be successful. Hard, physical contact, therefore, is expected on every play.

Hockey, like football, demands that body contact be part of the game. The ability to "check" an opponent is an essential part of the game if a team expects to be competitive at all. Yet hockey, unlike football, is not characterized by continuous body contact. Most bodychecking occurs when an opponent has or is near the puck. Penalties are often called if a player simply levels an opponent for no reason. Normative violent contact in hockey seems to center around the man with the puck, whereas in football, possession of the ball by a player is not necessary for contact to be initiated. In summary, hockey allows high levels of contact between participants, but less than in football.

Although some basketball players obtain "enforcer" reputations among their peers, the amount of legitimate body contact allowed in professional basketball is lower than in hockey or football. When picks are set and players "jockey" for position under the boards, there is physical contact. But the violent nature of the contact between players as evidenced in football and hockey is not evident in basketball.

Normative body contact between players is the least in baseball. With the exception of collisions at home plate and an occasional hard "take-out" slide into base, baseball players have little legitimate physical contact with other players.

The hypothesis of an inverse relationship between legitimate body contact in a sport and the amount of illegitimate violence holds true except for hockey. Perhaps the reason for this lack of fit with the hypothesized relationship is that in hockey the amount of legitimized body contact is but one of the four variables which work together in explaining participant violence.

Player Retaliation: The More That a Sport Allows Legitimate Player Retaliation, the Lower the Amount of Illegitimate Violence. This inverse relationship between player retaliation and illegitimate violence is based on the premise that if players are allowed to retaliate immediately against an opponent, frustration cannot build up and brawling behavior will be less likely to occur. Conversely, if players are unable to retaliate immediately against an opponent, frustration will accumulate throughout the course of a game and illegitimate violence, taking shape in the form of brawling behavior, will increase.

The amount of retaliation between players in football is very high. Suppose, for example, that a defensive end "beats his man" and throws the quarterback for a substantial loss. The offensive tackle who was victimized does not need to wait until late in the game to retaliate and make the defensive end "pay" for his sack. Because the match-up system exists between players in football, the offensive tackle knows that he can block extra hard on the very next play to retaliate against the very same defensive end. His frustration level does not have the chance to build up over the course of the game because he has the opportunity to retaliate almost immediately.

Basketball players also have a very high opportunity for retaliation against their opponents but with much less physical contact than in football. Because scoring a goal in basketball occurs very frequently, the ball changes hands quite often. If a forward is faked out by his opponent who then scores an easy lay-in, he has the chance to do the same almost immediately. Because of the matchup system in basketball, where quite often one is guarded by the man he guards, a player has the ability to retaliate by going down floor the next time and scoring on his opponent. This is particularly true of professional basketball, where the 24-second shot clock is used. In addition, basketball has an immediacy of retaliation since players who are recipients of dirty play (flagrant elbows, verbal aggression) can go down floor on the very next possession and do the same.

Hockey presents an interesting situation in terms of the amount of retaliatory power a player has. Hockey is less likely than football and basketball to have woven into its structure the match-up phenomenon. Typically, defensemen play zones and do not follow other players in a man-to-man fashion all over the ice. Hockey is a very "fluid" game, where offensive possessions may change every few seconds. For this reason, the potential for man-to-man match-ups is less likely. Consequently, the potential for one player to retaliate against a specific other is low. So, for example, if a right-wing scores a goal by beating a defenseman, the defenseman does not have the retaliatory power to go back down the ice and score immediately on the same man or check him hard into the boards. He must wait until the same man has the puck, and then he may legally retaliate in a physical way. Since legal retaliation is relatively low in hockey, retaliation often takes illegitimate forms—high-sticking, tripping, or outright fighting.

Legitimate retaliatory power in baseball is virtually nonexistent. Perhaps even more than in hockey, match-up situations between players do not exist, and body contact is not even allowed. For a player to retaliate in baseball, a hard slide must be administered or a base hit must be achieved. Brush-back pitches and beanballs are techniques employed in order for one team to retaliate against another. The following quote by Pat Zachry, then a pitcher for the Mets, exemplifies retaliation through a brush-back pitch. After giving up back-to-back home runs, Zachry admitted throwing at Ron Cey to even the score. Zachry states: "I don't think it hurt him as bad as it hurt his feelings. . . . After two home runs, a guy should expect something inside" (Wulf, 1980). Legitimate retaliatory power among players in baseball, though, is very low to nonexistent.

The hypothesized relationship concerning the amount of legitimate retaliatory power and the amount of illegitimate violence that occurs in each sport would seem to hold true. In football and basketball, two sports that have high or very high amounts of retaliatory power among players, forms of illegitimate violence, i.e., brawling behavior is relatively low. Conversely, in hockey and baseball, two sports that have low or nonexistent amounts of retaliatory power among players, illegitimate forms of behavior are often evidenced.

Reward Structure: The Greater the Opportunity for Rewards During a Contest, the Lower the Incidence of Illegitimate Violence. We hypothesize that there is an inverse relationship between the amount of rewards amassed throughout the game and the incidence of illegitimate violence. In other words, the greater the number of rewards achieved throughout the game, the less the tendency for players to aggress illegitimately.

Football is one sport where a team is rewarded throughout the course of an event. Rewards are not necessarily measured in terms of whether points are put on the scoreboard. Rather, events that take place during the course of a game may aid in decreasing the level of frustration experienced on the part of the players. For example, the offensive team in football may not obtain the ultimate goal—a touchdown—but other rewards exist that serve to reduce tension and frustration. Among these rewards are: (1) first downs; (2) completed pass plays; (3) successful trick plays; (4) field goals; (5) long runs; and (6) "coffin-corner" placements on punts. The defensive team also has rewards which are present throughout the course of a game which decrease frustration levels. Among these rewards are (1) quarterback sacks and drops for losses; (2) tipped passes; (3) interceptions; (4) holding the offense on four downs to little or no yardage; (5) goal line stands; (6) blocked field goals or punts; and (7) recovering fumbles. Both the offense and defense, then, have the potential for rewards throughout the course of the game. And, we assume, the greater the rewards, the less frustration which should reduce the likelihood of illegitimate aggressive outbursts.

The structure of basketball also presents teams with the opportunity to amass rewards throughout the course of a game. In addition to lots of scoring opportunities by all players, regardless of position, special rewards may be obtained offensively by: (1) hitting a three-point shot; (2) scoring on a spectacular slam-dunk; (3) making free throws and baskets; (4) running plays in your offense to perfection; (5) making a beautiful pass for an assist; or (6) starting the fast break with an outlet pass off a rebound. Defensive rewards can consist of: (1) blocking a shot; (2) stealing a pass; (3) harassing your opponent into a turnover; (4) boxing-out for a rebound; and (5) drawing a charging foul. As in football, basketball has the potential for rewards throughout the course of a game. This high reward system may lessen tension and decrease the potential for illegitimate violence among participants.

The structure of baseball also presents teams with the opportunity to accumulate rewards throughout the course of a game. The same logic applies to baseball that applies to football and basketball; namely, opportunity for rewards throughout the course of a game may lessen tension and lead to fewer aggressive illegitimate incidents. Potential rewards for the offense in baseball include: (1) singles, doubles, triples, or especially home runs; (2) perfectly executed bunts and sacrifice flies; (3) stolen bases; (4) walks; (5) perfectly executed hit-and-run plays; (6) successful hard slides to break up double-plays; and (7) runs-batted-in. The rewards for the defense include: (1) strike-outs; (2) put-outs; (3) double or triple-plays; (4) throwing an opponent out trying to steal; or (5) throwing a runner out trying to take an extra base. In each case, rewards throughout the game may tend to lessen the potential for aggressive illegitimate action. Although we have already argued that bench-clearing brawls often occur in baseball, we still feel that rewards throughout the game dissipate tension on the part of players. The reasons why baseball still abounds with bench-clearing fights will be addressed later. Recall that participant violence in sport may be understood by analyzing the four variables' interactive effects, not their individual effects.

Of the four major sports in America, hockey has the least potential for rewards throughout the course of a game. A few goals (and assists) occur and there are good defensive plays, steals, and checking during the course of a game, but in general the rewards for players are less frequent than in the other sports. Perhaps this is a partial explanation for the extreme violence that occurs in hockey.

III. Why Sports Are Violent: The Interaction of Structural Variables

We have already discussed the four variables which each of the four major sports have in common. These common characteristics of sport can lend some valuable insight into determining why the four major sports vary in the incidence and magnitude of illegitimate violence by participants.

Although football is a contact sport, it may also be considered to be non-violent in the sense that bench-clearing brawls rarely occur. The middle range amount of scoring, the very high level of player retaliation, the very high level of body contact, and the high number of rewards allowed throughout the game help decrease the pent-up frustration experienced by the athlete. Perhaps football allows too much "legitimate" body contact for an athlete's own safety, but because the other three factors work together to allow the venting of frustration and tension in legal ways, football remains relatively free of illegitimate brawling behavior.

Professional basketball is basically a nonviolent game because the very high amounts of scoring, structural opportunities for player retaliation, and amounts of rewards throughout the game help to diffuse the pent-up frustrations experienced by athletes. In addition, basketball also legitimizes a middle range amount of body contact, which serves to reduce tension.

Baseball, a sport that has long been considered nonviolent, has a good deal of illegitimate violence. Bench-clearing brawls occur with alarming frequency. Yet when the structure of the sport is analyzed, the violent nature is no longer surprising. First of all, the amount of scoring is low. This means that the athletes see little reward for their work, at least in terms of what the scoreboard shows, and tension is heightened by the crucial effects of each play because it may determine the outcome of the game. Second, legitimate body contact between players is rare, which allows even more frustration to build up. And third, the amount of legitimized player retaliation is very low. Apparently, the very high rewards throughout the game are not gratifying enough for players. Some other outlet for frustration needs to be given. The real need for an additional outlet can be evidenced by the fact that when a batter charges the mound to fight, both benches clear almost *immediately*. Seemingly, this brush-back pitch was all that was necessary to send athletes' frustration levels over the edge. Baseball exhibits far more brawling behavior than either basketball or football and the structure of the sport promotes this violence.

Hockey exhibits the most illegitimate violence of the four major sports. The high incidence of violence in hockey is explained in part by the National Hockey League's unwillingness to take a firm stance against it. It could be argued that the league actually encourages violence because that increases spectator interest and revenue. But the structure of the sport is also responsible. Like baseball, hockey has low amounts of scoring. This could add to the high tension and frustration level of players. But more important, hockey is the only one of the four major sports which does not have a high number of rewards throughout the course of the game. Football, basketball, and baseball all have rewards in between scores built into their structure, but hockey has few. When this is added to the high amount of legalized contact and the relatively few opportunities for legitimate player retaliation, then the reasons for the high incidence of illegitimate violence in hockey become more clear.

IV. Summary

Table 1 presents a summary of the four structural variables examined here and a crude rank ordering of each by sport. Our thesis is that the lower the compo-

Table 1
The Rank Order of Structural Variables by Sport

Sport	Structural Variables				
	Amount of Scoring	Amount of Legal Contact	Amount of Appropriate Player Retaliation	Number of Rewards	Rank Total
Football	3*	4	4	3	14
Basketball	4	2	3	3	12
Baseball	2	1	1	3	7
Hockey	1	3	2	1	7

*These numerals represent ordinal rather than interval measurement.

site ranks of these variables, the more likely that illegitimate violence will occur. Clearly, our hypotheses are speculative. The rank orderings in Table 1 are not interval data and are subject to empirical verification. The structural variables delineated here are likely not to equal weight, and there are probably others that should be included in a definitive analysis. Despite these shortcomings, however, this article presents an important step in understanding why sports vary in the degree of illegitimate violence that occurs because it focuses on the structure of each sport.

This article has attempted to make the case that participant violence in the four major sports exists as a result of the structure of each sport. We believe that the existing theories currently used to understand participant violence explain only a small portion of why violence exists. These theories have attempted to explain violence: (1) as a "microcosm" of society; (2) as caused by commercialization and economic incentives; (3) as caused by violent crowd behavior; (4) as a genetic predisposition to aggress; (5) as a learned behavior; and (6) as caused by psychological deprivation and repression. These theories are limited because they do not address the important issue of why sports vary in illegitimate violence. Second, the sociological explanations for illegitimate violence have addressed only the types of violence found in contact sports such as football and hockey. Table 2 provides these existing theories of violence with the structural elements of sport considered in this paper added. We contend that the structure of each sport is the one important variable through which all other variables must be channeled in understanding why illegitimate forms of participant violence in sports occur.

The value of this article is that the causes for illegitimate participant violence have been analyzed sociologically by determining what structural characteristics exist in contact as well as non-contact sports that promote illegitimate violence. The addition of the structural elements adds to our understanding of why violence varies by sport. Our hope is that this discussion will encourage

Table 2
Factors Leading to Participant Violence in Sport

Social Factors	Biological and Psychological	Sport Situational	Structure of Sport
Societal values	Genetic	Spectator behavior	Amount of scoring
Economic incentives	Psychological	Importance of game	Amount of legitimate body contact
Economic conditions		Propinquity of opponent	Amount of retaliatory power
Cleavages in society (ethnic, religious)		Media intensity	High versus low rewards
Violence in society History Contemporary Punishment School Media War and militarization		Stage of contest Behavior of coaches, officials Drugs	

research on the structure of the various sports as the independent variable and that it will also encourage research that finds better measures of the dependent variable—illegitimate violence.

References

Bandura, A.K., and R.H. Walters
    1963a "Aggression," *Child Psychology,* Chicago, National Society for the Study of Education, Part 1; 364–415.
    1963b *Social Learning and Personality Development.* New York: Holt, Rinehart and Winston.
Berkowitz, L.
    1964 "The Effects of Observing Violence," *Scientific American* 210 (February): 35–42.
Blumer, Herbert
    1959 "Collective Behavior," in *Principles of Sociology,* revised edition, Alfred McClung Lee, Editor. New York: Barnes & Noble.
Brown, J. Marshall, and Nancy Davies
    1978 "Attitude Towards Violence Among College Athletes," *Journal of Sport Behavior* (May):61–70.
Cataldi, Peter, Jr.
    1978 "Sport and Aggression: A Safety Valve or a Pressure Cooker?" in *Sport Psychology,* William F. Straub, Editor. Ithaca, N.Y.: Movement Publications:59–62.

Coakley, Jay J.
1978 *Sport and Society: Issues and Controversies*. St. Louis: C.V. Mosby Company.

1981 "The Sociological Perspective: Alternate Causations of Violence in Sport," *Arena Review* 5 (February):44–57.

Dollard, J. and others
1939 *Frustration and Aggression*. New Haven: Yale University Press.

Edwards, Harry, and Van Rackages
1977 "The Dynamics of Violence in American Sport: Some Promising Structural and Social Considerations," *Journal of Sport and Social Issues* 1 (Summer/Fall): 3–32.

Eitzen, D. Stanley
1981 "The Structure of Sport and Society," in *The Social World*, Ian Robertson, Editor. New York: Worth:59–62.

Eitzen, D. Stanley, George H. Sage
1982 *Sociology of American Sport*, second edition. Dubuque: William C. Brown Company, Publishers.

Freischlag, J., and Charles Schmidke
1978 "Violence in Sports: Its Causes and Some Solutions," in *Sport Psychology*, William F. Straub, Editor. Ithaca, N.Y.: Movement Publications:161–165.

Furst, Terry R.
1971 "Social Change and the Commercialization of Professional Sports," *International Review of Sport Sociology* 6:153–170.

Gelles, Richard J. and Murray A. Straus
1979 "Determinants of Violence in the Family," in *Contemporary Theories About the Family*, Volume I, Wesley R. Burr, Editor. New York: Free Press:549–581.

Goldstein, Jeffrey H.
1982 "Sports Violence," *National Forum* 62 (Winter):9–12.

Graham, Hugh Davis and Ted Robert Gurr, editors
1979 *Violence in America*, revised edition. Beverly Hills, Calif.: Sage.

Hatfield, Frederick C.
1973 "Some Factors Precipitating Player Violence: A Preliminary Report," *Sport Sociology Bulletin* 2 (Spring):3–6.

Kramer, Jerry
1968 *Instant Replay*, Dick Schapp, Editor. Cleveland: The World Publishing Company.

Pilz, Gunter A.
1979 "Attitudes Toward Different Forms of Aggressive Behavior in Competitive Sports: Two Empirical Studies," *Journal of Sport Behavior* 2 (February):3–27.

Rubenstein, Richard E.
1970 *Rebels in Eden*. Boston: Little, Brown.

Sears, R.R. and others
1953 "Some Child-Rearing Antecedents of Aggression and Dependency in Young Children," *Genetic Psychology Monographs* 47 (February):132–234.

Silva, John, III
1978 "Understanding Aggressive Behavior and Its Effects Upon Athletic Performance," in *Sport Psychology*, William F. Straub, Editor. Ithaca, N.Y.: Movement Publications:177–186.

Sipes, R.G.
1973 "War Sports and Aggression," *American Anthropologist* 75 (February):64–86.
Skolnick, Jerome H.
1969 *The Politics of Protest*. New York: Ballantine.
Smith, Michael D.
1973 "Hostile Outbursts in Sport," *Sport Sociology Bulletin* 2 (Spring):3–6.

1974 "Significant Others' Influence on the Assaultive Behavior of Young Hockey Players," *International Review of Sport Sociology* 3–4:45–59.

1978 "Hockey Violence: Interring Some Myths," in *Sport Psychology*. William F. Straub, Editor. Ithaca, N.Y.: Movement Publications:187–192.

1979 "Hockey Violence: A Test of the Violent Subculture Hypothesis," *Social Problems* 27 (December):235–248.
Steinmentz, Suzanne K. and Murray A. Straus
1973 "The Family as a Cradle of Violence," *Society* 10 (September/October): 50–56.
Stone, Gregory
1955 "American Sports—Play and Dis-play," *Chicago Review* 9:83–100.
Storr, A.
1968 *Human Aggression*. New York: Atheneum.
Sugden, John P.
1981 "The Sociological Perspective: The Political Economy of Violence in American Sport," *Arena Review* 5 (February):57–62.
Sykes, Gresham
1971 *The Society of Captives*, Second Edition. Princeton, N.J.: Princeton University.
Thirer, Joel
1978 "The Effect of Observing Filmed Violence on the Aggressive Attitudes of Female Athletes and Non-Athletes," *Journal of Sport Behavior* 1 (February): 28–37.

1981 "The Psychological Perspective: Analysis of Violence in Sport," *Arena Review* 5 (February).
Vaz, Edmund W.
1974 "What Price Victory? An Analysis of Minor Hockey League Attitudes Toward Winning," *International Review of Sport Sociology* 2:33–57.
Underwood, John
1979 *The Death of An American Game: The Crisis in Football*. Boston: Little, Brown.
Wulf, Steven
1980 "They're Up in Arms Over Beanballs," *Sports Illustrated* (July 14):26–31.

6
Gambling

With more than half of the American public engaging in gambling, it is not surprising that sports betting is among the biggest growth industries in the United States. America's betting explosion has resulted in a $25 billion a year gambling spree. With the media's cooperation, gambling has become acceptable. Although it is obvious that there is a mania for sports gambling, there has been all too little analysis and information on the subject.

The media were full of stories about Tulane University's point-shaving scandal in 1985. Blame was placed on the commercialization of sport, payoffs, drugs, and all the combined ills of society. But point-shaving scandals have been in the headlines since 1951, and the patterns of these scandals were the same in 1985 as they were in 1951. Accusing fingers are often pointed at urban environments, such as New York City, as partial causes, yet in 1951, in the late 1950s, in the 1960s, and in the 1970s, many players from *all* areas of the nation were involved. The Tulane scandal had many of the same patterns with a new twist—the introduction of drugs.

"Hot Rod" Williams, the Tulane star, was charged with sports bribery. On his admission to the university with nowhere near the academic standards usually required for admission, Williams allegedly received a $10,000 bonus from an assistant coach. How different is it for an athlete to accept cash illegally for keeping games close or to accepting even more cash illegally from an official of the university?

In 1961, after a scandal involving twenty-two colleges and thirty-seven players, the presidents of the major universities in North Carolina dropped the Dixie Classic, an important revenue-producing holiday tournament. In 1985, the president of Tulane dropped basketball. There was no change in the sports and gambling climate in 1961, and it is unlikely that the national climate will change in 1986 because Tulane has dropped basketball.

Many have blamed the media for creating a climate in which gambling is more acceptable. Jimmy ("The Greek") Snyder, Larry Merchant, and Pete Axthelm emerged as TV personalities as a result of their "approach" to the games, and newspapers regularly published pointspreads.

In his article, "Sports, Gambling and Television: The Emerging Alliance" (*Arena Review*, vol. 7, no. 1), H. Roy Kaplan examines the direct relationship between the money involved in TV sports and the direct and indirect promotion of gambling through TV sports. Kaplan cites statistical evidence in support of his contention that TV encourages and promotes gambling on sports as a means of increasing the viewing audience.

The argument that printing pointspreads in newspapers promotes illegal gambling and related illicit activities was made many times during the 1985 scandal at Tulane University. Phil Straw's "Pointspreads and Journalistic Ethics" (updated and expanded by Straw from an article in *Arena Review*, vol. 7, no. 1) examines the views of sports information directors, sportswriters, sports editors, and basketball coaches on this issue.

Sports, Gambling and Television: The Emerging Alliance

H. Roy Kaplan
Florida Institute of Technology

Television and Sports

Sports are ubiquitous in our society. They are played and observed by millions of people on a daily basis, from joggers to racing car enthusiasts, fishermen to golfers, tennis players to pool shooters. The sports pages provide more enjoyment to many people than any other part of the newspaper (and are frequently the only section readers peruse). Many specialized publications have risen to cater to sports enthusiasts, e.g., *The Sporting News, Inside Sports, Pro, Sports Illustrated.* Books written by sports celebrities are commonplace and frequently top the best seller lists.

Millions of fans attend games involving the four major team sports (football, baseball, basketball and hockey), although horse racing and auto racing outdraw them as spectator sports. Paid attendance for professional football in 1980 was 14,017,000 (college was 35,541,000), basketball was 10,677,000 (college was 30,692,000), baseball was 43,746,000 and hockey was 11,511,000 (*Statistical Abstracts of the United States, 1981:* 235). 1985 was a record year for attendance in baseball and basketball.

The media tell us a lot about the role sports play in our lives. One has only to turn to the sports section of the newspaper to find reviews of current scores and games as well as gossip about players, coaches, owners, fans, playing facilities and, increasingly, gambling information. Indeed, the sports sections of many newspapers rival that of the news in many tabloids. We have become a society obsessed with sports.

The greatest popularizer of sports, especially professional sports, has been television. As much, if not more, time is devoted to sports on local "news" telecasts than prime news. Broadcast time allocated to sporting events may amount to as much as eight hours a day, as it did for NBC on the 1982 July 4th weekend. By the late 1970's, ABC, CBS and NBC were devoting more than 24 hours of broadcast time each week to sports (Yeager, 1979:119). The burgeoning cable television industry is feeding the demand for sports programming with several channels (ESPN, USA and Sportschannel) almost exclusively broadcasting sports (see: O'Donnell and Gissen, 1982:111). Cable television penetration in the United States market reached 33.4 percent of households in 1982, according to the Nielsen organization (*Broadcasting Magazine*, 6/21/82: 104). Entertainment and Sports Programming Network (ESPN) alone reaches nearly 14 million people and increased 86 percent during 1981 (*Broadcasting Magazine*, 1/11/83:117).

The trend toward increased television viewing in general and sports in particular, can be expected to continue, according to a study by the CBS Office of Economic Analysis which revealed that the average American adult spends 3,350 hours per year (65 hours per week) at "passive leisure activities," including 1500 hours (45 percent) watching television and 1200 hours listening to radio (36 percent). Newspapers accounted for only six percent of adults' passive leisure time, records and tapes 5.7 percent, magazines 4 percent, books 2.1 percent and other assorted activities such as video games and video cassettes less than one percent. The study revealed that leisure time has increased more than 25 percent since 1970 and television and radio's shares each grew by 300 hours (*Broadcasting Magazine*, 7/12/82:97).

Today there is almost no limit to the amount of time a person can devote to watching such stimulating sports events on television as the New York City Marathon, Palm Beach Polo, Chicago's Golden Gloves quarter finals, replays of Notre Dame football and basketball and the Mohammed Ali track meet. The very breadth and triviality of much of this sports broadcasting testifies to their importance to our society. The motivation for this obsession has been explored elsewhere (Lasch, 1978; Kaplan, 1981; Lipsky, 1981), and appears to be a combination of escapist, self-indulgent, thrill-seeking on the part of a bored, apathetic and programmed public. And it is through the mass media, especially television, that this programming or socialization into the viewing sports culture takes place.

Major team sporting events consistently outdraw other television shows. Six of the all-time television ratings are held by Superbowls and two by World Series as Table 1 shows. Superbowl XVI in 1982 on CBS was the highest-rated live television program in history and the third highest-rated program overall (behind episodes of "Dallas" and "Roots"). Over 105 million people watched at least part of Superbowl XVI and the viewing audience averaged 84 million a minute (*Broadcasting Magazine*, 2/1/82:34).

Table 2 contains television ratings by sports for the year 1980. Aside from the Superbowl, World Series and baseball's all-star game. Monday Night Football on ABC was the largest weekly sports attraction. Indeed, this program rated ninth among all shows for the 1981–82 television season (*Broadcasting Magazine*, 7/12/82:32). The popularity of this program testifies to the avid interest in football in the American public, but viewer interest is also linked to and heightened by the tremendous appeal these games have to gamblers. With the exception of the Superbowl, Monday Night Football attracts the largest amount of money wagered of any sports contest. Money and gambling are

Table 1
All-time Top Television Programs

Program	Date	Network	Households
Dallas	11/21/80	CBS	41,470,000
Roots	1/30/77	ABC	36,380,000
Super Bowl XIV	1/20/80	CBS	35,330,000
Super Bowl XIII	1/21/79	NBC	35,090,000
Super Bowl XII	1/15/78	CBS	34,410,000
Gone With the Wind, Pt. 1	11/ 7/76	NBC	33,960,000
Gone With the Wind, Pt. 2	11/ 8/76	NBC	33,750,000
Roots	1/28/77	ABC	32,680,000
Roots	1/27/77	ABC	32,540,000
Roots	1/25/77	ABC	31,900,000
Super Bowl XI	1/ 9/77	NBC	31,610,000
Roots	1/24/77	ABC	31,400,000
Roots	1/26/77	ABC	31,190,000
World Series Game 6	10/21/80	NBC	31,120,000
Dallas	11/ 9/80	CBS	31,120,000
Roots	1/29/77	ABC	30,120,000
Jaws	11/ 4/79	ABC	29,830,000
Dallas	11/ 7/80	CBS	29,720,000
Super Bowl X	1/18/76	CBS	29,440,000
Super Bowl IX	1/12/75	NBC	29,040,000
Dallas	12/ 5/80	CBS	29,020,000
Roots	1/23/77	ABC	28,840,000
Shogun, Pt. 3	9/17/80	NBC	28,710,000
Three's Company	3/13/79	ABC	28,610,000
Dallas	1/23/81	CBS	28,320,000
World Series Game 7	10/17/79	ABC	28,150,000
Dallas	1/ 2/81	CBS	28,090,000

Source: *The World Almanac & Book of Facts, 1982*, New York Newspaper Enterprise Association, Inc., 1981.

inextricably intertwined in the world of sports today, and it is the thesis of this article that the wedding of these and their transmission in the media, especially television with its mass markets, has heightened interest in sports telecasts.[1]

Money on the Mind

Fusing sports with gambling is as old as recorded history. Although not at first, wagers were eventually made on the outcome of Olympic events in ancient Greece (Kiernan and Daley, 1965), and later the Roman gladiatorial

Table 2
Sports on Television

	Household Rating %	% Viewing Audience			
		Men	Women	Teens	Children
Football					
NFL Superbowl	44.4	50	32	9	9
ABC-NFL (Monday evening)	20.2	59	28	7	6
CBS-NFL	15.7	56	28	9	7
NBC-NFL	15.2	56	27	8	9
College bowl games	17.1	52	32	8	8
College All-Star game	12.0	54	28	8	10
NCAA regular season	11.8	56	26	8	10
Baseball					
World Series	32.6	50	38	6	6
All-Star game	26.8	49	32	12	7
Regular season	8.0	52	32	8	8
Horse Racing					
Average all	8.6	43	44	7	6
Basketball					
NBA average	6.0	53	28	11	8
NCAA average	7.6	56	28	8	8
Bowling					
Pro tour	8.5	43	43	6	8
Auto Racing	6.0	49	35	8	8
Golf					
Tournaments	4.3	52	37	5	6
Tennis					
Wimbledon	6.6	51	35	7	7
Tournament average	4.8	47	41	7	5
All-sports Series					
ABC Wide World of Sports	10.8	45	36	9	10
CBS Sports Spectacular	5.9	46	35	8	11
Sportsworld	5.5	48	33	8	11

Source: *The World Almanac, 1982*, New York Newspaper Enterprise Association, p. 865.

games pitted contestants against one another for the greatest purse of all—life (Tucker, 1928). The earliest organized athletic contests were surrounded by religious asceticism and rigid training regimens. As the games became more glamorous, secularization crept in and with it the growing adoration of champions. Ultimately, abuses of the strict amateur creed occurred. The earliest recorded fix of an athletic event occurred in the 98th Olympic Games when Eupolus of Thessaly, a boxer, was convicted of bribing three opponents to let him win (Kiernan and Daley, 1965:16).

Today's sports bear little resemblance to their ancient Olympic predecessors that featured a foot race which covered approximately 200 yards. Modern sporting events are no less glorified than their Greek and Roman counterparts, but organization and professionalism have replaced their spontaneity and amateurism. One would be hard-pressed to find an athlete who does not contemplate the prospect of turning his or her skill to a financial advantage. The media thrive on accounts of multi-million-dollar salaries paid to professional athletes. The annual salary of professional baseball players in 1981 was $185,651; basketball players averaged $215,000, and football players $83,800. Those figures had doubled by 1985.

American society today is a sports-crazed coliseum where the game is played out every day by the owners, managers, coaches, athletes, promoters, agents and media representatives for mega bucks. And what has this intense commercialization wrought? Recent headlines are perhaps indicative: "Leading Jockeys Cited in Race-Fixing Report" (*New York Times*, 3/28/82:32); "How I Put the Fix In" (by the mastermind of the Boston College point-shaving scheme in *Sports Illustrated*, 2/16/81:14–21); "The Shame of College Sports" (*Newsweek*, 9/22/80:50–59).[2] The Tulane point-shaving scandal in 1985, resulting in basketball being dropped there, was only the latest in a long list of gambling scandals.

Without belaboring a point, all is not well in the world of sports in the United States today. Both amateurs and professionals are suffering from increasing commercialization which threatens the viability of athletic endeavors and the integrity of participants. In a society which makes winning paramount and rewards success with adoration, economic and even political recompense, the esthetic, play and consensual elements of sports frequently finish out of the money in the race for fame and fortune. The media, especially television, not only reflect some of the morbid and pathologically destructive tendencies such as violence, denigration of sportsmanship and gambling, but encourage them.

At the heart of the issue lies the eternally corrupting element: money. Sports are big business and have taken on the characteristics of business enterprises. More than a decade ago, Paul Hoch (1972) calculated that the sports industry in the United States generated more than $25 billion annually. Inflation alone would double that figure today.

The Commercialization of Sports in Television

It is in television that the fusion between sports and commercialism is personified and where enormous sums of money are involved. Professional sports, with the exception of hockey,[3] have a big stake in television, deriving much of their revenue from lucrative television contracts. Of an estimated $751 million gross revenues in the National Football League in 1982, television and radio accounted for 58 percent ($332 million). In baseball they account for 30 percent or $119 million of the $397 million in revenues, and 27 percent or $46 million of the $168 million in basketball revenues (Waggoner, 1982:53).

The most recent television contract signed between the National Football League and the three major commercial networks in March of 1982 was worth over $2 billion and compensates each of the 28 NFL teams $14.2 million per season for five years. Ed Garvey, head of the NFL Players' Association noted, "Under the current labor structure, a team could conceivably make $4 million or $5 million profit next year without selling one ticket" (*Time*, 4/5/82:80).[4]

The situation is similar in baseball according to Marvin Miller, formerly Executive Director of the Major League Baseball Players' Association:

> . . . the combination of the national television money, that is for the World Series, All-Star game, the game of the week, Saturday afternoon and Monday night, and the league championship playoff, which is negotiated nationally, the combination of that, plus the local radio and television, which in baseball is negotiated separately by each club . . . is equal to roughly 1½ times the total of all of the players' salaries and the clubs' contributions to the pension plans. In other words, before the first fan parks his car, and buys a hotdog, or scorecard, or pays admission, the radio and television money has met the entire salary bill and entire pension contribution and has almost 50 percent left over. (*Inquiry*, Part 1:382.)

But television networks more than recoup these expenditures. The NFL contract permits the stations to air 24 minutes of commercials per game at approximately $300,000 per minute, generating revenues as high as $7 million per game. The January 1982 Superbowl ads cost $690,000 per minute and were expected to cost approximately $800,000 in 1983. ABC's Monday Night Football advertising time goes for $58,000 for 30 seconds. Thirty seconds during a World Series game costs $185,000. NBC's Saturday Baseball Game of the Week costs $32,000 for 30 seconds. ABC's Baseball-Allstar Game in 1982 went for $150,000 for a half-minute (*Broadcasting Magazine*, 3/1/82:47–54).

Sports Betting and Television

The stakes are very high, and so is the pressure to assure high viewer ratings. The 1982 football television season began in August with weekly professional pre-season games and expanded when the regular professional and college season began in September. In addition to the traditional Saturday afternoon coverage of college games, there were five Thursday night and 13 Saturday night games scheduled to be telecast. The professional season, with its combination of Sunday, Monday, Thursday and Saturday games dragged on through February 1986, with the Pro Bowl. With the United States Football League spring schedule, the season was expanded to encompass the entire year. Their full season, if they survive, will limit that.

Obviously, network and league executives must wrestle with the vexing dilemma of overexposure—reaching a point that might reduce, perhaps significantly, the viewing audience. This plagued the post-strike NFL in the 1984 season. Despite the flourishing of television sports, networks compete to keep the public watching and their share of viewer interest in this lucrative market. According to the Nielsen ratings, NBC and CBS each lost half of their Sunday viewer audience because of games cancelled during the NFL players' strike in 1982. ABC's Monday Night Football cancellation precipitated a 25 percent decline in viewing. But all the interest and favorable ratings cannot dispel the fact that viewing habits change. At what point will sports programming reach the saturation point?

In their search for ways to entice viewers, the networks have hired experts to diagnose plays, analyze games and comment on the inner workings of the sports. Commentators and color reporters are recruited from the ranks of professional players to give anecdotal information and inside views. Football epitomizes this trend, with so many retired quarterbacks doing the color one wonders if it's part of the Players' Association Pension Plan.

But it takes more than anecdotal quips and tactical insights to keep fans glued to their sets for five or six hours. Other "experts" therefore discuss odds, betting lines, effects of injuries on the outcome of games and other gambling-related items. While such information has traditionally appeared in magazines and newspapers, the infusion of gambling into television not only lends an air of legitimacy to sports betting, but broadcasts this information to a much larger audience than that reached by other media, capitalizing on the known proclivity of the public to gamble on sporting events.

Sports and Gambling in America

Gambling is as American as apple pie. In a national survey done for the Commission on the Review of the National Policy Toward Gambling, the University of Michigan's Survey Research Center found that 61 percent of the population bet in 1974 and nearly half the population participated in a form of legal or illegal commercial gambling (National Commission, 1976:58). Sports betting is the most widespread form of gambling, accounting for over 50 percent of illegal gambling in the United States. Estimates of the amount of money wagered range from a few billion dollars to over $500 billion (by noted gambling author, John Scarne). Howard Samuels, former head of Off Track Betting in New York, estimated sports betting accounted for over $50 billion in New York alone. The Commission on the Review of the National Policy Toward Gambling thought it ranged from $10 billion to $40 billion nationally, with perhaps 5½ million people placing their bets through bookies (*Inquiry*, Part II:15).

League officials consistently deny that sports betting is widespread and are vehemently opposed to its legalization. For example, Bowie Kuhn, Commissioner of Baseball, has stated:

> Remember that most people in this country do not gamble. That is the fallacy of the oft heard argument that you might as well legalize gambling because people are going to do it anyway. No doubt a small percentage will but not the vast majority who are not gamblers. (*Inquiry*, Part I:154)

But the facts indicate otherwise. Indeed, gambling, both legal and illegal, seems to be increasing and along with it the number of compulsive gamblers. Recently, the American Psychiatric Association listed compulsive gambling as an illness in its *Diagnostic and Statistical Manual*. Estimates of the number of compulsive gamblers range from one to nine million and the costs of compulsive gambling are staggering. Taking the conservative 1.1 million figure, Politzer, Morrow and Leavey (1981:38) of the Johns Hopkins University Compulsive Gambling Center calculated that the social and economic costs of compulsive (or pathological) gamblers was over *$34 billion annually*.

League officials and owners of professional teams frequently voice their opposition to gambling, claiming that the public's confidence in the integrity of the games would erode, fixes of games might ensue, the public's interest would be diverted from who wins the games to the point spread (see Cady et al., 1/21/75), players might be tempted to bet, the number of gamblers might increase and the family orientation of the games would be threatened. (See Kuhn in *Inquiry*, Part I:153–158, and testimony of officials of major league baseball, the NFL, NHL, NBA, NCAA and NJCAA before the National Commission on Gambling, February 19 and 20, 1975.) Yet the Commission on the Review of the National Policy Toward Gambling concluded that the extent of gambling makes these concerns anachronistic. Commissioner Ueberroth's reinstatement of Mickey Mantle and Willie Mays reversed Bowie Kuhn and seemed to acknowledge this.

Indeed, James Ritchie, the Executive Director of the Commission, stated that, "If all illegal gambling vanished, professional sports would rue the day. It is gambling that has created the interest in pro sports to the extent that it does. In Mr. Rozelle's security office, the way they determine whether they have a problem is by calling Las Vegas to see if the point spread fluctuates'' (*Inquiry*, Part II:15).

So beneath the official veneer is the fact that sports betting is one of the biggest industries in the United States, and the broadcasting industry knows this. Televising information which might be of interest to bettors in the viewing audience, e.g., odds, injury reports, weather conditions, betting lines and discussion by sports and gambling personalities of strategy and possible outcomes, not only capitalizes on the public's gambling interest, it transforms a passive spectator activity into an active risk-taking adventure.

The argument could be made that television is fulfilling a need by providing such material as a public service. If the information was not made public and shared, gamblers would seek it through more secretive illicit means. But they do anyway, much to the embarrassment of prominent sports figures who counted bookmakers among their friends (see Denison, 1973, and Cady et al., 1975). Hence, such broadcasts must be aimed at the broader general audience with the intent of informing, enlivening and perhaps even proselytizing new viewer/bettors.

The Federal Communications Commission, charged with policing the television industry, ruled in 1964 that broadcasts of horseraces must be delayed half an hour to inhibit gamblers and prevent pyramiding bets, but it has consistently refused to act to stem the rising intrusion of sports betting information, despite the urging of the House Selection Committee on Professional Sports and the Commission on the Review of the National Policy Toward Gambling (which also criticized the sports industry for not assuming a more definitive role in controlling broadcasting activities that enhance sports betting) (National Commission:24, 177).

The FCC's reluctance to intervene in the broadcasting of such information stems from the sentiment of its members that the hiring of sports personalities such as former athletes, journalists and gamblers, e.g., Jimmy ''the Greek'' Snyder, Larry Merchant (author of *The National Football Lottery*) and Pete Axthelm (who promoted his gambling column in *Inside Sports* with television advertisements proclaiming, ''They [fans] know that sports are more than just a game'') lies within the First Amendment rights of broadcasters. (See the statement of Werner Hartenberger and William Ray of the FCC in *Inquiry*, Part II:54–62).

While one may agree with the noble intent of the FCC, the public also has the right to be protected from the pervasive intrusions of these subtle inducements to gamble that can have disastrous consequences for the diverse viewing population. It is useless to argue whether the networks are catering to demand or creating a need by forging this alliance between sports and gambling. The fact is that they, their advertisers, and the sports industry benefit from what appears to be a strategy, the ramifications of which deserve closer scrutiny by the FCC, sports officials and the public.

Notes

1. Violence, too is accentuated by the media, but this theme goes beyond the scope of this paper (see Yeager, 1979).

2. See also Denison, 1973, and Cady et al., 1975, for other references to links between sports, commercialism and gambling.

3. The National Hockey League does not have a contract with the three major commercial television networks in the United States, much to its chagrin, although the USA cable network recently negotiated a two-year contract with the league for the rights to broadcast 33 regular season games and all post-season games for $8 million. Some Canadian hockey clubs have television broadcasts, but the share of the U.S clubs in these revenues from 1973–76 was only $35,000 per club. The demise of the World Football League was hastened by its inability to secure a television contract—a fact not overlooked by the fledging United States Football League which negotiated a $20 million contract with ABC to show 20 games over two years (*Broadcasting Magazine*, 5/31/83: 48–49).

4. In 1982 the NCAA negotiated a contract with CBS and ABC calling for $263.5 million for televised football games from 1982–85 (*Facts on File* 1981:643), and an additional $17.6 million contract with the Turner Cable Network. Also in 1982, the Big East Basketball Conference signed a $2 million contract with CBS (for three games), NBC (five games), USA (27 games), ESPN (15 games), Turner's WTBS (three games) and William Tanner (nine games) (*Broadcasting Magazine*, 6/14/82:104).

References

Cady, Steve, and Joseph Durso, Gerald Eskenazi, and Sam Goldaper. This series on sports betting appeared in the Sports Section of the *New York Times,* January 19–22, 1975.

Denison, George. "Big-Time Gambling's Menace to Pro Sports." *Reader's Digest,* August, 1973:91–95.

Hoch, Paul. *Rip Off the Big Game.* Garden City: Doubleday and Company, 1972.

Inquiry into Professional Sports. Hearings before the House Select Committee on Professional Sports. Ninety-Fourth Congress, second session, Parts 1 and 2. Washington, D.C.: United States Government Printing Office, 1976.

Kaplan, H. Roy. "The Commercialization of Sport," in *Sports: Win, Place or Show,* Robert M. Cooper (editor). Memphis: Southwestern at Memphis Press, 1981.

Kiernan, John and Arthur Daley. *The Story of the Olympic Games, 776 B.C. to 1964.* New York: J.B. Lippincott Company, 1965.

Lasch, Christopher. *The Culture of Narcissism.* New York: W.W. Norton and Company, 1978.

Lipsky, Richard. *How We Play the Game: Why Sports Dominate American Life.* Boston: Beacon Press, 1981.

National Commission on the Review of the National Policy Toward Gambling. Final Report, "Gambling in America." Washington, D.C.: United States Government Printing Office, 1976.

O'Donnell, Thomas and Jay Gissen. "A Vaster Wasteland?" *Forbes,* May 24, 1982: 109–116.

Politzer, Robert M. and James S. Morrow, and Sandra B. Leavey. "Report on the Societal Cost of Pathological Gambling and the Cost-Benefit/Effectiveness of Treatment." Paper presented at the Fifth National Conference on Gambling and Risk Taking, October 22–25, 1981, Lake Tahoe, Nevada.

Tucker, T.G. *Life in the Roman World.* New York: The Macmillan Company, 1928.

Waggoner, Glen. "Money Games." *Esquire,* June, 1982:49–60.

Yeager, Robert C. Seasons of Shame: *The New Violence in Sports.* New York: McGraw-Hill, 1979.

Point Spreads and Journalistic Ethics

Philip Straw

Latest Line

PRO BASKETBALL

Favorite	Points	Underdog
WASHINGTON	8½	Utah
ATLANTA	5½	Kansas City
Milwaukee	3	NEW YORK
SAN ANTONIO	7	Golden State
CHICAGO	2½	Portland
HOUSTON	10	Dallas
LOS ANGELES	8	Denver
Philadelphia	7	SAN DIEGO

COLLEGE BASKETBALL

Favorite	Points	Underdog
HOLY CROSS	9½	UMass
AMERICAN	2½	St. Joseph's
RHODE ISLAND	10½	Brown
Penn	1	PRINCETON
NOTRE DAME	4	Fordham
St. Peter's	2½	MANHATTAN
Houston	2	RICE
TEXAS A&M	7	TCU
DRAKE	2½	New Mexico St.
WICHITA ST.	14½	W. Texas St.

Home team in capital letters.

I can't argue with the fact that it is a device used in conducting what is—by and large—an illegal activity. But I believe . . . it is a device that has evolved into legitimate news.

—Vince Doria, *Boston Globe*

A newspaper should come to grip with the moral influence it has on its readers and react correspondingly.

—Bill Dwyre, *Los Angeles Times*

Introduction

Make no mistake about it: sports betting is big business. It goes far beyond innocent office pools and friendly wagering. In 1974, the U.S. Justice Department conservatively set the level of illegal sports gambling in the country at nearly $35 billion annually. In Nevada alone, the only state where sports betting is legal, the 1983 gross wager exceeded $690 million, the bulk of it on professional football. If sports betting were legalized nationally and had a counterpart for comparison regarding its size and impact in the private sector, its revenue portfolio would top that of Citicorp, the largest private bank in the world.

Jim Smith, writing for *Newsday* in 1983, said that "media attention to point spreads, odds and betting information is an important contributor to the sports betting boom. The media has created a climate of acceptance for betting on sports events." A 1982 survey by The Associated Press Sports Editors association revealed that 67 percent of 127 papers surveyed carried pro football betting lines and 50 percent had college lines. Jimmy ("The Greek") Snyder, Pete Axhelm, the syndicated tip service "The Latest Line," and nearly 400 handicapping sheets nationwide all contribute to the "climate of acceptance," noted by Smith.

Handicapping books, newspaper features and newsletters are aimed at a constituency bent on beating the odds. Some sports editors regularly receive (without asking) *The Experts*, a slick $60-yearly California newsletter giving systematic techniques promising to turn a profit for its readers. In his March, 1982, editorial, publisher Ernie Kaufman called basketball "the easiest sport to beat. Wagering on basketball is, in my opinion, absolutely the easiest of the three major sports (basketball, baseball, football) to win money." Later, in the same come-on, Kaufman said: "I'll stick to my guns in support of the big, brown, bouncing ball as being the most reliable source for sports-betting profits." Kaufman theorized that "things go better with buckets" (as in basketball, not fried chicken).

"We're the equivalent to Kiplinger's or Standard & Poors: a newsletter, an advisory service to people interested in informed opinions about the outcome of sporting events," Mort Olshan, publisher of the Los Angeles-based *The Gold Sheet*, told *Newsday*'s Smith. *The Gold Sheet*, founded 30 years ago, has more than 25,000 subscribers nationwide.

Sixteen years ago, Congress called together a blue ribbon panel (the Commission on the Review of the National Policy Toward Gambling) in response to widespread concern over the increasing number of people trying to whip the odds, on anything. The Commission was told to study the problem, make recommendations about trends and offer suggestions for adoptable policies that would curb or, at least, control gambling's tumbleweed. The Commission's final report—presented to Congress in 1976—said, in essence, that gambling regulation should be left to the states. Having shrugged in the face of the issue, the Commission disbanded and no in-depth assessment has been made since to monitor the growth and influence of sports betting in America. According to *Washington Post* reporter Bart Barnes, who researched betting for a two-part 1982 *Post* series: "Inevitably, with the increase in betting, there has to be an increasing concern that gambling will threaten the character and, ultimately, the integrity of professional and amateur sports."

A study conducted by the University of Michigan's Institute for Social Research uncovered some noteworthy trends in sports betting: more men than women bet on sports; more whites than blacks; a greater proportion of individuals from the Northeast and North Central regions bet than persons from other areas; heavy sports gamblers tend to be better educated. Sports bettors, it has been strongly suggested, read the daily newspapers. More accurately, they tend to read the sports pages with religious regularity.

Gambling's growing shadow and its probable adverse impact on the athletic establishment has led to renewed campaigns to stop betting's cancer before it reaches (again) the college campus or the court room. Of all sports shaken by hints of fixes and rigged outcomes, none has been so badly bruised as college basketball. Four times in the last 30 years damaging scandals have swept up players, known criminals, bettors and middle men as a series of depressing incidence left college basketball's credibility crippled. North Carolina coach Dean Smith has, according to *Post* writer Barnes, "been trying unsuccessfully for years to persuade newspapers not to print spreads on college basketball games." With some resignation to the seemingly overwhelming presence of gambling, Barnes, whose editor encourages the publication of spreads, recently editorialized: "It may well be that Smith is trying to do the impossible."

This is an essay about the publication of point spreads by daily newspapers. While it cannot ignore the sports world, this essay's primary focus is on the newsroom, not the gym or football field. To print or not to print: that is the question, and its answer unavoidably involves a discussion of journalistic ethics—to abide or not to abide. Dr. John C. Merrill, the scholarly dean of those who have examined ethics and the newsman, writes in *Ethics and the Press:*

> Ethical concern is important for it forces the journalist to commitment, to thoughtful decision among alternatives. It leads him to seek the *summum bonum,* the highest good in journalism, thereby heightening his authenticity as a person and journalist.

Merrill's thoughtful comments apply to the sports editor and his decision to print point spreads as they are read, used and recited by gamblers of all sorts, on all sports. The publication of point spreads is clearly a matter of judgement. Even with corporate fences and guidelines, it remains a distinctly personal decision as noted by social researcher and media critic Wilbur Schramm:

> The longest step that can be taken is perhaps to emphasize the individual sense of responsibility rather than the corporate sense—that is, the responsibility of the communicator as a public servant and as a professional, quite apart from his obligations to the business that employs him.
>
> Although legal and administrative responsibility for a communicator's actions rests with his employers, the mass media—and especially the journalists within mass communication—do not really operate like other businesses.
>
> More freely than employees in any other business do journalists respond to questions about their practices with "I would do this" or "I wouldn't do it that way."

Ethical considerations can't be casually dismissed, as Merrill says, by hiding behind the simplistic assumption that anything's OK (i.e., ethical) if it appears in print. The frequent publications of point spreads can't be waved off so easily. If they appear in print before a game or match, there is a consequential legitimacy lent to an illegal act and an editor has to be prepared to defend his decision to print, or not to print. His defense, in no small way, will reflect editorial priorities just as it will comment on the ethics of the sports page and the people who paste it up daily. Ethics for the journalist, as Merrill notes, is coupled to personal values, principles, to commitment, to the selection of alternatives, all with honor at stake. Given the intensity of sports, 1982, in America, along with the sharpening profile of gambling in our society, the sports editor can't avoid Merrill's call to commitment or his argument for thoughtful alternatives.

To print or not to print: *that is, indeed, the question.*

Keeping It Close: Basketball's Darkest Days

Going into the 1949 National Invitational Tournament (NIT) (in New York's Madison Square Garden) against Loyola of Chicago, talent-rich Kentucky had won 29 of 30 games (including the 1948 NCAA title) and was considered the best team in the nation. During the first four post-war seasons the Wildcats won 130 of 140 games. Considering the record, Loyola should have been easy pickings. "The bookmakers made UK a 10-point favorite," according to Dave Kindred's history of Kentucky basketball, "and the point spread was duly reported in both the New York and Louisville newspapers, for in the years immediately after World War II the country was caught up in a giddy sports and gambling spree, all fun and games after so much terror."

"It was a gambler's catechism in the late forties," Stanley Cohen observed in *The Game They Played*. The smart money during the period, Cohen implied, knew not to bet against the Yankees in baseball, Notre Dame in football or Kentucky in basketball. But there was something awkward, something eerie, in 1949 about Kentucky's winning, or, at least, *the way* they won. "Kentucky was not always the choice of those inclined to wager on the outcome of a game," Cohen wrote. "Though they had won 93 percent of their games over a four-year period, their percentage was not nearly so good against the spread." Kentucky—a good five baskets better than Loyola of Chicago, lost by eleven, 67–56. "Something's wrong with this team," UK coach Adolph Rupp remembered worrying following the defeat. Nineteen months after the game, three Kentucky starters admitted sharing nearly $2000 in bribes to shave points in the NIT opener against Loyola. In trying to keep it close, but win, the game got away from Alex Groza, Dale Barnstable and Ralph Beard and Kentucky was dropped in a stunning upset.

While the indictment of Beard, Barnstable and Groze shattered Kentuckians (and nearly ended Rupp's career), the revelations of gambling's growing grip on the college game wasn't without warning. Players from Bradley, Manhattan, Long Island University and City College of New York had shaved points to the benefit of bettors long before Kentucky arrived at the Garden. Reacting to the fixes, Kentucky's legendary Rupp (who had boasted that gamblers couldn't touch his players "with a 10-foot pole") said New York was full of sin and corruption. He fingered "big city newspapers that printed point spreads" as an element in a widening point-shaving quicksand that eventually included 32 players from seven colleges. In the five years preceding the Korean War, college basketball staggered from ongoing disclosures of game rigging. A grand jury convened in February, 1951, to investigate the betting web and shaving scandals learned that at least 86 games had been manipulated between 1947 and 1950 by players who had been influenced by payoffs.

Players were paid to keep the outcome of the game within the bookies' pregame point spread. "The involved players," Kindred explains, "were committed" to the preservation of the spread, as published. A missed layup, a bad pass, an innocent fumble all appeared incidental and relatively unimportant to dizzyball fans and non-bettors more concerned with school loyalty than the margin of victory. "Naturally it was possible, in these circumstances," Kindred wrote, "to lose a game—either by design or by a troubled conscience [or] by simply being outplayed on a given night." A 1949 (Louisville) *Courier-Journal* headline read: "Bookies Give Up Net Play." In the story, reporter Pete Johnson wrote that local bookmakers had been stung so many times by upsets that they were no longer taking bets on basketball. The latest upset, Kindred found, had been St. Xavier's victory over Valley—a high school game.

During the stormy early days of basketball's scandals, sportswriters "had heard all the rumors about fixed games." They had, according to historian Larry Fox, "covered a lot of 'upsets' that defied explanation, but the laws of libel prevented them from printing the rumors and voicing their own suspicions." Besides, writers reasoned at the time, if coaches could be fooled by their own players, how could an outsider tell—for sure—when a game was rigged? Max Kase, the astute sports editor of the New York *Journal-American*, shared his colleagues' suspicions and eventually found a cooperative bookmaker (tired of taking a financial beating on games) to confirm his impressions. Kase—who later was given several awards for his work in exposing bribery in college basketball—got names, identified go-betweens and fed his information to New York District Attorney Frank Hogan. He got an exclusive and won wide praise for his investigative work while, all along, the sports pages of the *Journal-American* continued to print point spreads considered by Adolph Rupp to be so damaging, so influential, so sinful.

Even the wrongdoing of the 1950s did not end any further player-gambler collusion. "The lesson was not learned," Zander Hollander wrote years later. In 1961 another scandal erupted, this time touching 22 colleges and 37 players. There was more. In 1965, two Seattle University players were arrested for fixing and in February, 1982, former Boston College player Rick Kuhn was sentenced to 10 years in prison for conspiring (with four others) to manipulate the scores of six BC games during the 1978–79 season. In the point-shaving conspiracies 30 years before the Boston College nightmare, five players received jail sentences ranging from six months to three years while nine others were given suspended sentences. Kuhn was allegedly paid $2500 for each of the six games although gamblers won bets on only three.

In imposing the stiffest sentence ever given a college athlete, Judge Henry Bramwell rejected defense requests for leniency, saying a lengthy prison term might prevent future rigging. District Attorney Frank Hogan made the same point 30 years before. At sentencing, Judge Bramwell read into the record a series of rhetorical questions (example: "Does the court have a responsibility to protect the integrity of intercollegiate athletics?") all of which he answered "yes." According to Bramwell's law clerk, Mary Mullen, the judge's questions did not include any specific reference to the responsibilities of the press or the publication of point spreads by newspapers. "That [issue] certainly came up in one of the colloquies between the defense counsel and the judge," Mullen confirmed, "but it was only one item in a series of things."

Defense lawyers said after the trial that the hypocrisy of society's standards ("Do as I say, not as I do") were as much on trial as the individuals they represented. "Printing point spreads is wrong, just as listing injury reports is wrong. I made that very point," James O'Malley, an attorney for Kuhn's co-defendants, said one month after sentencing. "I feel very strongly about that. Society obviously approves of gambling. It's wrong, and it isn't fair to punish one person for what society condones." Reminded that point spreads were being published before the first major basketball fix, O'Malley commented: "It takes a sports editor with guts to drop them. But why don't they? It is probably the most widely read item in the paper. Such information is useful only to gamblers and gambling is illegal. It's apparent where they [editors] place their priorities."

Almost three years after Kuhn was sentenced for the Boston College scandal, another erupted. In 1985 the integrity of college athletics, admission standards, the impact of point spread publication and the priorities of higher educational institutions were called into question and carefully examined once again following the implication of five Tulane University basketball players in a point-shaving scheme for payoffs. Tulane President Eamon Kelly shut down the school's basketball program and withstood criticism from athletic backers that the scandal was an exception. History had already shown President Kelly that just the opposite was more likely to be true.

A Point of Emphasis: Publication and Personal Opinion

Not realizing that the game had been canceled months earlier, Las Vegas odds-makers made Davidson's basketball team a 5½ point favorite over The Citadel on January 27. To his annoyance, Davidson's sports information director Emil Parker got a firsthand reminder the next day of the extent of gambling involvement in college sports. By Parker's count, more than 50 "fans", frustrated by the absence of a score in their newspaper, called him to ask how the game came out.

Parker allows that he might have succumbed to the temptation to give the callers a phony score except that he was "afraid of waking up and finding a mile-long black limo parked in my driveway." The make-believe score Parker had in mind would have had his school failing to cover the point spread under circumstances calculated to cause apoplexy among at least some of the callers: Davidson 149—The Citadel 144 in triple overtime. (*Sports Illustrated*, February 8, 1982)

Every March, some of college basketball's most respected coaches get together with some of journalism's most widely read sportswriters and they talk about point spreads in the paper. Members of the National Association of Basketball Coaches of the United States (NABC) journey to the NCAA tournament knowing what to expect in the ritualistic conference with representatives of the U.S. Basketball Writers Association. But the coaches attend anyway, loosening their ties and, according to NABC executive directory Joe Vancisin, "generally letting down their hair."

Officials of the two organizations have been meeting like this for over 30 years, since the first point-clipping scandals rocked the college game in

1950–51. "Each year we appeal to them to not print point spreads," Vancisin said. "But we don't seem to make any headway." Vancisin said that the two groups generally agree on the seriousness of sports betting but part company when the conversation turns to the role and responsibility of the press. "We're told: 'This is what our readers want.' It sells papers, I guess." The coaches organization was formed in 1927 and includes nearly 2300 members, all coaches. Most, according to Vancisin (a former Yale head coach), have strong opinions on the topic. Indiana's Bobby Knight once refused to answer post-game questions at a press conference until a writer for a known tout sheet was ushered from the briefing room.

A past NABC president is North Carolina's Dean Smith who, through Vancisin, contends that the publication of betting lines makes sports gambling legitimate to the reader. "Don't newspapers have a social responsibility," Vancisin wondered aloud two weeks before the 1982 pow-wow with writers in New Orleans. "Don't they have a responsibility to improve society? They continually hide behind the First Amendment."

Bill Brill, executive sports editor of the *Roanoke Times & World News* and immediate past president of the 1000-member writers association contends that "people find them [point spreads] interesting. I do not believe point spread information inspires gambling. People like to know who is favored. If there were no odds, there would be no upsets." Brill—who has faced Vancisin's heat on previous occasions—agrees that conditions could exist that would lead to the total elimination of point spreads from the sports pages. According to Brill: "If there ever was any indication that, somehow, these published odds actually affected the outcome of a contest." Evidence to confirm any such association has not yet surfaced. Former *Washington Post* ombudsman Robert McCloskey, whose paper features the syndicated "Latest Line," observed in 1982: "My greatest concern in this aspect [of reporting] would be when athletes, themselves, got involved in the practice [of sports betting]. If it could be proven that athletes were directly influenced by the publication of spreads, then I would suggest that we knock it off."

Is it unethical?

McCloskey: "I guess it is if I think that gambling, per se, is unethical. It is obvious that this information is of interest to the readers of the sports page." Former *Post* columnist Dave Kindred, who led a sometimes-lonely crusade to abolish point spreads from the sports page, said "our paper is among the leading offenders." McCloskey, on the other hand, indicated that the issue had not been one of burning importance at the *Washington Post*. He said his closest prior encounter to the issue involved a discussion about the appropriateness of *Post* classifieds including ads for inflated Rolling Stones concert tickets.

The point spread issue was brought to the attention of McCloskey's replacement, Sam Zagoria. At first unaware of the gambling information tucked away in agate type on *Post* sports pages, Zagoria discussed the issue with editors and writers and offered his observations in an April 10, 1985, *Washington Post* co-ed essay:

> I wonder why newspapers publish information that contributes to illegal betting. I wonder if such listings do not swell the betting pot so that there is more incentive to bookmakers or gamblers to find ways to convert their bets to sure things. Should we not ask newspapers, rarely shy about commenting on the ethics of others, whether they are behaving ethically [themselves]?
>
> In my opinion, gambling is not a victimless crime, because for some it is a sickness, and newspapers should not be cooperating in the illicit conduct.

Zagoria was disturbed by a *Post* layout that included a sidebar to the 1982 NCAA basketball title game story which was devoted entirely to the point spread on the Georgetown–North Carolina championship match-up. "While undergraduates and other purist fans will remember North Carolina's 63–62 victory over Georgetown for the high drama and the artistry on the court, gamblers will remember it as the night the bookies cleaned up," observed *Post* columnist Andrew Beyer. "They [the gamblers] were the only winners on the NCAA title game." His article, boxed on the *Post* sports page with a welcome-home story about Georgetown, detailed the betting ebb and flow effected by the game. Bettors, it was obvious, were not concerned about the outcome of the game, only the margin of winning or losing.

Post writer David Remnick commented in September 1983 that broadcasting point spreads on a television pregame show has commercial appeal, but it also raises the ethical questions that can't be shrugged off. Remnick wrote:

> Gambling may be called a victimless crime by officials of the Justice Department, but no one who is familiar with the tolls so often exacted by gambling on the gambler can call it a victimless activity. Remember Art Schlichter? Sure, thousands may gamble and only a few will ruin their lives with it, but that few should be sufficient to give a station or newspaper pause. Gambling on football games is illegal in most states. Neither the press nor television should be in the business of providing point spreads or any other sort of help.

In an address before the Associated Press Managing Editors Conference in 1984, psychologist Dr. Julian Taber challenged editors to place moral responsibility above profit motives. "Clinically," Taber stated, "it seems clear to me that the typical sports pages in the U.S. feed, encourage, sponsor and promote gambling and little else. The effect of all this gambling information on the gambler is clearly to support and give public sanction to his addiction."

Taber continued:

> The only honest thing [for editors] to do, really would be to rename the sports
> section and call it what it really is: The Gambling Section. That would sell
> newspapers and lighten the image of sports as a gambling vehicle.

Taber suggested that sports betting information be clearly labeled as potentially hazardous to the reader's mental health. "I wish you would print in your paper everyday some simple caution to the effect that any use of your sports laboratory for gambling purposes could prove hazardous," Taber told the editors. "And if your guilt or sense of ethical responsibility tells you to, I wish you would editorialize more about the need to support treatment programs for gamblers. These are the kinds of responsibilities that go with freedom."

In June, 1985, the athletic directors of the 10 Mid-American Conference (MAC) universities asked publishers of newspapers within the region to drop gambling information. The action was prompted, in part, by the Tulane point-shaving scandal uncovered only weeks earlier. The prestigious Atlantic Coast Conference (ACC) took similar action under serious consideration, with Commissioner Robert James saying "we do have some problems from the legal standpoint [in possibly withholding press credential from publications which regularly publish spreads on college games], but [we] hope to overcome them to the point of taking steps at least to reward those who have not participated in the publication of gambling information." It was suggested to James that the ACC endorse a resolution urging coaches and sports information directors to reconsider their interviewing and public information policies with publications that print betting information on ACC contests. Southwest Conference Commissioner Fred Jacoby said that point spread publication "further enhances the opportunity for the exploitation of college athletes by gambling interests."

The Mid-American Conference appeal prompted the *Columbus* (Ohio) *Citizen Journal*'s Sandy Schwartz to react, then ask for reader reaction to the proposal. The *Citizen Journal* regularly carries the syndicated point-spread column, "The Latest Line." Schwartz doubted the effect of the proposal but applauded the Conference's intent just the same. That was on June 10, 1985. The reader's survey was completed three weeks later and Schwartz built another story around the responses. "*Citizen Journal* readers have spoken: 82 percent want to see "The Latest Line" in its present form [carrying both college and pro contests] in the *C-J* every morning," Schwartz reported. The paper received more than 150 responses, with 82 percent wanting the line kept, 13 percent wanted it dropped altogether, and 5 percent wanting the line confined to professional sports. Reader reaction reflected a classic "everyone's doing it, it must be OK" justification from those asking the newspaper to ignore the MAC request. One reader told Schwartz: "Should you drop "The Latest Line" I can assure you of at least five people who will cancel their home delivery." The newspaper, which also covers Ohio State and Big Ten athletics, and devotes extensive attention to the off-field trials of former OSU quarterback and gambler Art Schlichter, offered no comment on any aspect of the ethical questions involved in point spread publication and the welfare of college sports.

Unlike years past, Joe Vancisin might have an ally in Frank Boggs, a former leader of the nation's basketball scribes. Boggs, sports editor of the *Colorado Springs Sun*, argues that the publication of point spreads is, indeed, unethical. "In most states gambling is illegal, so it seems to me that the publication should be considered unethical," Boggs said in response to a survey on the topic. Boggs's pages do not include betting spreads of any sort. His stories rarely mention who is favored "nor do we say that a team has little or no chance to win. 'Upset' is a word we hesitate to use. We simply report the outcome."

Do newspapers have a responsibility to print point spreads?

Boggs: "No. Nor do we have a responsibility to print the phone numbers of prostitutes." Boggs turns a coin over, saying "I feel that it [printing odds], at least, does not discourage gambling. I don't think gambling has ever benefitted athletics. It didn't at Boston College, did it?" As a rather somber afterthought on the issue Boggs added: "Of course, I'm in the minority."

In 1975, St. Johns University sports information director (SID) Bill Esposito stoked the conscience of his fellow publicists by urging college SIDs to unite and deny information to papers and tout sheets which advertised handicapping services. His idea was simple: we, the moral, law-abiding creators and cookers of essential sports facts, figures and photos, can strave line sheets and betting pimps out of existence. In 1975, Esposito was president of the 1000-member College Sports Information Directors of America (CoSIDA). As a student manager of St. Johns basketball team in 1950 he vividly remembers when the first point-shaving case erupted. As CoSIDA president, he tacked together a gambling awareness committee, went to the SID's annual conference in Houston in 1975 and asked his colleagues to join him in a noble cause.

"It has been a total failure," Esposito said three years ago. "It ended in absolute disarray. We needed strength in numbers among the SIDs and we never came close to getting it." Esposito said his campaign won wide support—in theory and intent. "But they didn't follow through. Basically, they [SIDs] are tub-thumpers. Their job is to create publicity for their programs. Many of the SIDs who agreed to the information ban told me later: 'Look, my coach wants the ink and I can't go against the coach.'" So much for principles and good ideas.

Esposito's awareness committee still exists on paper, but it has become, by his own account, a toothless tiger. "Yes, Bill," he's been frequently told along the college circuit, "We're still aware. We're still aware." "People say I expect things to be too absolute," Esposito says today. "Well, there are no shades of gray [in sports betting]. There can be no hint of gambling associated with sports."

Esposito's crusade was revived during the summer of 1985 at the CoSIDA convention in Boston. Jim McKone, the sports publicist at Pan American University in Edinburg, Texas, wanted the convention to approve a resolution urging SIDs to withhold information from tout sheets and publications carrying display advertising for betting services involving college sports. McKone traveled to the convention full of enthusiasm and returned deflated and defeated. McKone said he was "shot down completely" at the national workshop and threatened to give up his chairmanship of CoSIDA's Gambling Awareness Committee, the same post held by Esposito a decade before. The resolution, McKone said afterwards, did not even win the support of his Committee.

The NCAA, the czar of college athletics, has told its member schools they cannot issue press credentials for NCAA championship events to any publication carrying gambling ads. Because of that mandate, the editor of *Basketball Weekly*—with a circulation of nearly 40,000—buys a ticket and sits in the bleachers each year at the NCAA finals. Newspapers in general, the NCAA feels, have slowly resigned themselves to the presence of betting in America. "They simply have the attitude that gambling is here to stay. They have helped to make it an acceptable crime," Dave Cawood, chairman of the NCAA's Task Force on Gambling, said. "We can't stop what is printed, but we can establish policies on advertising, and we intend to enforce them."

Cawood has little patience with editors who defend the publication of odds by pointing to reader interest. "Newspapers have just as much responsibility NOT to print something as they do to print. When they run these things [spreads] they are contributing to a crime. It is an editorial judgement and they know it. Until gambling laws are changed, it is a crime—whether an editor wants to believe it or not," he says flatly.

Most newspapers running betting information are represented in the 28,000-member professional journalist society—Sigma Delta Chi (SDX). The society, based in Chicago, includes in its ranks journalists from cub reporter to sports editors to publishers. The SDX convention agenda has never included a discussion of ethics and the sports page. The social liabilities associated with the publication of point spreads and the responsibilities of the press and this particular issue have not been discussed or debated on the pages of *Quill*, the society's monthly magazine. "Frankly, this is the first time the issue has ever been brought up," SDX executive officer Russ Tornabene said when contacted in 1982. "I don't mean to downgrade it. It is important. But most people don't pay much attention to the finite information on the sports page." Tornabene agreed that the moral issue tied to the possible feeding of useful information to gamblers was "legitimate" and "does reflect the policy of the paper."

Eight months before bringing the 1982 SDX convention to order in Milwaukee, Tornabene said that tentative plans have been made to include "for the first time" a sports reporting panel on this year's docket. The listing is only tentative, Tornabene stressed, and is subject to change. There is little indication, at this time, that the society will tackle the sticky point spread issue. St. John's Esposito, always looking for an angle on the subject, suggested that Sigma Delta Chi become a leader in ultimately divorcing the sports page from the sports bettor. "There is a lot in the paper that shouldn't be," Tornabene agreed. "There is a lot of gore, for example."

Have You Thought About It? A Survey of Sports Editors

A six-question survey was sent to the sports editors of 19 major dailies representing a wide cross section of the nation. All papers are represented in Sigma Delta Chi, most of the sports editors belong (or are former members) to the U.S. Basketball Writers Association, and all have access to such items as "The Latest Line" (sports betting point spread information). Each editor was contacted by phone and the issue was discussed (in detail, in some cases) with each. A total of 17 responses were obtained, with only the *New York Post* (Jerry Lisker) and the *St. Louis Post-Dispatch* (Ed Wilks) failing to respond and return the survey.

A compilation of the survey results shows:

Questions

1. Are you convinced that point spreads (as published by daily newspapers) are being read by the public?

    Yes _____   No _____   n/a _____

2. Is the publication of a point spread unethical?

    Yes _____   No _____   n/a _____

3. In your opinion, are there *any circumstances* under which a newspaper should cease to publish point spreads?

    Yes _____   No _____   n/a _____

4. Opinion question

5. Do you feel that your newspaper has a responsibility to print point spreads?

    Yes _____   No _____   n/a _____

6. Do you personally encourage, permit or oppose the printing of point spreads?

    Encourage _____   Permit _____   Oppose _____

Every respondent (with one exception) feels that point spreads are being followed—for whatever reason—in the paper. The key question about ethics found only four editors calling point spread publication unethical while the balance felt otherwise. Some contend that ethics has nothing to do with the publication of such information. Eleven editors said, yes, there are circumstances ("if my managing editor says so") to cease publication of spreads, four couldn't point to any conditions necessitating a halt and two didn't respond to the question. Only two felt that they had a responsibility to print, while 12 said they didn't but selected (oftentimes) to do so in response to reader interest in the topic. Six encourage the publication of spreads, 8 permit it (implies that someone else is making the decision, and the sports editor is simply approving it) while three oppose the use of spreads.

Newspapers surveyed:

Kansas City Star (Dale Bye)

Atlanta Constitution (Paul Bodi)

New York Times (Joe Vecchione)

Washington Post (George Solomon)

The Milwaukee Journal (Jim Cohen)

Des Moines Register & Tribune (David Westphal)

Miami Herald (Paul Anger)

Baltimore Sun (Ed Brandt)

Detroit Free Press (Joe Distelheim)

Cleveland Plain Dealer (Harding Christ)

Chicago Tribune (George Langford)

Philadelphia Inquirer (Jay Searcy)

Dallas Times Herald (Kenn Finkel)

Roanoke Times & World News (Bill Brill)

Colorado Springs Sun (Frank Boggs)

Boston Globe (Vince Doria)

Los Angeles Times (Bill Dwyer)

Observations

To print or not to print: that was the question.

To print or not to print: that remains the question.

While the publication of point spreads by newspapers cannot by singled out as the major factor in the web of sports betting which is expanding annually in America, it can be stated with some basis that running betting lines in the corners of the sports page is *a contributing factor, an accessory to the crime.* Published point spreads are not the primary spoke in gambling's machinery; they are, perhaps, but a bolt; a small, but important part of a complex, illegal activity.

I found it very disturbing that some coaches (primarily in college basketball) roundly condemn sports betting and readily recognize its adverse impact on the players and the game, yet—somehow—justify their continued cooperation with publications that provide information useful to gamblers who tinker with the health and welfare of collegiate athletics. There appears to be a righteousness about some coaches that bumps against reality. Many coaches who belong to the National Association of Basketball Coaches—which faults the publication of spreads—look the other way when the opportunity to get some ink for their programs clashes with their moral, organizational stance against sports gambling and everything associated with it. Bill Esposito and Jim McKone who campaigned to cut off information to tout sheets and like publications, should have had more support from the coaches and athletic directors as well as sports information directors.

A conflict of interest? A matter of priority? Is it newsworthy? Is it ethical? The questions can't be avoided by editors, and their association with sports betting can't be ignored. Contrary to the contentions of some editors, *there is a question of ethics—is this right? is this wrong? is this responsible journalism?—tied to the publication of spreads.*

We refer to ethics and principles and lofty standards daily without digging below the surface, without looking into the nooks and crannies and determining with certainty just what it takes to keep a principle, an ethic, a standard as upright and imposing as McDonald's golden arches. John Merrill wrote that before any journalist selects his ethics he has to first decide whether or not to be ethical. He has to, in fact, make a commitment to personal principles and strive to uphold them. It isn't easy, but it is necessary.

An editor is paid to be selective and that responsibility means that he has to choose between what he can defend as proper and what he can eliminate (from his pages) as useless or wrong. His highly subjective skills that result in the publication of certain information or the removal of certain items from his pages are factors that should remind him of his position as a keeper and guardian of the public's trust. Protecting that trust involves a recognition of the obvious: if something appears on the pages of a paper, the reader can generally assume it is considered legitimate by the editors. *Be it ever so indirect, the publication of point spreads implies approval of sports betting.*

To justify the publication of point spreads on the basis of reader interest suggests that it is an editor's job to merely give his readers everything they want. An editor is also paid to give his readers what they need. Reasoning which finds an editor dishing up information simply because of "reader interest" can be compared to making a pyromaniac a fireman because he likes hot places. An editor is paid to be selective, to use sound judgement. Those who exercise that judgement and fulfill their responsibilities with diligent consistency and purpose deserve credit and praise. At some point, principles ought to outweigh profits.

Perhaps the most disturbing theme that surfaced from some sports editors contacted on this issue (should point spreads be printed?) was a "bigger than both of us" attitude reshaped in the newsroom to justify running betting lines on sports. I found it difficult to accept from such journalistic monuments as the *Washington Post* shoulder-shrugging responses ("Everyone's doing it") that were more characteristic of a teenager arguing that he be allowed to smoke, drink and run wild on Friday because that's the way things are today. One expects more of journalism. One should expect more of responsible editors. Ethics, as Merrill noted, reflect personal values and perhaps, as Frank McCulloch expressed, journalists "need to be prodded. We need to be told we're not doing well enough. We even have to feel threatened."

Those in the newsroom, broadcasting booth and on college campuses who profess a sincere desire to clean up athletics and restore integrity to the business of sports in America have a responsibility both to the athletes and to the public to examine every aspect of the sports establishment and the environment in which it exists. No one realistically contends that ceasing point spread publication will, in itself, end gambling on games. But that factor, in itself, does not justify the continuation of providing point spreads on the air or on the sports page.

Conscientious athletic conferences and universities, as well as the leadership of professional sports leagues, should put tout sheets, tipsters, bookies and bettors and editors on notice: we do not condone the broadcasting or publication of point spreads and we will not contribute to, or cooperate with, any effort to undermine the integrity of amateur or professional athletics. Until a resolution reflecting such a stance is taken, and upheld, by athletic directors, sports information directors, coaches, and commissioners, the betting community and editors feeding readers will assume that it has the approval of athletics to continue a practice which is unethical and unjustified.

7
Drugs

Nineteen eighty-six was a big year for drug stories in sports. In the first two months, seven New England Patriots were named as having a "serious drug problem" on the day after the Super Bowl, Michael Ray Richardson was banned by the NBA after his fourth failed test for cocaine, Baseball Commissioner Peter Uberroth announced sanctions against twenty-one known users in Major League Baseball, and fifty-seven of the top senior collegiate prospects for the NFL draft tested positively for drugs.

This rash of stories brought back memories of fallen heroes of other times, whom we had managed to forget before the "epidemic." Mercury Morris, one of the premier running backs of his time in the National Football League (NFL), watched his former team, the Miami Dolphins, from a prison cell. Thomas ("Hollywood") Henderson, once the most famous defensive player in the NFL, sat is prison on the other coast after fighting drugs himself. Basketball stars like Michael Ray Richardson, David Thompson, John Lucas, and John Drew fought battles with cocaine.

Seven members of the U.S. Olympic cycling team admitted to blood-boosting during the games. They had received transfusions in the hope that their increased red blood cell count would result in heightened energy during the races. The seven included Steve Hegg, who won a gold and a silver medal, and silver medalists Rebecca Twigg and Pat McDonald. Coaches and team staff were blamed for encouraging the practice, which, some said, could have killed the athletes. It was also revealed that eighty-six Olympic hopefuls screened in the months leading up to the 1984 Games tested positively for banned substances. The United States Olympic Committee (USOC) said that thirty-three athletes tested positively for stimulants and fifty-three others tested positively for anabolic steroids.

Steroids have become a serious problem in the professional ranks, in colleges, and in high schools. Athletes take the steroids in the belief that they will increase their strength and performance. An article by William Oscar Johnson in *Sports Illustrated* (May 13, 1985) estimated that 40 to 90 percent of NFL players use them, a figure roundly denied by both the league and the Players Association. The illegal trade in steroids is a multimillion-dollar-a-year business in the United States, and suppliers of the drug say that half of their dealings are with college athletes. It was revealed in 1985 that thirty-two past and present Vanderbilt University football players were involved in a case of illegal distribution in Nashville—a network of distribution that went throughout the South at least. The *Sports Illustrated* article indicated that these drugs are becoming more and more common with high school athletes.

The effects of steroids, which can be devastating, include possible liver and kidney damage, decreased sperm count, impotence in men, and masculinization in women. A study of ten nationally ranked women athletes who had used steroids found that all had deepened voices, nine had increased facial hair, and eight had enlarged clitorises. Doctors believe such side effects may be irreversible. Finally, in the extreme form, steroids can kill. In 1984, Dr. Robert Goldman, director of sports medicine research at the Chicago Osteopathic Medical Center, attributed the deaths of six athletes to the use of steroids.

Most of the notoriety of "recreational" drug use has focused on the pros and on college athletes, yet studies have shown that an estimated 5.6 million high school athletes are also abusing chemicals, like their peers. However, according to the Minnesota Department of Welfare, although high school athletes use drugs roughly in the same proportion as young nonathletes do, studies have shown they are apt to use those drugs three times as often. Among the reasons given by young athletes for drug use is that the pros, who in many cases serve as role models, are portrayed by the media as fast-living, drug-consuming high rollers: "If its OK for them, it's OK for me." Upon his conviction in 1983 for possession of cocaine, Kansas City Royal Willie Wilson told a reporter, "I didn't sign a contract to take care of anybody else's kids or to be a role model for anybody else. . . . To go around taking care of millions of other kids is just something I never asked for."

The fact is, however, that athletes *are* role models for America's youth. Although executives with incomes comparable to those of athletes may consume drugs in the same proportion, they are not role models. That is what made the Pittsburgh drug trial so noteworthy.

The *New York Times* published a 3-month investigative report on drugs in baseball. This penetrating four-part series, written by Murray Chass and Michael Goodwin, is included here in its entirety. The Pittsburgh trial implicated both current stars—such as Dave Parker, Bill Madlock, Lonnie Smith, Keith Hernandez, Joaquin Andujar, Gary Matthews, and Enos Cabell—and former stars—such as Willie Stargell, Willie Mays, and J.R. Richard. The trial set the sports world reeling as no other event could. The way to prevent such episodes was not on the books, and until it is, the future of sports will be clouded.

Drug Abuse in Baseball

Murray Chass and
Michael Goodwin
New York Times

The use of cocaine by major league baseball players has been so wide-spread in recent years that scores of players have been implicated in criminal investigations as users, purchasers and, sometimes, as sellers of the drug. However, the players generally have not been prosecuted, and in some cases law enforcement officials have taken unusual steps to protect the players' identities.

Court documents and interviews with more than 100 players, baseball executives and law-enforcement officials during a three-month investigation by the *New York Times* also uncovered the following facts:

- Players representing nearly all 26 major league teams have been named in connection with cocaine use in criminal cases across the country, with some teams having several players named.
- In at least four cities, drug dealers or their couriers had access to base-ball clubhouses and conducted sales there.
- The practice of shielding players from prosecution and identification has caused resentment among some defense lawyers, who feel that their clients have become scapegoats.
- In Kansas City, as many as 20 players and one batboy representing nine teams were implicated in a 1983 cocaine case although it culminated in only four Royals being sent to Federal prison.
- Two players—Dale Berra of the Yankees and Dave Parker of the Cin-cinnati Reds—were among the players named as cocaine purchasers in a statement given to Federal prosecutors by a defendant in an ongoing case in Pittsburgh. Both players disputed the assertions.
- At least eight players—including Keith Hernandez of the Mets—are expected to testify in the trial next month of one of the seven defendants in the Pittsburgh case.

Until now, public knowledge about the extent of cocaine use in baseball was confined to the cases of the dozen or so players who have publicly acknowledged cocaine use and several others who have been charged individually with possession of the drug. Most of those who have acknowledged using cocaine have been those who have received treatment for addiction. Baseball officials say that an unspecified number of additional players have undergone such rehabilitation treatment, and they say others may have done so without telling anyone in baseball.

With the exception of the case in Kansas City two years ago in which four players were sentenced to prison terms, no players have been prosecuted as a result of large-scale investigations.

Estimates of the extent of cocaine use among players vary widely, with some people connected with the game saying they believe the problem peaked a few years ago and had now declined to where only a few players used it. On the other hand, a Government source familiar with the Pittsburgh case said that some of the players interviewed by the Federal Bureau of Investigation said that "40 to 50 percent of all players use drugs."

In between are estimates such as one put forth by a player agent, Ron Shapiro, who said he believed 8 percent of all players "have been addicted." Bill Lee, a former player who acknowledged using several different kinds of drugs during his career, said in his recently-published book, *The Wrong Stuff*, that he believed "15 percent of major league ballplayers have a serious drug addiction." In an interview, Lee described that figure as a "guesstimate."

Commissioner Peter Ueberroth, while declining to estimate how many players used cocaine, said he considered drug use the No. 1 problem facing the sports and has warned that it could lead to corruption of the game by gamblers and drug dealers. Asked whether he believed the cocaine problem was less or greater than it was several years ago, he replied simply: "Greater."

One owner, who requested anonymity, said an agent had told him a year ago that he could field an all-star team in each league with players who were using cocaine.

The investigations in which the players were implicated have all taken place from 1982 on. The cases extend across the country and implicate, among others, three members of the 1982 Yankees, two current and four former members of the Milwaukee Brewers and two current members of the Baltimore Orioles.

Officials "Cleaned House"

Cocaine use has not been limited to cities where criminal investigations have taken place. Baseball officials across the country said they were aware that their teams had serious drug problems at one time or another.

In Montreal, for example, John McHale, president of the Expos, said that eight or nine of his players were using cocaine in 1982. Told of McHale's comments, Whitey Herzog, the manager of the St. Louis Cardinals, said his team had an even bigger drug problem than the 1982 Expos when he took over in 1980. Ballard Smith, president of the San Diego Padres, said that in 1982, "we probably had half-a-dozen guys we felt strongly were involved" with drugs. All three officials said they "cleaned house," meaning they released or traded most of the players involved.

A former member of the San Francisco Giants cited the names of four players on the 1985 team as frequent cocaine users. One of the four—Chili Davis—conceded that he had experimented with the drug and that F.B.I. agents had warned him in 1983 that he was under surveillance.

"That was enough for me," Davis said. "You know, a word to the wise."

The former manager of another National League team, who asked not to be identified, recalled a conversation where a player told him a person couldn't get a good cocaine habit on a salary of $200,000 a year.

Baseball may learn in the next few weeks about the cocaine habits of some players through the cases of seven men charged in Pittsburgh with a total of 165 counts of cocaine possession and distribution.

While six of the cases are expected to end with guilty pleas, the one defendant government officials believe will go to trial is Curtis Strong, a Philadelphia caterer who is charged with 16 counts of cocaine distribution and who had access to the Phillies' locker-room. The officials said those likely to be called to testify in his trial, scheduled for next month, include Hernandez, Berra, Parker, Lee Lacy of Baltimore, Lonnie Smith of Kansas City, Al Holland of California, Jeff Leonard of San Francisco and Enos Cabell of Los Angeles.

They are among the 11 active players and one former player who testified before the grand jury with immunity from prosecution and, in separate interviews, each declined to discuss his testimony. However, Hernandez, through Jay Horwitz, the Mets' director of public relations, said "With the possibility of the case going to court, I find it both improper and inappropriate for me to say anything at this time."

Four of the 11—Smith, Leonard, Rod Scurry of Pittsburgh and Tim Raines of Montreal—have acknowledged receiving rehabilitation treatment. Lee Mazzilli of Pittsburgh and John Milner, a former player with several teams, also appeared before the grand jury.

Several people close to the case said Strong traveled to other National League cities to supply players with cocaine.

Adam Renfroe, Jr., Strong's lawyer, said his client would not have any comment, but added: "The reason a lot of guys are pointing to him, was my guy is the least likely one who can hurt them. I'm not going to tell you my guy doesn't know any of the guys involved. But this stuff is all over the country. Why is he being singled out? It's ludicrous to say he's the one."

Guilty Plea Expected

Dale Shiffman, an unemployed photographer indicted on 111 counts, is scheduled to go on trial today, but sources close to his case said he is expected to plead guilty barring a last-minute breakdown in plea bargain negotiations. The case against Shiffman was built in part with the aid of a cooperating witness whom the F.B.I. said made a government-monitored purchase of cocaine from the defendant. Sources close to the case identified the witness as Kevin Koch, who was in his seventh season as the Pittsburgh Parrot, the team mascot, when he resigned in June. The sources said Koch acted as a go-between for Shiffman and players who purchased cocaine from him, picking up the drug from Shiffman and delivering it to players in the clubhouse.

Contacted by telephone, Koch declined to discuss the case. "I don't have any comment," he said. "I appreciate the call, but I have nothing to say. I've talked to the people I've had to talk to. There's really nothing I can say." Then he added, "I'm planning on writing a book myself."

Berra, a former Pirate, and Scurry, a Pittsburgh relief pitcher, had been expected to testify at Shiffman's trial, people on both sides of the case said. A prosecution source said their names may still surface today as part of a guilty plea by Shiffman. The two players, sources on both sides said, also have been mentioned as possible witnesses if another defendant, Jeffery Mosco, goes to trial.

When Scurry was asked about his involvement in the Pittsburgh investigation, he said, "I have nothing to say."

In addition, the sources said, Berra was involved with three other defendants, including Shelby Greer, a sales representative for a telecommunications company in Philadelphia. Sources familiar with Greer's statement to authorities said it named Berra as a cocaine customer and reported that one night Berra ransacked Greer's apartment looking for drugs. Other sources said Mosco attended Berra's wedding last winter and had stayed at Berra's townhouse in Pittsburgh when, in his days as a member of the Pirates, he wasn't using it.

Berra acknowledged that he rented his townhouse to Mosco and a friend of Mosco one winter, but he took issue with Greer's statement.

"Shelby Greer's statements are not fact," Berra said in an interview. "I don't feel I have to comment on anything as ridiculous as that. I never ransacked Greer's apartment. It's ridiculous and it's not true."

Meanwhile, a Yankee source said Berra, after being traded to New York, had agreed to undergo testing for drug use and has passed two tests this season at times selected by the club.

Parker, who other players said was a friend of Greer, was another player who had substantial involvement in the Greer case, according to sources on both sides of the case and other people who are familiar with both. Two of those sources said that in his statement on drug trafficking in baseball, Greer, who was charged with 10 counts, said Parker once gave him $2,000 to buy an ounce of cocaine and told him to deliver it to him in San Diego.

Parker, in a telephone interview, said he had "nothing to say" about the Pittsburgh case. Asked specifically about his inclusion on the list of witnesses for the Strong trial, he said, "I'm not acknowledging anything." Asked about what Greer said in his statement, he said, "I don't even know what you're talking about."

Milner, whose last season was 1982, has been identified by sources on both sides of the case as a possible witness in the Mosco trial and also as a friend of Robert McCue, another defendant. Repeated efforts to reach Milner, a former member of the Pirates and the Expos, were unsuccessful. One of his lawyers, Chuck Berry of Pittsburgh, said he had been unable to locate him recently.

Treatment Called Unfair

Some lawyers in the case expressed the belief that their clients had been treated unfairly because the witnesses received immunity from prosecution. Michael Mullen, the lawyer for Thomas Balzer said neither Balzer nor Kevin Connolly, both of whom pleaded guilty to intent to distribute cocaine, would have been in court if it had not been for the cocaine buyers, whom he did not identify.

"Neither of these boys had the wherewithal to purchase such a large quantity of cocaine," Mullen said. "Somebody had to finance these things. Kevin operates a heating and air conditioning plant. He didn't generate enough income. If someone hadn't laid a large amount of money on Kevin, he wouldn't have been there and neither would Tom. The guys who supply the money get immunity and walk away. It really stinks."

Another lawyer involved in one of the cases, who asked not to be identified, said he believed at least some of the defendants were friends of the players, socialized with them and, eventually, began getting drugs for them at the players' requests. "They became gofers," he said. "They wound up getting stuff for them. The players provided a ready market for these guys. These guys didn't corrupt the players."

Throughout the Pittsburgh case, the United States Attorney, J. Alan Johnson, has steadfastly kept the identities of the players hidden, refusing even to acknowledge that players were involved.

In New York, three members of the 1982 Yankees were mentioned as cocaine users in a telephone call intercepted by law enforcement officials working on a 1982 Manhattan narcotics case. The conversation was between two men who later pleaded guilty to cocaine charges.

"The naming of the Yankees was peripheral to a general conversation about cocaine," said Moacyr Calhelha, a former assistant District Attorney in Manhattan.

Calhelha, now in private practice, said he had wanted to play the entire tape in court because he considered it strong evidence that the defendants were involved in cocaine trafficking. He also said that during the case, he and other prosecutors discussed subpoenaing the players to testify.

But they decided not to issue the subpoenas and Calhelha said that his superiors overruled him on playing the tape in order to protect the players' reputations. After a mistrial was declared, prosecutors said, they agreed to erase the names of players from all copies of the tape, an unusual step. The master tape was sealed, along with other court records, and the case was closed when the defendants pleaded guilty to reduced charges.

Sterling Johnson, New York State's special narcotics prosecutor, whose office was also involved in the case, defended his decision not to identify the Yankees or act against them.

"If two bad guys are talking about drugs and they mention someone, that is a way of really slandering a person legally," Johnson said. In response to another question about the players' role, if any, he said: "I'm not saying they were not involved. We just couldn't make a case against them."

The *Times* has chosen not to reveal the names as a matter of fairness because the members of the Yankees never were questioned by law enforcement agencies or called to testify.

10 Players Are Mentioned

In the Milwaukee case, which resulted last year in Anthony J. Peters, a former ice cream salesman, being sentenced to 22 years in prison for running a cocaine operation that authorities said grossed $17 million a year, the names of at least 10 players from the Brewers, Chicago White Sox and Cleveland Indians were mentioned in grand jury testimony as cocaine users. Witnesses testified that Peters had access to the Brewers' clubhouse and an Internal Revenue Service agent, Ed Miller, testified that bank records showed financial transactions involving Peters and numerous players, according to court documents obtained by the *Times*.

At least three players—Dick Davis, a former Brewer; Paul Molitor of the Brewers and Claudell Washington, formerly of the White Sox and Mets and now with the Atlanta Braves—were interviewed by Federal agents and admitted buying from Peters and others and using the drug, the documents show.

"I have on a number of occasions purchased drugs from Dick Davis," Miller quoted Washington as saying in an affidavit the agent read to a Milwaukee grand jury. "The drugs I purchased were cocaine or pot."

Referring to checks from his account made out to Davis that were shown to him by Miller, Washington said in his affidavit: "The above-described checks would have been for the purchase of drugs through Dick Davis."

William Kedersha, an agent representing Washington, said his client would not comment on the case. However, Kedersha said: "He did use drugs at one point in time. He's not now." Asked whether Washington had ever attended a drug treatment center, Kedersha said yes, that Washington had spent time in such a center between the 1983 and 1984 baseball seasons.

According to a transcript of Miller's testimony obtained by the *Times*, Davis named eight players from various teams as customers of Peters and said that he and Molitor had "drug problems because of an identity crisis." Miller added: "Davis stated that he did in fact purchase cocaine from Peters in 1979 and 1980 on numerous occasions for himself and other major league ballplayers including Claudell Washington."

Davis also identified checks for several hundred dollars each drawn on Brewer road fund accounts as payments to Peters for cocaine and said that Harry Dalton, general manager of the Brewers, had warned him and Molitor to stay away from Peters and a Milwaukee bar where many of the drug sales to players were said to have taken place.

Davis, who is now playing in Japan, declined to discuss specifics of the case when reached by phone. However, he said: "That was a big mistake in my life and I'm glad I got through it. Unlike a lot of guys, I wasn't an over-user. I was just in the wrong place at the wrong time."

Miller, according to the grand jury transcript, said he interviewed Molitor in April 1983. Asked whether Molitor had acknowledged knowing Peters, Miller answered yes, and added: "Basically, it was a business relationship that Molitor maintained with Mr. Peters in order to purchase cocaine for personal consumption. . . . He said he purchased at various times, which numbered 30 or 40 times, he purchased up to an eighth of an ounce of cocaine from Mr. Peters."

Molitor, who is still a member of the Brewers, declined to be interviewed for this article, according to Tom Skibosh, the team's director of publicity. But Molitor was recently quoted in *USA Today* as saying, "I admit to bad judgment. I tried cocaine but that was it. It was a long time ago and I regret it, but those things come back to haunt you. Part of it was peer pressure. I was single and in Milwaukee and I hung around with some wrong people. I was able to get out before I got into serious trouble."

Despite a lengthy trial for Peters and several other suspects, none of the players was mentioned in open court as a cocaine user. Laywers for several of the defendants said they had agreed to a prosecution request that the players be kept out of the case. The defense lawyers agreed, they said, because they felt that the public would be more inclined to view the defendants as corrupters of sports heroes.

"I chose to avoid bringing out the ballplayers for my client's sake," said Tom Brown, who was part of Peters' defense team.

Miller, the I.R.S. agent, said: "Basically, the ballplayers were pretty well protected here. It's my personal opinion that during the time, there was baseball fever," a reference to the Brewers' appearance in the 1982 World Series. He added that another reason was that the case was geared to prosecuting cocaine dealers, not users.

The chief prosecutor in the case, Lawrence Anderson, an assistant United States Attorney, denied that there was an agreement not to name the players. However, he said he had viewed it to his advantage not to name the players because the publicity that would have resulted would have made it more difficult to pick an unbiased jury.

"I didn't need any more publicity," Anderson said. "It took a week to pick the jury as it was. My job is to convict this guy, not to provide interesting reading for sports fans."

However, according to a transcript of grand jury comments obtained by the *Times*, Anderson said: "As you know, Mr. Molitor's status is somewhat of a sports celebrity not only in this city but nationally, and I can't emphasize enough the secrecy involved in a matter such as this because if anything were to leak out, as you know, he could be damned by the press even if it turns out that he's not a target or even a witness in this investigation."

Sales Described

The case involving at least two members of the Orioles similarly resulted in jail terms for the nonplayers who were selling cocaine and immunity from prosecution in exchange for testimony for the players who were buying it, according to Gary Kimmel, a former high school teacher and businessman in Owings Mills, Md. He was recently released after spending 13 months in Federal correctional facilities for selling cocaine to various people, including, he said in an interview, Rich Dauer, an Oriole second baseman, and Sammy Stewart, a relief pitcher. Kimmel said he sold the drug to each of the players seven or eight times between the 1982 and 1983 seasons.

"It was usually a gram every couple of weeks," he said, describing his sales to the players. "When you look at cocaine, that's not what I would call abuse. That's just not that much."

Kimmel, now in the real estate business, said he could not remember how he met Dauer, but that he had met Stewart through a mutual friend. Dauer, he said, attended a poker game on several occasions built around television broadcasts of Monday night football games and that he had sold cocaine to him there. Stewart, Kimmel said, purchased cocaine from him as well as from the mutual friend. He said that he never saw the players use the drug together.

"I can totally understand what they had to do," Kimmel said, referring to the players' testifying against him to a Federal grand jury. "They're making $400,000 or $500,000 a year. When you're making $500,000, it's not that hard to tell what you have to."

Stewart has refused to discuss the subject publicly. Attempts to interview him at Yankee Stadium before an Orioles-Yankees game were rebuffed with comments such as "I have nothing to say."

Dauer, who first denied knowing anyone involved, later said through his agent, Ron Shapiro, that he had testified against Kimmel. Asked if that meant that Dauer was also acknowledging buying cocaine from Kimmel, Shapiro said: "If Kimmel wants to say he sold cocaine to Dauer, then you can put the pieces together."

Perhaps the largest case involving players took place in Kansas City during 1982 and 1983. Only four members of the Royals—Vida Blue, Willie Wilson, Jerry Martin and Willie Aikens—were charged, but Mark Liebl, a Kansas City man who pleaded guilty in the case, said players from around the American League were his customers. Liebl, who was sentenced to six years in Federal prison in Texas, said he sometimes delivered drugs to players at Royals Stadium.

Wilson, Martin and Aikens pleaded guilty to misdemeanor charges of attempting to possess cocaine after calls they made to Liebl were picked up by a government wiretap. Blue was charged with possession, also a misdemeanor. Blue agreed to testify against Liebl and others in the case, including Liebl's brother, and he received the same sentence as the other players—a year in prison with nine months suspended, and a fine.

In an interview and in a sworn statement to baseball officials, Liebl said he had used cocaine with nine members of the Royals organization, including some from the minor leagues, either at his house or at the homes of Blue and Aikens. He said he also used cocaine with eight other players from the Oakland A's, Chicago White Sox, Boston Red Sox and Minnesota Twins, as well as a Brewers batboy.

Liebl said that Blue was the first player he met and that after initially purchasing cocaine for others, Blue started bringing players to Liebl's house and having cocaine parties at his house. Liebl said that Blue had purchased the drug from him for at least one other player on the Detroit Tigers, that Aikens had attempted to purchase it for a member of the Baltimore Orioles and that Wilson had tried to purchase it for a member of the Seattle Mariners.

Aikens, then the Royals' starting first baseman but now in the Toronto minor league system, declined to comment except to say that the whole experience was "history."

Wilson, too, declined to comment directly on the case. However, in his confession, he acknowledged placing a phone call to Liebl's house in an effort to purchase cocaine. Later, he said he had made the call on behalf of a friend. Liebl said the friend was a Mariner player.

Experience with Cocaine

What struck Liebl about the players who used cocaine, he said, was that they all had experience with the drug before they met him.

"I can't think of one ballplayer where it was his first time with me," Liebl said in the interview. "There was no such thing. They all knew how to roll up dollar bills to snort it with. I remember talking to these guys about where they had their first experience and their first experience was always with another ballplayer."

Blue, a member of the Giants, declined to comment on Liebl, saying that he—like Liebl—was writing a book on the subject. However, regarding the issue of his introducing other players to Liebl, he said, "They were already doing cocaine."

Federal agents, who interviewed many of the people involved in the case as well as getting grand jury testimony from Blue and others, would not comment on what they learned about the players not indicted, except to say that all such information is forwarded to F.B.I. headquarters in Washington and kept for future reference.

Harry Gibbs, in charge of security for major league baseball, interviewed Liebl four times, including three times since Liebl has been in the Fort Worth Correctional Institute. Either Gibbs, someone from his staff or club officials talked to every player Liebl cited as a cocaine user, Gibbs said.

"A lot of the information he gave us has been proven correct," Gibbs said of Liebl. "It's more than somebody just winging it."

Bowie Kuhn, the former baseball commissioner, said that, in addition to the four Royals imprisoned, "a number" of the players mentioned in the Kansas City case had undergone treatment for addiction to cocaine. He declined to say which ones or how many.

Regarding the question of the extent of cocaine use among players, Kuhn was asked whether he believed there were people such as Liebl using cocaine with players and selling it to them in other cities.

"You'd be naive if you didn't think there are," he said.

Cocaine use among baseball players has been so pervasive in recent years that the drug's debilitating effects have tarnished individual performances, shortened careers and influenced the outcome of games and pennant races, club officials and players say.

John McHale, president of the Montreal Expos, said cocaine was the reason his team did not win its division championship in 1982, when the team generally was considered to be the best in the National League.

"I don't think there's any doubt in '82 that whole scenario cost us a chance to win," McHale said. "We felt we should've won in '82. When we all woke up to what was going on, we found there were at least eight players on our club who were into this thing. There's no question in my mind and Jim Fanning's mind—he was managing the club that year—that cost us a chance to win."

Executives and managers also acknowledge that cocaine has become a major factor in trade talks and has made managers suspicious when they see players make mistakes on the field.

Although people involved in the game have been reluctant to assess the impact cocaine has had on baseball, a three-month investigation by the *New York Times* found that the subject is one that players and club officials have thought much about, in part because of growing evidence of extensive cocaine use among players. In a series of interviews marked by unusual candor, several members of each group agreed to discuss their experiences and conclusions.

Players Describe Effect

Two top players who underwent drug rehabilitation, Tim Raines of the Montreal Expos and Lonnie Smith of the Kansas City Royals, told how the drug adversely affected their play. Smith told of hiding his cocaine in pockets in his socks. Raines told of carrying cocaine in gram bottles in his uniform pants pockets and of using it between innings in the restroom behind the dugout.

In 1982, the Expos finished in third place, six games from first in the National League's East Division. Raines, who the season before had established a major league record for stolen bases by a rookie, was one of the players McHale belatedly discovered was using cocaine.

"I'd Start Arguing"

"It certainly hurt my performance," said Raines, a 25-year-old outfielder, who underwent addiction treatment after the 1982 season. "I struck out a lot more; my vision was lessened. A lot of times I'd go up to the plate and the ball was right down the middle and I'd jump back, thinking it was at my head. The umpire would call it a strike and I'd start arguing. He'd say, 'That ball was right down the middle.' When you're on drugs, you don't feel you're doing anything wrong."

The question of how cocaine affects baseball is a complex one, if only because success in the major leagues is difficult to achieve and depends on many factors. The history of the game is filled with stories of promising youngsters who failed to achieve stardom or even mediocrity, and of established players who suddenly, without explanation, lost their abilities. Sometimes, alcohol has been cited as the villain and, sometimes, unspecified "off the field" problems have been blamed. Cocaine is the latest factor in the formula, different if for no other reason than it is illegal.

Moreover, the effects of cocaine can vary, depending on when, how much and how often an individual uses it. The effects can be dramatic if a player uses it just before or during a game. If a player restricts his use to non-game times and uses it only occasionally, there could be little or no effect, doctors say. For those who use cocaine regularly but not on the field, the effects might show up gradually.

"There is no doubt in my mind that the stimulant does improve performance but it is short-lived," said Dr. Howard S. Rubin, who has studied the drug's effect on athletes as president and clinical director of the California Institute for Behavioral Medicine. "After a brief time, it becomes destructive."

Questions About Use Arise in Trade Talks

A government source in Pittsburgh, where at least 11 active players, including Raines and Smith, and one former player testified before a grand jury, said a common tale told by players there was that they had a good game after using cocaine for the first time, then kept using it in the belief that it helped their performance. However, they eventually discovered that the drug hampered them and diluted their talent.

Perhaps the clearest example could be that of Willie Wilson, who was one of four Kansas City players imprisoned after the 1983 season on cocaine charges. Although Wilson said the issue of the drug's effect on his performance was irrelevant because he never used it during games, his .332 batting average that won the American League batting title in 1982 plummeted to .276 in 1983, the only time he has batted under .300 in the six seasons he has been a regular in the Royals' outfield.

John Schuerholz, general manager of the Kansa City Royals, stopped short of blaming cocaine for the team's failure to win the American League West title in 1982, when the team finished three games from first. The Royals learned later that several of their starting players had been using cocaine regularly.

"It's so hard to isolate the effect the problem had on the club," Schuerholz said. "We didn't win the pennant. We did have a drug problem. But that's not to say we could've won if we hadn't had the problem. I don't know if we would have won without the problem. But we've always challenged for titles."

Whitey Herzog, who took over a last-place team when he became the St. Louis manager in mid-1980, said that perhaps 40 percent of his players were using cocaine at the time. Asked what effect it might have had on their play, he said pointedly, "We were dead last when I got here."

One owner, who asked not to be identified, said he understood that use was especially prevalent among relief pitchers. If the owner's understanding is correct and those pitchers use cocaine during games, it would fit the pattern described by doctors who say the drug can give a user a 45-minute high. That stimulant would be enough to carry a relief pitcher through perhaps three innings.

It is easy, of course, for clubs to keep track of the players who have undergone rehabilitation. It is not so easy for them to know which players are users when the clubs become involved in trade talks with other teams.

Bill Giles, president of the Philadelphia Phillies, said possible drug use is a subject of immediate interest in trade talks. "That's one of the first things clubs ask," he said. "Is he healthy and is he clean?"

Or there is the approach noted by Tom Haller, general manager of the San Francisco Giants: "What you ask is whether this guy takes care of himself. I guess that's one way of asking if he's clean."

Schuerholz said that trades often are not made because of a suspicion of drug use. "I've heard people say on a lot of occasions, 'I won't involve myself with this guy because I've heard of this or that,'" Schuerholz said.

Dick Howser, the Royals' manager, added, "You probably spend as much time researching that as you do finding out about whether a guy can bunt or hit-and-run."

Murray Cook, general manager of the Expos, said clubs "try to get as much information as you can on anybody."

Cook also talked of the problem of sifting through and investigating the rumors. "That's happened with a lot of players," he said. "They've been painted with a brush. It's such a nebulous area, trying to determine whether or not a player is involved with drugs. It's easy to generalize. It's easy to say this player is performing in such a fashion, he's got to be using drugs. The drug situation is pretty unpredictable. It's hard to tell who's involved, who isn't. You've got to be very careful. It makes it very difficult."

The issue also creates difficulties for players. Chili Davis, a Giant outfielder, was one of four players on the current San Francisco team mentioned by a former Giant as having used cocaine in recent years. "I tried it before," Davis acknowledged. "It wasn't for me. It made my body deteriorate. It made me feel bad. The day after I tried it, I felt drained."

Davis, who had his worst season in 1983, said that he was approached by both the Federal Bureau of Investigation and Giants coaches that season. "The coaches," he said, "whisper, 'Hey, they think you're on cocaine. You're not getting mad when you make outs any more.'"

Davis said he stopped using the drug after being approached by the F.B.I. But some of the suspicion lingered.

Davis said, "Last year, an ex-player came up to me and said, 'They got you; they're watching you.' I said, 'What are they watching me for?' "

Nothing, though, was more difficult for the Expos than the discovery that cocaine had undermined their efforts a few years ago.

"It slipped in the back door and you didn't even know it was in the house," McHale said sadly.

Raines, the rookie sensation, was the only member of the 1982 Expos publicly identified as a cocaine user. He voluntarily entered a treatment center after the season. "Now that I look back," Raines said not long ago, "I probably was the only one that did undergo treatment, but I wasn't the only one that needed to."

McHale said some of the Montreal cocaine users "seemed to be so far gone" that the Expos didn't try to rehabilitate them. Raines, he said, "worked hard" at his rehabilitation.

"He probably cost us six, eight, 10 games doing things we couldn't believe he was doing," McHale said of the outfielder. "We moved him to second base for a while and there were times he held the ball without making a play. He'd be on first base and he couldn't run; they picked him off. He couldn't find balls in the outfield. After we found out what was wrong, we said why couldn't we spot it? You look for excuses, like maybe there's too much pressure on him, or maybe he has problems at home."

Raines said he became involved with cocaine through older teammates. He wouldn't discuss his testimony in Pittsburgh or identify any of his teammates who were involved with him, but added, "When I got anything, it was always from a player." Over all, he said he used the drug with "eight or nine" players, mostly teammates but also some players from other teams.

Raines described himself as a "sort of quiet guy" when he arrived in the major leagues in 1981. "I never knew what drugs were when I was growing up," he said. "Once I got into the big leagues, you just sort of want to fit in. I felt it was just an experiment I tried, and I got hooked. You can't just turn it on and off that easily. I just got in with the wrong people."

Raines said he never found it difficult to get cocaine. "Anytime there's a big party, there's going to be drugs around," he related. "That's the easiest thing to do, to meet someone."

Parties and players and cocaine seem to be a popular combination. When players attend parties, other people often want to ingratiate themselves with these stars by giving them whatever they want.

Ron Davis, a relief pitcher with the Minnesota Twins, recalled how, when he played for the Yankees, he and teammates would go to parties in New York. "I have seen a lot of cocaine around, not that any of our players took it," Davis said. "But it was there if you needed it. A guy would come up to you and say,

'Let's go into the back room, I got some stuff.' He was giving it to us for free if we wanted it. Some of us left. We didn't want to get blamed for using it.''

Sliding Head First to Protect His Cocaine

Raines, on the other hand, used—and used and used. During the 1982 season, he said, he had three months of particularly heavy use, using cocaine virtually every day. But he was careful about where he bought the drug.

"You're taking a chance as an athlete to try to obtain some and risk it being an undercover agent," he said. "I never went out and sought to get it from someone on the street. I never had the guts to do it. When I got anything, it was always from a player."

It didn't take Raines long to become a regular user.

"You find yourself liking it," he said. "You try it again and again. All of a sudden, it gets to the point where you have to have it. It's like an upper. You come down, you feel sluggish, sick. When you're high, you feel normal, but it's not really normal."

Players don't normally take naps in the dugout between innings either, but Raines at times did just that, being exhausted from staying up late using cocaine.

In 1982, Raines did not have what for him was a normal season. His average dropped 27 points to .277; he drove in only six more runs in more than twice as many times at bat as he had the previous season and he struck out nearly three times as often. He also had only seven more stolen bases than he had the year before in the strike-shortened season. In 1981, he stole one out of every 1.97 times he reached base; in 1982, he stole one out of every 3.26 times.

Raines said he often went into the bathroom behind the dugout to use more between innings. Where did he keep it?

"I had it in little gram bottles that I kept in my pocket," he related. "Actually, a lot of times, I would put it in my batting glove and then in my pocket. I was trying to find ways of not getting caught." When he slid into a base, Raines added, he was sure to protect his investment. "Usually," he said, "when I carried it in my pocket, I'd go in head first."

Delivering Cocaine by Federal Express

Lonnie Smith, who said he used cocaine for several years, was another player who took great care to protect his stash. A heavy user when he played the outfield for the St. Louis Cardinals in 1983, Smith told of the different ways he concealed his supply.

"The majority of the time, I hid it on me," he said. "I had these Playboy socks with pockets in them and I'd stick it in there. I had ways of folding my clothes, 10, 12 pairs of pants in a suitcase. I learned it from a Latin friend in Venezuela. People who wanted to check wouldn't take the time.''

During the offseason, he said, he and his supplier had a simple system of delivery. "We Federal Expressed it back and forth," Smith, 29, explained. "I Federal Expressed the money, he Federal Expressed the stuff. He would use a phony address for his address. I thought it was kind of creative in a way. He'd send me newspapers from Philadelphia and tape the stuff inside the papers.''

During the season, he said, his supplier, who lived in Philadelphia, where Smith began his major league career, would call "and ask me if I needed anything.'' The supplier, Smith added, also would travel to other cities, including New York and Pittsburgh, to deliver cocaine to him.

Smith wouldn't name his supplier, but he said he identified him to F.B.I. agents who interviewed him and to the Pittsburgh grand jury when he testified. Smith was said by government officials to be one of several players who would be called to testify at the trial next month of Curtis Strong, a Philadelphia caterer who was one of seven alleged dealers indicted by the grand jury. Asked if Strong was his supplier, Smith laughed and said, "I better not say. There's more than one dealer in Philly.''

Smith said marijuana had been "my drug of choice" but then "I got involved with cocaine and I started to have a problem. There's no doubt I was addicted. I started losing interest in things. I didn't care about the game. The majority of the time we were in a hurry to get the game over with and do it all over again.''

"Three or four" Cardinal teammates, he said, were using cocaine with him, but "at no point did I think any of them were as hooked as I was. They had more will power to control the habit than I did.''

He first used cocaine, he said, when he was playing winter baseball in 1977, before he reached the major leagues, but he said he didn't use it regularly until after the 1980 season, his first full season in the majors, "when I started making more money." The Cardinals won the World Series in 1982, and over the following winter Smith's drug use increased. "I really went over the bend with it because I didn't have anything to do," he said. "I did it almost every day during that winter.''

He estimated that from 1979 until he entered rehabilitation in June 1983 for four weeks, he spent about $50,000 or $60,000 on cocaine, "give or take a few thousand. I started buying in bigger quantities, eighths and quarters. I almost tried buying an ounce." At times, he said, he used the drug with friends and teammates, but "the majority of time, you do it solo. It's so expensive and it goes so fast, you like to hoard it.''

Smith acknowledged talking to players on other teams about cocaine on the field before games. "We would have conversations sometimes," he said, "trying to find out who had connections, who could get something. It was usually during practice before a game, loosening up, running sprints, talking to guys. I think that's how some of the information got around in the drug investigation.''

In 1983, Smith, never considered an outstanding outfielder, played even worse than usual defensively, finishing with a .941 fielding average compared with a .970 average the year before. His success at stealing bases was also not so great as in the year before.

"I think it slowed me down, not just running but my mental thinking," Smith said, discussing the effect cocaine had on his play. "I wasn't as alert. My body was getting run-down, burnt out, as they say. I think it affected me. Other people didn't because I was still getting hits.''

Smith wound up the season with a .321 batting average, 14 points better than the previous year. But over all, he said, the cocaine use affected his play.

"Look at my defense," he said. "It seemed like I was averaging two or three errors a game. I was getting picked off. Everything I swung at was away.''

"Whitey thought I was having problems but not drugs," Smith said, referring to Manager Whitey Herzog. "He thought I was having emotional problems. No one wants to believe a guy is doing bad because of drug problems. But the more I did it, the worse I felt. My need kept getting greater and I couldn't fight that need.''

He told of locking himself in a room, not answering the phone, not talking to anyone. "I was getting away from my family," he said. "My addiction was changing my thinking and my feelings, and I no longer was the same person.''

Using Meal Money for Purchases on Road

Smith's story is not different from those of others who have talked of their involvement with cocaine. The drug can become all-consuming, and the players addicted to it virtually lead their lives with it at the center. Law enforcement officials say some players would make sure their suppliers always were nearby so they wouldn't have to carry large quantities of cocaine with them. The players obtain cocaine from suppliers before games for use during the games, then make another purchase after the games for use then. They use alcohol and pills to come down from the cocaine high so they can sleep, then start with cocaine again when they wake up, again making sure the suppliers are on hand to deliver the morning's supply.

These officials also told of how some players have had their paychecks sent to their agents but still have had money to buy drugs. Among other resources, officials said, they have used the meal money they get when they are on the road and they have used money they get from shoe companies for wearing their shoes. Some players also have sold cocaine to other players as an accommodation, officials said, but there has been no indication—or at least known evidence—that any players have sold the drug for profit.

Whether or not there is evidence, clubs are careful about acquiring players who may have involvement with drugs. In fact, eyebrows around the league were raised earlier this season when the Royals obtained Smith from the Cardinals, considering the shattering experience the Royals had only two years ago.

"We checked him out thoroughly, and that's mild," Howser, the Kansas City manager, said. "A club that's been involved like we were has to be overcautious. That's the most embarrassing thing that has happened. If we're even suspicious that a guy is involved, we wouldn't go after him. I don't know that winning would be worth going through that again."

Sackful of Chicken Tips Off a Manager

Howser was as surprised as anyone when several members of the Royals were implicated in the Kansas City drug case. He said he can look back at various incidents now and see that they might have been the result of drug use, but he said he had no way of knowing then.

"The peoples' work habits weren't as good," he said, "and when your work habits are bad, your skills decline. Their drive dropped off quite a bit. The tenacity, the ability to stay after it, they don't seem to be as tough mentally. They're kind of docile, milquetoast. The frustrating thing as a manager is you're around these guys for seven months and that slips by you."

He told of how one of the players who eventually was found to be involved walked into the clubhouse one day at 4:55 P.M. carrying a sackful of chicken. The players were supposed to be in uniform at 5 P.M.

"That's kind of a tipoff," Howser said. "The thing that disappointed me about this guy was he had good work habits; he came from a good organization. He was supposed to be in here early one day and when he didn't show up, we called him and he was asleep at 3 o'clock.

Speaking later of Willie Aikens, the first baseman who pleaded guilty to a drug charge and served time in prison, Howser said, "His work habits dropped off. He used to have a smile on his face, but his attitude changed. I thought he was mad at me or the organization."

Aikens who hit four home runs for the Royals in the 1980 World Series, has not played well since his drug experience and this season has played in the minor leagues. He declined to talk about his cocaine use. Asked if cocaine has ended careers prematurely, Howser said, "No question about it."

The known cases of cocaine use also have made managers suspicious about other players.

"I've checked lockers and their bags while they're on the field," Billy Martin, the Yankees' manager, said, speaking of the time he managed the

Oakland A's, "trying to find different stuff, people I've suspected. I've never found anything and I've tried hard."

Buck Rodgers, the Montreal manager, said he didn't have to look too hard when he managed the Milwaukee Brewers.

"One of my players came in late for a Sunday game in Minnesota," Rodgers related. "Being late was just part of it. He couldn't stop sniffing. He walked in and every player on the team watched him walk across and then everybody looked at me to see if I was watching. So everybody had some idea."

Suspicion has become a first reaction in certain instances.

"When a ballplayer shows some symptoms on the field," Jim Frey, manager of the Chicago Cubs, said, "when his personality as a player on the field changes, you question it because of today's culture. Sometimes you say to yourself, 'I wonder if maybe this fellow is using something.' That's a natural reaction."

On the other hand, Chuck Tanner, the Pittsburgh manager, whose team was the center of controversy during the drug investigation in Pittsburgh earlier this year, said he tries to resist suspicion.

"If every time a guy boots a ball, you wondered what it was, you'd go crazy," Tanner said. "Everybody makes an error. Every pitcher loses a game. Guys in the Hall of Fame lost games."

Even experience doesn't make a manager an expert, though. Rod Scurry, a Pirates relief pitcher, underwent rehabilitation for cocaine use and returned to the team. "It was up to me to take care of him after he came back," Tanner said. "So I'd ask him and he said he felt good. When he didn't show up, I was surprised. If I thought there was a problem, I would've tried to help him."

Scurry returned to rehabilitation a second time for substance abuse; though the Pirates never said the treatment was for drug abuse.

Players who have undergone treatment for cocaine use acknowledge that it is difficult to remain free of drugs afterward, not unlike an alcoholic with alcohol. Steve Howe, the relief pitcher released by Los Angeles earlier this season and recently signed by the Minnesota Twins, has been treated twice.

"You're always tempted," Lonnie Smith said. "If you socialize with people you run across the wrong people. You're tempted almost every day out of the year. It's not easy. There's no known cure for the disease."

They called it "the Cooperstown room."

The basement in Mark Liebl's suburban Kansas City home was decorated with baseball memorabilia—autographed balls, bats and photographs of players. But the sobriquet linking it to the Hall of Fame had nothing to do with the decorations.

It was called that because many prominent major league players went there to snort cocaine.

"I remember we made a joke that they ought to put the room in Cooperstown," Liebl said. "One of the players said that because a lot of baseball was talked and a lot of cocaine was done there."

The use of cocaine by major league players has been widespread in recent years, with players from nearly all 26 teams implicated in criminal investigations across the country. The drug has affected baseball in fundamental ways—impaired performances have influenced games and even pennant races, trades have been made or not made based on drug reports and careers have been shortened.

Nowhere has the extensive mix of baseball and cocaine been as dramatic as in Kansas City, where four key members of the Royals were sentenced to Federal prison after the 1983 season. The four—Vida Blue, Willie Wilson, Jerry Martin and Willie Aikens—are the only players to be sent to prison in this country on cocaine charges while still active major leaguers.

Liebl, the target of the investigation, was sentenced to six years after he pleaded guilty to conspiracy to distribute cocaine and to using the telephone for unlawful acts. He is in the Fort Worth Correctional Institute, the same minimum-security prison where the four players each served 81 days.

Yet the Kansas City case is significant in ways beyond the imprisonment of the players. For one thing, the full details, as pieced together through interviews and an examination of court documents, offer a rare glimpse of how the worlds of baseball and cocaine meet.

For example, cocaine orders were frequently placed in telephone calls made from the Royals' clubhouse, Liebl said, and the drugs were delivered to the players at Royals Stadium. The players talked about baseball, while using drugs, Liebl said, and talked about drugs while playing baseball.

Moreover, the case illustrates a pattern repeated in other cities—the players publicly identified represent only a portion of the actual number involved. The four Royals who went to prison were not the only players who were frequent cocaine users, Liebl said. He named 13 other players from the Royals and four other American League teams as people he had used cocaine with and said that Kansas City players had bought or attempted to buy cocaine from him for at least three other players on three more teams.

Liebl, who is writing a book on the subject, also said he believed that additional players he never met often shared in the drugs carried from his house. He said members of the Royals introduced him to players from teams visiting Kansas City and that the players talked about their sources in other cities.

"It's all over baseball," Liebl said.

Liebl's assertions were supported by baseball officials, who interviewed him several times and also talked to other players involved in the case. Former Commissioner Bowie Kuhn, who made an extraordinary trip to Texas to interview Liebl in prison, said he considered Liebl credible. Kuhn was present, often asking questions, when Liebl made a sworn statement of player involvement. A transcript of the statement, recorded in June 1984 by a Texas reporter, was obtained by the *Times.*

"Oddly enough, Liebl is a real baseball fan," Kuhn said in an interview. "He wanted to make the players happy, so he supplied them with drugs. But he was concerned about what was going on. It was a paradoxical thing."

Richard Block, baseball's arbitrator, in upholding Kuhn's decision to suspend Blue for the 1984 season, cited Liebl's accounts.

"We conclude that the testimony is clear and consistent," Bloch's decision says, referring to Liebl. "The testimony corroborates similar evidence, gained from the initial interview with Blue and the various statements of other affected players, of Vida Blue's substantial involvement.'

The players he used cocaine with, Liebl said, included three members of the 1982 Boston Red Sox, two members of the 1982 Oakland A's, two members of the 1982 Chicago White Sox, five other Royals and a member of the Minnesota Twins.

On one occasion, Liebl said, a teenage batboy from the Milwaukee Brewers attended a cocaine party at Blue's apartment. Liebl said that he objected to giving the batboy cocaine, but that Blue said it was fine.

"Till this day, I still have a terrible feeling about that," Liebl said in a recent six-hour interview in the visitors' room at the prison. "He let that little batboy snort cocaine. Boy, he should have never done that."

Although Blue, in an interview, refused to comment on this incident or anything regarding Liebl, saying he, too, is writing a book, a transcript of Bloch's decision shows that security aides from the commissioner's office investigated the allegation. The transcript says: "The incident concerning the Milwaukee Brewer batboy is confirmed in substantial part by testimony from Liebl and from the batboy. Clearly, there was a party in Blue's apartment. There is considerable dispute as to whether and to what extent the young man indulged in cocaine use that evening, but it is abundantly clear that cocaine was openly apparent and readily available."

Throughout the prison interview, and in numerous subsequent telephone conversations, Liebl expressed regret over his role in the entire episode. He said he was addicted to the drug and believed that at least some of the players, whom he considers friends, were also.

"Being in prison is tough, believe me, it's really tough," Liebl said. "But that cocaine hell was a lot tougher."

He believes baseball has a serious cocaine problem and that gamblers and drug dealers could influence the results of games through drugs. Liebl said he gave the names of the players he said were involved to baseball officials after being promised that the players would be offered help, but not punished. Baseball officials said all the players involved were interviewed, and Kuhn said "a number" underwent drug rehabilitation.

Although one might question comments from someone seeking parole,

Liebl is not, according to the prosecutor in his case, a typical drug dealer.

He's a nice guy, a kind of a Billy Budd type," said Amanda Meers, an assistant United States Attorney in Kansas City, Kan. "I don't mean in the legal sense because there was no question that he was guilty of selling cocaine. I mean in the sense of being naive."

She went on to say that Liebl made little or no money from his baseball customers. The profits he made, she said, were used to buy more cocaine, which he used himself or gave free of charge to players and others who befriended him.

"I didn't have the mentality to be a drug dealer," Liebl said. Then, recalling parties where as many as 30 people came to his house to snort his cocaine, he added, "I always said you didn't have to be pretty or famous to do cocaine at my house. You only had to be a friend."

His rule was simple: The cocaine used at his house was free. Anything taken out the door had to be paid for usually at $80 a gram. He went through "many thousands of dollars" that way and lost his business and the two homes he owned.

"Real Good Friendship Right Off the Bat"

As Liebl remembers it, the beginning of his association with baseball players was relatively inauspicious.

"It was a Sunday night, in April of 1982," Liebl recalled. "I was home resting on my couch, about 11 or so, and a friend called and asked what I was doing. I said I was getting ready to go to bed. He asked did I mind if he came over, he had somebody he wanted me to meet."

"About 30 minutes later, the doorbell rang," Liebl said. "It was my friend and Vida Blue."

A self-described "baseball nut," Liebl was awed to have the famous pitcher in his home. The introductions were made, pleasantries exchanged, and the three men got to the business at hand: snorting cocaine.

"I think Vida might have brought some that night, or he had some with him," Liebl said, "I can't remember which. But we started snorting."

At the time, Liebl, who is 6 feet 5 inches tall, was 32 years old and had been using cocaine occasionally for about two years, in part to chase away the blues brought on by a crumbling marriage. A native of Dodge City, Kan., he had catered to tourists on Boot Hill as a teen-ager and, after failing to finish college, had settled in Overland Park, near Kansas City. He had managed three sporting goods stores and worked in public relations for a beer distributor before buying a liquor store. His three-bedroom home had a swimming pool in the backyard, and he bought a second house, which he rented out. He and his wife had no children, he said.

Blue was from a small Lousiana town and had risen to instant stardom during his rookie season in 1971, when he had a 24–8 record for the Oakland A's. Blue was an enigma to many people. His celebrated contract disputes with the A's owner, Charles O. Finley, had soured him and he seemed to be getting little joy out of baseball when the San Francisco Giants traded him to the Royals before the 1982 season.

Two days after they met, Blue invited Liebl to a Royals game. Later that night they went to Liebl's house to snort cocaine.

"Vida and I struck up a real good friendship right off the bat," Liebl said. "I could tell him every number that every Oakland player ever wore. Gosh, he was amazed. Just as much as I was amazed about him being there, he was amazed at how much I knew."

Before long, Liebl, who was buying about four ounces of cocaine a month, was selling to Blue in quantities that Liebl knew were too large for one person. There are 28 grams per ounce.

"Vida was telling me other guys on the team were snorting," Liebl said, adding that the sales were usually for two or three grams.

One night Liebl was in a bar. At about 7:15 the phone rang. "They said it was for me," Liebl recalled. "It was Vida and the game was going to start at 7:35. He was in the clubhouse and he asked me if I was coming to the game. I said I wasn't planning on it. He said, " 'Well, if you do, could you bring some for Wilson and Aikens.' "

Staying Up All Night and Snorting Cocaine

Liebl said he still had not met any other players, but that was about to change. In June 1982, Blue suggested he join the team on a road trip to Anaheim, Calif., where the Royals were playing the Angels. Liebl arrived on a Friday evening and checked into the hotel where the Royals were staying.

"The team had already gone to the stadium," he said. "But Vida had a reservation for me. Then I went to the ball park, and he had tickets waiting for me. After the game, there was a couple of girls he knew. We went out with them, to a party, and went back to the hotel about 1 or so. Willie Wilson came to the room. That's the first time I ever met Willie and we started snorting cocaine."

Later, he said, Jerry Martin joined them and they stayed up until nearly 6 A.M., snorting cocaine.

Saturday's game was at night and Blue was the Royals' starting pitcher. But he was lifted after six innings, dressed in civilian clothes and, Liebl said, joined him in the stands behind home plate. At Blue's invitation, Liebl said, they went to the Royals' clubhouse, where they drank beer and watched the last few innings on television. The Royals lost.

"It was fascinating to me," Liebl said, "to be in a major league clubhouse like that during a ball game."

After the game, he said, they went back to the hotel, where they repeated the previous night's activities.

"Once again, it was Martin and Wilson that came by and we snorted cocaine all night long," Liebl said. "I remember those guys had to rush to pack their bags in the morning because it was getaway day after the Sunday game, and they had to rush to be ready by 10 o'clock."

Liebl took an early flight back to Kansas City, where he learned that the Royals lost again, 9–1. It was, he said, the clearest indication to him that cocaine was hurting the team. The Royals finished the season in second place, three games behind the Angels in the American League West.

On other occasions, Liebl accompanied the team on road trips to Texas and Boston. He said the pattern was the same—staying up all night, snorting cocaine with players.

"The Greediness of Some of These Guys"

Gradually, other Royals began to join in the parties, Liebl said. Aikens and the shortstop U.L. Washington were coming around, as was Don Hood, a pitcher. And then Liebl began meeting players from visiting teams, who were being brought to his house, or to Blue's or Aikens's apartments. At one point, Liebl said, Blue purchased cocaine from him for a member of the Detroit Tigers and Aikens tried to buy cocaine from Liebl for a friend on the Baltimore Orioles, but Liebl didn't have any at the time.

Washington, now with Montreal, declined in an interview to discuss the case. "It's all in the past," he said.

Hood, now out of baseball, cannot be reached, according to his agent, Alan Hendricks. "I think he's somewhere up in New York State, but he doesn't have a phone," Hendricks said.

Liebl also recalls a night in 1982 when he met a good portion of the Red Sox pitching staff. He said that a friend took him to a hotel where the team was staying and that they spent the night snorting cocaine with Dennis Eckersley, Mike Torrez and Chuck Rainey.

"We got there after the game, about midnight," Liebl said. "And I left the room at about 11 o'clock in the morning."

Asked to respond, Eckersley, now with the Cubs, said: "I have nothing to say. I have no idea why my name came up." Asked if the incident happened, he said, "I have no idea. No comment. Bad subject . . . terrible subject."

Torrez, a former Met and Yankee who is now out of baseball, said: "I don't know anything about it. I've been to a lot of parties where I thought people were using cocaine, but that's their business." He said he would "throw a lawsuit on somebody's butt if my name isn't used right."

Rainey is out of baseball and lives in San Diego, according to his agent, who said Rainey was on his honeymoon in Europe and could not be contacted. The agent, Stephen Freyer, of Boston, said he had been contacted by the Players Association last year regarding Liebl's account.

"Chuck definitely denied it," Freyer said. "That guy was singing like a canary down in Fort Worth. I believe Chuck."

When the White Sox came to town, Liebl said, Blue introduced him to Ron LeFlore and Steve Trout.

"It was a Friday night after a ball game and here again we snorted and snorted," Liebl said. "You talk about the greediness of some of these guys. We snorted till about 4 in the morning and, when they got ready to go, they wanted to get one-quarter ounce, seven grams, they said it was going to be for other players, too. I gave it to them, and they said, 'Well, we don't have the money on us, but we're going to be here till Sunday, and we'll get the money to you.'

"They never did get the money to me," Liebl continued. "I often wonder, who do they think they're fooling? You don't forget that you just bought $500 worth of cocaine and you haven't paid the guy. Boy, they were just a couple of jerks about it. They must have thought it was some pleasure for me that they were at my house. They were dead wrong. What if I had been a real nut and marched out there on Sunday afternoon to the airport when they're getting on the airplane and stuck a gun in their ribs and said, 'Where's my money?' And there's people like that, especially in that business."

Trout, now with the Cubs, said: "I don't understand it. That's a stupid question to be asking about. I have nothing to talk about."

LeFlore, who is out of baseball, said he did not recall meeting Liebl and added, "I don't know anything about it."

After mentioning that he did cocaine with Mike Norris and Tom Underwood at Blue's apartment when Oakland came to town, Liebl noted that so many pitchers were involved because "Vida was the one that always brought the players by. There was a little fraternity there. That's what's so damn dangerous about it—those are the guys throwing the damn ball."

Underwood, now with Columbus, the top Yankee farm team, disputed Liebl. "That's wrong," he said. "Evidently, I met the man without even knowing it." He said he was at Blue's apartment "to have a few beers" with Norris and Blue and that Liebl arrived as he was leaving, but that they had not used cocaine.

Norris, out of baseball, was twice arrested for possession of cocaine. The first charge was dropped, the second is pending. His agent, Steven Kay, of Oakland, said Norris was in a rehabilitation facility and would have no comment.

Discussing Baseball, Battles with Manager

The cocaine use went on throughout the 1982 season, Liebl said, with players coming to his house on an average of two or three nights a week when the Royals were home. The conversations often centered on how common it was for players to use amphetamine pills, known as "greenies," and what players on other teams used cocaine, Liebl said.

"Like I said, they didn't get their start from a friendly pusher man," Liebl said. "They all got their start from another baseball player."

They talked about other things. When Aikens began getting less playing time, he described the battles he and the Royals' manager, Dick Howser, were having. Martin, who, court records show, had previously sought rehabilitation treatment, liked to talk about his family, Liebl said. Blue liked to play baseball trivia.

"One time, Vida asked me, 'Hey, who was the last switch-hitter in the American League to win the Most Valuable Player award?'" Liebl recalled.

Stumped, he guessed, "Mickey Mantle?"

"No," Blue answered. "Me."

Liebl laughed when he told the story. "It was him," Liebl said. "He won it in 1971, before they had the d.h., and he was a switch-hitter. He was real clever on stuff like that."

The drug use by the group grew especially heavy in the winter months before the 1983 season, Liebl said, adding that he was buying and selling in ever larger quantities. He had become dependent on the drug, was having trouble sleeping and often suffered hallucinations and paranoia.

Sleeping Troubles and Hallucinations

Meanwhile, law enforcement authorities had become aware of what was going on in Liebl's house based on information gathered in Dodge City, his hometown. Joaquin Padilla, an undercover agent for the Kansas Bureau of Investigation, was investigating a man there named Dennis Young on suspicion of selling cocaine. At their first meeting, Padilla, posing as a businessman, bought cocaine from Young. According to an affidavit filed by Padilla, Young boasted that he had been to "some Kansas City Royals baseball games and had 'partied' with three members of the Royals, naming Vida Blue, Willie Wilson and Willie Aikens."

Padilla, who confirmed the account in an interview, then asked Young if he got the players' autographs.

"We don't need their autographs," Padilla reported Young as saying. "We got their noses."

The authorities, through detective work, began to focus on Liebl as Young's source of cocaine. Surveillance of Liebl's home, which involved Federal agents, showed that cars with license plates issued to Wilson, Aikens, Washington and others were frequently at Liebl's house until early morning.

The authorities applied for a wiretap authorization. The application named, among others, Liebl, Young, Aikens, Wilson, Blue, and Washington as "the persons committing the offenses." It was approved and, on June 3, the tap was installed.

Over the next 17 days, Wilson, Martin and Aikens were among the many people who called Liebl, hoping to purchase cocaine. All the calls were recorded by the Government and were the basis of the charges against the players.

A call made by Wilson on June 18 was an attempt to purchase cocaine for Al Cowens of Seattle, Liebl said. Wilson, who acknowledged making a call on that day in his written confession, has said that the call was for a friend, but he has not named anyone. Seattle was in Kansas City that day as part of a three-game series with the Royals.

Cowens did not respond to repeated telephone requests for an interview. Craig Detwiler, a Mariner spokesman, said he personally twice gave Cowens the messages, but added, "I wouldn't hold your breath" for a response.

Blue, while he did not call Liebl while the phone was tapped, was later charged with possession of cocaine on the basis of testimony presented to a grand jury. Because Washington and other players did not call while Liebl's phone was tapped, and there was insufficient evidence against them, they were not charged, according to law enforcement officials.

On June 20, 1983, Liebl and his girlfriend were preparing to go to a Royals game when the authorities came crashing through the door, guns drawn.

"I said, 'You just don't know how glad I am this thing's finally over,' " Liebl recalled with a laugh. "That's how bad that whole thing had become for me. I was relieved."

The police and drug agents searched the house and found a bag of cocaine, but told Liebl they were not arresting him because the investigation was ongoing. Eventually, the players were questioned and, after the season, Federal drug charges were filed against 17 people, including Dennis Young, Liebl, and his brother John. Most, including the players, pleaded guilty to reduced charges. Young and Mark Liebl are in prison together, while John Liebl is in another Federal prison.

Mark Liebl has served 17 months and hopes for parole later this year. His spirits seem good, thanks largely to his fiancee, who talks to him daily and visits him each Monday. Prison officials say he causes no trouble, is friendly to everyone, does his job well—he helps with bookkeeping—and spends his time jogging around the spacious prison grounds and playing first base on the softball team. He praises the facility's drug treatment program.

But he remains addicted to baseball. He calls everybody arrested with him his "fall partners" and follows the players' careers closely. He is still loyal to the Royals, but believes they erred in trading Aikens, who often batted cleanup.

"It's so easy to pitch around George Brett now," he says, sounding like a true fan. "The Royals need a good lefthanded d.h."

No one knows the extent of cocaine use in baseball and there is no basic agreement among the commissioner, the owners and the players on the proper way to approach a solution to the problem.

Everyone, though, is trying to deal with the issue. Commissioner Peter Ueberroth, for one, said in a recent interview that he was attempting to extend his mandatory drug-testing program to the winter leagues in Latin American countries.

"I'm going to go outside the United States and Canada, into the winter leagues," said Ueberroth. "There are places where players play where people look the other way. I don't know how much leverage I'll have. I'm running into resistance. But I'm getting a steady flow of information that some of the root causes are there."

Ueberroth, who believes drugs are the No. 1 problem facing baseball, added that "if we're going to shut down drugs in baseball, we have to shut them down everywhere. I've got to be concerned that we're curing the problem in the United States and Canada and not elsewhere."

Ueberrroth did not provide details of how he planned to implement such a program. But, he said, "Remember, they need baseball players." The winter leagues are stocked partly with young players from the major leagues and high minor leagues.

Some people in baseball suspect that players get their first taste of cocaine when they play winter ball in Latin American countries, Venezuela particularly.

"I think a lot of it starts in winter ball in Venezuela; you're right next to Columbia," said Joel Youngblood, an outfielder for the San Francisco Giants. "I think that's where a lot of players are introduced to cocaine. If you don't speak the language, what else is there to do except play ball and hang out by the pool. A lot of players were exposed to it, and it was cheaper."

Other people don't think players have to leave home to discover the drug.

"They have as much cocaine here as they do in the Dominican or in Venezuela," says Dock Ellis, a former major league pitcher, who admittedly has had vast experience with drug use and, more recently, experience in treating drug abusers.

Wherever the players first find it and try it, they have used cocaine to such an extent that many more players than previously known have been implicated in criminal investigations as purchasers and, in some cases, sellers of the drug. This fact was uncovered in a three-month investigation by the *New York Times* into cocaine in baseball. Use of the drug, the investigation also found, has affected individual performances and careers, games and pennant races, and it has influenced trades made or not.

The subject of drugs in baseball was basically dormant until earlier this year when two developments brought it hurtling into the public eye: A Federal grand jury investigating cocaine trafficking in the Pittsburgh area summoned at least a dozen current and former players to testify, and Ueberroth announced a mandatory drug-testing program for everyone in baseball except for major league players, who are covered under a joint program with club owners that provides for voluntary testing.

In announcing his program in May, Ueberroth said he was concerned about the integrity of baseball. In a *New York Times*/CBS Poll conducted between July 16 and July 21, 78 percent of those surveyed said they believed that drug taking among baseball players was a serious problem.

Ueberroth, showing little faith in the joint program, has tried to induce the players to agree to mandatory testing. But the players think the testing would be an invasion of their privacy. Further, they say the joint program has a mechanism for change if the three-doctor panel known as the joint review council believes alterations are necessary.

"I expect the program to be reviewed before next spring," Donald Fehr, acting executive director of the Players Association, said. "I don't know if there will be any changes. If I had to guess, we might want to get the joint review council involved with aftercare at an earlier stage so if there's a problem down the road, they would be better informed. We're also going to continue to develop the education side of the program."

Fehr said that "less than a handful" of players have appeared before the council since it was created a year ago, but he declined to give the specific figure or identify them, noting that the procedure is confidential. A player goes before the council if he and his club cannot agree on his involvement with drugs or a way to have his problem treated.

"Virtually all the cases that have come up since the program went into effect are relapse cases," Fehr said. "My general impression is the use of cocaine is way down. It has diminished in amount, frequency and the number of people involved. I think the worst is behind us. In the last year and a half, there has been growing public awareness that it is a dangerous drug."

Baseball, as other sports, was slow in reaching the realization that cocaine was a problem that had to be dealt with. Managers and coaches readily acknowledge that they had no idea what was happening when players were having difficulties in the field or at bat. They often attributed the mistakes and errors to problems "at home."

Now seminars are held for executives and managers to learn what symptoms to look for. Players hear lectures, as an educational tool, about the effects of cocaine. Clubs employ doctors to be on call for consultation with players who need help.

A Former Pitcher Recalls His Addiction

Ellis, who pitched in the major leagues for 12 seasons (1968–79), knows all about cocaine, not to mention other drugs as well. He tried them all, he said, at one time or another during his tenures with five teams, including the Yankees and the Mets.

"I was using everything," Ellis said. "I mean everything. For about eight or nine years, I was an addict."

Ellis, who after his baseball career worked in adolescent units at two hospitals, now operates the substance-abuse program for the California Institute for Behavioral Medicine, a private clinic in Beverly Hills. He said he sees a lot of athletes, entertainers, doctors and lawyers.

Baseball players are not alone in the use of cocaine. The National Institute of Drug Abuse estimates that 22 million Americans have used cocaine. And the United States Drug Enforcement Agency estimates that between 74 and 95 metric tons of cocaine were consumed in the United States in 1984, a 52 percent increase over 1983.

"I always say we have a mirror of society in sports," said Ellis, who once hit the first three Cincinnati batters in the first inning, he says, while under the influence of amphetamine-like pills. "It's there. It's not going to up and go away. I would say three or four years ago it was out of control. It was everywhere. I mean people were traveling with teams, I don't think it's as bad now as it was in the past. What has happened is teams have taken more of an interest in it and are trying to do something about it. It's also quieted down with all these investigations. Guys realize if they get caught, it could be the end of their careers."

Why do players use cocaine in the first place?

Sparky Anderson, a major league manager for 16 years, says it's fear.

"Guys are scared for their jobs," Anderson, the Detroit manager, said. "You see guys who are afraid. They're scared to death. They have to be afraid of something or else they wouldn't turn to it. No one with common sense would start unless it's fear."

Pressure on Players Is Called Relentless

Ellis said cocaine use begins in the minor leagues. "You leave home and you're a star," he said. "You've been a star wherever you've played. Then you're not a star anymore. There are a lot of guys as good as you or better. You're afraid of failure and you're afraid of success. That's where this stuff starts.''

As a minor leaguer, of course, a player doesn't earn a large salary and thus doesn't have the kind of money a regular cocaine habit requires. Major league salaries, now averaging about $360,000 a year, provide players with money for drugs that few professions afford. Often, people who want to be around players make cocaine available for nothing, making it even more readily obtainable, players say. Users especially like the initial results of their cocaine taste.

"Cocaine is like a greenie," said Ellis, who noted that he never paid for the drugs he used. "It's a stimulant; it's an upper. What it does, they think they can run faster; they see the ball differently, like a balloon. It gives them the feeling they can do anything, 'I can conquer the world,' like Superman.''

The long-range effect, though, creates a drastically different feeling, especially when a player uses cocaine regularly. Frequent usage becomes commonplace because the high attained from a one-time use lasts for about 20 to 30 minutes, Ellis said, or in some systems up to 45 minutes.

"It eventually gets to you," Ellis explained. "You're going to do well with it, but when you abuse it, which you naturally do, you're going to hurt yourself and someone on the field—an outfielder running for the ball and not seeing another outfielder and running into him, a third baseman picking up the ball and throwing it and hitting someone. Down the line it will affect you negatively.''

Dr. Roger Weiss, who runs the drug dependency center at McLean Hospital at Harvard University, has been retained by the Boston Red Sox for counseling. He said he has treated many people, including athletes, for cocaine abuse, but no members of the Red Sox.

"Athletes are different in the sense of having to be on all the time, the pressure of having to perform in the public eye relentlessly," Dr. Weiss said. "There's always so much attention to what they do, and I guess there's always some self-doubt underneath their confidence that can be eliminated with drugs.''

Regarding heavy users of cocaine, he added, "Their behavior is going to be quite erratic." Part of the problem, he said, is that people addicted to cocaine often resort to alcohol and Valium in order to sleep, eventually becoming addicted to those substances as well.

Players become aware of the effects of cocaine often too late. Even after going through rehabilitation, some suffer relapses, finding the emotional need for cocaine greater than the intellectual knowledge that it can be destructive.

"The problem," Ellis said, "is the stresses the individuals are dealing with. Until someone in management understands that, they're going to have failures after guys have treatment. They need someone to relate to. Until you can get a person to relate, you can't even deal with the guy and understand his stresses. When you treat the stresses involved and you have a carefully planned aftercare program, there's no guarantee the guy is going to stay clean, but he has a chance.''

The Los Angeles Dodgers created a stir earlier this year when they put a mandatory drug-testing clause in the contracts of Bill Russell and Mike Marshall. The Players Association contended that the clause violated the joint drug agreement, and the owners' Player Relations Committee, with which the agreement was negotiated last year, concurred. The Dodgers withdrew the clause.

Some players, though, have agreed to testing. Rich Dauer of the Baltimore Orioles is one, submitting after he was involved in the investigation of a drug dealer in Baltimore in 1983. Dale Berra, who testified before a Federal grand jury in Pittsburgh earlier this year, agreed to random testing after the Yankees acquired him from the Pirates last winter.

Some clubs initiated minor league drug-testing programs before. Ueberroth announced his plan, which, he has emphasized, is geared toward treatment and not punishment. Some officials attribute what they believe is a decline in the use of cocaine to these programs.

"The kids are afraid to use drugs because of the possible consequences," said Murray Cook, the Montreal general manager. "Organizations I've talked to have fewer and fewer players testing positive."

Yet not everyone agrees that cocaine use has diminished. One major league coach, who also played in the majors for many years, said he believed "if anything, it's worse." Bowie Kuhn, who was baseball commissioner for 15½ years until last Sept. 30, said that as he left office he "didn't get any impression that it had diminished."

"I'd like to think that it had, but the vibes I was getting was that there was and continues to be a substantial problem," he said.

The indictments in the Pittsburgh cases covered dates ranging from December 1979 to Jan. 11, 1985. Every one of the seven men charged was indicted on counts with dates at least as recently as 1984. In other words, the most recent investigation implicating baseball players comes close to the present.

Concern Expressed About Gamblers

This week some people in baseball, including Lee MacPhail, president of the Player Relations Committee, have pointed out that events that prompted investigations in such places as Milwaukee, Baltimore, Kansas City and Pittsburgh took place several years ago and so do not reflect the current state of affairs. But investigations by law enforcement agencies take time, both to be started and concluded.

Both Kuhn and his successor have expressed concern that cocaine use could lead to criminal involvement in baseball, that players dependent on the drug are potentially vulnerable to gamblers seeking inside information or trying to control the outcome of games.

"The integrity of the game is everything," Ueberroth said in calling for player support for his drug-testing program.

Ueberroth, however, also said he had no evidence of gambling influence.

"If there have been instances where there has been a legitimate factual concern, I haven't heard about them," Fehr, the players' union chief, said, "If people have facts to back that up, they should let us know. We have absolutely no interest in having gambling involved in baseball. If there are serious problems, we feel something should be done. But I don't know of any problems."

"A New Feeling" Evolves About Users

Some players have encountered problems in criminal cases but in investigations of drug dealers, not in relation to the outcome of games. Yet, in several cases, authorities have tried to hide the identities of the players. They reasoned that the players served to help them get to the dealers, who were their targets, and they didn't want to tarnish the players' reputations.

That view may be changing.

Stephen Trott, head of the criminal division of the United States Justice Department, explained that the United States has always seen cocaine as "Colombia's problem" but that Colombia points out that the United States is the marketplace for the drug.

"That's where people spend $80 billion a year on this thing," Trott said. "The demand side of the equation was written off. But the people who break the law and use drugs are part and parcel of the problem."

Discussing the practice of not identifying users, particularly baseball players, he said, "There's a new feeling evolving. We view users differently than we did 15 years ago, maybe five years ago. The Colombians say, 'We view our peasants who grow the plant as criminals. Do you view your people who use the plant as criminals?' They're right."

However, there is no indication that any change has taken effect.

In the Pittsburgh case, J. Alan Johnson, the United States Attorney in Pittsburgh, wanted to grant baseball players immunity from prosecution for testifying about people accused of dealing drugs.

One government source said there had been some disagreement between Trott and Johnson on the immunity question. Trott did not acknowledge that such disagreement existed.

"There were lots of talks with Jerry on immunity," he said, "I was the person he had to consult in the final analysis, I agreed with Jerry and he handled the cases as he saw it."

In the next few weeks, one of those Pittsburgh cases, in which many players may be called to testify against a defendant may provide a more detailed look at how the worlds of baseball and cocaine have met.

8
The Media

For decades, media coverage of sports kept us either uninformed or misinformed about how sport interacts with society. The sports media emphasized their function as provider of entertainment rather than information. They mythologized heroes while giving the consumer a steady stream of statistics. Gradually, the field of sports journalism evolved into sports promotion. This has been especially true of television and radio.

The media helped make sport the world's broadest cultural common denominator. Men and women, blacks and whites, Soviets and Americans, barefoot villagers from the hills of Kenya and sophisticated urbanites from Boston all seem to "think sports." The proportion of column inches devoted to sport in our nation's newspapers exceeds that of virtually any other area— more than international politics, national affairs, education, or the arts. The same is true of local nightly TV news programs. Weekend network programming is saturated with sports events, and some 24-hour cable networks televise nothing but sports.

The "Sports of the Times" columnist, Robert Lipsyte, stood up against the concept of journalists as promoters and entertainers and helped bring a new dimension to sports journalism. With a handful of other writers and sports editors, he began to challenge the surface hype and take an in-depth look at the reality of sport. In "Sportsworld Revisited" (*JSSI*, vol. 1, no. 1), he notes the historic role of journalists: "stewards of the mansion, preserving the status quo, parroting the owners, the mayors or the government's line." His article, updated for this book, provides an overall perspective on what he calls Sportsworld—the very subject this book is attempting to address in depth.

Led by the likes of Bob Lipsyte in print and Howard Cosell on TV, sports journalists are now complementing sports scholars and opening our eyes to the impact of sports on society and vice versa. The scholars, with analytical training but scant field experience, have benefited from the experience of the journalists. In turn, journalism departments at our major universities are infusing future generations of sports journalists with the desire to go beyond the surface stories. Whereas previous generations helped bury stories about academic abuses, drugs, gambling, racism, and sexism, a handful of current journalists are examining those subjects microscopically.

Even today, however, there is a poor body of information regarding the question of ethics in sports journalism. In their article, "Ethics in Sports Journalism" (*Arena Review*, vol. 7, no. 2), Garry Smith and Terry Valeriote examine this issue, including allegations that sportswriters are poorly trained and lack objectivity. They use a Canadian example, deriving their information from three Toronto dailies.

Sportsworld Revisited

Robert Lipsyte
CBS Television

For the past hundred years, most Americans have been led to believe that playing and watching competitive games not only are healthful activities, but exert a positive force on our national psyche. In sports, they believe, children will learn courage and self-control, old people will find blissful nostalgia, and families will discover non-threatening ways to communicate among themselves. Immigrants will find shortcuts to recognition as Americans. Rich and poor, black and white, educated and unskilled, we will all find a unifying language. The melting pot may be a myth, but we will all come together in the ballpark. The values of the arena and the locker-room have been imposed on our national life. Coaches and sportswriters are speaking for generals and businessmen when they tell us that a man must be psychologically "tough" to succeed, that he must be clean and punctual and honest, that he must bear pain, bad luck and defeat without whimpering or making excuses: real men play hurt, a pro doesn't rub.

A man must prove his faith in sports and the American way by whipping himself into shape, playing by the rules, being part of the team, and putting out all the way. (This is interesting terminology, by the way, and no coincidence. The jock in our society is not unlike the stereotyped woman, judged on beauty and performance, existing at male/owner sufferance, and replaceable.)

If an athlete's faith is strong enough, he will triumph. It's his own fault if he loses, fails, or remains poor.

Even for ballgames, these values with their implicit definitions of manhood, courage and success, are not necessarily in the individual's best interests. But for daily life they tend to create a dangerous and grotesque web of ethics and attitudes, an amorphous infrastructure—I call it Sportsworld—that acts to contain our energies, divert our passions and socialize us for work or war or depression. I think it's interesting to note that in 1929, a Columbia historian named John Krout wrote: "During depressions, with thousands out of work, sports helps refocus our attention on the great American values and ideals and also helps us to remember that life does not begin and end with the dollar."

Sportsworld, of course, includes sports spectaculars that are not, strictly speaking, sporting events: space shots and political conventions keep our eyes up while the ground beneath us crumbles away. This infrastructure, Sportsworld, is neither an American nor a modern phenomena. The Olympics of ancient Greece were manipulated for political and commercial purposes: at the end they held a cracked mirror to a decaying civilization. Sportsworld is no classic conspiracy, but rather an expression of a community of interest. In the Soviet Union, for example, where world-class athletes are the diplomat-soldiers of ideology, and where factory workers exercise to reduce fatigue and increase production, it is simple to see that the entire athletic apparatus is part of government. In this country, Sportsworld's power is less visible. Banks decide which arenas and recreational facilities will be built. Television networks decide which sports shall be sponsored and viewed. The press decides which individuals and teams will be celebrated. Municipal governments decide which clubs will be subsidized. And the federal government, through favorable tax rulings and exemptions from law, helps develop and maintain sports entertainments as a currency of communication that surpasses patriotism and piety, while exploiting them both.

Sportsworld, though determinedly anti-intellectual, has come under increasing scrutiny lately from psychologists, physicians and social scientists. But most investigations still study sports within its own insulated context, rather than exploring the possibility that if the glorious fun and games of sports—and let me say here that this is important only because at root sports *is* glorious, ennobling even, certainly the most fun a person can have with their body in public—if the fun and games could be separated from the "jock-ocracy" of Sportsworld we could take a major step toward the liberation from the false values, the stereotypes, the idols of the arena, that have burdened us all since childhood.

The killer word in my old neighborhood was "fag." Call a boy a fag and he would have to fight or slink away. The homosexual connotation of the word was implicit, but not primary. Since we believed that homosexuals were unmanly, somehow "feminine," the word really meant to us that a boy was "girlish," unfit for the company of men. We all knew that girls were smaller, weaker, less physically skilled. They had no place in the big leagues of life. They had no future. Sports taught us that.

A boy tried very hard to avoid being labeled a fag. He might play games in which he found no pleasure, he might root for professional teams that bored him. He paid constant lip-service to sports. Who you like betta, fella, Mantle or Mays? You could answer any way you wanted to, you could say Duke Snider, just so long as you didn't say, who cares? The schoolyard, the no-woman's land, was a male sanctuary, and the first of the arenas in which we would be tested for the rest of our manipulated lives. Sports was the first great separator of the sexes. Sometime after kindergarten, a girl was handed—symbolically or literally—the majorette's baton and told to go in the corner and twirl, honey. Her athletic moment was over. She now existed only as an encourager of males. There were, of course, girls who dropped the baton and picked up the bat, and beat us at our own games. But we were prepared for them. Athletically superior boys were supermen, but athletically superior girls were something less than real women. Locker-room jokes. She's playing because she can't get a date, she's a tom-boy, she's a dyke. And if she turns out to be world-class, well, we'll scrape the inside of her cheek and study her chromosomes and declare her a male.

At fourteen, reading about Babe Didrikson in Paul Gallico's popular *Farewell to Sport,* I had no reason to disbelieve his statement that she became one of the greatest of all American athletes merely as "an escape, a compensation." Didrikson, wrote Gallico, "would not or could not compete with women at their own best game . . . man-snatching."

In the sixties, as a sportswriter with a partially-raised consciousness, I accepted the statement as the routine sexism of my trade. After all, we barred women from press boxes then, much less locker-rooms. Only recently, while researching my book, I came across an even simpler explanation. Gallico, a fine and vain athlete himself, once raced Didrikson across a golf course. She ran him into the ground, and he never again wrote about her without mentioning her prominent Adam's apple or the down on her upper lip. Of course, a woman can't beat a man, unless he's a fag. Or she's not really a woman.

Once, I believed that women were culled from sports competition to protect their delicate bodies from harm. I am no longer so sure. Perhaps they were culled to protect the delicate egos of men who have been taught that their manhood depends upon the presence of an underclass. Past childhood, into our working lives, we are still in thrall to Sportsworld, although less obviously. And, adding insult to injury, we are taxed to support it.

Politicians have always realized that sports identification is helpful. Why else throw out the first ball of the season? But the best recent example of this kind of political sportspower occurred in New York, in 1969, when John Lindsay was running for a second term as mayor. Justifiably, his chances looked poor. But that fall, the Mets began a drive to the pennant, and I remember Lindsay, who hated baseball, arriving at Shea Stadium around the eighth inning of every game so he could be on hand for the locker-room interviews afterward. Lindsay was taller than most of the Mets, and handsomer. He materialized on television as somehow having been involved in the pennant race. The Mets manager refused to endorse Lindsay but when one of the pitchers poured champagne on the Mayor's head during a locker-room party, which was televised, it seemed as though the whole team was endorsing Lindsay. By the time the Mets won it all, got their ticker-tape parade and the keys to the city, it seemed as if the ball-club had actually pounded a few more beats into New York's sick old heart. Anyway, that's what the press told us. We're gonna be all right. If the Mets can do it, so can New York. We're number one.

It was the same Lindsay who made the deal—which may eventually cost

New York more than $150 million—to refurbish Yankee Stadium. It was a corrupt land swindle, but one based on the political axiom—and I have heard this from politicians—that a city cannot be major league unless it has a major league baseball team—no matter the quality of its public services, it's only major league with a ball-team plugging the city into what I call the good news network . . . datelines across America from cities . . . Boston, New York, Los Angeles . . . with terrible problems, whose only happy images come through sports. We're O.K., say the sports pages. Chief Justice Earl Warren said he turned to the sports pages first because "the sports page records people's accomplishments. The front page usually records nothing but man's failures." No wonder that twenty-five percent of the hard news in your newspaper is sports news, that no matter what else is happening in the world, there's always at least three or four minutes of sports on your evening news telecast.

When sports moves across international boundaries—the sexism, boosterism and emotional corruption of sports journalists, the commercial demands and political vulnerability of television, and the goals of political leaders, become more serious and complex. We are told that international sports is "a moral equivalent to war." I have problems with that concept because it seems to presuppose a substitution for a necessary event—sports for war as one substitutes chewing gum for cigarettes—rather than confronting the problem and finding bona fide alternatives.

The role of journalists in all this has been as steward of the mansion, preserving the status quo, parroting the owners, the mayors, or the government's line—whether it be in admitting girls to little league, which came about with little thanks to sportswriters, or in admitting China to the Olympic Games. Sportswriters can roughly be classified into three categories: as box-score maniacs, those involved in the technical aspects of the game; as gossips, and this is a very derogatory term among old-line sportswriters; as sociologists. A sociologist is one who dares to approach sports within the context of a larger society . . .

During the fourteen years I was in the sports department of the *New York Times,* we were known as the "toy department," and the rest of the paper was called "outside." Responsible newspapers tend to be slightly embarrassed at *having* sports departments—it's considered a sop to circulation, and the same standards of quality journalism do *not* generally prevail in the toy department as outside. In the *Times,* for example, all men are "mister"—except convicted criminals and sports figures. Thus, for example, the China-Taiwan-Canada machinations at the 1976 Olympics never got the same kind of serious coverage one would have expected of a routine United Nations debate. Nor has the background of the South African sports boycotts. This is a serious omission. Readers in general would have found out more about our two-China policy, would have been able to cut through the superficiality of the ping-pong diplomacy story, if we could have seen how sports was used, the past twenty-five years, to separate peoples on a global scale. And I've always felt that the quick labeling of the South African boycotts as responses to apartheid, miss the greater point—South Africa has no right in any Olympic or international competition for the same reason that Nazi Germany should have been boycotted in the thirties—the systematic exclusion of Jews in Germany and Blacks in South Africa from the clubs that feed the national teams was in direct violation of Olympic rules—rules we are only now coming to understand have meaning only when they are being bent and expediently used by the politicians and the multi-national corporations and the titled "aristocrats" who control sports.

One of the most hopeful signs, to me, lit up in a strange place—the academic world. In the last several years there has been an explosion of social science courses with sports orientations. I've spoken at a number of them, and I suspect that many were created to make sociology sexy, but the level of consciousness-raising, particularly among young men on varsity teams, carriers of the so-called jock ethic, has been gratifyingly high. A great deal of the current turbulence in professional sports is directly attributable to men affected by the so-called athletic revolution of the 1960s, when important sports figures such as Harry Edwards, Jack Scott, and Phil Shinnick were taking their higher degrees and using the classrooms as platforms for change. In a great tradition, this revolution came out of academia, but I've called it a so-called revolution, because I don't think it's really happened yet. I think it will. I think women will play an important role in it. And I think people involved in *ARENA* will be at the forefront of it, helping a generation to understand what a critical role sports plays in every aspect of its life, to understand that such old bromides as—politics has no place in sports—does not mean that we have to work to get politics out of sports—we never will—but that such politics as we now live under have to be changed, made responsive to our needs, if sports, or anything else, is going to help us live fuller and richer lives.

Ethics in Sports Journalism

Garry J. Smith
University of Alberta

Terry A. Valeriote
Coaching Association of Canada

Introduction

Sportswriters have traditionally been perceived as uncritical sports buffs. They are even derogated by other journalists who claim they work in the toy department of the newspaper business. It has also been suggested that the occupation is a sinecure for former athletes and that the writers are idol worshippers who are grateful for their jobs because they get free entry into sports events and they get to mingle with star athletes (Andelman, 1974).

The credibility of sportswriters has also been questioned because they often have no special training for their jobs; they have sacrificed their objectivity by accepting gifts and other treats from the sports establishment (Smith, 1976); and they have been chided for the notable absence of social commentary in their writing (Edwards, 1969).

Despite these well-intentioned critiques, there has been little scholarly examination of the sportswriter role. In an effort to either validate or refute these allegations, a study was conducted in the City of Toronto which involved personal interviews with a sampling of sportswriters from all three daily papers. The purpose of the study was to determine whether or not sportswriting could be considered a profession. As part of this occupational analysis, the authors investigated how sportswriters were trained and educated, how they performed their roles, and the types of problems they encountered in their work. This article represents only a portion of the overall study.

Review of Literature

The sportswriter has a demanding role primarily because he must interact with a variety of groups on a daily basis, all of whom may have differing expectations of him. The writer must be responsive to his employer, his competitors, the athletes, the owners and sports promoters as well as the public. The resultant of these interlocking roles is often a confused sportswriter. The sports journalist has dichotomous responsibilities, if he performs up to expectations for one group he automatically disappoints another group. On the one hand, he is supposed to be objectively reporting sports news to the public; on the other hand, he is expected to glorify a particular sport for the benefit of a promoter. Usually, these two functions are in direct opposition to one another. McFarlane (1955) claims what sometimes happens is that there is a form of compromise in which both roles can be played simultaneously. What often occurs is that the sports journalist abrogates his public service role and becomes a shill for the promoter (Smith and Blackman, 1978).

Sportswriters have been known to accept gifts and favors from the groups they are paid to cover. More than thirty years ago, McFarlane (1955) revealed that sports promoters in Montreal obtained favorable publicity from the writers. Some writers received free drinks, meals, gifts, all-expense-paid trips, money for sportswriter's banquets, and even cash payoffs. McFarlane pointed out that:

> . . . these affairs are all designed to create situations wherein generosity will be recognized by the recipients. Therefore, the recipients will be under certain obligations to the donors. (1955, p. 82)

Smith (1976) in a study of Edmonton sports journalists found similar occurrences. Along with the previously mentioned handouts, sportswriters were producing articles for sport programs, broadcasters were serving as public address announcers at sporting events and Christmas gifts were willingly accepted.

Various reasons have been advanced to account for the writers' involvement in these situations. Primarily, it happens because the sportswriter tries to get close to the promoter in order to gain "inside information." In the process though, he becomes hooked because he begins to owe the promoter favorable publicity, particularly for information that has been given "off the record" (McFarlane, 1955). Some writers are simply lazy, unprincipled, or weak-willed, while others feel they are so underpaid that they will take any extras they can get.

In addition to direct handouts, there are other subtle forms of manipulation that can be used to sway sportswriters. Beddoes (1970), a former sportswriter with the Toronto *Globe and Mail*, reflected how Punch Imlach, who was then coaching the Toronto Maple Leafs, tried to keep the sportswriter under his thumb. If Imlach liked the sportswriter, "he would give you a news story when you required one, tip you off to something that is happening. That is what I consider a news favor. I consider that a form of payoff" (Beddoes, 1970, p. 70).

To be a credible sports journalist, it is essential that the writer maintain an arms length distance from the people being covered. This is a difficult task because the reporter must interact regularly with the athletes and promoters who view him as being a propaganda arm of the program. Andelman (1974) is critical of writers who fall into this trap. He points out that political writers are in a similar position, yet they are able to maintain their objectivity. Dickey (1974) qualifies this viewpoint with a dose of realism:

> If film critic Pauline Kael pans a movie or criticizes an actor, she does so with the knowledge that she need not see anybody she had criticized. A sports-writer may have to go to an athlete he has criticized for a story the next day. Only a political writer has the same kind of problem, and his is eased by the fact that few politicians are in a position to scare him physically. The average athlete has no problem scaring the average sportswriter. (Dickey, 1974, p. 88)

Sportswriters who have taken a critical stance are often ridiculed by the sports establishment, barred from the locker room or even physically abused (Smith, 1976).

Sports journalists have also been taken to task for their lack of social consciousness. Edwards (1969, p. 32) maintains that sportswriters are "insensitive to the magnitude and impact of the social problems that are festering beneath their own noses." They neglect to fully expose problems like racism, drug abuse, violence, cheating and so forth that are commonplace in the sports world. Shecter (1970) believed that sportswriters had a strong need to be in the presence of athletes, thus they tried to steer clear of critical articles. He also noted that "there is a strong possibility that the newspaper needs the team more than the team needs the newspaper" (1970, p. 59).

Two other prominent sports journalists concur with Shecter's viewpoint, but they provide different explanations for the phenomenon. Cosell (1974, p. 204) found that, in general, sportswriters "were neglecting the great issues in sports on the grounds that the fans were not interested." In *I Never Played the Game*, Cosell was even more direct in his attack on both the sports media in general and specific sports journalists. Whereas, Red Smith, the late New York sports columnist, flatly stated that many sportswriters are substandard:

> I don't like to admit it, but there are as many incompetents . . . among sports-writers as among doctors and grocers and shoe salesmen. Some of them are childish, they think the world is bounded by the outfield fences. Well, obviously, anyone who thinks that way is not only a knothead with a serious case of arrested development, but is gonna be a lousy sportswriter too. (Stein, 1978, p. 63)

In recent years, the image and status of the sportswriter has diminished somewhat because of the immediacy of radio and television. Through these media, the public hears and sees firsthand about the happenings and results of sporting contests. The result is a double-edged sword for the sportswriter; the importance and significance of what he writes may now not be as vital to the public as it once was, also the players and owners give the sportswriter less time because they gain greater exposure through other media, especially television.

Despite the disparaging comments made about the sportswriter's role, there are indications that the field is becoming more professional. Douglas Fisher, a Canadian political columnist and co-author of the 1969 Canadian Task Force Report on Sport, stated that the quality of sportswriting was equivalent to the writing on politics:

> I would say that the level of sports journalism, particularly in the larger newspapers, is comparable to the level of political journalism. Neither one is consistently excellent but it is fair. (Fisher, 1969, p. 3)

One may question whether Fisher was being complimentary when he compared sportswriters to political writers, but he at least sees them as being equal, whereas most critics do not.

Lately, the trend has been for writers to be less awe-struck by sports heroes and less a pawn of the sports promoters. Sport is not viewed as being sacrosanct, but merely as an activity that amuses and entertains people and for those reasons alone deserves coverage. No longer in wonder of sports figures, proponents of this school of writing take the position that it would not be a calamity if high profile sports ceased to exist. They also believe that the press has the power to make or break a particular sport. The philosophy of this type of writer is rather bluntly stated by Shecter: "No press, no interest, no baseball, no twenty-two year old shit-kicker making thirty-five grand a year, at an animal occupation" (Poe, 1974, p. 175).

A blend of reporting styles now exists but there is still a greater emphasis on hero making. Whatever the mixture, the newspapers seem to have found a combination that allows them to survive against the powerful competition from the electronic media.

Results and Discussion

In an effort to assess the professional standards of sportswriters, personal interviews were conducted with thirty-five sportswriters representing all three daily newspapers in Toronto (Valeriote, 1980). The data reported in this section pertains to the ethical standards of the sportswriters and their newspapers.

The sports reporters were asked whether sports promoters ever tried to influence the way they wrote their stories. In general, the writers felt that attempts at influence were made sporadically. Usually this was by a single member of an organization and not part of any systematic plan. For example, the Toronto Argonauts football coach once stated to the reporters, "You're either for us or against us.'' He mentioned this because he wanted the writers not to report player injuries. A now defunct Toronto hockey team offered portable T.V. sets to the writers as Christmas gifts. In these types of situations, the writers said that they were not influenced. They did not accept gifts and they wrote what they pleased despite what persuasive techniques were used by the sports promoters.

Each of the three newspapers had policies which bore on the relationship between the sportswriters and the teams they covered. These are as follows:

The Toronto Globe and Mail

All travel, meals and hotel costs for the sportswriters were paid by the paper and not the teams. On the road, the writers made every effort to travel separately from the team and stay at a different hotel.

Pre-game meals that were offered to sportswriters by the pro teams were paid by the *Globe*. The paper also did not allow its baseball writers to act as official scorers at the Blue Jay baseball games. They felt that this would make the writer a part-time employee of the baseball league and might compromise his objectivity especially in a case where he should be critical of the league. The *Globe and Mail* had a good record in this regard. They were part owners of the Blue Jay baseball team, yet it did not stop them from questioning the personnel decisions and operating procedures of the team.

Moonlighting in the form of writing "creampuff" articles for game programs was not permitted by the *Globe*. Two of their feature columnists did have regular radio and television shows but management did not consider this to be a conflict of interest.

Rarely was a writer ever removed from a beat even though there had been pressure at various times from the pro football and hockey teams. One writer's assignment was changed because his sources of information dried up. Apparently, this writer described how a hockey player had been drunk and acted boorishly on the team's flight home. Although it was true, the athletes subsequently refused to talk to the reporter. This same writer is now one of the paper's main political correspondents in Ottawa.

The Toronto Star

The *Star* paid for the writer's travel, meal and hotel costs. The paper did allow writers to accept pre-game meals, but not gratuities or gifts. The baseball writer from the *Star* was also the official scorer for the Blue Jays and was paid $35.00 per game by the American League.

The Toronto Sun

Like the other two papers, the *Sun* had a general policy against accepting gifts from sports promoters. The *Sun* generally paid for the travel, meals and acommodations for its writers, however, two writers claimed to have accepted free plane tickets to cover a golf tournament, and an auto racing event. The *Sun* also did not allow their writers to act as official scorers.

Soccer writers from all three newspapers were offered a bribe of $200.00, plus a lifetime pass to a burlesque show in return for favorably publicizing a soccer match. All three returned the money and turned down the lifetime pass.

What constituted a satisfactory relationship between the sportswriter and team players or team management was always a point of contention with the sports editors and sportswriters. One editor felt that coaches and athletes generally considered the media to be a "pain in the neck" or at the very least "a necessary evil." The writer has to walk a very fine line: "You try to find the key that makes a player open up while at the same time retaining your self-respect." One writer who was mentioned frequently by his peers as being the best in the city was quite cynical about the media–sports establishment connection. He commented that "the owners treat you like children, the players like scum, the public relations man and the coach like you're their best friend."

Although their policies differ slightly, each of the papers was aware of the potential pitfalls of there being too close a liaison between the sportswriters and the teams. The crucial point is that the writers must be able to get the information for their story without compromising themselves.

Many of the sportswriters noted that the intensely competitive nature of the job caused some writers to lose their perspective to the point where they might violate ethical journalistic practices. Toronto is one of the few North American cities that still has three daily newspapers. On the one hand it keeps writers from getting lazy because they don't want to get scooped by a rival, but on the other hand they may also resort to "yellow journalism and half truths just to come up with a sensational headline." All of the writers that were interviewed were very sensitive about their competitors from the other papers. It was standard procedure that when one paper's edition was off the press, it was immediately being scrutinized in the offices of the other papers. The writers tried to avoid being beaten on a story because this raised the ire of the editor. If it happened too often, the writer would be gone. So when it appeared that a writer had been scooped, his first reaction was to try and discredit the initial story, or failing this, try to find a fresher angle to write about.

The sportswriting role has been assailed by scholars who feel that the writers lack initiative or commitment to expose excesses and abuses that occur in a sporting context (Edwards, 1969; Beddoes, 1970). To a large degree, this would be a valid criticism of the Toronto sportswriting scene. The writers were asked to articulate what they felt was the role of sport in society. The majority of writers had not done any deep thinking on this subject. The standard reply was that sport, especially professional sport, was entertainment and that one did not need a well-defined philosophy of sport to be a good sportswriter. This would appear to be a rather narrow approach to the job in light of the social and cultural significance of sport in society. Professional sport is generally held up as a role model for amateurs because the professionals supposedly represent the best. The sportswriters in Toronto however, in equating professional sport with entertainment, fail to recognize the leadership role of the professionals.

One of the best known Toronto sportswriters offered this philosophical comment on sport:

> Sport is an enjoyable and entertaining human pursuit in which courage, excellence, cowardice, physical skill, laziness, enterprise and other human virtues and failings are seen under circumstances of little long range importance.

The last part of his statement belies the fact that sport is a powerful instrument of socialization in our society.

All of the sportswriters could think of articles that had appeared which were designed to have social impact. For example, stories had been written about drug use, irregularities in boxing, and racism in sport. One article on sports agents which exposed how hockey players' funds were being mismanaged even resulted in a conviction. So while socially responsible, investigative-type articles did exist, their appearance was haphazard and there was no follow-up to see whether conditions really changed.

The violence in hockey situations is an example of a long-standing blemish in sport where sportswriters have little or no impact. A significant percentage (72 percent) of the sportswriters claimed that the sports pages in Toronto assisted in fostering violence in hockey. They felt that many of the stories and the photos used actually promoted rather than criticized the violence. A photo depicting a violent action is often used as an attention getter. The editors justify the use of these photos as "being good action shots" or they have "artistic merit." The stories often glorify violence in the game; for example, "So and so really cleaned his clock" or "There were wrist shots and fist shots at last night's exciting game at the Gardens." Phrasing such as this makes heroes out of violent players and plays up the violence as being a pleasurable aspect of the game.

The main reason this approach is taken is that editors think it helps to sell newspapers. If that is what the public wants, that is what they will get, seems to be the attitude of the editors. It does point out, however, that sports journalists do not see the necessity of playing a leadership role in trying to change public opinons.

Conclusion

The results of this study indicate that while journalistic practices have improved over the past decade, sports journalism still lacks many of the ingredients that would make it a profession. Editors are now careful to institute policies that minimize the influence of sports promoters. On the other hand, the excessive competition between reporters and the reluctance to be outspoken on social issues continue to corrode journalistic standards. Even in Toronto, where the overall level of sportswriting is reputed to be the best in the country, there is considerable room for improvement. As a starting point, sports journalism could move closer to a profession if there were academic standards, formal training procedures, qualifying exams and a code of ethics.

References

Andelman, E.
1974 *Sports Fans of the World Unite!* New York: Dodd, Mead and Company.

Beddoes, R.
1970 "Special Senate Committee on Mass Media." Ottawa: Vol. 24.

Cosell, H.
1974 *Like It Is.* Chicago: Playboy Press.

Dickey, G.
1974 *The Jock Empire.* Radnor, Pa.: Chilton Book Company.

Edwards, H.
1969 *The Revolt of the Black Athlete.* New York: The Free Press.

Fisher, D.
1969 "Special Senate Committee on Mass Media." Ottawa: Vol. 24.

McFarlane, B.
1955 "The Sociology of Sports Promotion." Unpublished M.A. Thesis, McGill University, Montreal.

Poe, R.
1974 "The Writing of Sports." *Esquire,* October.

Shecter, L.
1970 *The Jocks.* New York: Paperback Library.

Smith, G.
1976 "A Study of a Sports Journalist." *International Review of Sport Sociology.* Vol. 3 (11).

Smith, G. and Blackman, C.
1978 Sport in the Mass Media. C.A.H.P.E.R. *Sociology of Sport Monograph Series.* Ottawa.

Stein, H.
1978 "Sports Writing's Poet Laureate." *Sport Magazine,* March.

Valeriote, T.
1980 "An Occupational Analysis of Sportswriters." Unpublished M.A. Thesis, University of Alberta, Edmonton.

9

Sports in the International Arena

J ust as sports are supposed to do so many good things for our national society, the same has always been assumed in the international arena. Sports contact between nations has been expected to build bridges and end animosities.

For years, arguments were made to the effect that sports contacts with South Africa would lead to changes in the apartheid system. South Africa offered "compromises" that beguiled some and provided a rationale for others to continue sports contacts. It was only after their exclusion from the Olympic movement in 1970 that more and more actors began to realize that only isolation would effect real change. The bridge building argument with South Africa was out, but then South Africa has always been a unique case.

My article, "A Political History of the Modern Olympic Games," is an updated and expanded version of an article first published in the *Journal of Sport and Social Issues* (vol. 2, no. 1). It not only gives a perspective on the role of politics in the modern Olympics but also discusses how the context of that role changed from an American viewpoint with the United States–led boycott of the Moscow Games. A critical question was why the United States chose to get involved only in 1980. It had had the opportunity to make important statements in 1936 at the Nazi Olympics, in 1968 when black Americans raised their voices in protest, and in 1976 when the African nations boycotted the Games to protest apartheid.

The United States was active in the 1950s, trying to keep the People's Republic of China out of the Games; throughout the 1960s and into the 1970s, we frequently denied visas to athletes from the German Democratic Republic and Cuba but allowed South African athletes into the country; and in 1976, President Ford threatened to pull out of the Montreal Olympics unless Taiwan was permitted to compete. What does it say to the world when we consistently play political sport in the face of a "communist threat" but never do so when racism or facism is the issue?

Harry Edwards's article, "The Free Enterprise Olympics" (*JSSI*, vol. 8, no. 2), views our most recent Olympics from several points of view including the issue of Soviet participation, domestic political agitation, minority alienation, and the profit motive in the Games. He also looks to the future, considering the Seoul Games in 1988.

Vincent Mosco and Levon Chorbajian, the current co-editor of the *JSSI*, provide an extensive analysis in "1976 and 1980 Olympic Boycott Media Coverage: All the News That Fits" (*Arena Review*, vol. 5, no. 3). This article, which focuses on the Olympics coverage of *Time* magazine and the *New York Times*, presents the authors' argument regarding how the print media serves the purpose of its national audience.

Finally, because of the importance of South Africa's role on the international stage in the mid-1980s, I have written a new article for this chapter— "Sports and Apartheid: The World Closes In." This article not only traces the development of the boycott against South Africa but also gives a detailed description of life inside South Africa. Ultimately, it concludes that a boycott cannot make the situation for black South Africans any worse than it already is—it can only hasten change.

A Political History of the Modern Olympic Games

Richard E. Lapchick
Center for the Study of Sport in Society,
Northeastern University

In recent times—as we have been forced to watch a succession of political events associated with the Olympic Games—politicians, sportswriters, editorial writers, and most of the American public have expressed shock at the mixing of politics and sport. The black protest in 1968, the assassination of Israeli athletes in Munich in 1972, and the African boycott of the 1976 Games all heightened the battle cry. However, when President Carter called for the boycott of the 1980 Moscow Olympics, the cry of "Let's keep politics out of sport" was silenced. The same people who had criticized others were suddenly on the patriotic bandwagon and ready to go along with the boycott to protest the Soviet invasion of Afghanistan. By 1984, a subsequent Soviet boycott of the Los Angeles Games was all too predictable.

In fact, the modern Olympic spirit, even from inception in 1896, has never been free of political influence. While the political strings were initially petty, the 1936 Berlin Olympics opened a new era where politics has vied with sport for the spotlight in the Olympic Games.

This article is an attempt to trace the history of that entanglement and to analyze what this might mean for the future of the international sport.

The Early Years: 1896–1933

When Le Baron Pierre de Coubertin helped to rekindle the Olympic flame in 1896, he was largely moved by the noble thought that international sports competition would move men and nations to view each other as peaceful friends. Sports could be the area where a common understanding might be reached. In 1894, de Coubertin stated that:

> The aims of the Olympic Movement are to promote the development of those fine physical and moral qualities which are the basis of amateur sport and to bring together the athletes of the world in a great quadrennial festival of sports thereby creating international respect and goodwill and thus helping to construct a better and more peaceful world.[1]

Years later it was discovered in de Coubertin's personal correspondence that the decline in the French spirit after the Franco-Prussian War was a prime motivating factor in his work to rebuild the Olympic Games. He even worked behind the scenes to keep Germany out of the first Games.

However, there was at least a verbal commitment that international sport must be free from all government pressures. This was incorporated into the Olympic Principles. Participation could never be determined by race, religion or politics. The late Avery Brundage, who dominated international sport for three decades from his post in the International Olympic Committee (IOC), summed up the need for such a principle as the root of the Olympic Movement:

> Were this fundamental principle not followed scrupulously, the Olympic Movement would surely founder. It is essential to the success and even to the existence of any truly international body that there are no restrictions of this kind. . . . As it is, the Olympic Movement furnishes a conspicuous example that when fair play and good sportsmanship prevail, men can agree, regardless of race, religion, or political convictions.[2]

Indeed, sportsmen have chosen to believe in these principles ever since de Coubertin. On the level of individual competition, it has long been believed that sport is an area where there was equal opportunity for all, based purely on the ability of the athlete, with no reference to the athlete's personal background and/or beliefs. On the level of international competition, it has long been said that nations compete with each other for the sake of sport only. Avery Brundage said:

> We must never forget that the most important thing in the Olympic Games is not to win but to take part.[3]

In essence, ". . . sport, like the fine arts, transcends politics."[4]

These are the ideals of sport in general and of the Olympic Movement in particular. The reality has been something less than the ideal.

The first overt act of politics in the Olympics took place in 1908 when the United States team refused to dip the American flag to King Edward VII at the opening ceremonies of the 1908 Olympics in London. For the next 25 years the politics of international sport were played at this low-keyed, almost petty level. But the Hitler regime changed all of that very quickly.

The Growth of the Olympic "Political Spirit": 1933–1967

In May of 1933 the German Reichssportfuhrer, Hans Von Tschammer-Osten, announced the Nazi sports policy:

German sports are for Aryans. German Youth Leadership is only for Aryans and not for Jews. Athletes will not be judged by ability alone, but also by their general and moral fitness for representing Germany.[5]

The Reichssportfuhrer thus sowed the seeds that inexorably dragged politics into sport.

In June of 1933, Osten approved the anti-Semitic resolutions in German sports clubs, which, taken with the municipalities, controlled most of the sports facilities in Germany.[6] It became impossible for German Jews to train properly.

In November of that year, Osten ruled that Jews could not be members of athletic governing boards, thus effectively cutting them out of sports administration.[7]

In August of 1935, Jews were forbidden to join in the new Nazi consolidated sports clubs.[8] It was ruled that they could not compete abroad and, therefore, could not represent Germany.[9]

Jewish spectators were also frequently prohibited. In August of 1935 Jews were forbidden to attend the Winter Olympic Games in Garmisch as signs on the gates proclaimed. "Jews are not admitted."[10] (These signs were subsequently taken down after international protest.) In October, a United States swimming team swam in Berlin before an all-Aryan audience. A sign over the box office read, "Jews are not wanted."[11] The segregation of sports was complete, encompassing athletes, administrators and spectators.

In the 1930s, protests against staging the Games in Berlin were held in Canada, Britain, Sweden, France, the Netherlands, Poland, Palestine, and, of course, the United States.[12] Despite the protests, these countries all sent teams to Berlin.

It was in the United States that the Berlin boycott movement had the widest base. Led by prominent public figures, the Fair Games Committee was formed.[13] Other groups were involved in the boycott crusade between June of 1933 and January of 1936: twenty Olympic champions; various Catholic and Protestant groups, numerous Jewish groups, six U.S. Senators, seven governors, forty-one university presidents, the American Federation of Labor, the Women's League for Peace, the National Association for the Advancement of Colored People, and other black groups, the American National Society of Mural Painters, which withdrew its Berlin exhibit, and the Amateur Athletic Union (AAU).[14] The last was particularly important: without the AAU's sanction, no American athlete could go to Berlin. In November of 1933, the AAU decided it would boycott the Games unless the Germans changed their policy immediately.[15]

Reichssportfuhrer Osten clearly showed the importance which Germany attached to the American's participation in Berlin:

> The protest of the AAU is a complete impossibility and represents the dirty handiwork of conscienceless agitators who want systematically to undermine Germany's position abroad.[16]

Osten knew that if the American's withdrew, many others would follow and the Games might collapse in Hitler's face. It was not to be as Avery Brundage, then President of the American Olympic Committee (AOC), stepped to center stage. As the AAU appeared ready to finalize its decision, Brundage said that American athletes must meet this

> un-American boycott offensive with historic American action. . . . To those alien agitators and their American stooges who would deny our athletes their birthright as American citizens to represent the United States in the Olympic Games of 1936 in Germany, our athletes reply in the modern vernacular, 'Oh, yeah!'[17]

He went on to say that American athletes must follow

> the patterns of the Boston Tea Party, the Minute Men of Concord, and the troops of George Washington at Valley Forge. . . . Regardless of AAU action, we (AOC) are going to send a team abroad.[18]

The American protest against the Berlin Games was clearly not the work of one particular ethnic or religious group; it represented a cross-section of society that spanned religious, economic, and political boundaries. The movement brought together 20,000 people in August of 1935 at Madison Square Garden to ask for the withdrawal of the American team from the 1936 Games.[19] This remains the largest single group ever to come together at one time to protest a sports-related event.

The importance of sport to Hitler was shown in the press (*Der Angriff*) after the German soccer team played in London in December of 1935 amidst widespread British protests:

> For Germany, it was an unrestrained political, psychological, and, also, sporting success. . . . It is hardly a secret in well-informed circles that a resumption of closer contact with Great Britain is earnestly desired.[20]

The Reichssportfuhrer, as early as 1933, had said:

> Sports are something to conjure with in international relations and it is my duty to improve these relations.[21]

Later, when the American Olympic Committee voted to participate in the Berlin Olympics despite the controversy then raging in the United States, Reichssportfuhrer Osten said that the decision marked, "a turn in the international campaign of hate against Germany."[22]

As the opening of the Games neared, the official Nazi party newspaper, *Volkischer Beobachter*, revealed the propaganda value of the Games and the national exhibit 'Germany'. "The exhibition will present a concrete demonstration of the National Socialist principles and program."[23]

Despite Brundage's pledges—made both before and after the Berlin Games—that the Olympics were run solely by the German Olympic Committee and the IOC, the German government actually paid for all the sports facilities and the army paid for the Olympic Village, which later became an army facility.[24]

The use of the Games as blatant propaganda was highlighted by the dedication:

> Germany's thousands of years of history find their ultimate meaning in Adolf Hitler. Adolf Hitler fulfills a thousand year old German dream.[25]

The official Olympic poster had a map of Europe that included German-speaking sections of Southeast and Central Europe within Germany's borders.[26]

When the Austrian team arrived in Berlin, they were greeted by the German national anthem.[27] The opening ceremonies showcased the British and French teams giving the Nazi salute to Hitler. The 100,000 spectators cheered them wildly; however, the crowd showed tremendous displeasure with the American team when they refused to salute Hitler.[28]

When black American athletes began to roll up victories, *Der Angriff* attacked the AOC for bringing 'black auxiliaries' to the Games.[29] The victories by these blacks caused a huge storm in Berlin. An English report was circulated that the blacks had leg operations to increase their speed. The Germans claimed they were effective because of their peculiar bone structure, while the South Africans openly depreciated their achievements.[30]

The original German plans were to have no Jews associated with their Olympic team. Hitler had even asked Lewald, the head of the German Olympic Committee, to resign because of his Jewish ancestry. However, the Americans made their first threat to withdraw and Lewald was quickly restored in an advisory capacity. It was announced in 1935 that Avery Brundage would personally conduct an investigation into charges of discrimination against Jews in Germany. The Reichssportfuhrer immediately requested that the Jewish federations name 50 Jewish candidates for the German olympic team.[31] *Before* Brundage undertook his investigation, he told American athletes to prepare for the Games.[32] As Brundage left Germany, Rudolf Hess, minister without portfolio in Hitler's cabinet, ordered that Nazis could not fraternize the Jews.[33] Many felt that this meant the end of the Games in Berlin. Brundage expressed great interest in the order as he left.

The American Olympic Committee, which met with Brundage and voted to accept Germany's invitation to participate in the Games, claimed that sport was the wedge that would lead to the end of discrimination in Germany. In a setting that added irony to the situation, the AOC meeting was held in the New York Athletic Club, which barred Jewish membership.[34]

With all the major nations deciding to participate, the Jewish fencing star, Helene Mayer, became the only Jewish member of the 477 person German team. With the threat of isolation gone, the Germans made no real compromise. In 1959, Brundage recalled the situation and analyzed it in the following manner:

> In 1936 there was an organized and well financed attack on the Games of the XIth Olympiad, because certain individuals and groups did not approve of the German Government at that time. . . . The outcome, however, was a great victory for Olympic principles and the United States was represented by one of its largest and best teams.[35]

Brundage obviously felt that having one Jewish team member out of 477 was a worthwhile compromise, and all that followed for the Jewish people in Germany did not dampen his enthusiasm for the 1936 Games. It does not take a great deal of insight to see that there were certainly no lasting compromises in terms of an end to discrimination against Jews in Germany. One must decide if the month long journey away from discrimination merited the tremendous propaganda value Hitler enjoyed as a result of the Games.

For the Germans had their sports propaganda success as they rolled to an impressive athletic triumph. Thus, Nazi Germany utilized their sports and sports festivals as tools of propaganda so effectively that they were able to lull sportsmen and diplomats alike into believing that Germany was a fine nation in the family of nations. After the conclusion of the Games, Brundage addressed the pro-Nazi American-German Bund before 20,000 in Madison Square Garden:

> We can learn much from Germany. We, too, if we wish to preserve our institutions, must stamp out communism. We, too, must take steps to arrest the decline of patriotism. Germany has progressed as a nation out of her discouragement of five years ago into a new spirit of confidence in herself. Everywhere I found Germans friendly, courteous, and obliging. The question was whether a vociferous minority, highly organized and highly financed, could impose its will on 120,000,000 people.[36]

This was a reflection of the effectiveness of the propaganda. Richard D. Mandell, in his study, *The Nazi Olympics*, maintains that this was a major turning point for Hitler, giving him tremendous self-confidence in the international spectrum. The lesson was not lost for other nations have used sports ever since as a vehicle for national prestige or to spotlight political causes.

The "Two Chinas" Question

The question of "Two Chinas" has been addressed in the Olympics since the IOC admitted the People's Republic of China (PRC) in 1954 while retaining the membership of the Republic of China (ROC)—also known as Taiwan or Formosa. The IOC began to maneuver on this question once it became clear that the PRC would not compete *with* the ROC.

When Canada refused to admit Taiwanese athletes as representatives of the Republic of China for the Montreal Games, the question was settled de facto. With the exception of the Socialist nations, Canada was universally condemned for bringing politics into sport. There was no issue in 1980 because of the Western boycott of Moscow. The PRC was alone in 1984 at the Los Angeles Games, and the issue was finally resolved.

The controversy was at its height when the IOC convened in May of 1959 to rule that the "Republic of China no longer represents sports in the entire country of China," and must reapply as Taiwan.[37] It was assumed that Taiwan would not accept this and the PRC would be the only representative of all of China. However, the United States Department of State immediately issued a formal position on the IOC decision:

> It is evident that Communist pressures have been directed to obtaining the expulsion of the Chinese Nationalists. . . . We trust that public and sports organs, both here and abroad, will recognize the Communist threats for what they are.[38]

On the same day, a resolution condemning the IOC was introduced in the House of Representatives by Francis E. Dorn of New York. Representative Melvin Laird (later to become the Secretary of Defense) introduced an amendment to the bill prohibiting the use of any U.S. Army equipment or personnel in the 1960 Winter Olympic Games, to be held in Squaw Valley, California, if any "free nation" was banned.[39] President Eisenhower himself condemned the IOC action and, suddenly, Avery Brundage became an advocate of re-admitting Nationalist China as the "Republic of China."[40] This represented a complete turnaround of position for Mr. Brundage.

When Canada recognized the People's Republic of China in October of 1970, all "Republic of China" passports became unacceptable for entry into Canada. The Canadians informed the IOC of this fact more than a year prior to the Games. The IOC did nothing until Canada reiterated its position on May 28, 1976. Lord Killanin, then head of the IOC, did not call a special meeting of the IOC to discuss the issue but instead waited until IOC delegates gathered in Montreal seven weeks later.

Their compromise offer had no substance: there was no reason to believe that Taiwan would compete under an Olympic banner or as Taiwan. Therefore, the IOC knew what the result would be. The American position was that we were behind the compromise under the guise of a threatened withdrawal on principle. Gold has always been heavier than principle. When the Americans had their threat to withdraw on the table, the American press praised the position for its idealism. To withdraw in this case would be honorable.

Early Soviet-American Battles in Political Sport

The American view of world communism did not differentiate between the People's Republic of China and the Soviet Union. Therefore, in retaliation for 'communist pressures,' the United States refused visas for East Germans to compete in the modern pentathlon world championships in Harrisburg, Pennsylvania.[41] In February of 1960, the State Department refused visas for the East German press and members of their Olympic staff to attend the Winter Olympics on the grounds that, "admission was not in the best interests of the United States."[42] No one, including major political leaders, wanted to recall the United States had acted in the same way, for more blatantly political reasons, as the Canadians had. Somehow, this condemnation of the Canadians by the United States seems hollow with the knowledge of these past events.

For decades, the Soviet Olympic Committee has fought for the inclusion of communist nations such as East Germany, North Korea and Communist China. The United States Olympic Committee has, dutifully, opposed the same.[43] Both France and the United States refused visas to East Germans as recently as 1962.

Later in that same year, the Fourth Asian Games were marred by President Sukarno's refusal to admit teams from Nationalist China and Israel. When India implied that the Games became 'unofficial' as a result, Indonesian Trade Minister Suharto broke off trade relations and 4,000 Indonesians 'raided' the Indian Embassy in Jakarta. Prime Minister Nehru accused the Chinese Communists of playing up anti-Indian feelings in Indonesia.[44] Demonstrating its pro-Western bias, the IOC chose to ban the Indonesian team from the 1964 Tokyo Games for not admitting Nationalist China and Israel. However, it barely mentioned the actions of France, the United States or the Philippines (which had barred Yugoslavians).[45] The entire Arab League then threatened to boycott the Tokyo Games unless the ban on Indonesia was lifted.[46] President Sukarno left no room for doubt about his intentions for the use of sport, saying, "Indonesia proposes now to mix sports with politics and we are thus establishing 'the Games of the Newly Emerging Forces.'"[47] All of this was in the name of sport.

In the United States, Mr. Edward Herbert, Chairman of the House Armed Services Subcommittee, said that a $2,000,000 bill for athletes was "to make the United States the most powerful nation in the world athletically."[48] In an incredible statement for a man of his position, the then Vice-President, Hubert Humphrey, said:

> What the Soviets are doing is a challenge to us, just like Sputnik was a challenge. We are going to be humiliated as a great nation unless we buckle down to the task of giving our young people a chance to compete.[49]

This was in reference to the unofficial team defeat (although nations are not supposed to keep a national count of victories, most nations do) of the United

States Olympic team at the hands of the Soviet Union in Tokyo. He went on to say that we must conclusively prove that a free society produces better athletes than a socialist society. This is not to say the Soviet Union did not have a similar aim in proving that a socialist society produces better athletes than a free one—all in keeping with the tradition set by Hitler in 1936.

The Racial Factor in the Games: 1968–1976

I, therefore, want to make it quite clear that from South Africa's point of view no mixed sport between whites and non-whites will be practiced locally, irrespective of the standard of proficiency of the participants. . . . We do not apply that as a criterion because our policy has nothing to do with proficiency or lack of proficiency.[50]

When Prime Minister Vorster of South Africa reaffirmed his government's position on mixing races in sport *during* the IOC investigation of South African sport, many assumed that this statement alone would keep South Africa out of the 1968 Mexico Olympics. The Africans were sure that the IOC would keep South Africa out in 1968 as they had in 1964. They turned out to be poor judges as the IOC, meeting in Grenoble during the Winter Olympics, voted South Africa back into the Games. Although the African nations had threatened a massive boycott of the Olympics if South Africa participated, the IOC apparently felt it to be an idle gesture. It was anything but idle.

The Organization of African Unity (OAU) strongly urged the Supreme Council for Sport in Africa to call for its 32 member nations to boycott the Games in protest of South Africa's apartheid policy. They did so two weeks after the Grenoble verdict.[51] Most Socialist and Third World countries threatened to join the Africans. By March 10th, four weeks after Grenoble, the *New York Times* reported that only ten nations—all predominantly white—were certain to go to Mexico.[52] Many American athletes began to pick up the idea as the American Committee on Africa (ACOA) tried to enlist support.[53] This, of course, was at the height of the black American boycott. After two months of delay, with their small empire evaporating in the heat of political battle, the IOC reversed its decision. Avery Brundage never admitted that the change was a result of the boycott or because the South Africans violated the Olympic principles. He merely maintained that the Mexicans could not guarantee the safety of the South Africans in Mexico City.[54]

At the end of July, Avery Brundage called Mexico, "the most stable and fastest growing country in Latin America," and claimed that "the Olympic Movement had no little part in making it so."[55] Within days of this statement a student strike began in Mexico City that provoked the worst government crisis in 30 years. As the opening of the Games neared, thirteen were killed and hundreds injured in the three-day riot. It was an ironic scene: Olympic posters saying, "With peace, everything is possible," were plastered everywhere in the city.[56] Brundage, it seems, was slightly premature in his evaluation of the stability of Mexico, but he was not premature in saying that the Olympic Movement had helped to make Mexico what it was. Of the several reasons given by the students for the riots, one was that the incredibly high cost of staging the Games was a national disgrace.

The Olympic-political event best remembered in America was the 1968 black American boycott movement led by Harry Edwards. When that did not materialize to the degree that Edwards hoped, he changed strategies and planned demonstrations at the Games. The best remembered photo of the 1968 Games was the clenched-fist portrait of John Carlos and Tommy Smith during the playing of the Star Spangled Banner after a presentation of medals. Their actions were followed by the gestures of a dozen other black athletes who won medals in track and field events. Sports officials were outraged at the conduct of the black athletes. A survey taken four years later showed that the controversy surrounding these events lingered on: only 32 percent of the whites questioned (8 percent were undecided) felt the athletes' gestures were justified. Even among blacks opinion was divided as only 57 percent approved (9 percent were undecided).[57]

In a press conference at the close of the Games, Avery Brundage was asked what progress the Olympics had made in human relations. He replied:

> Right here in Mexico, thanks to the Juegos Deportivos, the Mexicans have proved that boys and girls are able to become better citizens, as they are stronger and healthier and have acquired a sense of discipline and national morale.[58]

Mr. Brundage had apparently not noticed the riots of a few days before which took strong police action to stop in time for the Games.

Brundage's most curious statement came in response to a question asking him how the Olympics could survive as long as politics continued to become more and more involved in the Games. His response was, "Who said that politics are becoming more and more involved in the Olympics? In my opinion this is not so. . . . You know very well that politics are not allowed in the Olympic Games."[59] Even as sport became more and more political, the czars of the sports world continued to ignore the trend. Sportswriters and the public seemed very willing to go along with the ruse until the next political-Olympic event when they could condemn the activists for bringing politics into sports as if it were the end of the virginity of a pure and angelic child. They did not have to wait long.

In May of 1970, the IOC met in Amsterdam to consider the expulsion of South Africa from the Olympic Movement in protest of that country's apartheid sports policy. No nation had ever been expelled from the Movement itself and it was thought highly unlikely that the African-led plan would succeed.[60]

The difference was that the South Africans had gone too far by refusing a visa to the Black American tennis star, Arthur Ashe, so that he could compete in the 1970 South African Open Tennis Championships. This had the effect of raising American political consciousness about apartheid sport.

The second precipitating event was the insistence on the part of the South Africans on going ahead with plans to send an all-white cricket team to tour Britain in the spring of 1970. There were massive plans for protest in Britain led by the Stop The Seventy Tour (STST) committee. STST had rallied 50,000 demonstrators to various rugby fields in the winter months while a South African rugby team toured Britain. Then Prime Minister Wilson ended up cancelling the tour to avoid the certain conflict.

When the IOC vote was tallied, the South Africans were out. This seemed remarkable in May of 1970, but what really was remarkable was that South Africa, with all the evidence and seemingly the majority of world opinion against them, was able to remain in the Olympic Movement *until* 1970.

The best explanation is that the IOC was dominated by representatives from white member nations who did not oppose South Africa's continued good standing. The IOC, according to its own publication, OLYMPISM, was a self-recruiting elite: membership on the committee was the result of election by existing IOC members. The statement, "It is customary to favour nationals of countries with a long Olympic tradition behind them," is reminiscent of the grandfather clause in the post-Reconstruction era of the South in the United States.[61] The custom was a convenient way of excluding representatives from nations that were colonies during the period when "a long Olympic tradition" could have been formed. In fact, the first two representatives from Africa were white men: Reg Alexander of Kenya and Reg Honey of South Africa. De Coubertin commented on the nature of membership in the IOC. "The second characteristic of Olympism is that it is an aristocracy, an elite.[62] He also added, "It is not sufficient to be an elite; it is also necessary for this elite to be a chivalry."[63]

Since 1960, 61 percent of the representatives from non-white nations were admitted to the IOC. However, this meant only a minor change in the racial composition of the IOC as the non-whites had only 33 percent of the voting power on the IOC in 1970. To achieve their 67 percent control, it was necessary for eleven of the white nations to have two or more representatives on the IOC. Moreover, of the national olympic committees (NOC's) without an IOC representative (which, in effect, means they are powerless), only 12.4 percent were from white nations while 87.6 percent were from non-white nations.[64]

To the idealistic sportsman, sportswriter, and fan who might feel that such statistics are meaningless because sport and the Olympic Movement are above politics and race, the results of the following survey should be instructive. The information was gathered in a survey completed in the spring of 1970 in which the NOC's were asked for their position on South Africa's participation in the

Olympics. Sixty-eight percent of the white nations were not opposed to South Africa's participation. However, 98 percent of the non-white nations opposed South Africa's participation without complete sports integration in South Africa.

Thus, it can be seen that the South African issue developed along rather strict racial lines. Race and politics had become an integral part of international sport.

The Africans had a firm grasp on their power by 1972. According to Abraham Ordia, President of the Supreme Council for Sport in Africa (SCSA), the new goal was to have South Africa's neighbor, Rhodesia, expelled from the Olympic Movement. The SCSA made the mistake of trying to do this by going through the back door: they made demands on the Rhodesians they were certain would never be agreed to by the Smith regime. Much to their surprise, Smith agreed and the Rhodesian team arrived in Munich ready to participate under the stringent conditions put forth by the Africans. It was at the IOC meeting prior to the Games that the SCSA reversed its stand: the Rhodesians would have to be thrown out of the Movement or there would be another boycott.[65] The IOC complied.

The tragedy of the Israeli athletes in Munich cast a shadow over the Games and their future. The Montreal Olympic Village was an armed camp in an attempt to prevent new terrorist acts. While SportsWorld expressed shock at the Munich terrorism, it is not altogether surprising that such a thing could happen. It has been the theme of this article that the Olympics have become so big and attract so much international attention that they have become the ideal stage for political actors with causes: the French, the Americans, the Nazis, the People's Republic of China, Taiwan, the South Africans, the black Africans, the Socialists and the Capitalists. Why not terrorists?

Even with all this background, many doubted that there was any reason to fear an African boycott in 1976. After all, the threat of an American boycott over the "Two Chinas" issue had been resolved. The Western press condemned the African nations who withdrew. The American press had not even mentioned the real issue involved New Zealand's rugby team being in South Africa. With the election of Prime Minister Muldoon, New Zealand had resumed full sports relations with South Africa. The most controversy, however, had been raised by the rugby tour. While the difference between British and New Zealand teams competing in South Africa may have been lost on the average sports fan, the essence of that difference was not lost on the world's political leaders. Prime Minister Muldoon had made it a policy of his government to compete with South Africa. No other government did this.

It had been known for months that the African nations would withdraw from the Olympics if New Zealand sent its rugby team to South Africa. The Supreme Council for Sport in Africa announced this early in the spring. The Conference of the United Nations Special Committee Against Apartheid supported the Council's resolve at its May Havana meeting. The Organization of African Unity, meeting in Mauritius, also encouraged the African teams to boycott the Games. Therefore, the statements of surprise that 24 African nations did not march in the opening parade were rather unworldly. The fact that other Third World nations joined them is no less surprising if one simply examines the history of the modern Olympics.

Looked at from the point of view of the Africans and their supporters, they took a very strong and idealistic stand in order to keep racial politics out of sport. These countries sacrificed hard training, substantial amounts of money, and the prestige that comes from competing in the global spotlight that accompanies the Olympics. Dennis Brutus, a main moving force behind the boycott, believes that the IOC deliberately dragged out the China issue to divert the attention away from the African threats.[66] It almost worked as it appeared that there would be no boycott. But because the IOC was so involved in the China issue, New Zealand was never put on the agenda and nothing could be worked out prior to the Games. It can be reasonably assumed that the IOC believed that since no nation had ever actually taken itself out of the Games, the Africans would not do so and the issue would go away. As has frequently been the case, the IOC was proven wrong.

The Cold War Olympics: 1980 and 1984

With the African boycott behind us in 1976, the threats for the future seemed more real. Still, for the American media, the United States was the "good guy"; it was others who had dragged politics into sport. That perception changed very quickly when President Carter announced the United States boycott of the Moscow Games in retaliation for the Soviet invasion of Afghanistan.

The press was on his side, but Carter had to convince two other groups to go along. The first was the athletes. Led by such Olympians as Anita DeFrantz, many athletes resisted the pressure. An informal poll of the USOC Athletes Advisory Counsel indicated that most athletes wanted to compete. However, confronted by the national wave of patriotism, they ultimately succumbed to the pressure. The president also cajoled U.S. allies into joining the boycott, promising incentives to developing nations, especially in Africa, if they would shun the Games. That was a tough sell, because the United States had never backed the African nations in their protest against the inclusion of South Africa in international sport. In addition, the Russians were offering their own incentives *for* participation.

The boycott had mixed results. Many European and some developing nations joined in the boycott. However, by making his point, Carter forever made it impossible to say that politics and sport are not to be mixed.

The 1980 Games were depicted as a failure in the Western media, yet the contrary is arguable. Thirty-six new world records and seventy-four new Olympic records were set—more than in any previous Olympics. Eighty-one nations participated, more than 60,000 foreign tourists went to Moscow, and an estimated 1.5 billion saw the Games on TV. Moreover, the Soviets are still in Afghanistan more than a half decade later.

Retaliation by the Soviet bloc nations in the 1984 Los Angeles Games was almost guaranteed by the events of 1980. The fact that the Soviet boycott was announced so late was also predictable. Only the rationale was clouded by the "security" issue, although it was a real issue at the time. Reportedly, the Soviet press implied that the Los Angeles Games were a failure because so many of the world's top athletes were not present. However, more nations participated than ever before, more people saw the Games, and they were the first profitable Games. At least in America, they were depicted as the most successful Games ever.

The Future

Potential problems in holding the 1988 Olympics in Seoul appear greater than ever before. However, it is possible that the realism that has been forced upon us will make us better able to deal with them. The importance of the role of sports in international politics should no longer be overplayed.

While the political involvement has consistently been decried by the sports world, even the idealist, Avery Brundage, must share much of the blame. He, too, had frequently viewed the role of sports in international politics as being far more important than it is in reality. In his own unique historical perspective, Brundage largely attributed the downfall of Ancient Greece and Rome to an improper sports outlook:

> Twenty-five hundred years ago the Greeks made a breach in the city walls to receive their home-coming Olympic champions. A city with such heroes for citizens needed no fortifications. When they began to give large special awards and prizes, however, they created a class of athletic loafers instead of heroes. The Games were finally abolished and the glory of Greece departed.[67]

> . . . the Romans did not descend into the arena, which was left to professionals, gladiators, grooms, etc. They were spectators, not participants, and lacked the discipline of sports training. Eventually a victim of her own prosperity, Rome fell to the barbarians, the hard and tough Goths and Vandals, invaders from the North.[68]

The lofty role that Brundage saw fit for modern sport, as led by the IOC, was revealed in his speech to the 62nd IOC Session in Tokyo in 1962:

The Olympic Movement is a 20th Century religion, a religion with universal appeal which incorporates all the basic values of other religions, a modern, exciting, viril, dynamic religion, attractive to Youth, and we of the International Olympic Committee are its disciples.[69]

Even after all of this the sportsworld was ready for a sublime Olympics in Montreal. Naivete is still in its ascendancy in the IOC.

In 1959, George Orwell said of international sport:

It is bound up with hatred, jealousy, boastfulness, disregard for all rules and sadistic pleasure in witnessing violence—in other words, it is war minus the shooting.[70]

While the reality may not be quite that negative, politics is and has always been part of the Olympic Movement. If we want to change that—and many do not—then a complete overhaul must begin. But the time for expressions of astonishment, wonder and shock should have passed many years ago. We have known the reality; now it is ours to face.

Notes

1. Monique Berlioux, ed., *Olympism* (Lausanne: International Olympic Committee, 1972), p. 1.

2. Speech to the 55th Session of the IOC in Munich (May 23, 1959), from *The Speeches of President Avery Brundage, 1952 to 1968* (Lausanne: International Olympic Committee, 1969), pp. 41–42.

3. Speech to the 53rd Session of the IOC in Sofia, September 22, 1957, in *Speeches of Brundage*, p. 34.

4. Speech to the 60th Session of the IOC in Baden Baden, October 16, 1963, in *Speeches of Brundage*, p. 65.

5. *New York Times*, May 29, 1933.

6. Ibid., June 13, August 27, 1933.

7. Ibid., November 23, 1933.

8. Ibid., August 12, 1935.

9. Richard D. Mandell, *The Nazi Olympics* (New York: Macmillan Co., 1971), p. 59.

10. *New York Times*, October 21, 1935.

11. Ibid.

12. See: *New York Times*, November 5, 22, 1933, August 26, December 8, 1934, March 18, October 4, November 12, 16, 1935, March 9, 13, 31, May 10, 17, June 16, 20, 1936.

13. *New York Times*, October 11, 1935.

14. See: *New York Times*, May 31, June 6, 1933, August 12, September 3, 27, 1934, 1934, July 22, 31, August 5, 23, September 1, October 4, 18, 16–27. November 26, 27, December 1–4, 1935, January 4, 25, 1936.

15. Ibid., November 21, 1933.
16. Ibid., November 23, 1933.
17. Ibid., December 4, 1935.
18. Ibid.
19. *The Times* (London), August 12, 1935.
20. Ibid., December 6, 1935.
21. *New York Times*, August 6, 1933.
22. Ibid., September 30, 1934.
23. Ibid., April 23, 1936.
24. Ibid., May 31, 1936.
25. Ibid., July 18, 1936.
26. *The Times* (London), July 18, 1936.
27. Ibid., August 1, 1936.
28. *New York Times*, August 2, 1936; *The Times* (London), August 3, 1936.
29. *New York Times*, August 6, 1936.
30. Ibid., August 7, 1936.
31. Ibid., June 28, 1934.
32. Ibid., August 11, 1934.
33. Ibid., September 19, 1934.
34. Ibid., September 27, 1934.
35. Speech to the 55th Session of the IOC in Munich, May 23, 1959, in *Speeches of Brundage,* p. 41.
36. *New York Times*, October 5, 1935.
37. Ibid., May 29, 1959.
38. Ibid., June 3, 1959.
39. Ibid., June 4, 1959.
40. Ibid., August 1, 1959.
41. Ibid., September 17, 1959.
42. Ibid., February 7, 1960.
43. Ibid., March 17, 1961.
44. Ibid., September 3, 1962.
45. *The Times* (London), February 8, 1963.
46. Ibid., February 21, 1963.
47. Ibid., October 29, 1963.
48. *New York Times*, May 23, 1966.
49. Ibid.
50. Prime Minister John Vorster, address to Parliament, April 11, 1967, from "Report of the IOC Commission on South Africa" (Lausanne: IOC, 1968), p. 68.
51. *The Times* (London), February 27, 1968.
52. *New York Times*, March 10, 1968.
53. ACOA, press release, April 10, 1968. ACOA Collection.
54. IOC *Newsletter #8,* (May 1968), p. 151.
55. *Star* (Johannesburg), July 31, 1968.
56. *The Times* (London), September 26, 1968.
57. Survey conducted in August 1972 in the following cities: New York, Philadelphia, Washington, D.C., Denver, Norfolk and Los Angeles.
58. IOC, *Newsletter #15,* p. 577.

59. Ibid., p. 578.

60. *Star* (Johannesburg), May 14, 1970.

61. Monique Berlioux, *Olympism*, p. 8.

62. Ibid., p. 10.

63. Ibid., p. 2.

64. All figures were compiled from the official *Olympic Directory, 1969* (Lausanne: IOC, 1969).

65. Abraham Ordia, interview, May 26, 1976.

66. Dennis Brutus, interview, July 5, 1976.

67. Speech to the 48th Session of the IOC in Mexico City, April 17, 1953, in *Speeches of Brundage,* p. 10.

68. Speech to the 51st Session of the IOC in Cortinna d'Ampezzo, January 23, 1956, in *Speeches of Brundage,* p. 22.

69. Speech to the 62nd Session of the IOC in Tokyo, October 6, 1964, in *Speeches of Brundage,* p. 80.

70. *New York Times,* October 4, 1959.

The Free Enterprise Olympics

Harry Edwards
University of California at Berkeley

The slogan coined by ABC to promote its broadcasts of the 23rd Olympiad in Los Angeles is, "The Olympics: The Tradition Continues." No slogan could be more fitting.

Predictably, developments and relations beyond the sports arena assumed preeminence over the athletic and cultural events that the Games were intended to showcase. This is neither unique nor inconsistent with recent Olympic history.

Beginning with the 1952 Helsinki Games—the first in which the Soviet Union entered a team—the attention of the world gradually shifted from the performances of individual athletes competing for global recognition to a titanic "Cold War" ideological struggle acted out in the sports arena by the U.S. and the U.S.S.R. Over ensuing years, the athletes and Olympic officials of both countries have been reduced to little more than footsoldiers in a quadrennial propaganda battle carried out under camouflage of international sports competition and pageantry. Due largely to the example set by the U.S. and the U.S.S.R., the potential political uses of the Olympics were widely recognized by the start of the 1968 Games. And, with each successive Olympiad, the political acts have escalated. "Black Power" protests and Mexican students' demonstrations at the 1968 Games were surpassed in both media drama and impact by the armed attacks upon Israeli athletes at the 1972 Munich Games. In 1976, governments and heads of state raised the political ante again when thirty-six nations boycotted the Montreal Games. And, in 1980, the first superpower boycott of the Games occurred when the United States declined to participate in the Moscow Olympics.

Because of increasing opportunities for athletes and corporations to "cash in" on Olympic performances and because of the ever more prevalent presumption that Olympic victories provide demonstrable proof of a nation's viability, if not superiority, the pressure to win medals has intensified. In turn, this pressure has given rise to increased incidents of performance-related drug use among athletes, biased judging among Olympic officials, payoffs to athletes by corporate sponsors, and Olympics-related political intrigue both within and between nations. There was nothing to suggest that the thrust toward escalating problems at the games would diminish in 1984. To the contrary, in an era when problem plagued Olympics have indeed become traditional, the Los Angeles Games were plagued by political controversy, commercial exploitation and ethical violations.

Political developments in the international realm headed the list of problems confronting the Los Angeles Olympic Organizing Committee (LAOOC). And it is precisely this fact that prompted Peter V. Ueberroth, President of the LAOOC, to state what no other U.S. Olympic official has ever dared to admit: "We must now face the reality that the Olympics are a political event as well as an athletic event."

Of course, in the wake of the U.S. boycott of the 1980 Moscow Games and what amounts to a deep freeze in already "Cold War" U.S.–Soviet relations, LAOOC's political attention has focused principally upon the intentions of the Soviet Union and its allies. Not only were LAOOC officials faced with the challenge of placating and assuaging Soviet sensibilities about the 1980 U.S. Olympic boycott, but the officials also had to convince the U.S.S.R. that relative to the 1984 Games, the politics of Olympic participation are more conducive to Soviet interests than the politics of Olympic protest. The LAOOC's task was made more difficult because of heightened anti-Soviet sentiment in the U.S. following the Soviet's downing of Korean Airlines Flight 007, and because of Soviet and East-bloc consternation and outrage over the arrival and deployment of U.S. cruise and Pershing-2 Missiles in Western Europe, over the U.S. invasion of Grenada, and over the U.S. C.I.A.'s less-than-covert action against the government of Nicaragua. With the Soviet announcement that its athletes would not participate in the Los Angeles Olympics, the true magnitude of the LAOOC's task became evident. And so did the consequences of its lack of success. A Soviet absence meant the loss of what was to be the centerpiece of the summer games, head-to-head U.S.–U.S.S.R. "sportpolitical" competition. In addition, given that most Soviet allies and client states would inevitably follow the U.S.S.R.'s lead in boycotting the L.A. Games (much as U.S. allies and client states joined in the American boycott of the Moscow Games), the Soviet Olympic boycott constituted another step toward a permanent East–West split in the international Olympic movement. And, most important for the Los Angeles Games, the Soviet boycott resulted in a loss of revenues to the already financially strapped LAOOC. ABC's contract to televise the Games contained a clause calling for a 60 million dollar "downward renegotiation" in financial arrangements with the LAOOC in the event of a Soviet boycott. Millions more would be lost to other business interests directly dependent upon Olympic delegations' and spectators' attendance at the Games.

And, as if these were not enough political headaches, the LAOOC managed to alienate and provoke the ire of local Black and Latino communities by implementing what are viewed by these groups as insensitive, racist, and exploitive employment and licensing policies. In exchange for their cooperation in convincing the International Olympics Committee of the suitability of Los Angeles as a Games site, minority leaders were promised by Mayor Tom Bradley in 1979 that at least 20 percent of all Olympic concessions and production licenses would be awarded to minority contractors. But, the promise was not kept. In the Black community, for instance, with the dubious exceptions of Ken Norton's "Key Chains" and "Moochie's Lap blankets" (for use in Los Angeles in July and August?), the Games have brought little in the way of financial benefits. Typical of the "employment opportunities" offered Blacks was the position offered to Stan Wright, a former U.S. Olympic track coach who has been officially active in the United States Olympic Movement for almost thirty years. Coach Wright was told by an LAOOC official that a volunteer usher's position was available—if he wanted it.

"A lack of money" is the most frequent response to monetary inquiries as to why promises of employment and licensed sub-contractor opportunities have not been realized. But some minority leaders are quick to point out that a lack of money has not prevented top LAOOC officials, all of whom are white, from voting themselves hefty bonuses—estimated by some news services to be as high as 100,000 dollars for some officials.

In the words of one resident of the overwhelmingly Black and Latino Coliseum-Exposition Park area that is the hub of Olympic competitions, "It's as if we're hosting a party, only we're not invited." Minority communities in Los Angeles have assumed as a result, what several Los Angeles news reports describe as a "fortress approach" to the Games—meaning that when Olympic participants and spectators travel through these areas, they keep moving—and fast.

Even were there no issues of Soviet participation, domestic political agitation, or minority alienation, the Los Angeles Games would have had their problems.

The 1984 Olympics are the Games that nobody wanted. The only other city in competition as a possible Games site was pre-revolution Teheran, Iran. And since few people welcomed the likelihood that Mr. Khomeni would become Chief Olympics host, Los Angeles was awarded the games virtually by default.

The already clouded future of these Games, then, darkened considerably more when Los Angeles residents voted not to support them financially.

Enter Peter V. Ueberroth and the Los Angeles Olympic Organizing Committee with their concept of corporate sponsored, commercialized, "free enterprise" Olympics. Not only did Ueberroth and his staff propose to stage the Games under a "new and innovative free-enterprise format" requiring "no city, state, or federal government funding," but they projected a "budgetary surplus" or profit. What struck many as astonishing was that Ueberroth and company proposed to stage the games at a *total cost* of about 500 million dollars—less than half the 1.1 billion dollars *debt* left by the six billion dollar Montreal Olympics, and only a small fraction of the nine billion dollars spent by the Soviets to stage the "spartan" Moscow games.

Traditionally, the games have been awarded to cities, not private corporations such as the LAOOC. Similarly, expenditures by Olympic organizing committees have been determined by one consideration: *Whatever is required to successfully stage the games.* However, because its budget was limited to the monies raised through sales of Olympic sponsorships, concessions, and other marketable interests, the LAOCC was forced to adopt a "bottom line" philosophy on every decision surrounding the staging of the 1984 games. That is, the questions, "How much will it cost?" and "How much will it produce?" overshadowed practically all other considerations. This situation made the Los Angeles Games the most commercialized Olympics in history. Everything which could be sold was sold to raise money and to secure facilities and services. However, some critically negative consequences of this bottom line strategy were evident throughout the LAOOC effort. For instance, because budgetary considerations compelled the use of existing facilities as Olympic venues, events associated with the games were spread out over *three states* with the preponderance of Olympic competitions taking place in five *Southern California counties* stretching over an area *190 miles long and 40 miles wide* and encompassing *19 Olympic sites* that are connected by *705 miles* of the most traffic congested freeway system in the United States. The thousands of athletes participating in the Games were housed in dormitories at the University of California at Los Angeles, the University of Southern California, and the University of California at Santa Barbara—"Olympic Villages" that required some athletes to travel as far as 40 miles to their competitions.

Aside from logistical difficulties, these arrangements resulted in monumental security problems not only because of the size of the area to be secured but because of coordination problems and jurisdictional disputes among the 17,000 local, state, and federal law enforcement officers and military personnel charged with security responsibilities during the Games. Though fully one-fifth of the total Olympic organizing budget—100 million dollars—was allocated for security, according to "California Poll" results released in May, a majority of the state's citizens found little basis upon which to feel very secure in attending the Games. Nearly two-thirds (65 percent) reported that they "expect an increase in terrorism and street crime in Los Angeles during the Olympics."

Despite unprecedented political, logistical and financial problems, the greatest threat to the integrity and conduct of the Los Angeles Olympics may well come from competing athletes themselves. Since 1952, under the heady influence of nationalism and in pursuit of personal glory and pecuniary interests, amateur athletes throughout the world increasingly have resorted to use what they believe to be performance enhancing drugs. While estimates as to the extent of illegal performance-related drug use among international sports competitors vary, there is no shortage of evidence that there exists a widespread problem.

In August of 1983, after strict testing exposed over a dozen drug-abusing competitors at the Pan American Games in Caracas, Venezuela, there was an embarrassingly extensive exodus of athletes whose events had not begun. Yet other athletes were suspected of "competing to lose" in their events in order not to be among the top three finishers who were automatically tested for drug use. In the European Championships just before the Moscow Olympics, five women distance runners tested positive on anabolic steroid use, among them the top three competitors in the world.

The LAOOC made provisions to test specifically for some 178 drugs among the hundreds banned for use by Olympic competitors. And to get the job done, the most sophisticated drug testing machinery in Olympic history has been developed and installed. As one LAOOC official commented, "If the human palate were as sensitive to flavors as this drug testing machinery is to banned substances, we would be able to taste a pinch of sugar dissolved in an Olympic-sized swimming pool."

But even this may be insufficient to guarantee ethical competitions. With each successive Olympiad, there have been rumors of new, exotic and bizarre drug use techniques among athletes searching for the winning edge. In 1984, most speculation in this regard revolves around the use of "blood doping." Blood doping is a technique whereby an athlete's own blood is drawn in small doses over time, frozen, and then thawed and reinjected 6 to 10 days before the competition to boost the count of oxygen-carrying cells and thereby increasing performance. There is also talk of a pituitary substance derived from human corpses which supposedly enhances muscle size and strength, and is purportedly being used by some athletes in place of the more easily detected anabolic steroids.

Beset with problems, some once supremely optimistic individuals inside the LAOOC were privately admitting that the "free enterprise" Games format involved great risks. Others associated with the LAOOC effort pointed out that though people tend to look back upon the 1932 Los Angeles Olympics with nostalgia, those games were far from trouble free. The Great Depression was worldwide, the burgeoning specter of political upheaval and war was already evident in Europe, and Prohibition was seen by many as a direct threat to foreign spectatorship and tourism. As Gwenn Wilson, now 86 and formerly associate director of the 1932 Olympics, states, "Nobody thought we could do it. Nobody thought we could successfully stage the Games."

However, for all the difficulties and complexities of the times, the 1932 Games were nonetheless of a simpler age: those games had *no* security budget; the total cost for food, lodging, and transportation for each athlete was $3 a day (as opposed to $35–$45 a day per athlete in 1984) and there was no commercialization of Olympic symbols, concessions, or events; there was no drug testing; there was no law enforcement jurisdictional problems to contend with; and there were no candidates for national boycotts.

The Los Angeles Games were marred by the Soviet bloc boycott which undercut the level of competition in a number of athletic areas and reduced spectator interest in the Games. But in retrospect the businessmen, bankers, real estate developers and others of the administrative leadership of the LAOOC were fortunate in escaping some of the uglier possibilities which confronted them—particularly in the area of political violence. Whether the Los Angeles Games were a success or a failure will be debated by partisans for some time to come. But the larger question which looms ahead is the future of the Games themselves. The 1988 summer Olympics are scheduled for Seoul, South Korea, a nation with explosive internal political rifts. Because the symbolic implications of South Korea are lost to neither the Eastern nor Western bloc of nations, we can expect the trend of mounting Olympic contradictions to continue with the Seoul Games. Facing such a prospect, it may be time to ask ourselves if the Olympic Games as a 19th century western institution finally has been outpaced and overrun by the course and complexity of 20th century political events?

1976 and 1980 Olympic Boycott
Media Coverage: All the News That Fits

Vincent Mosco
Queen's University

Levon Chorbajian
University of Lowell

Introduction

In 1976, 28 African nations withdrew from the Montreal games. This withdrawal highlighted three decades of struggle against the athletic policies of the Union of South Africa. South Africa is a nation dominated by a white minority which controls 87 percent of the land resources and monopolizes political rights at the expense of the African majority. Africans supply labor in mining, agriculture and industry and live in generally depressed conditions. White per capita income exceeds black by a factor of 30. Every other index of living standard shows a similar pattern of oppression in this system maintained by an elaborate police-state apparatus.[1]

The *apartheid* system of strict racial separation is reflected in South African athletics. South Africa never allowed Africans to represent it at the Olympics and, internally, separation of facilities, teams and administration was the standard in sport. Protests within South Africa on the issue of sports dates to the late 1940s. In the intervening decade the movement against *apartheid* sport became international with major protests against touring South African teams. In England and New Zealand these protests were broadly based, backed, as they were, by student organizations, trade unions, religious bodies and selected Labour Party officials.

International opposition eventually produced results with the Olympic movement and international sporting bodies beginning to sanction South Africa from the late 1950s on. South Africa was excluded from the 1964 and 1968 Olympics, and it was expelled from the Olympic movement in 1970. With this success attention turned to those nations which continued sporting contacts with South Africa. The major offender here was New Zealand, and when the International Olympic Committee voted not to exclude New Zealand from Montreal, the walkout ensued.[2]

The 1980 boycott was sponsored by the United States in response to the Soviet invasion of Afghanistan. The boycott was taken with an eye to quite narrow political goals, not the least of which was President Carter's sagging re-election hopes. In addition, and very importantly, the possibilities for large-scale U.S. corporate investment in the Soviet Union promised by detente were not taking place, and the focus shifted back to the Third World with a renewed emphasis on Third World stabilization. The American hostage crisis in Iran and the Afghanistan question allowed public mobilization behind increased militarization and an openly interventionist foreign policy.[3]

It is clear that the events of 1976 were the outgrowth of years of popular struggle in South Africa and many other nations. These struggles were conducted on the athletic front in conjunction with efforts at the political, economic and diplomatic levels. By contrast the boycott of the 1980 Moscow Olympics spearheaded by President Carter had no similar popular history and it did not concern the issue of sports or the Olympics at any level other than that of presidential fiat. Nonetheless the 1980 boycott movement did keep over 50 nations, including Japan, West Germany and Canada, from attending the Moscow Games.

Time and the 1976 Olympics

The hard, intense quality of *Time* is reflected in its textual and graphic material. Interesting in this regard are the *Time* covers in the weeks preceding the 1976 Olympics. The June 14 issue announces: "Italy: The Red Threat." On the cover we find a jagged, granite-featured drawing of a man with the caption, "Communist Leader Berlinguer." The next three issues in this bicentennial year have American themes. June 21 features "Our Next President," where our choices are presented with Carter on the left and Reagan and Ford on the right. The June 28 issue is titled, "Rediscovering America," and the cover features a young blond woman on the back of a motorbike with a considerable display of red, white and blue clothing and decalling throughout. The June 5 theme is "America's New Immigrants." On the cover we see such words as "tall ships" and "Bicentennial," symbolizing history, nationhood and unity." . . .

This pattern of four issues creates a mood of patriotism and identification of the nation with feelings of warmth and security in a frightening and alien world. The portraits of Carter, Reagan and Ford are flattering and intended to reassure the reader. "Rediscovering America" focuses attention on the U.S. in a year when the Olympics are across the border in Canada. The new immigrants invidiously compare the U.S. to the nations from which they came, nations portrayed, correctly or not, as poor, dictatorial and unfree. The *Time* essay in this issue is entitled, "Loving America," and informs the reader that "one ultimately loves America not for what it is, or what it does, but for what it promises" (p. 36).

The Olympics carry an implication of internationalism. This ideal is undercut by promoting a fear of foreign people, places and beliefs with the cover and feature stories on Italian Communism and insects. By creating a warm, reassuring mood on things American while frightening readers on the non-American, the political controversies stemming from the Montreal Games can be more easily portrayed as alien, Communist and Third World. By the time the August 2 issue arrives and we see Nadia Comaneci on the cover, the reader, from the covers alone, has been encouraged to understand the caption, "She's Perfect: But Olympics Are In Trouble," in the manner in which *Time* wishes it to be understood.

The 1976 protests cannot be understood without reference to South Africa, but in *Time*'s Olympic coverage there is scarcely any presentation of such material. The June 28 issue does contain an article, "The Soweto Uprisings: A Soul Cry of Rage," which is factually sound and sympathetic to the struggles of non-white South Africans. However, the article is undercut in the July 19 issue where all three letters to the editor on South Africa are hostile to the popular struggles taking place there. One letter says, "Thank God that South Africa has laws to quell such disturbances as the one in Soweto." This July 19 issue contains the first major article on the African boycott.

The first nation to walk out was Tanzania. *Time* describes the Tanzanian action as "a gesture" and sees its main implication as the inability of Filbert Bayi, holder of the world 1,550m record, to compete. The reason why we will not have the pleasure of seeing Bayi, according to *Time,* is because millions of live and TV viewers make the Olympics "the world's biggest stage"; inevitably this leads to "the oil and water mixing of politics and sport" (p. 54).

In keeping with its preference for spotlighting individual personalities the next article, "Matter of Race," features Bayi and his main competitor, John Walker, of New Zealand. The article begins in pleading, nostalgic tones:

> Politics and providence permitting, one of the most memorable foot races of modern times would have been the 1,500 meter final on Saturday, July 31st. (p. 57)

The article states that "misfortune intervenes." This "misfortune" is briefly described with a background of the Tanzanian protest. Brief references to New Zealand, rugby and South Africa appear. It is pointed out that OAU rejected a Tanzanian resolution for a walkout but Tanzania "decided to take action on its own" (p. 57).

Bayi is quoted as supporting the protest and putting the struggle against *apartheid* above his personal disappointment. *Time* immediately questions Bayi's statement. "Such self-abnegation cannot have come easily" (p. 57). *Time* then describes Bayi's intense desire and rigorous training habits, thus highlighting the tragedy of the Tanzanian walkout.

Walker speaks his piece next, and the occasion is again taken to question Bayi's sincerety.

Walker seemed more disturbed, or perhaps more candid than Bayi about the Tanzanian decision. "We're sportsmen," he fumed last weekend. "It's bloody crazy to make us into politicians." (p. 57)

The July 26 article, "Game Playing in Montreal," focuses on the Taiwan issue. *Time* takes the official Washington line in supporting Taiwan in its dispute with the Canadian government over the question of national nomenclature. The Canadians are strongly criticized for their insistence that Taiwan compete as Taiwan and not as China. According to *Time* the Taiwan issue and the African boycott make "the Montreal Games one of the gloomier landmarks in Olympic history" (p. 39).

In the August 2 article, "The Games Up in the Air," there is great excitement over Nadia Comaneci. However, despite being the first person to ever receive a perfect score of 10 in gymnastics, "never before have the Olympics seemed less perfect" (p. 44). Taiwan and the African boycott may have done "irreparable damage" (p. 44). Once again we are treated to tales of the anger and heartbreak of disappointed athletes. Consistent with *Time*'s other coverage of the Games this article takes the preservation of an idealized "non-political Olympics" as its goal and never considers the validity of the protest. Thus the Games are presented as needlessly politicized.

This same issue of *Time* features an essay, "Are the Olympics Dead?" The author admits that politics and the Olympics have a long history. He even views this as appropriate "to the degree that nationalism equates with patriotism" (p. 48). However, matters have gotten out of hand: "The magnitude of the African boycott has placed the Games at the mercy of political blackmailers" (p. 49). The essay ends with a State Department official telling us: "One thing is certain, if politics is not removed—and quickly—the Olympic Games have no future" (p. 49).

Time's Olympic coverage ends in the next two issues with letters to the editor. None of the seven letters so much as hints of support for the African boycott. Typical of the tone of these letters is one appearing in the August 16 issue which deplores what "we have come to expect from Third World dictatorships."

The *New York Times* and the 1976 Olympics

Olympic coverage in the *New York Times* reveals a broader and more extensive scope which we would expect in a daily and also a somewhat greater willingness to present contrary views, particularly in the letters-to-the-editor department. In the case of its news articles, however, we encounter less a case of the absence of bias than the greater subtlety of bias. In the case of editorials in 1976 and 1980, *Time* editorials, with only two meaningful exceptions, fit right in with the official U.S. government position. There is scarcely a difference between *Time* and the *Times* in this department. Because the *Times* is a daily and because its Olympic coverage represents a considerable body of material, this material will be covered by type—editorials, letters to the editor, and news stories and features.

The *Times* ran seven editorials and columns on the political issues of the 1976 Olympics which appeared between July 7 and August 2, 1976. For the most part these editorials dealt with the Taiwan controversy, but they often made reference to the African protest, or, if not, they clearly communicated the *Times'* position on political controversies and the Olympics. Two important points need to be made concerning these editorials. First, by any reasonable standard there is not sufficient background information anywhere in the *Times* to allow the reader to make an informed, independent judgment on the *Times'* editorial positions. Second, without a single exception all of these editorials strongly condemn both the idea of political controversies bearing on the Olympic process in general and the Canadian position on Taiwan and the African protest over South Africa and New Zealand specifically.

The July 7 editorial, "Olympian Politics," deplores the "intrusion" of politics into the Games. According to the writer this has occurred "all too frequently." If this principle were to be legitimized the "Olympics would be turned into a shambles . . . " (p. 32).

The July 17 editorial, "The Flickering Flame," complains of "political stubbornness" and deplores "the trend of extreme nationalism, commercialism and professionalism which . . . has long been tarnishing the Olympic ideal" (p. 22). In the July 20 issue, "Destroying the Olympics" trots out the old standby of the non-political Olympics: "The whole concept of open, global sporting competition is being debased before the world's eyes" (p. 30). This editorial is highly critical of the African nations and dismisses their protest as being "totally outside the Olympic framework" (p. 30).

On July 25 C.L. Sulzberger offers us the article, "End of a Tradition." Sulzberger incorrectly informs his readers that the idea of a a purely sportive Olympics "was honored until recently." He criticizes the Trudeau government and the African nations for their actions at the Montreal Games and writes:

> . . . it would be pity, but not an international disaster, if the neo-Olympics were to vanish from the contemporary scene . . . because they have developed into a nasty bedlam of argumentation wholly extraneous to the idea of sport and sportsmanship. (Sec. IV, p. 17)

The August 2 Op-Ed piece, "The Dying Flame," refers to "thoroughly distasteful displays of political chauvinism" and describes the Games as "seriously marred" (p. 22). This editorial specifically refers to the protest of the African nations and criticizes their protest for making "an irrelevant point" (p. 22).

The *Times* published only three letters to the editor with references to the African boycott. One is a strong letter in favor of the boycott (July 23, p. 30). Two briefer letters are opposed to the boycott. On this limited basis *Times* letters to the editors were somewhat more balanced than those of *Time.*

The *Times* ran several dozen articles and feature stories on the African protest and walkout from Montreal. While several of these articles contain information on the New Zealand rugby tour and the opposition of the African nations to *apartheid* sport, nowhere does the *Times* present the motivation, organization and history of the protest movement against *apartheid* sport. The effect is to sever the Montreal protest from its historical roots and to lessen the likelihood of the protest assuming legitimacy in the mind of the *Times* reader. At a more insidious level the reputation for thoroughness and objectivity enjoyed by the *Times* allows it to successfully ignore the background of the protests and thereby to convey upon the walkout itself a rash and impetuous quality.

The first article on the African protest appeared on May 23. The article, "African Threat Casts a Cloud on Olympics," contains many forms of bias and distortion which are recurring features of later pieces on the African boycott. The initial sentence assumes a mocking, comic posture:

> The threats are flapping again, like kites in a strong wind. Just as they did in Mexico City. Just as they did in 1972 before Munich. It has recently become a recurrent theme. If this is an Olympic year, it must be time for a boycott. (Sec. V, p. 1)

The author pays considerable attention to the Bayi-Walker matchup in the 1,500 meters. This stress on specific athletic contests and personalities is a recurring feature of the *Times,* distracting attention from the underlying issues which fail to be thoroughly reported. The author also employs the image of "pure" sport to situate for the reader the meaning of the proposed boycott: "Sport, itself, is only tangential to the threat. It has to do with politics" (Sec. V, p. 1).

We learn that the Supreme Council for Sport in Africa bases its position "on what it considers to be New Zealand's violation of various United Nations resolutions . . ." (Sec. V. p. 1). The U.N. resolutions in question are not listed, nor are their contents amplified. The resolutions themselves are quite clear and unequivocal, but the author's use of an equivocal, hedging language allows him to cast doubt on the Supreme Council's position. The article closes with the view that the boycott will pose to the affected athlete a severe "injustice" (Sec. V, p. 8). To reinforce this view, the photo accompanying the article is one of a smiling Bayi and Walker at the 1974 Commonwealth Games.

In several instances opponents of the boycott are offered coverage with no space given to defenders of the boycott. More commonly the *Times* does quote speakers on both sides of an issue. While these quotations can have the effect of affording those in favor of the African boycott the space to state their opinions, the presentation of views and counterviews has the effect of lending both views an equal legitimacy which would be gainsaid through an historical analysis of the issues. But as we have seen, this analysis is nowhere provided by the *Times;* nor is it always the case that the African boycott position is accorded equal space. A single, brief article, "UN Official Calls Boycott 'Noble Act'" (July 27, p. 24), is the only one in which the pro-boycott position receives monopoly or majority coverage. In every other instance the coverage is equal or inferior. "Olympic Games Started; Guyana Joins Boycott" (July 19, pp. 1, 16) quotes four prominent officials opposed to the boycott and one in favor. In "Olympic Games Lose 17 Nations" (July 20, pp. 1, 27), Jean-Claude Ganga of the Supreme Council defends the boycott, but greater space is accorded Lance Cross, New Zealand representative to the IOC, who opposes it.

Finally, every human interest story related to the boycott promotes anti-boycott sentiment. "Guyana Pullout Turns Boxer's Golden Dreams to Nightmare" (July 19, p. 16) sympathetically documents the hopes, aspirations and sacrifices of a boxer from Guyana who cannot compete because of the boycott. The disappointment of athletes from boycotting nations is also a major theme in the article, "U.S. Blacks Won't Join Boycott" (July 21, p. 25).

Time and the 1980 Olympics

Coverage of the 1980 boycott by *Time* and the *Times* was considerably more extensive than in 1976. We also find a significant qualitative difference in the 1980 reportage. While both publications took strong positions against governments employing the Olympics to pursue political goals in 1976, both publications in 1980 sought to provide justification and legitimization for the U.S. boycott of the Moscow Games.

In late 1979 and early 1980 *Time* both reflected a growing neo-Cold War mentality and participated in promoting militant anti-Soviet and anti-Third World attitudes among its readers. On December 24 *Time* spoke of the "rising Soviet threat" in an article on the NATO decision to strengthen its nuclear strike force. The first issue of the new year, January 7, featured a major story on the Soviets in Afghanistan, "the most brutal blow from the Soviet Union's steel fist since the Red Army's invasion of Czechoslovakia in 1968" (p. 72). On the cover of the January 14 issue we see "Moscow's Bold Challenge," with President Carter telling us: "My opinion of the Russians has changed most dramatically." For the first time we read of the Olympics as Carter hints of a boycott in his discussion of sharp controls over exports of technical equipment and grain to the Soviet Union.

The next three issues contain articles on the boycott. In the January 21 article, "Should the Torch Be Passed," we read statements by Carter and Vice-President Mondale endorsing a boycott. The author then quotes Don Miller of the U.S. Olympic Committee as an example of those who say the Olympics should be above politics. To disprove this point, the Moscow Games are equated with those of Berlin in 1936: the Soviets want the Games "as a way to greatly increase their nation's prestige, even as a way to legitimize their system" (p. 21). The January 28 issue contains the article, "Olympics: To Go or Not to Go," informing readers that "there is probably no single action short of war that would punish Moscow more than to have the Olympics taken away or spoiled" (p. 15). Also featured with the article is an extremely hostile anti-Soviet cartoon.

On March 4 we see the fourth consecutive cover featuring a neo-Cold War theme. Carter appears with the caption, "Taking Charge: An Assault Will Be Repelled By Any Means Necessary." The article, "On Your Marks, Get Set, Stop!" refers immediately to the boycott: "It had been launched as a trial balloon—and it took off immediately" (p. 20). Ignored is the still considerable resistance to the boycott idea. It is noted that the USOC is opposed, but its efforts are described as being "in vain." In the closing paragraph the understandable disappointment of the athletes is noted and an effort is made to transcend this disappointment with the concluding words:

> . . . there was growing agreement in the U.S. with Jimmy Carter's declaration that for this Olympics, under these conditions, there were "deeper issues at stake." (p. 22)

In the February 11 issue there are five letters to the editor on the boycott, four in favor and one opposed. There also appears a two-page *Time* essay titled, "The Boycott That Might Rescue the Games." In contrast to 1976 those who argue that the Games should be above politics are labelled "purists" and they are said to "argue a bit romantically":

> To say that the Olympic Games have nothing to do with politics is the equivalent of saying that disco dancing has nothing to do with sex. (p. 72)

Readers are told that not to boycott "would be an act of diplomatic negligence" (p. 75).

Time resumes its Olympic coverage on March 31 with the article, "A Resounding Chorus of Maybes." The themes of organizing the boycott and opposition to it are detailed. On April 26 *Time* reports on the French and West German votes on the boycott. France will not boycott and the West Germans will. The French decision is described as a "ploy." Carter is quoted as describing the West German decision as "courageous."

The June 9 issue contains one letter to the editor, a pro-boycott letter focusing on the NBC decision to cancel its TV coverage of the Games. Says its author:

> I just hope that the athletes understand the importance of what NBC has done: a large corporation has put the nation's values and policies above material gain.

Neither the letter-writer nor *Time* mentions that NBC's insurance coverage will compensate it for much of its loss.

With the July 21 issue we have the first coverage of the Moscow Games with an article titled, "Bearish Beginning in Moscow: The Clouded Games Get Under Way in a Grand Setting." A considerable portion of the article is devoted to American swimmers, boxers and track and field stars and speculation on how they would have fared in Moscow.

Time articles on July 28 and August 4 stress the boycott, Soviet security and press censorship and the negative impact of the boycott on the quality of the Games. The August 4 issue also contains the second of *Time*'s two-page essays on the Moscow Games. "The Games: Winning Without Medals" is strongly supportive of the boycott. The author asks, "Is the U.S. a Spoilsport?" and goes on to answer in a resounding negative. In stark contrast to 1976 *Time* asserts that the Olympics are not and have never been free of political considerations. Readers are told that "the countries participating in the Moscow Olympics are symbolically abetting the Soviet takeover of Afghanistan" (p. 68).

The August 11 issue offers further coverage of the Games in the article, "That Warsaw Pact Picnic." Italian and French efforts are highlighted since "there is little else for the West to cheer about" (p. 24). The article notes a million-dollar Washington tribute for 380 American athletes. The U.S. National Swimming Championships in California are also noted. Readers are told that 8 of the 17 Olympic distance winners in California bettered the times set in Moscow. *Time* then takes a look ahead to the Los Angeles Games in 1984, where U.S. Olympians will have a chance to show their stuff.

Time concludes its Olympic coverage with letters to the editor in the August 25 issue. Consistent with past issues where there have been equal numbers of pro- and anti-boycott letters, or more commonly a larger number of pro-boycott than anti-boycott letters, there are three letters in favor of the boycott, one against and one neutral.

The *New York Times* and the 1980 Olympics

The *New York Times* coverage of the 1980 Olympics and its attendant controversies begins with the first word of a possible boycott stemming from an emergency meeting of NATO in early 1980 and continues through the month of August. Altogether the *Times* runs over two dozen editorials and columns, close to 40 letters to the editor and over 300 news stories.

Editorial writers and columnists are unflinching in their support of President Carter and a boycott of the Moscow Olympics. Of the 29 editorials and columns which appear on the boycott, only three take a position opposing the boycott. One of these is Michael Harrigan's "On an Olympic Boycott" (January 12, p. 19). Harrigan opposes the boycott but from a strong anti-Soviet, Cold War perspective. If we discount Harrigan, we are left with Phil Shinnick's "Former Olympic Athlete Says U.S. Should Go to Moscow" (March 16, Sec. V, p. 2) and James Riordan's "Olympic Flame, Yes. Smudgepot, No" (June 29, Sec. IV. p. 19). Both are well reasoned anti-boycott pieces, but they are swallowed in a mass of pro-boycott editorials.

The *Times'* premier sports columnist, Red Smith, devotes portions or all of seven columns to the boycott and takes a consistently strong pro-boycott position. Smith's first boycott column appears on January 4. Smith begins his "Boycott the Moscow Olympics" (p. 16) by lauding a Conservative MP who urged Prime Minister Margaret Thatcher to lead a world-wide Olympic boycott. Smith stresses that politics has always played a part in the Olympic movement. He also discusses the 1936 Berlin Games at length, pointing to the dangers of allowing totalitarian regimes to have a propaganda field day with the Games. "The Games We Need Not Play" appears on January 16 (p. 20), in which Smith again urges a boycott and criticizes Carter for moving too slowly on the matter.

As events unfold Smith is right there to interpret them for the public. In "Petitions, Girls and Euclid Avenue" (February 29) Smith comments on an anti-boycott petition signed by members of the U.S. Winter Olympics Team and presented to Carter:

> . . . with all due respect for the young people who competed so earnestly at Lake Placid, there is no clear evidence that sliding downhill, chasing a puck or describing figure skating on ice automatically qualifies one as an authority on foreign relations equipped to advise the President and his staff. (p. 22)

Smith has his final say in "His Lordship's Tantrum" (July 21, Sect. III, p. 7). Lord Killanin, outgoing President of the IOC, has blasted the U.S. for leading a boycott of the Moscow Games. Smith will not let it pass, nor will he deal with the substance of Killanin's criticism. Killanin, readers are told, "goes out on a note of petty spite, having a tantrum because the United States chose not to attend his farewell party" (p. 7). Smith is joined by Dave Anderson, Russel Baker, George Vecsey, Tom Wicker, the op-ed page and others. Each endorses the boycott and not one has a critical word to say about it.

"The Games Nations Play," the op-ed editorial (January 8, p. 18) informs us that "taking the politics out of the Moscow Olympics is about as feasible as taking the alcohol out of vodka." Another op-ed piece, "Let's Forget the Moscow Olympics" (January 24), makes a point repeated on numerous occasions in *Times* editorials:

> A boycott of the Moscow Games stands as one of the few nonviolent measures readily available to the President . . . American withdrawal from the Olympics will hurt . . . the Soviet Union for a very long time, draining joy from a keenly anticipated event. (p. 6)

In "Laurels for Moscow?" (February 11) Anthony Lewis criticizes the Olympic movement for *ignoring* political issues in the past. His prime example is Berlin in 1936. "Olympic bureaucrats," according to Lewis, have time and again "turned a blind eye to . . . political savagery . . . " (p. 19). *Times* editorials repeatedly inform the public that the Soviet Union seeks to employ the Olympics for political purposes, that we can severely and justifiably foil their intentions by boycotting and that such a boycott is consistent with the political nature of the Olympic Games. Of all the coverage of the 1976 and 1980 Olympics in *Time* and the *Times* it is only in the 1980 *Times* letters to the editor that we have a balance in the presentation of points of view. Of the 32 letters which could be categorized as favoring or opposing the boycott, 16 are in favor and 16 are opposed.

Not so for photographs. The *Times* runs two photographs which strongly reinforce the boycott decision. The first appears on July 21 (p. 3), featuring a smiling Yasir Arafat. The caption employs the guilt-by-association technique to discredit the Games then in progress, i.e., Mr. Arafat is a terrorist, and these are the kinds of people who go to and are welcomed by Moscow:

> TOURS OLYMPIC SITE: Yasir Arafat, Chairman of the Palestine Liberation Organization, visiting Yugoslav athletes yesterday in Moscow. During the 1972 Olympic Games in Munich, a terrorist group linked to Mr. Arafat's own organization, Al Fatah, staged a raid in which 11 Israeli athletes and coaches died. . . . (p. 3)

The second photo appears in the July 31 issue. Congress passed and Carter signed a bill authorizing the distribution of medals to American athletes who were barred from going to Moscow. We see Carter distributing these medals, and the caption quotes Carter's words:

> If our Olympic team had been in Moscow these past days, with all the pageantry and spectacle, it would have been impossible for us credibly to maintain our effort to seek freedom in Afghanistan. (p. D 20)

Of the hundreds of news articles published by the *Times*, only a small handful report critically on the boycott or allow Carter's critics to freely express themselves. We do not wish to say that objective reporting was absent; there were dozens of news articles which reported without partisanship. On the other hand it must be recognized that the publication of a newspaper requires discretionary actions on the part of the editorial staff. These decisions on reporting or not reporting a story, content, headline and location can and do affect what we read as "the news." With very few exceptions these discretionary actions give *Times* news articles a pro-boycott bias, often subtle, but *in toto* forming a larger, consistent pattern.

Among the forms of bias found were: allowing pro-boycott forces to express their viewpoint without publishing counter-viewpoints; publishing a larger number of pro-boycott than anti-boycott statements within an article; publishing misleading headlines; and mocking or denigrating anti-boycott spokespersons. There are only five articles which present the anti-boycott position sympathetically or allow anti-boycott forces to express their viewpoint without rebuttal. The largest number of news articles are objective reports of developments, but the articles leaning in favor of the boycott far outnumber those few which called it into question.

Articles dealing with Soviet charges that the U.S. is using the boycott for political purposes contain rebuttals from U.S. officials or editorial comment. Statements by administration officials are often presented without balancing points of view. "Response by Alliance to Soviet Is the Focus of U.S.–British Talks" (January 15) quotes Deputy Secretary of State Warren Christopher as saying, ". . . in the United States . . . there is growing feeling of the inappropriateness of holding the games in Moscow . . . " (p. 9). No differing point of view appears. Additional news articles employed to offer forecasts of the effects of the boycott are often of the "hurt" or "punish the Russians" variety. Possible negative consequences of a boycott rarely appear.

Several articles publish the views of athletes and coaches. Despite the fact that most of the athletes initially opposed the boycott, a larger number of pro-boycott viewpoints is published in every single case. In "Athletes Give Some Opinions on Matter of an Olympic Boycott" (January 20, Sec. V, p. 2) a poll of coaches and potential and former Olympians is reported. Five favor the boycott and three oppose it. In "President Proposes Deadline of Month for Olympics Move" (January 21, p. 1) two athletes and a coach present their opinion on the boycott. All three support it. In "Pros Feel for Olympians But Back Boycott" (January 22, pp. B 11, B 14) seven professional athletes express their opinions. All seven support the boycott.

When the topic of the article is itself critical, officials and others are allowed considerable space to reassert their pro-boycott positions. An example appears on February 26 in the article, "Olympians Welcomed by Carter, Offer Petition Opposing Boycott" (pp. 1, C 11). Carter receives a group of U.S. Winter Olympians. During the visit skating star, Eric Heiden, presents Carter with a petition opposing the boycott. This portion of the article is followed by a lengthier one in which Carter is able to present his position on the boycott. Heiden is the only person who presents an anti-boycott viewpoint, while Carter is backed by hockey coach, Herb Brooks, and goalie, Jim Craig.

The *Times'* coverage of the boycott movement in Canada and Australia is instructive. Three news articles appear on the boycott movement in Canada. In all three articles only the points of view of those supporting a Canadian boycott are published. In Australia the national Olympic Committee voted to attend the Moscow Games contrary to the government's wishes. The curious use of the word "unit" in the headline, "Australian Unit Votes to Go to the Olympics" (May 24, p. 7), implies that this vote was taken by some small, insignificant body with a final binding vote to come at some later date. In fact, it was a vote of the National Olympic Committee which had final jurisdiction over the fate of the Australian team. No one supporting Australian participation in the Moscow Games is quoted or mentioned in this article, even though that is the winning position. On the other hand Conservative Prime Minister Malcolm Fraser is accorded the opportunity to criticize the decision:

> I pray that the Olympians who do go to Moscow will not pay the price that many of those who went to the Berlin Olympics paid once World War II started.

A similar comparison can be made of the reporting on the French decision not to boycott and the West German decision to boycott. The article "France's Olympic Group Approves Sending Team to Games in Moscow" (May 14, p. 1) quotes Secretary of State Edmund Muskie as being "very disappointed." The West German article is optimistic and upbeat with its title, "West Germans to Boycott Games, Step Likely to Influence Neighbors" (May 16, p. 10), in which it is clearly stated that the West Germans are not going. We find no talk of "units" or "groups." But why is the West German decision "likely to influence neighbors"? The boycott effort was least successful in western Europe, making it clear that if either of these decisions did, in fact, "influence neighbors," it was the French decision to go to Moscow. The boycott also received exposure in political news articles and always from the pro-boycott point of view. Examples are in "NATO Accuses Soviet of Imperiling Peace With Afghan Thrust" (May 15, pp. 1, 10) and "U.S. Scolds France on Soviet Talks and Britain Over Sanctions on Iran" (May 21, pp. 1, 16).

Conclusion: Olympian Myths and Corporate Realities

Despite its reputation for objectivity, an analysis of Olympic coverage of the 1976 and 1980 boycotts reveals the *Times*, much like *Time*, to be guilty of serious biases. This absence of objectivity is *not* principally due to error, negligence, or the myopia of particular journalists and editors. These exist, to be sure, but if they were the root sources of bias and misrepresentation, the gap between objective and reported reality would be a random one, errors here and there, willy-nilly. But it is precisely this pattern of accidental, random error which is absent. In its stead is a pattern in which the press legitimizes existing societal power relationships and patterns of exploitation.

In the 17th century the philosopher-statesman George Savile wrote, "A man that should call everything by its right name would hardly pass the streets without being knocked down as a common enemy." This is not a dilemma which ordinarily confronts the media. They are perhaps the greatest myth-makers of all, simultaneously the servants of power and powers in their own right. These issues and their bearing on the coverage of the Olympic boycotts are best clarified through a brief examination of two key issues: the organization of the mass media and the particular crisis facing the ruling class of the United States in the post-Vietnam era.

Media spokespeople are fond of pointing to a vast landscape of thousands of newspapers, magazines, and radio and television stations, a varied tableau said to guarantee the diversity of points of view essential to a democracy. A closer look at the media landscape gainsays these claims by revealing near monopoly and monopoly control of media markets. Nearly 99% of American cities have only one daily newspaper,[4] and newspaper chains control 65% of all dailies and 75% of daily circulation.[5] In the magazine field we find even greater concentration with the top four in circulation controlling 20% of revenues and the top eight controlling 30%.[6] The same pattern prevails in the electronic media. Over 50% of the AM radio stations are affiliated with the four major radio networks and over 75% of FM stations are owned by AM stations.[7] In TV we find the greatest level of concentration with 85% of all commercial stations affiliated with one of the three networks.

The New York Times Corporation and Time Incorporated are large, diversified media empires. Each publishes newspapers, magazines, and books. The *Times* owns radio and TV stations and wire services. *Time* is invested in film production and distribution, cable TV, and a number of non-media areas. As major economic enterprises operating in a capitalist context where profit is the *raison d'etre* of production and distribution, the *Times* and *Time* are subject to the same pressures as news outlets throughout the United States, namely censorship and self-censorship in order not to offend advertisers and the affluent reader-listener, and viewership which the media deliver to their advertising clients.[8] In such a context certain parties can be expected to receive favorable coverage. These include the middle class, community institutions, local elites, businesses, multinational corporations, and the institution and many of the personalities of government. In 1976 South African blacks struggling for political and economic rights in a nation of heavy investment by U.S. multinationals did not receive fair and accurate coverage in the media. Consistent with a broader pattern of serving the interests of power, Jimmy Carter, a president with a dwindling base of national support, received nearly uncritical support for his Olympic boycott only four years later.

The second factor to consider is the post-1975 political crisis. The Vietnam War was enormously unpopular, initially among students and later among broad sectors of the population. From the ruling class point of view, future foreign interventions in other lands would be difficult to sell to the public yet this intervention was necessary to the growth and security of the multinational corporations. These corporations derive considerable profits from investments in the Third World. These profits are made from lowly paid, unorganized workers who labor under specific conditions imposed—since workers do not willingly accede to them—through repression, i.e., anti-labor legislation, martial law, right wing death squads, and broad, sweeping human rights violations. On a day to day basis the U.S., allied with conservative military *and* civilian regimes, supplies weapons, trains officers, and provides other skills, personnel and equipment to this repressive apparatus.[9] If these forces fail to hold the line, direct intervention by U.S. military forces becomes a real option. But if the public is war weary and war wary, how is intervention to be accomplished? A partial answer to this question lies with the mass media, which play a key role in attempting to blunt the possibility of a critical perspective on U.S. foreign policy. It is within this context that the media coverage of the Olympic boycotts is to be fully understood.

The media have been frequent and willing handmaidens of the ruling class, lending their resources to shift public opinion toward militarism, justifying both foreign intervention and shifts in federal expenditures from social services—health care, education, welfare, recreation, mass transportation, and elder services—to high profit weapons development programs. We have seen how the boycott coverage of 1976 and 1980 promotes the interests of the powerful while attacking those of the downtrodden, but it also reveals more. Looking at a lengthy series of foreign news items over the past decade, the Olympic boycotts assume their place alongside the Iranian hostage crisis,[10] the Bulgarian-Soviet "plot" to assassinate the Pope,[11] the "international terrorist conspiracy,"[12] Korean Air Lines Flight 007,[13] alleged Soviet chemical and biological warfare deployment in Afghanistan and southeast Asia,[14] and the Soviet-Cuban "threat" to Central America[15] in a pattern of manipulated, jingoistic, and, in some cases, fabricated "news."

Notes

1. Bernard Magubane, *The Political Economy of Race and Class in South Africa*, New York: Monthly Review Press, 1979. Ann and Neva Seidman, *South Africa and U.S. Multinational Corporations*, Westport, Conn.: Lawrence Hill, 1978.

2. Richard Lapchick, *The Politics of Race and International Sport*, Westport, Conn.: Greenwood Press, 1975. Ramadnan Ali, *Africa at the Olympics*, London: Africa Books, 1976. Peter Hain, *Don't Play With Apartheid*, London: George Allen & Unwin, Ltd., 1971. Joan Brickhill, *Race Against Race: South Africa's 'Multinational' Sport Fraud*, London: International Defense & Aid Fund, 1976. Derek Humphry, *The Cricket Conspiracy*, London: The National Council for Civil Liberties, 1975. Richard Thompson, *Retreat From Apartheid*, Wellington, N.Z.: Oxford University Press, 1975. J.L. Kember, ed., *New Zealand, South Africa and Sport: Background Papers*, Wellington, N.Z.: Institute of International Affairs, 1976. Tom Newnham, *A Cry of Treason*, Palmerston North, N.Z.: The Dunmore Press, Ltd., 1978.

3. Fred Halliday, "Revolution in Afghanistan," *New Left Review*, No. 112 (November/December, 1978), pp. 3–44. Fred Halliday, "War and Revolution in Afghanistan," *New Left Review*, No. 119 (January/February, 1980), pp. 20–39. Also on Afghanistan, the July/August, 1980, issue of *MERIP Reports*. On Carter and the rightward shift of U.S. foreign policy see Thomas Ferguson and Joel Rogers, "The Empire Strikes Back," *The Nation*, November 1, 1980, pp. 436–40.

4. Benjamin M. Compaine, *Who Owns the Media? Concentration of Ownership in the Mass Communication Industry*, White Plains, N.Y.: Knowledge Industry Publications, 1979, p. 18.

5. Ibid., pp. 21, 22, 33.

6. Ibid., p. 147.

7. Vincent Mosco, *Broadcasting in the United States: Innovative Challenge and Organizational Control*, Norwood, N.J.: Ablex, 1979.

8. Ben Bagdikian, *The Media Monopoly*, Boston: Beacon Press, 1983, pp. 3–4, 29–44, 107–135.

9. Michael T. Klare and Cynthia Arnson, *Supplying Repression: U.S. Support for Authoritarian Regimes Abroad*, Washington: Institute for Policy Studies, 1981.

10. See Reza Baraheni, "The Savak Documents," *The Nation*, February 23, 1980, pp. 197–202, for an alternative analysis not reported by the dominant, mainstream mass media.

11. For an alternative analysis see "Disconnecting the Bulgarian Connection," a special issue of the *Covert Action Information Bulletin*, Spring, 1985, pp. 2–38.

12. For an alternative analysis see Edward S. Herman, *The Real Terror Network: Terrorism in Fact and Propaganda*, Boston, South End Press, 1982.

13. For an alternative analysis see David Pearson, "KAL 007: What the U.S. Knew and When We Knew It," *The Nation*, April 18, 1984, pp. 105–124.

14. For an alternative analysis see Levon Chorbajian and Richard Krushnic, "Political Genesis of the Chemical Warfare Debate," paper presented at the annual meetings of the Eastern Sociological Society, Boston, March, 1984.

15. For an alternative analysis see Charles Clements, *Witness to War: An American Doctor in El Salvador*, New York: Bantam Books, 1984; Alexander Cockburn, "Remember El Salvador," *The Nation*, June 1, 1985, pp. 662–663; James McGinnis, *Solidarity with the People of Nicaragua*, Maryknoll, N.Y.: Orbis Books, 1985.

Sports and Apartheid: The World Closes In

Richard E. Lapchick
Center for the Study of Sport in Society,
Northeastern University

S outh Africa and its system of apartheid have been in the news lately, more than at any other time in recent history. Bishop Desmund Tutu won a Nobel Peace Prize while, inside South Africa, the struggle has reached new heights—with murders, riots, boycotts, and a general intensification of the efforts of the forces opposed to the regime. In the United States, thousands of citizens have been arrested in protests against apartheid, and college campuses have come alive with anti-apartheid activities.

It is not unreasonable to ask "Why now?" For those who have known about apartheid for many years, that question is difficult to answer. Many of us thought such protest should have happened a long time ago. Until now, however, the issue that has received the most public notice has been the sports boycott. The international leaders of the boycott effort, following a call from nonracial forces inside South Africa, have had to fight a number of myths.

Sports Myths

The first myth is that sports and politics don't mix. That was an appealing cry even if one had to ignore the reality of so many examples of just such a mix—from the founding of the modern Olympics by de Coubertin to the Nazi Olympics, the battle over the "two Chinas," and other cases. However, no one could make such an argument after President Carter withdrew the United States and led the boycott of the Moscow Games to protest the invasion of Afghanistan. The Soviet boycott of the Los Angeles Games in 1984 was inevitable. Thus, sports and politics clearly are and have been mixed. The case of South Africa is only the most spectacular example.

The second myth is that sports break down racial and international barriers. Sports were supposed to be the way out of poverty for millions of American blacks, when in fact they have helped perpetuate that poverty as the masses have pursued the 12,000 to 1 odds a high school athlete faces to become a pro.

A third myth is that sports boycotts are ineffective. After the U.S. boycott of the Moscow Olympics, the Soviets were still in Afghanistan, and the Soviet reciprocation in Los Angeles left a hot cold war. However, the boycott against South Africa has been unique because of its universality. South Africa has not participated in the Olympics since 1960, and it is excluded from twenty-two of the twenty-six Olympic-related international sports federations. The European Economic Community and the Commonwealth nations have taken actions at the heads-of-state level to stop sports contacts between their countries and South Africa. The United Nations, which finds it almost impossible to reach a unanimous decision, has come down hard against sports contact with South Africa, as has the Organization of African Unity.

Opposition to Sanctions Against South Africa

Supporters of the Reagan administration and like-minded opponents of sanctions against South Africa criticize the forces for sanctions on three levels. First, they ask why, with so many problems in the United States, we should focus on South Africa, thousands of miles away. Although I could cite innumerable reasons, among the most prominent is that racism in America is closely linked to racism in South Africa. The same banks that have "red-lined" urban communities in the United States have lent funds to South Africa. The same companies that are laying off workers in America are exploiting cheap labor in South Africa. Many of the same people who are training Ku Klux Klansmen in weapons camps here were mercenaries in Angola, Zimbabwe, and Mozambique. South Africa counts on ignorance to keep the uninformed on its side.

More often, the question is why we should single out South Africa when the world is riddled with monstrous dictatorships. Those who ask why we do not boycott other dictatorships miss the point of South Africa's uniqueness—its viciously systematic construction of legal, political, economic, and social terms that define a society based totally on racial discrimination. Those who argue against a boycott forget that the great majority of South Africans are boycotted for life by their own government, denied the most elementary human rights—the rights to vote and to own land.

However, the most frequently heard argument against sanctions is that they would hurt black South Africans the most. I will respond to this argument more thoroughly later.

South Africa Today

To understand the boycott issue, we must understand how South Africa functions today. First, everything is divided according to race:

Groups	Population	Percent of Population
Africans	21 million	72.7
Whites	4.5 million	15.5
Colored	2.6 million	9.0
Asian	0.8 million	2.8

Beyond this, men are divided from women, rural people from urbanites, and each ethnic group from every other ethnic group. Steve Biko became such a critical actor on the scene because he said, "We are all one against apartheid, there are no Asians, Coloreds or Africans. We are all Black." Thus, he adapted black power to black consciousness—and he payed with his life.

A recent story in the *New York Times* highlighted the absurdity of the race laws. One of those laws is the Group Areas Act, which divides all neighborhoods by race. The story focused on Bibi Moola, a woman of Indian descent. Her house in Mayfair straddled a white suburb and an Indian area known as Fordsburg. Mrs. Moola may not use her front door because it lies in the white part of the house. The side entrance is in the Indian area of town.

"I never have a bath," she said in a wry joke at her own expense. The reason is that the dividing line runs through her modest bathroom. The wash basin is, for her, legal because it is on the "Indian" side. The bathtub, however, lies on what is technically "whites only" land so use of it is officially illegal.[1]

Such stories would be absurd save for the untold agonies they cause.

The Military

It is generally acknowledged that it is no longer a question of *if* but *when* and *how* blacks will take control in South Africa. South African whites clearly believe, however, that force will forestall the inevitable, and they have prepared mightily:

Despite the arms embargo, there has been a 4,500 percent increase in military expenditures between 1960 and 1981.

Legislation in 1982 spelled out another doubling of such expenditures by 1987.

The Reagan administration gave $28.3 million in arms to South Africa in its first three years.

Every white South African up to age 55 must serve in the military.

There is mandatory training with guns for children in elementary schools.

Between 1961 and 1981, the armed forces increased from 106,000 to 592,000, and military spending went from R75 million to R3 billion.

Most observers believe that South Africa has the atomic bomb.

Censorship

With its rigid censorship laws, we know what the South African government allows us to know. During the period of the scandal in the Ministry of Information, the South Africans spent $72 million illegally in the United States and Europe. They tried to buy the *Washington Star* and did buy a string of local papers.

Internal censorship is even more dramatic, with the application of banning orders. You have no trial if you are banned; you become a "nonperson." You cannot have social contact outside your family; you cannot write; you cannot speak; you cannot teach (75 percent of those banned have been teachers); and in 85 percent of the cases, you are under house arrest. Banning orders are routinely extended, as in the case of Winnie Mandela, the wife of imprisoned Nelson Mandela; Ms. Mandela has been under a banning order for two decades as of this writing.

But justice has always been a sometimes thing in South Africa. On any given day, 440 of every 100,000 South Africans are in prison, as compared to 189 in the United States. Furthermore, although 50 percent of the accused whites are acquitted, 85 percent of accused blacks are convicted. In 1980, 1,131 people were detained without trial for up to 18 months. Of those, 714 were children. In 1985, hundreds of children were detained. Fifty-nine political prisoners have died in detention in South Africa since 1963. Steve Biko is merely the best known of them.

Finally, the heinous pass laws, the likes of which are not on the books in any other nation in the world, have resulted in the imprisonment of 13.5 million black South Africans.

Income and Employment

White South Africans earn almost ten times as much per capita as blacks ($400 per month for whites versus $40 per month for blacks). Fifty-seven percent of the economically active men are migrants. Unemployment is officially at 500,000, or 9.2 percent of the economically active population; unofficially it is at 1.5 to 2 million, or 27 percent. Africans make up 71 percent of the work force, yet they earn only 29 percent of the income; whites constitute 18 percent of the work force and earn 59 percent of the income. More than 60 percent of urban Africans and 75 percent of rural Africans live below the official poverty level, which many believe is inhumanly low.

Bantustans

South Africa said that is would grant "independence" to all ten designated "homelands," or Bantustans. So far, it has done so in Transkei, Bophutatswana, Venda, and Ciskei. No government except the South African government recognizes the Bantustans, because it is there that perhaps the greatest human tragedy of all takes place. Although half of the Africans live in the Bantustans, only 13 percent of their income is generated there. Thus, most adult males leave; 75 percent of the adults living there are women who are single parents. Unemployment in the Bantustans fluctuates between 40 and 80 percent.

The 13 percent of the land that is designated for the African people is among the poorest in South Africa, and these barren lands don't produce enough food. The result is that up to 50 percent of the children born in Bantustans die before their fifth birthdays from malnutrition-related diseases. Yet South Africa *exported* more than $2 billion worth of food in 1980.

The life expectancy for whites in South Africa is 69 years; for blacks it is 54 years. Infant mortality rates are 190 per 1,000 for Africans—six times the rate for whites. Tuberculosis is virtually nonexistent among whites, whereas the TB rate for blacks is 285 per 100,000. There is one doctor for every 390 whites in the country and one black doctor for every 90,000 Africans in the Bantustans.

The result of the Bantustan policy is a fractured nation—families, communities, careers, and lives torn apart.

Education

The South African regime has stated that discrimination is based not on race but on the educational backwardness of Africans. Therefore, a look at the educational system there should tell us how rapidly things might change.

All public educational facilities are strictly segregated. Schools for Africans are vastly inferior to those for whites and follow a curricula designed to prepare them for a subservient life. For example:

Education for whites is free and compulsory; it is neither for blacks.

The government spends $1,115 per white child versus $170 per black child.

The teacher/pupil ratio is 18 to 1 for whites, 39 to 1 for Africans.

Less than 10 percent of African children complete high school.

Only half of school-age African children actually attend school.

Less than 1 in 1,000 Africans gets technical training.

There are almost 2,000 percent more white university graduates than Africans (10,000 percent more on a per capita basis).

African universities focus their curricula on divided cultures.

An education specialist wrote in the January 30, 1985, edition of the *New York Times:* "Whole communities lack even minimal educational facilities. I have visited "lucky" homelands and urban areas where schools do exist—and a sad spectacle they are; terribly overcrowded, understaffed and with minimal facilities."[2] Few teachers have university degrees; some, but not all, have finished high school. Yet South Africans say that they don't discriminate on the basis of racism—and the American press wonders why hundreds of thousands of black children boycott classes while the Reagan administration prepares to give substantial assistance to the existing educational system.

The Reagan Administration and the Future

It is no wonder that the now-defunct *Rand Daily Mail,* on the day after President Reagan's election, noted: "South Africa has been the real winner in the American elections as not only has Ronald Reagan been elected but all of South Africa's opponents have been buried in one mass grave." (This was a reference to such anti-apartheid legislators as Senators Church, Bayh, Durkin, Magnuson, and Clark).

The Reagan administration argues that actions against South Africa will hurt blacks the most. But many Africans ask, *"How much worse can it get?"* Even if it were true, no loss of material standards can be measured on any scale of human values against the prospect of the recovery of human dignity. The battle is not against "petty apartheid" but *for* land (blacks have no land rights and daily face the policy of forced removals) and the vote (blacks have not voted since 1936).

Even with President Reagan agreeing to limited sanctions in 1985, the anti-apartheid movement in the United States was stronger than ever before, as it reflected the horror inside South Africa. American anti-apartheid campaigns, such as sports boycott and the campaigns to end bank loans and investments, are symbolic and, ultimately, are steps of patience. As South Africa's first Nobel Prize winner, Zulu chief and African National Congress (ANC) leader Albert Luthuli, said:

Who will deny that 30 years of my life have been spent knocking in vain, patiently, moderately and modestly at a closed and barred door? What have been the fruits of moderation? The past 30 years have seen the greatest number of laws restricting our rights and progress, until today we have reached a stage where we have almost no rights at all.[3]

We must face the fact that it may take a revolution to change things in South Africa—as it did in Mozambique, Angola, and Zimbabwe. We should not be diverted by the presence of the USSR or Cuba. The United States has 350 companies operating in South Africa and is much more dominant. The Western press, however, continually treats the struggle of the people like a football game without a life of its own, with each team wearing the uniform of its sponsor and nothing more. References to the ANC, the most widely recognized liberation movement, are usually prefixed by "pro-Soviet."

A victory for the ANC cannot simply be a function of military success or external support. Ultimately, it will be the passions, sacrifices, and consciousness of the people themselves that will shape their own history. The cry inside South Africa is that it is time to choose. Nelson Mandela—the man who most agree would be elected prime minister if the people had a choice but who has been imprisoned for more than 20 years—made his choice early in the 1960s:

> During my lifetime I have dedicated myself to the struggle of the African people. I have fought against white domination, and I have fought against black domination. I have cherished the ideal of a democratic and free society in which all persons live together in harmony with equal opportunities. It is an ideal which I hope to live for and achieve. But if needs be, it is an ideal for which I am prepared to die.[4]

Sports Boycott as One Response

South Africa is offering huge dollars to attract athletes. *It pays for integrated sports.* For example, John Tate received $2.5 million to fight there and then got only $300,000 to box in the United States. Likewise, Mike Weaver made $2.5 million there but brought in only $500,000 when he got home. Sri Lankan and West Indian cricketers earned enough in 6-week tours that they were able to afford never being allowed to play again in their own countries because of their sanctions-busting. On the other hand, John McEnroe twice refused $1 million to compete in South Africa.

It was no accident that Errol Tobias, the only "nonwhite" on the 1981 Springbok Rugby team that came to America after its tumultuous tour of New Zealand, was the spokesperson on tour. Tobias told the press, "I represent *progress,*" claiming that the protesters didn't understand that he would not have been on the team a few years before.

The problem for Tobias was that the press was now more educated. He couldn't answer when he was asked such questions as, "Can you vote?" "Can you live where you want?" "Can you send your kids to the best schools?" "Can you have a drink with your teammates in all but a few places in South Africa?" He did not know how to respond to those who pointed out that 99 percent of rugby in South Africa is segregated and that 230,000 African rugby players were not eligible for the team because they were affiliated with the South African Council on Sport, the nonracial body in South Africa.

These are among the reasons South Africa is boycotted in sports. Yet cases of individuals hit the heart of the matter. Few non-American athletes in the 1984 Olympics received more publicity than two ex-South Africans: Zola Budd and Sydney Maree.

Maree and Budd are victims of the politics of apartheid, and it is regrettable that such athletes cannot compete for their country. Sympathy for them appeared to be widespread, however, and the apartheid government is counting on that sympathy to help it break out of its sports isolation. It had counted on such sympathy for Tobias, but it's unlikely to materialize because American citizens understood better what apartheid is all about. It was harder with the cases of Maree and Budd. It was ironic that, in the end, an injury kept Maree on the sidelines and that the image of Budd in our minds is her ill-fated race with Mary Decker.

The fates and freedoms of such superstars as Sydney Maree and Zola Budd must be balanced against more critical freedoms. In South Africa, the boycott is weighed on the same scale with the lives of 24 million black South Africans who have no freedoms at all. The collectively imposed sacrifice of individuals like Maree or Budd may eventually speed up the historical forces that will inevitably bring freedom to black South Africans. If that does happen, and if even one life is saved that might have been lost in an armed fight for that freedom, then even Sydney Maree and Zola Budd might one day think that their individual sacrifices were well spent.

A message from the late M.N. Pather, then Secretary-General of SACOS, on the evening of the demonstration in Albany against the South African rugby team in the only public match allowed during its American tour, captured the essence of what overseas protest can mean back home in South Africa:

> You have given us hope that Americans care about our rights. I wanted to come to protest myself, but you were my voice. Today we are a little bit more free in our minds and hearts than we were yesterday.[5]

Notes

1. *New York Times*, October 31, 1984.
2. Ibid., January 30, 1985.
3. Speech by Chief Albert Luthuli, "The Road to Freedom is via the Cross," November 1982, published in *Luthuli Speaks* (United Nations Center Against Apartheid).
4. Speech by Nelson Mandela, "The Rivonia Trial," in *Nelson Mandela* by Mary Benson (London: PANAF Books, 1980).
5. N.M. Palmer telegram to Richard Lapchick, September 1981.

Conclusion

The popular media have inundated us for decades with the positive aspects of sport. Until recently, however, they only rarely have examined problems in sport so that sports can be seen not as a panacea for all of society's ills but as a reflection of both positive and negative aspects of society. This book has attempted to counterbalance all of the writing about the unbridled joys of sport with a critical look at those problem areas.

There is little question that sport has the potential for delivering significant benefits to individuals, organizations, and nations—it already does so. Doubt still exists, however, regarding whether sufficient reform will occur to convert the most attractive possibilities of sport into realities. The foremost conditions for meaningful reform are, first, to recognize the imperative need for change and, second, to understand the situation in depth so that proper mechanisms for change can be designed and implemented.

The 1968 Olympic protest by America's black athletes, followed by a period of campus protests, sensitized even hardened sports administrators and owners to the reality of the need for change. However, all they seemed to offer were higher salaries for the pros and greater inducements for college athletes.

Beyond the initial protests, owners and administrators weren't challenged over a sustained period of time. It was a time when society and athletes were getting a little richer each year. The boat sat still in the water; however, the rocking began when the economy soured in the late 1970s. People started to protest various forms of U.S. policy into the 1980s, professional athletes began to strike, and new scandals seemed to appear whenever someone opened an athletic department door. The same problems that plagued sport in the 1950s were still there in the 1980s.

We have always looked for the positive and tried to ignore the negative in society and, not surprisingly, in sport. That is why each new scandal brings cries of anguish but rarely brings about change or acknowledgment of root problems. Today's scandal is viewed tomorrow as yesterday's aberration or exception. Nevertheless, the most important condition for change is recognition of the imperative need for change.

No one is in a position to propose changes that would eliminate all of sport's problems. Sport that is free of problems could exist only in a society that is free of problems, so it is only realistic to look for ways to *alleviate* those problems. The best way to do that is to empower the athletes themselves so that they can control their own destiny.

Historically, scholars, journalists, and activists have helped to keep us informed. To move ahead now, more information must be generated so that appropriate actions can be taken. The dissemination of information will be the catalyst for change.

Education and Athletics

Knowledge of the graduation rates of athletes has forced university presidents into action. If that action is sustained, educational institutions might be able to regain their position, along with the family and religious organizations, as the guardians of our nation's moral values. However, some major steps will have to be taken first. For example, the NCAA will have to pass and implement penalties for not graduating athletes that have equal weight with penalties for unfair recruiting practices. Education can no longer be viewed as a secondary issue to athletic performance.

I firmly believe that college athletes do deserve "special treatment." Part of their enrollment is an obligation to give thousands of hours of their time to the school for its benefit during their four years of eligibility. Their time brings the school entertainment, prestige, and, very frequently, handsome revenues. To argue against special treatment would seem patently unfair. However, what I mean by special treatment is the assurance of academic preparedness—not the exemption from such preparedness.

Athletes must be given the time and resources to complete their education. Provision for the continuation of athletic scholarships after eligibility is critical. Real academic standards must be imposed for collegiate athletes. The NCAA's Proposition 48, even in a modified version, is an important beginning toward this goal.

The situation is still worse for the high school student. It is painful to see some of the millions of America's youth lose their chances for a meaningful education because they have bought the dream that they can beat the 12,000 to 1 odds and become a pro—with the emphasis on eligibility, not educational skills. They don't see that 98 percent of them won't even get a scholarship to play in college. Thus, too many of our children are lost educationally while trying to live a dream.

Parents who push their children into youth sport programs at the earliest possible ages must be the primary agents for change. They should attend parent—teacher conferences and PTA meetings as often as they go to their chilren's games. They should reward their children for good grades as much as for points scored. It all begins where everyone always said it did—in the home.

Texas has adopted a no-pass, no-play rule that has been called the most controversial piece of legislation since civil rights laws were adopted in the 1960s. It is controversial because it demands academic standards—low ones at that—of young athletes. But students are being lost every day. They need our help.

The pressures on coaches may not be so great at the high school level, but they are there. Why else would coaches be pushing for seasons that never end? Why are coaches the backbone of the opposition to the concept of no-pass, no-play? The answers are just as obvious as the reasons are understandable. Coaches survive by winning. Eligibility is not education, however. Too many high school coaches have adopted the same distorted values as some bigtime college coaches. Too many student-athletes are simply athletes by their junior or senior years. They have to be reached by the seventh or eighth grade—before it is too late.

The athletes also do their part. Hoping to realize the dream of a pro career, young athletes cut academic corners to remain eligible. And considering that only about 1 out of every 12,000 athletes playing high school football, basketball, or baseball goes on to become a pro, that leaves a potential 11,999 with less than an adequate education—facing, at best, an uncertain future. That is why these athletes have to be empowered to act responsibly and reasonably on their own behalf.

A group of national leaders has now gotten together to move for the adoption of minimal academic standards for high school athletes in the United States. Less than 100 of 16,000 school districts have such standards, and the movement toward such standards has become even more controversial than the adoption of Proposition 48 by the university community.

State interscholastic athletic associations across America have opposed the adoption of standards for years, but there is a national momentum for the adoption of such standards. The critical point is that standards must be implemented in a way that will be fair to high school athletes. We can learn from the mistakes made by some school districts, particularly in Texas. The young athletes deserve a warning and a probationary period, so that teams aren't decimated and lives disoriented—but they also deserve to have standards demanded of them.

The positive effects of educational demands on athletes will, of course, be greatest for black athletes. Above all others, they must comprehend that sports is not the way to success or the way out of poverty. Black athletes in particular—but not only black athletes—must know the odds against "making it" in the pros or even getting into college.

Women in Sport

Similar problems of distorted values are emerging in women's sport as it becomes more and more big-time. All of the suggestions made in the preceding section should be applied to women athletes so that we can avoid the catastrophes that might occur if women adopted the horrible example of male athletic programs. This is likely to happen, however, only if women gain more prominent positions of authority in athletic departments and in sports management. That would mean reversing the current downward trend in women's participation in sports administration.

Violence

The soccer riot that occurred on May 29, 1985, in Brussels made the Western world sit up and take notice of violence in sport. The riot, which left 38 dead and nearly 400 spectators injured, increased fears that such violence could happen in North America. It also forced many involved in sport to view sports violence as a cumulatively building phenomenon leading to potential catastrophe for individuals and groups.

The relationship between consumption of alcohol and fan violence at sporting events appears to be direct. This problem will continue, however, until economically profitable alcoholic beverage concessions are dropped and tighter security is established at stadium entrance gates. An encouraging sign, even if it is only a partial step, is the creation of nonalcoholic sections in some sports stadiums. Such a step might at least contain the violence. However, it might also imply that fans can do *anything* in the other sections.

League and team officials will have to impose more severe penalties to stop player fights. Unless players know that their incomes will be negatively affected, they are not likely to be deterred from fighting.

Gambling

America's involvement in sports betting seems unlikely to be halted in the face of our $25 billion annual gambling binge. So long as the media cooperates, gambling will continue to be acceptable. Universities must also accept responsibility. So long as they continue to admit athletes who are unprepared academically and pay them illegally—as Tulane allegedly did with "Hot Rod" Williams, it will be difficult for some athletes to perceive a significant difference between illegally accepting cash for keeping games close and illegally accepting even more cash for attending a university.

If any real progress is to be made against gambling, newspapers will have to stop regularly publishing pointspreads. Television will also have to halt its direct and indirect promotion of gambling through TV sports. This won't be easy, because TV producers believe that encouraging and promoting gambling on sports is a means of increasing the viewing audience. Considering the money involved, I am not optimistic that these changes will occur. Sports gambling seems to be here to stay, and it is poised to grow even bigger.

Drugs

Along with our sudden "discovery" in 1985 that drugs are a major part of sports came calls to stop the spread. Young people were clearly taking notice, as cocaine-use stories ran rampant through the sports pages, following revelations about "blood-boosting" by Olympic athletes and widespread use of anabolic steroids. With an estimated 5.6 million young high school athletes abusing chemicals, we face a monster that is perhaps too large to contain. Like gambling, the income from this growth industry is a powerful and largely uncontrolled force.

The fact is that athletes are role models for America's youth. Until the pros who use recreational drugs are punished effectively within the structure of sport, youthful jocks will assume that they, too, can get away with it—just like their heroes. Wayward pros can't be forgiven two, three, and four times without their followers becoming convinced that the warnings are false.

Performance-enhancing drugs are possibly even more difficult to contain because they promise to deliver the dream. Educators must do their jobs and let the public know what else these drugs deliver—possible life-long suffering and irreversible damage.

No matter how valuable a service it might render, mandatory drug testing appears to be a violation of the Constitution. Therefore, schools, universities, pro teams, and leagues must work toward voluntary drug testing for the greater good of the public. Furthermore, athletes must face sanctions for abusing illegal substances to stop some of the flow.

Sports in the International Arena

There is really no way that sports will ever be totally separated from politics at the international level. Sports contacts between nations are not likely to end animosities where they already exist or to bring peace and understanding to the global community where it did not already flourish.

The Olympic Games have always been our best hope to change this, although politics and nationalism have frequently blocked that hope from becoming a reality. Many leaders have proposed that no national teams be represented and that a permanent neutral site be chosen to avoid boycotts such as those that have taken place in the last two Games because of the host nations. Despite all the problems of the Games, however, the financial success of the Los Angeles Games will probably allow future Olympics to take place with minimal, if any, change.

The primary objective of this book has been to move its readers to think critically about sport. The articles were meant not to dampen the readers' love for the game but simply to make them think about what is happening off the field. If we can all do this, and if we care enough to act upon what we see, then we are in for some good games—and we may watch them from a better world.

Selected Bibliography

Intercollegiate Athletics

Benagh, J. *Making It to #1*. New York: Dodd, Mead, 1976.

Cady, Edwin H. *The Big Game: College Sports and American Life*. Knoxville: University of Tennessee Press, 1978.

Denglinger, K., and L. Shapiro. *Athletes For Sale*. New York: Crowell, 1975.

Durso, J. *The Sports Factory*. New York: Quadrangle, 1975.

Hoch, Paul. *Rip Off the Big Game*. New York: Anchor, 1972.

Locke, Tates, and Bob Ibach. *Caught in the Net*. New York: Leisure Press, 1982.

Rooney, John F. *The Recruiting Game: Toward a New System of Intercollegiate Sports*. Lincoln: University of Nebraska Press, 1980.

Scott, J. *The Athletic Revolution*. New York: Macmillan, 1971.

Tippette, G. *Saturday's Children*. New York: Macmillan, 1973.

Underwood, John. *The Death of an American Game: The Crisis in Football*. Boston: Little, Brown, 1979.

International

Auf der Maur, Nick. *The Billion-Dollar Game*. Toronto: Lorimer, 1975.

Espy, Richard. *The Politics of the Olympic Games*. Berkeley: University of California Press, 1979.

Gilbert, Doug. *The Miracle Machine*. New York: Coward, McCann and Geoghegan, 1980.

Griffiths, J. *Sport: The People's Right*. London: Writing and Readers Publishing Cooperative, 1979.

Hoberman, J. *Sport and Political Ideology*. London: Heinemann, 1984.

James, C.L.R. *Beyond a Boundary*. New York: Pantheon, 1983.

Kolatch, Jonathan. *Sports, Politics, and Ideology in China*. New York: Jonathan David.

Leaver, Janet. *Soccer Madness*. Chicago: University of Chicago Press, 1983.

Lowe, Benjamin, David B. Kanin, and Andrew Streak. *Sport and International Relations*. Champaign, Ill.: Stipes, 1978.

Lucas, John. *The Modern Olympic Games.* New York: A.S. Barnes, 1980.

Mandell, Richard D. *The Nazi Olympics.* New York: Macmillan, 1971.

Pickering, R.J. *Cuba: In Sport Under Communism.* London: C. Hurst, 1978.

Riordan, James. *Sport in Soviet Society.* Cambridge: Cambridge University Press, 1977.

Schaap, Dick. *An Illustrated History of the Olympics.* New York: Ballantine, 1976.

Seagraue, Jeffrey, and Donald Chu. *Olympism.* Champaign, Ill.: Human Kinetics, 1981.

Law

Appenzeller, Herb, Teri Engler, Nancy N. Mathews, Linda Rielees, and C. Thomas Ross. *Sports and Law.* St. Paul, Minn.: West, 1984.

Grayson, Edward. *Sport and the Law.* London: Sunday Telegraph, 1978.

Johnson, Arthur T., and James H. Frey. *Government and Sport: The Public Policy Issues.* Totowa, N.J.: Rowman and Allanheld, 1985.

Markham, Jesse W., and Paul V. Teplitz. *Baseball Economics and Public Policy.* Lexington, Mass.: Lexington Books, 1981.

Sobel, Lionel S. *Professional Sports and the Law.* New York: Law-Arts, 1977.

Weistart, John C., and Cym H. Lowell. *The Law of Sports.* Indianapolis: Bobbs-Merrill, 1979.

Literature

Berman, Neil D. *Playful Fictions and Fictional Players.* Port Washington, N.Y.: Kennikat Press, 1981.

Dodge, Tom. *A Literature of Sports.* Lexington, Mass.: D.C. Heath, 1980.

Higgs, Robert J., and Neil D. Isaacs. *The Sporting Spirit: Athletes in Literature and Life.* New York: Harcourt, Brace, Jovanovich, 1977.

Higgs, Robert J., and Laurel Thorn. *The Athlete in American Literature.* Lexington: University Press of Kentucky, 1981.

Messenger, Christian K. *Sport and the Spirit of Play in American Fiction: Hawthorne to Faulkner.* New York: Columbia University Press, 1981.

Oriard, Michael. *Dreaming of Heroes.* Chicago: Nelson-Hall, 1982.

Professional Sport

Dolson, Frank. *Beating the Bushes: Life in the Minor Leagues.* South Bend, Ind.: Learus Press, 1982.

Garvey, Edward. *The Agent Game: Selling Players Short.* Washington D.C.: Federation of Professional Athletes, AFL-CIO, 1984.

Kahn, Roger. *The Boys of Summer.* New York: New American Library, 1973.

Kramer, Jerry. *Farewell to Football.* New York: World, 1969.

Lineberry, W.P. *The Business of Sports.* New York: H.W. Wilson, 1973.

Meggyesy, D. *Out of Their League.* Berkeley, Calif.: Ramparts Press, 1971.

Murdock, Eugene C. *Ban Johnson: Czar of Baseball.* Westport, Conn.: Greenwood Press, 1982.

Plimpton, George. *Mad Ducks and Bears.* New York: Random House, 1973.

Rentzel, L. *When All the Laughter Died in Sorrow.* New York: Bantam, 1972.

Rozin, Skip. *One Step from Glory: On the Fringe of Professional Sports.* New York: Simon and Schuster, 1979.

Russell, Bill, and T. Branch. *Second Wind: Memoirs of an Opinionated Man.* New York: Random House, 1979.

Racism

Archer, R., and Antoine Bouillon. *The South African Game: Sport and Racism.* London: Zed Press, 1984.

Axthelm, Peter. *The City Game.* New York: Harper and Row, 1970.

Chalk, Ocania. *Black College Sport.* New York: Dodd, Mead, 1976.

de Broglia, C. *South Africa: Racism in Sport.* London: Christian Action, 1970.

Edwards, H. *The Revolt of the Black Athlete.* New York: Free Press, 1969.

Gilmore, Al-Tony. *Bad Nigger: The National Impact of Jack Johnson.* Port Washington, N.Y.: Kennikat Press, 1974.

Hain, P. *Don't Play with Apartheid.* London: Allen and Unwin, 1971.

Henderson, Edward B. *The Negro in Sports.* Washington, D.C.: Associated Publishers.

Horrell, M. *South Africa and the Olympic Games.* Johannesburg: South Africa Institute of Race Relations, 1968.

Jordan, P. *Black Coach.* New York: Dodd, Mead, 1971.

Lapchick, Richard E. *The Politics of Race and International Sport: The Case of South Africa.* Westport, Conn.: Greenwood Press, 1975.

Lapchick, R. *Broken Promises: Racism in American Sport.* New York: St. Marten's/ Marek, 1984.

Newnham, T., *Apartheid Is Not a Game.* Auckland, New Zealand: Graphic Publications, 1975.

Newnham, Tom. *A Cry of Treason: New Zealand and the Montreal Olympics.* Palmerstown North, New Zealand: Dunmore Press, 1978.

Olsen, J. *The Black Athlete.* New York: Time-Life Books, 1968.

Orr J. *The Black Athlete.* New York: Lion Books, 1969.

Peterson, R. *Only the Ball Was White.* Englewood Cliffs, N.J.: Prentice-Hall, 1970.

Robinson, J. *I Never Had It Made.* New York: G.P. Putnam's Sons, 1972.

Ragosin, Donn. *Invisible Men: Life in Baseball's Negro Leagues.* New York: Atheneum, 1983.

Rust, A., Jr. *Get That Nigger off the Field.* New York: Delacort Press, 1976.

Tygiel, Jules. *Baseball's Great Experiment: Jackie Robinson and His Legacy.* New York: Oxford University Press, 1983.

Wielgus, Chuck, and Alexander Wolff. *The In-Your-Face Basketball Book.* New York: Everest House, 1980.

Sociology

Arnold, Peter J. *Meaning in Movement: Sport and Physical Education.* London: Heinemann, 1979.

Baker, William J., and John M. Carrell. *Sports in American Society.* St. Louis: River City, 1981.

Ball, D.W., and J.W. Loy. *Sport and Social Order.* Reading, Mass.: Addison-Wesley, 1975.

Ballinger, Lee. *In Your Face! Sports for Love and Money.* Chicago: Vanguard, 1981.

Blanchard, K., and A. Cheska. *The Anthropology of Sport: An Introduction.* Hadley, Mass.: Bergin and Garvey, 1985.

Boyle, Robert. *Sport: Mirror of American Life.* Boston: Little, Brown, 1973.

Brohm, Jean-Marie. *Sport, A Prison of Measured Time: Essays by Jean-Marie Brohm.* London: Ian Links, 1978.

Brooks, George A. *Perspective on the Academic Discipline of Physical Education.* Champaign, Ill.: Human Kinetics, 1981.

Cantelon, Hart, and Richard Gruneau. *Sport, Culture and the Modern State.* Toronto: University of Toronto Press, 1982.

Coakley, J. *Sport in Society: Issues and Controversies.* St. Louis: Mosby, 1978.

Curry, T., and R. Jiobu. *Sports: A Social Perspective.* Englewood Cliffs, N.J.: Prentice-Hall, 1984.

Edwards, Harry. *Sociology of Sport.* Homewood, Ill.: Dorsey Press, 1973.

Eitzen, D.S., and G.H. Sage. *Sociology of American Sport.* Dubuque, Iowa: Wm. C. Brown, 1978.

Eitzen, S. *Sport in Contemporary Society: An Anthology* (2nd ed.). New York: St. Martin's Press, 1984.

Figler, Stephen K. *Sport and Play in American Life.* Philadelphia: Saunders, 1981.

Gerber, Ellen W., and William J. Morgan. *Sport and the Body: A Philosophical Symposium.* Philadelphia: Lea and Febiger, 1979.

Gruneau, Richard. *Class, Sports, and Social Development.* Amherst: University of Massachusetts Press, 1983.

Guttman, Allen. *From Ritual to Record: The Nature of Modern Sports.* New York: Columbia University Press, 1978.

Hart, Marie, and Susan Birrell. *Sport in the Sociocultural Process.* Dubuque, Iowa: Wm. C. Brown, 1981.

Higgs, Robert J. *Sports: A Reference Guide.* Westport, Conn.: Greenwood Press, 1982.

Hoberman, John M. *Sport and Political Ideology.* Austin: University of Texas Press, 1984.

Ibrahim, H. *Sport and Society.* Long Beach, Calif.: Hwong, 1975.

Issacs, N.D. *Jock Culture USA.* New York: Norton, 1978.

Krotee, M.L. *The Dimensions of Sport Sociology.* West Point, N.Y.: Leisure Press, 1979.

Landers, D.M. *Social Problems in Athletics.* Urbana: University of Illinois Press, 1976.

Leonard, W.M. *A Sociological Perspective of Sport.* Minneapolis: Burgess, 1980.

Lipsky, Richard. *How We Play the Game—Why Sports Dominate American Life.* Boston: Beacon Press, 1981.

Lipsyte, Robert. *Sportsworld: An American Dreamland.* New York: Quadrangle, 1976.

Loy, J.W., G.S. Kenyon, and B.D. McPherson. *Sport, Culture and Society.* Philadelphia: Lea and Febiger, 1981.

Loy, J.W., B.D. McPherson, and G. Kenyon. *Sport and Social Systems.* Reading, Mass.: Addison-Wesley, 1978.

Luschen, Gunther R.F., and George H. Sage. *Handbook of Social Science of Sport.* Champaign, Ill.: Stipes, 1981.

Mandell, Richard D. *Sport: A Cultural History.* New York: Columbia University Press, 1984.

Michener, J. *Sports in America.* New York: Random House, 1976.

Mihalich, Joseph C. *Sports and Athletics: Philosophy in Action.* Totowa, N.J.: Rowman and Littlefield, 1982.

Mitchell, Richard G. *Mountain Experience: The Psychology and Sociology of Adventure.* Chicago: University of Chicago Press, 1983.

Nixon, H.L. *Sport and Social Organization.* Indianapolis: Bobbs-Merrill, 1973.

Nixon, H.L. *Sport and the American Dream.* New York: Leisure Press, 1984.

Pankin, Robert M. *Social Approaches to Sport.* East Brunswick, N.J.: Associated University Presses/Fairleigh Dickinson University Press, 1982.

Ponomaizyou, J.I. *Sport and Society.* Moscow: Progress Publishers, 1974.

Scott, Jack. *Athletics for Athletes.* Hayward, Calif.: Otherways, 1969.

Scott, Jack. *The Athletic Revolution.* New York: Free Press, 1971.

Snyder, Eldon E., and Elmer Spreitzer. *Social Aspects of Sport.* Englewood Cliffs, N.J.: Prentice-Hall, 1978.

Suinn, Richard M. *Psychology of Sports: Methods and Applications.* Minneapolis: Burgess, 1980.

Talamin, J.T., and C.H. Page. *Sport and Society.* Boston: Little, Brown, 1973.

Theberge, Nancy, and Peter Donnelly. *Sport and the Sociological Imagination.* Fort Worth: Texas Christian University Press, 1984.

Tutko, T., and W. Bruns. *Winning Is Everything and Other American Myths.* New York: Macmillan, 1976.

Umphlett, Wiley. *The Sporting Myth and the American Experience.* Lewisburg, Pa.: Bucknell University Press, 1975.

Yiannakis, A., T. McIntyre, M. Melnick, and D. Hart. *Sport Sociology: Contemporary Themes.* Dubuque, Iowa: Kendall/Hunt, 1979.

Violence

Goldstein, Jeffrey J. *Sports Violence.* New York: Springer-Verlag, 1983.

Horrow, R.B. *Sports Violence.* Arlington, Va.: Carrollton Press, 1980.

Smith, Michael D. *Violence and Sport.* Toronto: Butterworth, 1983.

Tatum, Jack, and Bill Kushner. *They Call Me Assassin.* New York: Everest House, 1979.

Williams, J., E. Dunning, and P. Murphy. *Hooligans Abroad: The Behavior and Control of English Fans in Continental Europe.* London: Routledge and Kegan Paul, 1984.

Women

Boutilier, M., and L. San Giovanni. *The Sporting Woman.* Champaign, Ill.: Human Kinetics, 1983.

Bouton, Bobbie, and Nancy Marshall. *Home Games: Baseball Wives Speak Out.* New York: St. Martin's/Marek, 1983.

Gerber, E. *The American Woman in Sport.* Reading, Mass.: Addison-Wesley, 1974.

Hall, M. Ann, and Dorothy A. Richardson. *Fair Ball: Toward Sex Equality in Canadian Sport.* Ottawa: Canadian Advisory Council on the Status of Women, 1984.

Kaplan, Janice. *Women and Sports.* New York: Viking, 1979.

Oglesby, Carole A. *Women and Sport: From Myth to Reality.* Philadelphia: Lea and Febiger, 1978.

Parkhouse, Bonnie L., and Jackie Lapin. *Women Who Win: Exercising Your Rights in Sports.* Englewood Cliffs, N.J.: Prentice-Hall, 1982.

Twin, Stephanie. *Out of the Bleachers: Writings on Women and Sport.* New York: Feminist Press, 1979.

Youth

Albinson, J.G., and G.M. Andrew. *Child in Sport and Physical Activity.* Baltimore: University Park Press, 1976.

Magill, Richard A., Michael J. Ash, and Frank L. Small. *Children in Sport: A Contemporary Anthology.* Champaign, Ill.: Human Kinetics, 1978.

Martens, Rainer. *Joy and Sadness in Children's Sports.* Champaign, Ill.: Human Kinetics, 1978.

Small, F.L., and R.E. Smith. *Psychological Perspectives in Youth Sports.* New York: Halsted Press, 1978.

Yablonsky, Lewis, and Jonathan J. Brower. *The Little League Game.* New York: Times Books, 1979.

About the Editor

Richard E. Lapchick is director of the Center for the Study of Sport in Society at Northeastern University. The Center has been hailed as one of the most important agents for change in American sport today. He is the son of Joe Lapchick, the Original Celtic center who is also known for his coaching of St. John's and the Knicks and for his part in integrating the NBA. Influenced by his father, Richard Lapchick has been very active in civil rights issues, many in the area of sport.

In 1968 he was the first recipient of the Martin Luther King Fellowship for studies in race relations, which he used to complete his Ph.D. in international race relations at the University of Denver. From 1970 to 1978, he was associate professor of political science at Virginia Wesleyan College. He served at the United Nations from 1978 to 1983, becoming a senior liaison officer while working on issues involving South Africa, the Middle East, and women's rights.

Lapchick has been a leader of the international campaign to isolate South Africa until apartheid is eliminated. He is the author of *The Politics of Race and International Sport: The Case of South Africa* (Greenwood Press, 1975), and has been national chairperson of ACCESS, the American Coordinating Committee for Equality in Sport and Society, since 1976.

He is also the author of *Broken Promises: Racism in American Sport* (St. Martin's, 1984) and coauthor of *Oppression and Resistance: The Saga of Women in Southern Africa* (Greenwood Press, 1982), as well as numerous articles for both academic and popular audiences.